How to Organize
Effective
CONFERENCES
and MEETINGS

7th edition

How to Organize Effective CONFERENCES *and* MEETINGS

DAVID SEEKINGS
with JOHN FARRER

KOGAN
PAGE

First published in 1981
Second edition 1984, reprinted 1985
Third edition 1987
Fourth edition 1989
Fifth edition 1992
Sixth edition 1996
Seventh edition 1999

Kogan Page Limite
120 Pentonville Road
London
N1 9JN
UK

Kogan Page Limited
163 Central Avenue, Suite 4
Dover
NH 03820
USA

British Library Cataloguing in Publication Data

A CIP record for this book is available from the British Library.

ISBN 0 7494 3077 X

Typeset by Jean Cussons Typesetting, Diss, Norfolk
Printed and bound by Clays Ltd, St Ives plc

CONTENTS

PREFACE

Welcome to this, the seventh edition of *How to Organize Effective Conferences and Meetings*.

I began writing the first edition in 1980: it is sobering to think how much has changed since then – a fact reflected in the previous five revisions and in this latest update. The meetings industry has not been slow to adapt to change (which is hardly surprising since – being a 'people' business – it has to respond to the changing needs of its audiences); nor has it been slow to use new technologies. Much of this latest edition has been extensively revised to reflect these developments.

That said, apart from minor updating, some sections are much as they were in the original edition. That is because there is much that does not change: meticulous attention to detail in planning and execution to avoid disasters which waste time and money – and which can destroy the event.

This book is for anyone who is involved in organizing conferences and meetings – large or small – whether they are new to the task or already have a great deal of experience. Whatever our level of knowledge and experience we can all learn new tricks of the trade; we all need to go back to basics from time to time to make sure we are not becoming casual in our approach; and we all need to keep up to date.

Our task is often a lonely one. We probably had to learn as we went along, with little outside help or guidance, and we seldom have the opportunity of meeting other people who organize conferences. How can we be sure we are 'doing it right'? And how can we be sure we are not missing a trick or two if we cannot benefit from the knowledge or experience of others?

This book helps fill that gap.

A high proportion of people in the conference business are female. I hope they will not be offended by the liberal use of masculine nouns and pronouns throughout the text. This stems from my desire to avoid ugly and cumbersome English. No discrimination, prejudice or bias is intended.

So many people have advised and helped me with the various editions of the book that it would be almost impossible to list them all: to each and every one of them I extend my personal thanks – and the thanks of the many readers who have benefited from the advice and tips they have so willingly passed on: in many ways this book is a tribute to and reflection of their accumulated knowledge and experience.

Special thanks go to those who have helped me with this particular edition. In particular, I must thank Sharp Electronics (UK) Ltd who kindly allowed me to draw extensively upon the text of their excellent booklet, *The Sharp Guide to Presentations*, when updating Chapter 6 'Modern Techniques in Presentation and Production'.

Last – but far from least – I would like to thank John Farrer, who has taken on the mantle of co-author and who has been responsible for the revision and updating of this edition. John has almost unrivalled experience in the conference industry and is – unlike me – still very much a current practitioner. He was therefore well placed to revise the text to reflect both the industry and current practices as we embark upon the new millennium. John would like to thank The Right Solution, who kindly provided a copy of their 1999 UK Conference Market survey from which we have extracted data to produce the very informative graphs about both corporate and association meetings in Chapters 1, 2, 4 and 5.

We hope you enjoy reading the book. We hope you find it useful. But above all, we hope you enjoy organizing your conferences and that they are successful.

David Seekings
Ely, Cambridgeshire
July 1999

1

APPROACHING THE TASK

INTRODUCTION

Conferences and meetings are essential business and social activities. We meet with other people to learn, to exchange information, to take decisions ... and to enjoy ourselves.

We meet in groups of almost every size from two to thousands. We tend to take it for granted that meetings are 'necessary' and that they are usually 'successful' (although success can sometimes be difficult to measure – and in any case depends upon whom you ask, the organizer or the delegate).

It is axiomatic that people hold conferences and meetings to 'communicate'. If you look up the word 'conference' in a dictionary, you will find a definition which uses terms like 'a formal interchange of views' and 'a meeting of two or more people for discussion of matters of common concern'. Both these definitions imply *two-way* communication; indeed, many would argue that if it is to be successful, communication *must* be a two-way process.

In spite of this, it is probably true to say that most people who arrange conferences view the process as one-way communication, seeing their events as gatherings where they impart information to those who attend.

We see things from a very different perspective if we look from the delegates' point of view. What benefits do they hope to derive from attending meetings?

Some benefits are obvious, some less obvious:

- People usually expect to *learn* something, and look for the learning experience to be pleasant – even entertaining.
- They want to *enjoy* themselves (who ever deliberately sets out not to do so?) and, in this context, it should be noted that comfort, organization (or lack of it), efficiency and presentation all directly influence delegates' enjoyment.
- They also tend to seek *stimulation* and *reassurance*; this is especially so for people who work alone (for example, salesmen and many professional people).
- People also seek *peer group approval* and prestige (being seen in the 'right' company).
- They go to conferences to *network* and, often, to do business.
- They may also attend for a *morale booster*, for a *break from routine*, or as a reward for outstanding performance.

In short, people go to conferences and meetings for many reasons and, if our conferences and meetings are to be successful (ie 'effective'), we must arrange them so that all these needs are met. The success we seek will elude us if we fail to do so.

Having said that, there are those who argue that modern communications – video-conferencing, Internet, interactive video and the like – threaten to make the conference obsolete. Why, the argument goes, spend all that money and time assembling a group of people for a conference when the information could just as well be provided in each individual's place of work?

A brief look back to the above list of benefits people hope to derive from attending meetings provides the answer: conferences are about people interacting with each other face-to-face. Whilst video-conferencing and the other technologies have their places, they will never make the traditional conference obsolete.

In short, conferences and meetings will continue to be a very important human activity for a long time to come. And all conferences have to be organized by someone.

This book is designed to help would-be conference organizers, be they new to the job or already well versed in their task, to make sure that events they arrange are successful. As you read the text, and as you organize your events, always remember your delegates. Imagine what *they* will expect and try to meet all their needs. Organizing a conference is not simply about good administration, or efficiency, or just about putting a message across. Rather, it is about making the event as good as it possibly can be from the delegates' point of view.

CONFERENCE ACTIVITY IN THE UNITED KINGDOM

Whatever the time of day or night, someone, somewhere, will be holding a 'conference'. In fact, throughout most of the year, our hotels, conference centres and corporate and institutional meetings' facilities are almost fully occupied with gatherings of every type and size.

No-one really knows how many conferences are held each year in Britain. A survey into the UK conference market by Coopers & Lybrand Deloitte suggests that the total UK conference market is in excess of 115 million delegate days. This figure, which at best is probably little more than an informed estimate, fluctuates in tune with recession and recovery. For example, training is invariably one of the first targets for savings in a recession, but this only creates pent-up demand which has to be satisfied as the recession eases. Thus, taken overall, conference activity remains strong.

Hard facts and figures about meeting patterns have historically been difficult to ascertain but The Right Solution recently completed an extensive survey on behalf of the Meetings Industry Association. The graph below shows the trends of both association and corporate meetings. In the chapters on Choosing the Venue, The Budget, and Presentation and Production we also draw on the survey's findings.

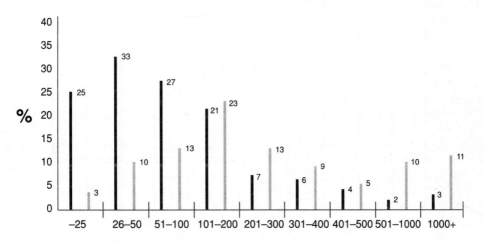

Figure 1.1 *Number of delegates attending typical events*

━━━━ Corporate   ▨▨▨▨ Associations

Trends in conference activity

The number of delegates attending association meetings is rising (see Figure 1.1 on previous page). In 1998, when 49 per cent had between 50 and 300 delegates at their main annual meeting, the largest number of meetings by a long way had between 101 and 200 delegates, which supports our view that the average meeting size in the UK for all types of meetings is 150.

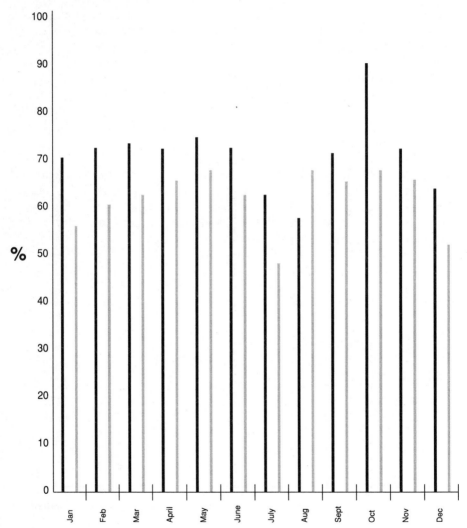

Figure 1.2   *Months when meetings held*

Corporate   Associations

There used to be two clearly defined conference seasons but now, with many more conference hotels and more alternative accommodation in academic institutions, we will see that the pattern is changing and conferences are round-the-year activities.

By the same token, conference activity used to be confined to the middle of the week. Now it is much more evenly spread – see Figure 1.3.

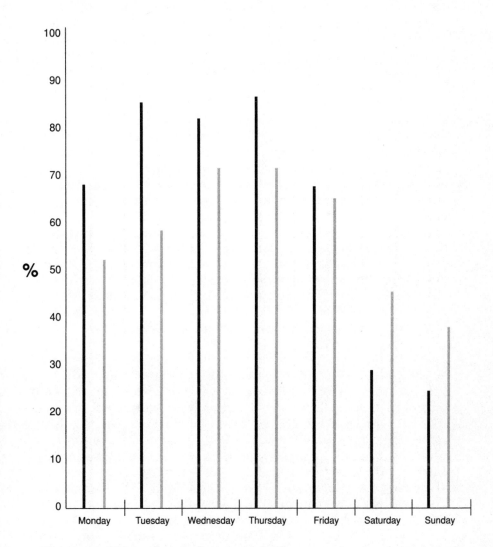

Figure 1.3   *Days of week when events held*

— Corporate   ⬛⬛⬛ Associations

Total expenditure on domestic conferences and related activities (travel and production costs – which account for 25 per cent of expenditure) is estimated to be between £5 and £6 billion. The UK conference market is clearly big business.

The value and importance of the conference market is reflected in what is sometimes called the 'conference industry':

♦ The hotel groups compete fiercely for conference business, advertising heavily in the national press, in specialist publications such as *Marketing, Conference & Incentive Travel, What's New in Marketing* and *Meetings and Incentive Travel*, and they are also significant users of direct mail and other promotional channels.

♦ Large sums are being spent to upgrade and improve existing venues. In London, the P & O Group – probably best known for its cruise ships and Channel ferries – invested £100 million in its Earls Court Olympia complex to provide a 450-seat conference centre with raked seating and a revolving stage along with 1,000,000 sq ft of exhibition space. Elsewhere, before becoming part of the Granada group, Forté invested heavily in upgrading the conference facilities in its chain of around 200 hotels – a pattern now being followed by many other groups.

♦ Major conference centres include the Government's Queen Elizabeth II Conference Centre in Westminster, the £160 million International Convention Centre in Birmingham (funded in part by a £50 million grant from the European Community), a £38 million conference centre in the heart of Edinburgh, and the 2,500-seat Sheffield Arena – originally built for the student Olympics and now an American-style, multi-purpose venue for sports, entertainment, conferences and exhibitions.

♦ The first stages of ExCel, the major new international conference and exhibition centre in London's Docklands, have been completed. New hotels are planned to complete the rejuvenation of this area, and with the extension to the Docklands Light Railway (DLR) there could be major moves from the current tired sites in West London. Easy connecting flights to and from the City airport will make this area very competitive to the large continental exhibition centres. Attracting the same type of business will be the major redevelopment at the new Eurostar terminal in the King's Cross/St Pancras area of London. This development, if and when it comes on-stream, will bring yet another dimension to London's facilities.

♦ There has also been heavy investment in new residential conference centres, often in converting country houses to accommodate residential training courses.

Until recently, the inexperienced conference buyer had no way of knowing how venues compared with each other (unlike the hotel and catering industries which are judged by a host of independent guides ranging from the *Cellnet Egon Ronay Guide* to the *Michelin Guide*, the comments and grading of which can make or break the top hotels and restaurants). Whilst the industry has failed to introduce an independent grading system for conference facilities, CD ROM systems such as Viewpoint (published by CID Publishing) make it easier than hitherto to compare the offerings of individual venues.

Conferences and meetings are clearly big business. The investment involved is large: the Queen Elizabeth II Conference Centre in Westminster cost £55 million *excluding* the cost of fixtures and fittings – an increase of around 20 per cent in real terms over the original estimates. The Harrogate Conference Centre exceeded its original budget by a far wider margin (the final cost, agreed in late 1988, was £34m compared with the original mid-1970s estimate of just under £8m). What is more, the Centre does not even cover its running costs. That said, the Harrogate District Council (which financed and operates the Centre) point out that the Centre and its exhibition halls are well filled by industry standards. Consultants estimate the complex brings £50m – £60m a year into the area: hotels which would otherwise remain empty are filled with conference delegates and everyone, from local taxi drivers and florists to specialist suppliers, benefits from the additional income brought into the town by conferences. Similarly, the 1,200 seat Edinburgh International Conference Centre (EICC) opened in 1995 and is expected to attract an additional 100,000 business visitors to the city each year.

The popular image of a 'conference' is probably that of the annual party political or trades union conferences – a thousand or so delegates gathered in Blackpool or Brighton under the scrutiny of the media – or, perhaps, of a huge medical conference involving learned dissertations, simultaneous translation, extensive social programmes and scores of parallel activities.

The largest conference ever held in Britain was the 75th Rotary International Convention which attracted over 23,000 delegates from 148 countries. It is estimated that the event was worth £25 million to Birmingham when pre- and post-convention tours are taken into account. Another type of large meeting has developed as a result of the Conservative Government's privatization programme. The annual general meetings of companies like British Telecom, British Gas and Lloyds TSB can attract several thousand shareholders: what is more, bearing in mind that every shareholder has the right to attend, the organizers are faced with the problem of being ready to cope with an unknown number of shareholders on the day: in theory, some 5 million people could turn up for a British Gas AGM!

The millennium saw a whole new range of celebratory meetings. One that set the scene was a one-day event in Central London for 20,000 people: an organizer's challenge only acceptable with the aid of the facilities offered through the Internet.

But most meetings are very much smaller and attract little or no public interest. This is not to say that they are unimportant. Indeed, small meetings make up the bulk of conference activity. Go into almost any hotel, on any day of the week, and the notice board in the foyer will read like a catalogue of top company names. Training meetings, product launches, sales briefings and corporate think-tanks – these are all conferences and meetings which are organized by people who have other work to do. This book is specifically designed to help them in their task.

Hotels have found that conference business can be very profitable. A recent survey suggests that about 31 per cent of hotel profits are generated from conferences. What is more, large luxury hotels, which only represent 15 per cent of all venues, account for 50 per cent of the market in terms of delegate days.

In spite of the special rates offered to conference buyers (the 24-hour delegate rate – which includes accommodation and all meals – can be less than the bed and breakfast rate), the reasons why conference business is so lucrative are easy to see. The average conference delegate spends twice as much in the hotel as the ordinary tourist – and the delegate from overseas spends more than twice as much as the British delegate. Meetings tend to be held in the off-peak holiday seasons when rooms would otherwise remain empty: the first quarter of the year is the peak period for conference activity (although the summer has its own peak of university-hosted events – another example of utilizing otherwise empty rooms).

Budgets for the larger conferences can involve significant sums of money: for example, the budget for a major international conference for 3,000 delegates in London can easily exceed £300,000 *excluding* delegates' accommodation – which can add a further £800,000 or more on a five-day event, making a total budget of well over £1 million. The sums involved in many corporate events are equally impressive: the Ford Motor Company invested well over £1 million (excluding travel and accommodation) in a series of presentations to over 13,000 people from its European dealer network prior to the launch of a new model in its range. The budget for a series of product launches shown to tractor dealers and farmers was over £1 million.

High-budget product launch spectaculars of the sort mentioned above have spawned a whole industry of production companies and 'high-tech' audio-visual support services. Indeed, the never-ceasing quest for new and original shows and productions is the driving force behind many of the technological advances described in a later chapter (Chapter 6, 'Modern Techniques in Presentation and Production').

With all this activity in mind, it is not surprising that people talk about the 'conference industry'. But the conference industry is unlike any other in that it is not really an industry at all. When we speak of other industries, such as the motor or film industries, we are referring to readily recognizable groups of companies. People who work in these companies usually identify themselves with their industries and would normally regard themselves as 'professionals'. This is not quite the case in the conference industry. True, there are professional conference organizers and there are several 'professional bodies' for conference organizers. Some large companies and professional bodies do have their own full-time conference staff and others engage professional consultants to help them arrange specific events. But most conferences and meetings are arranged by people who have other jobs to do. A survey undertaken for *Marketing* magazine revealed that, out of a group of 115 corporate executives responsible for organizing conferences, there were no less than 42 different job titles of which only six included the words 'conference' or 'communications'. It is not unusual for the task to be given to marketing managers, personnel directors and even personal assistants to senior executives. These people often have little experience of arranging meetings and are almost invariably short of the time and knowledge needed for the task.

It is not difficult, in the technical sense, to arrange a conference, and few of the tasks cannot be accomplished by a competent executive. However, there is a lot to do and many different things to remember and, if he or she lacks the time, knowledge and other resources needed to do the job properly, then things will almost certainly go wrong. The price of failure can be great. Everyone at the event will immediately be aware of the disasters – the speaker who fails to arrive, the projector which breaks down, the meal which is late or uneatable, the noise outside the room which makes it impossible to hear the speaker, and the seats which are unbearably uncomfortable. At best these things are minor distractions, at worst they can ruin the event. Such failures are not only very public, they are also unforgivable.

This book is designed to help anyone who has to arrange a meeting, whether large or small, corporate or public, long or short.

DEFINITIONS

You will have noticed that, so far, the words 'conference' and 'meeting' have been used to describe much the same sort of event. There is no standard terminology to define the different types of gathering, but the following meanings are commonly accepted in our worldwide industry and are the ones intended in this book:

Conference, Convention and Congress   In the UK the word 'conference' is used to describe almost every type of meeting although professional congress organizers (PCOs) tend to use the word to describe the larger event. Conferences often last for several days and may attract hundreds or even thousands of delegates (*qv*); they may involve complex social programmes, exhibitions and displays. Many of the larger conferences have international audiences and are events of national and international interest.

In the hotel industry the word 'conference' is used to describe any meeting in an hotel (eg 'Your conference is in the River Suite').

In America, the word 'convention' is preferred, and in continental Europe 'congress' is the usual English equivalent.

For many, the word 'convention' implies a gathering of greater importance, size and formality – perhaps to formulate policy and select candidates for office. The annual UK party political conferences could well be described as conventions.

Meeting   A meeting can be a much smaller event, often involving a few executives discussing business round a boardroom table. However, the word 'meetings' is also used in a wider sense to describe conferences, meetings and seminars in a collective manner.

Seminar   The word is used to describe small to medium sized gatherings – from as few as a dozen or so up to around 150 people (although this upper figure might lead to the event being called a conference). Seminars are normally one- or two-day events designed to educate and inform delegates and to discuss matters of common concern.

Symposium   This is similar to a seminar except that it is normally concerned with a single subject and the occasion is usually less formal since the flow of information is two-way. However, the Oxford English Dictionary definition, 'an after-dinner drinking party, with wine and conversation' is a little wide of the mark!

Colloquium   This is a meeting at which one or more academic specialists deliver lectures on a topic and then answer questions on the subject. It is invariably an 'academic' event.

Workshop   This is similar to a symposium and involves a small gathering of people to discuss specific topics, to exchange ideas or to solve particular problems. Note the distinction between the workshop and symposium, where the flow of information is between all the delegates, the seminar and colloquium, at which the flow of information is primarily from the rostrum to the delegate, and the meeting, which is usually called to discuss matters and to reach collective decisions. The words 'seminar' and 'workshop' are sometimes viewed with suspicion when used to describe public events (see below for a definition of 'public'). This is particularly true overseas where events with these descriptions have sometimes turned out to be poorly structured and of limited value. This is not to say that all such gatherings have diminished in value. Workshops which were an integral part of the programme at one international congress on management development were so successful that follow-up workshops, at which participants could explore issues in greater depth and cross-examine speakers (in a way not possible in large, plenary sessions) were arranged at regular intervals over an extended period. Details of this event structure can be found in Chapter 3.

Training Programmes   Many people do not associate training programmes with conferences and meetings, but they are included here because so many of them are held in hotels and because they need as much careful planning and organization as many other gatherings. Typically, a training programme will involve 15 to 20 executives and will last five working days. There is a severe shortage of specialist residential centres which is why the majority of residential training programmes are held in hotels.

Launch   (as in 'Product Launch', 'New Product Launch'). A 'show' (*qv*) to introduce an audience, whether internal management and staff, sales force or external dealers and customers, to a new company product or service.

Show or Production   These words are used to describe spectacular events involving the full razzmatazz of AV, multi-media and even live performers (dancers and so on), although the word show is also used to describe more modest set piece AV presentations during a meeting.

Incentive   An event – often held overseas – specifically designed to reward attendees. Although increasingly these have an element of serious content, the principal purpose is 'motivational' and incentives are primarily for salesmen (and often their partners) at the end of a sales campaign.

Corporate hospitality   Although not strictly either a conference or meeting, corporate hospitality (or, as it is sometimes termed, 'corporate entertaining') involves inviting groups of people – usually clients – to both public events (eg Henley Regatta or Wimbledon) and private activities (such as hot air ballooning, tank driving and grouse shooting).

Trade fair   A gathering – especially of buyers and sellers – for a trade or competitive exhibition, often with accompanying social events, a conference or workshops and entertainment.

Programme   This word is usually used to describe the schedule of events within a conference, but it is sometimes used to describe an event (eg training programme) or series of events (eg launch programme).

Road show   A programme where the same event is staged in several different venues.

Presentation   This word is sometimes used as an alternative to 'conference' or 'meeting', but more usually to describe the formal process of telling the audience something.

Public events   These are attended by members of the general public (although normally from specific market segments or from specific groups – eg associations).

External events   These are arranged by an organization, particularly companies, to disseminate information to external audiences (eg to wholesalers, distributors, dealers, consumers, the press).

Internal events ('in-house', 'in-company').   Attendance at these is confined to personnel within the organization (eg sales force, work force, departments and groups and people attending internal – as opposed to external – training courses).

Delegates   One of the terms used to describe people who attend conferences, seminars and similar events. See also 'participant'.

Participant   Similar to the term 'delegate', but used particularly for people attending training programmes.

Session   The word used to describe an unbroken period within a conference.

Plenary session   A session at which all delegates are present.

Syndicate or break-down/break-out sessions   Parts of the conference programme where delegates are invited to split into smaller groups (often called 'syndicates') for discussions or specialist workshops. The workshop sessions at the management development congress described earlier are a typical example of break-down.

Poster sessions   Times allowed in major conferences where authors of papers which are not presented stand by noticeboards displaying abstracts of their papers ready to meet delegates and answer questions.

Assembly   A company of people gathered for deliberations and legislation, worship or entertainment.

Conclave   A private meeting or assembly.

Summit   A conference of highest-level officials (eg heads of governments).

PLANNING MEETINGS

Many meetings are not properly planned. The survey undertaken for *Marketing* magazine mentioned earlier indicated that company management, in particular, often fails to prepare adequately for meetings: planning and organizing time was often found to be insufficient, as was preparation and rehearsal time for presenters, and objectives were often not identified.

Thus, even those events deemed to have been successful are often successful by chance rather than design. This state of affairs is hardly surprising given the difficulties which face most organizers. If objectives are not set, if insufficient time is allowed to arrange the event, if the event is not evaluated to determine its effectiveness, and if the person responsible for making the arrangements lacks the necessary experience, then failure is almost inevitable. The fault rarely lies with the organizer: more often it lies with the person or persons who take the original decision to hold a conference at all.

'WE MUST HAVE A MEETING...'

Pronouncements like, 'We must have a meeting...' or, 'It's time we started planning the annual sales conference' are all too often the trigger for panic and hasty planning. No real thought is then given to how long the conference needs to be to achieve the objective or even whether a conference is needed at all.

The thought process all too frequently runs like this:

'Bob, it's time we got down to planning the annual sales conference.'
'Ah yes, the annual booze up. We must go to a good hotel – last year's was a disaster. Remember?'
'Only too well. How many days do we want?'
'Oh, it's always only two – the MD insists it should be no longer.'
'Right, let's see how we can fill the time. What did we do last year?'

We need answers to five basic questions before we make any arrangements or take decisions about a proposed event. The whole plan for the event, its style, type, length, content and its eventual worth, rests upon the answers to these questions:

- ◆ *Why* do we need to hold a conference?
    - – to impart information?
    - – to collect information?
    - – to change attitudes?
    - – to boost morale through a difficult period?
    - – to motivate? ... and so on;
- ◆ *What* do we want to achieve?
- ◆ *Who* should attend?
- ◆ *When* should the event be held?
- ◆ *Where* should it be held?

WHY?

Why do we want to hold a meeting? This is a most fundamental question which is often never asked. As we have already seen, all too often it is first decided to hold a meeting and only then does someone try to decide how the time should best be spent.

Meetings are expensive. They absorb precious time and money. It is estimated that it takes over 300 executive man hours to arrange a two-day conference for about 200 people. Add to that the secretarial time, administrative costs and cost to the organization of gathering 200 people together (and do not forget the 'lost opportunity' cost penalty of taking these people away from their normal work) and the magnitude of the expense becomes apparent. It can take up a lot of executive time to arrange even a small meeting, while a large international conference can take several years to organize and can absorb around 3,000 executive man hours.

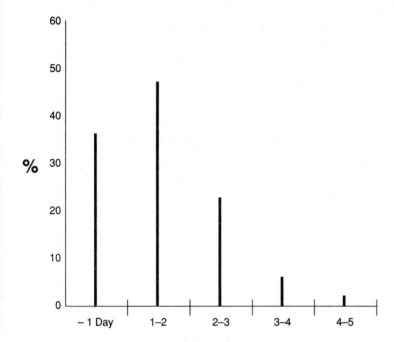

Figure 1.4 *Length of corporate events*

Faced with such costs, it is sensible to ask whether a meeting is needed at all. Can the information be put across in some other way – for example, by means of a news sheet or video film, a video conference or a series of factory/site visits by senior executives?

Corporate videos are used extensively these days. A short, well produced corporate video can cost as little as £20,000. Used by local managers in the company's various locations, a video can be just as effective a way of communicating an internal message as a conference – and far cheaper. By the same token, it may be cost effective to link up a number of corporate locations with video conference facilities, especially where frequent discussions are required. The savings in time and travel costs can be dramatic.

However, before deciding whether to opt for a corporate video or a video conference instead of a meeting, we need to think about the additional benefits we can derive from meetings.

Meetings and conferences satisfy definite social needs. People need to feel part of an organization and group identity is readily fostered by gathering them together. For example, a company sales force is usually

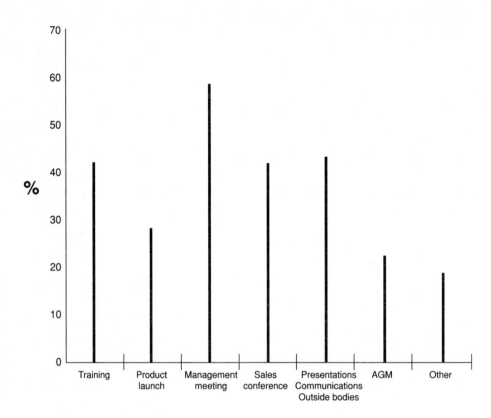

Figure 1.5   *Purpose of corporate events*

scattered far and wide. An annual sales force conference, or a special gathering to launch a new product, can do much to revitalize salesmen and rekindle their belief in their company. One travelling representative spoke enthusiastically about a company conference he had attended – the high-class hotel at which he had stayed, the late night drinking parties and, significantly, all the new things he had learnt about his company. Although he was middle-aged and a little tired and jaded, he was full of new enthusiasm for his company and its future. How else could his imagination have been so captured except through the obviously successful (and well organized) company sales conference he had just attended?

So meetings can do much to foster group identity and corporate spirit. They can also earn publicity. Think of the 'free' press and television coverage the annual political party conferences attract. A well organized product launch can capture the imagination of press and public alike, and new ideas and policies can be promulgated to large audiences through the medium of the public conference. The BBC has long been aware of this and regularly arranges local 'meet the BBC' events up and down the country. These expose senior management and local and national broadcasters to the criticisms of the viewing and listening public. As a public relations exercise they are invaluable and they probably also bring in a lot of information which helps shape future programme schedules.

Thus, meetings and conferences can do much more than pass on information. Even where the main objective is to pass information to delegates, the total information flow is very much greater than that covered in the formal sessions. It is widely recognized that the informal discussions at social functions and over drinks at the bar are equally important and, occasionally, even more valuable. Delegates learn from each other and the sensible conference organizer will allow plenty of time in the programme for exchanges of this kind, thereby satisfying many of the delegates' needs we identified earlier in the chapter.

The decision whether or not to hold a conference will not therefore be based purely upon the relative costs of putting across certain information. Most companies realize that, in spite of the financial cost of their conferences, product launches and management meetings, the value in human and intrinsic terms can far outweigh the cost and administrative disadvantages. And even the actual cost is often soon repaid by better performance and increased sales.

Nevertheless, it is wise to analyse the reason for holding the event in question. Sometimes the answer is obvious. It might be for a new product launch or an annual general meeting which is unavoidable. But, if the meeting appears to be at the whim of a senior executive, or is traditionally held and the tradition has never been seriously challenged, it will be worthwhile thinking again.

In any case, you must now consider the next question: *what* is to be achieved?

WHAT?

This question is all about setting objectives and deciding how these objectives can be met.

Objectives

The aim, or objective, of the proposed event is often implicit in the previous question. It will be much easier to work out succinct objectives if you have taken the trouble to find out why the event is needed. Objectives should be short statements rather than long-winded dissertations. Lengthy objectives are usually woolly and obscure – and woolly and obscure objectives lead to woolly and obscure meetings. How often have you been to a meeting where there is no agenda and no apparent objective? Without these, discussion is usually unstructured and aimless. Indeed, the meeting often turns out to be a waste of time because no decisions are taken or useful information exchanged. The same applies to any conference, meeting, training programme, seminar or workshop and also for incentives and corporate hospitality.

It is often possible to set down the objective in a single sentence. For example, the objective for the product launch might be 'to introduce the new model to the dealer network'.

Sometimes, subsidiary objectives may be set, in which case the objectives may extend to a short paragraph:

> To REWARD the sales force for their outstanding achievement in the past year. To INSPIRE confidence in the future and to BRIEF the sales force on the new product development programme. To MOTIVATE the sales force to meet next year's targets.

Always try to distil the objective into a sentence or short paragraph by using phrases like: 'To launch the new…', 'To inform executives of…', 'To teach…', 'To train…', 'To inspire…', and so on.

There is, of course, no reason why the objective for a public event should not be to make a profit. Many people are in the meetings and seminar business to make money and the need to plan events that are successful and profitable sharpens the mind wonderfully. (The organization of conferences for profit is dealt with in more detail in Chapter 9.) However, if you plan to market a public event, it is necessary to set parallel objectives which establish the product you wish to sell.

How to meet the objective

Having established the objective or objectives, it is possible to decide what has to be done to meet them. The whole length, style and content of the event is dictated by this consideration. This point is seldom realized. Typically, it is decided to hold, say, a two-day event and then someone tries to think of ways of filling the time. This approach almost invariably leads to the situation where either there is not enough time to cover the subject matter or, worse, there is too much time and some way has to be found of filling the programme.

The objectives will help you to decide what information has to be passed to the delegates and, perhaps, what information or contribution is required of them. Having decided the information flows involved, it is possible to sketch out a programme. The number of formal and informal sessions will be dictated by the amount of information to be exchanged. An outline requirement for audio-visual aids, demonstrations, displays and the need for group or syndicate sessions will emerge at this stage.

You might think it is not necessary to go into this sort of detail so early on. Notice, however, that a number of important parameters are set by the programme. It dictates the length of the event, some of the facilities needed (exhibition space, and seminar or syndicate rooms), the speakers, video and other audio-visual materials, etc. Until you have this information, it is not possible to complete the preliminary planning and costing. We return to programme planning in Chapter 3, but the subject has been introduced here to illustrate the importance of the programme in the initial planning process.

The objectives and programme also point to the sort of venue you will need. You will know from the programme what facilities will be needed, and the type of meeting will help you to decide what style and quality of venue you want. However, one further piece of information is required before we can decide exactly what sort of venue will be needed.

WHO?

Who should attend the event? This, too, is a function of the objectives. Sometimes the answer is self-evident. It might be easy to decide that all the sales force should be gathered in for a new product launch, but it is often less easy to work out who should attend other events. Careful thought is necessary to answer questions such as: Do all the area managers need to attend? How many members of the association will come? How many places can we sell on this seminar?

In all but events being 'sold' commercially, it is usually possible to be precise about the expected numbers: an estimate has to be made for commercial events. The chosen figure defines the size of venue needed and the age, seniority and background of the delegates will point to the standard of accommodation required.

WHEN?

It is not always easy to decide when to hold the event. Even when, by tradition, an annual conference is held at a certain time of the year, it is worth challenging tradition and looking at alternative dates. The main things to consider when you choose dates are discussed below. Most of them are interrelated.

Planning time

This is a factor which is often ignored but which is very important. The bigger the event, the longer it will take to plan and arrange. The lead time for some major international conferences is several years and even small seminars and training programmes have to be planned six to nine months ahead. There are many reasons for this. Everything takes more time than expected. If planning has to be rushed, mistakes are made, quality is reduced and costs go up. Finding venues at short notice can be a serious problem. The best places tend to be booked up well in advance. Other factors affecting the lead time include finding speakers, printing, preparation of audio-visual aids and the marketing plan for public events. Ensure that you make realistic estimates of the times these activities will take. Allow for holidays and add a safety margin.

It is always better to compromise on dates, or even to cancel an event, rather than rush the planning. One client asked a conference organizer to arrange a couple of public seminars against a very tight schedule. There was no room for any slip in marketing the seminars, printing the brochures, or even finding and briefing speakers. The organizer advised him to forget the idea if his timetable could not be changed. He was surprised but he must have seen reason because a few weeks later he approached the same organizer again and proposed a much more comfortable lead time.

Key dates

The timing of the event may be affected by key dates which cannot be altered. For example, the dates might be predetermined by the production schedule for a new product or by the legal requirement to hold an annual meeting before a certain date. The only flexibility available to the organizer where these restraints apply is the date on which he starts the planning process. This must be as early as possible.

Another key date factor is the availability of the people you want to come to the event. Whether you are marketing a seminar or arranging an in-company conference or meeting it is necessary to time the event so as to ensure the people will be free to attend. At the simplest level, this involves ringing round the secretaries of a few executives to ensure they are available on the chosen date. The shorter the notice, the more difficult it is to find a time and date which suits everyone. At certain times of the year it is even more difficult to find suitable dates – for example, you will find it is almost impossible to get a group of people together during the summer holidays.

The same difficulties apply for the larger events. It is necessary to give people plenty of notice in order to ensure that they keep the date free in their diaries. The peak holiday seasons and bank holidays should be avoided, as should seasonal factors when arranging events overseas, for example the monsoon season, or Ramadan. Check what other events are on, not only within the organization but also elsewhere, before fixing firm dates. It would be folly to try to arrange a seminar for public school headteachers during the week of their annual conference – but it has been tried!

Finally, check the availability of speakers and equipment which are vital for the event. At one conference, which involved the demonstration of a particular piece of equipment, it was only when the organizer contacted the appropriate production department that he discovered that no one had told them the equipment was needed. They were able to prepare it in time, but it was a close run thing. Just as it is no use planning a display of equipment if it will not be available, so it is wise not to fix dates before clearing them with VIPs involved, such as chairmen, key speakers and so on.

Tradition

Many company and association conferences and meetings are traditionally firmly fixed in the calendar. It is worthwhile reviewing such practices since it is often possible to make substantial savings by staging events during 'off peak' times of the year. This theme is dealt with in more detail in Chapter 4.

One-day events

There is some mystique in deciding what day of the week to use for one-day events. One executive always avoids Wednesdays, because a mid-week meeting ruins two weekends! Many people confine their one-day events to Tuesdays, Wednesdays or Thursdays. It is true that Friday can be a little difficult because people like to clear their 'in-trays' at the end of the week. Similarly, a very early start on Monday causes problems for some people. Nevertheless, Mondays and Fridays are not nearly as difficult as many people claim. It is quite easy to persuade even senior executives to come to seminars on these days, possibly because everyone else avoids them. It is usually much easier to book a decent venue on a Monday or Friday, or even over a weekend, for the same reason. (See also Figure 1.3, page 5.)

Perhaps the key, at least in the early stages of planning, is to be as flexible as possible over dates. This is especially so when answering the last of the five basic questions – where will the event be held?

WHERE?

Choosing the venue is one of the most important and difficult tasks which face the conference organizer. This is such an important and complex subject that it merits a chapter of its own (Chapter 2).

THE DETAILED PLAN

It is only after you have gone through the above outline planning process that you are ready to begin detailed planning. One of the earliest tasks, which is, to some extent, parallel to the above, is to work out a budget (Chapter 4). Deadlines and time-scales for the planning process have to be fixed and, for public events, a marketing plan will be needed. All this is normal executive work but, as already pointed out, it does require some specialist knowledge and a great deal of time.

Over 90 per cent of all conferences and meetings are arranged on a do-it-yourself basis by people who have other jobs to do. The remainder are handled either by permanent in-house conference staff or by professional conference organizers specially engaged for the task. Whoever is given the task has a difficult and demanding job. His role is to turn the sometimes vague ideas of one or two people into a successful event. If he is to succeed he must have the authority to use the resources he needs, sufficient time in which to do the job and the necessary experience or training to enable him to find his way around what is a complicated and demanding discipline.

The rest of this book is concerned with the task facing the conference organizer.

EXECUTIVE CHECKLIST

- ◆ Are all the meetings held in your organization strictly necessary?
- ◆ Are all your meetings and conferences successful – if not, why not?
- ◆ How well are your conferences and meetings planned – is too much left to the last minute… and to chance?

- What can be done to improve the planning of conferences, meetings, seminars and training programmes in your organization?
- Do you approach the task of organizing meetings with an open mind? Do ask yourself the five basic questions:

  1. Why do we need a meeting?
     - to impart information?
     - to collect information?
     - to change attitudes?
     - to boost morale through a difficult period?
     - to motivate... and so on;
  2. What do we want to achieve?
  3. Who should attend?
  4. When should the event take place?
  5. Where should it be held?

- How well defined are the objectives for your events? Do you always set objectives?
- Do you design a programme to meet those objectives?
- Do you evaluate your meetings?

2

CHOOSING THE VENUE

Choosing the venue is one of the most important – and difficult – tasks the conference organizer has to face. It would not be untrue to say that the majority of meetings are held in unsuitable venues. The most common fault lies in the venue itself, but poor catering, the wrong location and inadequate services are examples of other factors which affect suitability.

The choice of the venue – the standard, location, style and visual appearance – is as much a production decision as the staging of the event itself. If the delegate's first impressions of the venue are poor ('What a dump... it can't be a very important event if it is held in *this* place'), then he is likely to put the event in the same low category.

A really bad venue can actually destroy a conference. If your delegates become obsessed with their own comfort, bad food and poor service, they will concentrate on such topics instead of the business in hand. It is therefore no use accepting second best, be it for a small training programme for junior managers or for a major conference. It is the responsibility of the organizer to ensure that the venue selected matches the event in question.

Recently, a weekend board meeting was held in a Midlands hotel conveniently situated close to the M1 motorway and accessible to directors attending from London in the south and Bradford in the north. Although only a small meeting, a brief description of the day's proceedings reveals many lessons for the unwary. A working breakfast had been ordered for 8 o'clock and the meeting was to last all day. When the delegates arrived – on time in spite of fog and frost – they found the hotel totally unprepared; the meeting room could not be unlocked until the housekeeper came in at 9 o'clock and the group was told it could 'go into the coffee shop for breakfast'. Worse was to come. The room, when it finally opened, turned out to be a converted bedroom. The requisite boardroom table was crammed into the room along with a sofa, easy chairs, a television and other items of furniture. In the attached bathroom the bath was full of blankets, and there were no blotters, pads or pencils (these arrived later in the morning).

Lunch was a disaster. The hotel treated the group in the same manner as the rest of the day guests and served a leisurely one-and-a-half hour, heavy and soporific Sunday lunch. Finally, because it was Sunday, there was no-one available to handle complaints and put matters right.

This example – though trivial in its scale – is by no means isolated. Indeed, hotels are often justly criticized for their casual approach to their conference business. But in this example, both the hotel and the group holding the meeting were to blame – the hotel for its unprofessional and lackadaisical attitude towards the meeting and the organizer for selecting what was clearly an unsuitable venue.

Lest you think this example is too trivial to be important, this further case study reinforces the lesson. A mid-winter conference was held in a seaside hotel on the North Sea coast. A fading edifice which had clearly had its heyday in the Edwardian era, the delegates were of the firm opinion that the establishment must have been the inspiration for the BBC TV classic comedy, *Fawlty Towers*. A gale was blowing off the North Sea and it was bitterly cold (inside and outside the hotel), the service was dismal, the food institutional (and at best lukewarm) and the whole event became a rather grim survival exercise.

Ten years later, one delegate remembers the event – and the hotel – vividly. But he cannot recall why he went or what the conference was about. This is a classic example of an event actually being destroyed by the unsuitability of the venue. Just as a good venue can add so much to your event, so a bad venue can destroy it.

The planned approach to venue selection is described in this chapter, and some of the pitfalls to avoid are illustrated and discussed.

Venue selection is probably the task with which the inexperienced organizer most needs help. He is faced with a difficult and time-consuming exercise. Reliable and useful information on hotels and conference centres is hard to come by and it is often difficult to relate requirements to actual places. The problem is exacerbated by a general shortage of really first-class venues and by the fact that those which are good are invariably booked up well in advance. It is therefore necessary to start early and allow plenty of time.

Nevertheless, the inescapable fact is that lead times for both association and corporate meetings are decreasing (see Figures 2.1 and

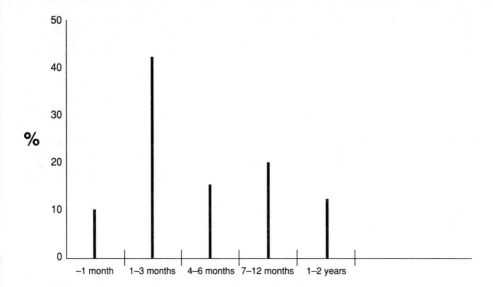

Figure 2.1   *How far in advance events are booked – corporate*

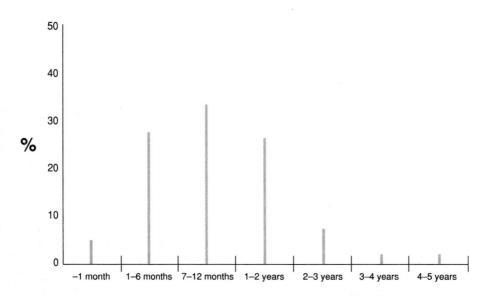

Figure 2.2   *How far in advance events are booked – associations*

2.2 – no doubt due to the ever-increasing pace of business life, but the major scientific, medical and association meetings are still booked up to four or five years ahead, mainly to ensure that the right venues are reserved and to allow time for the 'call for papers' and for their assessment and selection.

THE SPECIFICATION

Before reaching for the *Yellow Pages*, or ringing the nearest hotel, it is wise to draw up a detailed specification listing what you will need for your meeting. In Chapter 1 we saw that the answers to the basic questions 'why?', 'what?', 'who?' and 'when?' give a good idea of the type of event, its style, length, content and where it should be held. The following paragraphs discuss the main points to consider.

Budget

This is mentioned first because it will almost invariably be a major consideration. But you are faced with a chicken-and-egg situation: you cannot set a budget until you have found a venue and know how much it will cost you, but the choice of venue is directly related to how much you are prepared to spend.

Perhaps the best approach is to decide upon what general standard of venue you want. We have seen that a poor venue can destroy your event. And we also know those who attend the event will have expectations of their own: senior managers *expect* a quality venue whereas junior staff may feel far more comfortable at a less expensive venue.

Then, with the overall budget at the back of your mind, you can begin to reconcile the conflicting pressures you will inevitably encounter.

For most organizers, location is far and away the most important consideration.

Geographical considerations

Decide roughly where you want to go. Are you looking for something more exotic – for example, it is often part of the plan for an incentive conference to go to an exotic or unusual place – or for geographical convenience: good communications, well placed for all delegates, and so on?

In this way you will soon have a good idea of where to look. One company always arranged its annual sales conference in Manchester. The sales manager was adamant that the Manchester should be used even though he realized that it would almost certainly be possible to find better facilities elsewhere. His reasons were cast iron. His sales force had to come from all over the United Kingdom and from Ireland. He knew from previous experience that Manchester was the most accessible and cheapest place at which to gather the sales force together.

It is not possible to lay down firm rules. The country – or even the town – is sometimes part of the specification for the event. For example, the sponsors of most major international conferences make firm decisions to go to specific countries many years in advance. (This is, incidentally, a decision-making process of which the major conference cities are well aware and there is intense international competition to attract the more prestigious conferences: competition which itself can impinge upon, and even distort, the venue choice decision process.)

However, when the decision is left to the organizer, or only the vaguest guidance is given, he must ask himself questions like: 'Is there a natural town or area for the event?', 'Do we want a rural or cosmopolitan setting?', 'Will access be a problem?', and so on. Accessibility and methods of travel are important considerations, especially if delegates are to arrive by air or train, since their transfer from the airport or railway station to the venue can be a major problem. The rail operating companies do not offer the special conference discount fares once available through the old British Rail (although they do operate group fares for 10 or more people travelling together). Even so, rail travel can be an attractive alternative to going by car – especially in winter.

For those who do prefer to travel by car, the improved motorway network makes most venues within striking distance of a motorway a practical proposition.

Secrecy and security   These factors may dictate where the event can – or more often, cannot – take place. For example, a number of years ago when Sky, the satellite television company was negotiating to buy out its rivals, BSB, privacy was essential. Had the two sides been observed meeting up either in a London hotel or in each other's offices, rumours could have leaked to an already jittery City, share prices might then have moved and the deal might have been called off. The setting chosen for the meetings was a secluded country house hotel 80 miles from London. Set deep in the countryside, cloistered behind high walls, privacy was preserved throughout the delicate and protracted negotiations.

Overseas events   Similar considerations to those described above will, of course, also apply to overseas events, but many other factors such as airline schedules, costs and even the time of year must be taken into account. For example, it is probably too hot to hold a conference in Egypt in midsummer, but the weather is very pleasant in the winter months. The overseas venue should not automatically be ruled out when budgets

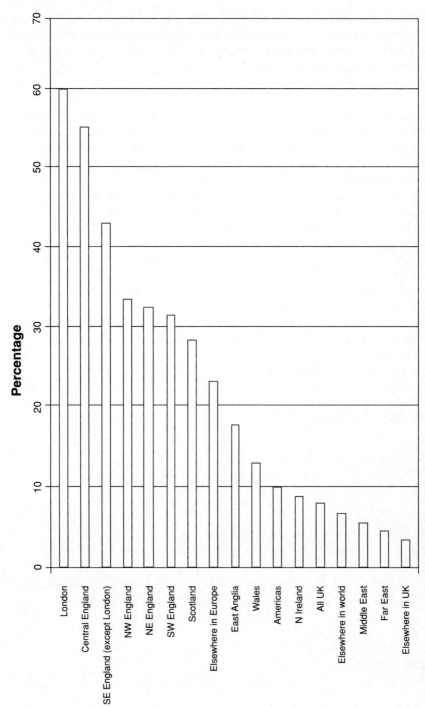

Figure 2.3 *Destinations used – corporate events*

are tight. It can actually be cheaper to hold a conference abroad than in Britain. That said, there are many pitfalls, for example company restrictions on the numbers of people who may travel together on one aircraft: these may make it impossible to use some destinations. Organizing conferences overseas is discussed in more detail in Chapter 8.

Environment   The type of event itself will also tell you much about the geographical location. Many residential management programmes are held in rural settings where the delegates can benefit from the atmosphere of informality and peace, probably in marked contrast to their normal places of work. Such a change of environment makes it easier for them to put work problems aside and concentrate on the programme. In contrast, an international conference may well have to be held in London, Paris or Rome so that delegates can see the tourist sights. However, the organizer of the international event should not neglect the less obvious places. Many provincial towns and cities in Britain are excellent tourist and conference centres and, by the same token, the choice facing the organizer of a conference in, say, America, is very much wider than New York or Chicago.

These considerations will give the organizer a good idea of roughly where to look for the venue. The decision process may be complex, especially for international events where air fares have to be negotiated and outline transport plans drawn up.

How big must the venue be?

This is the first question to answer in drawing up a detailed specification. It is not just a matter of deciding how many delegates are expected and finding somewhere big enough in terms of seating capacity and the number of bedrooms. As we saw in Chapter 1, the type of programme (session types, breakdown sessions, AV content, residential or non-residential) will dictate the type of venue and the support facilities you will need.

It is of course necessary to work out how many people will actually be involved – delegates, speakers, exhibition and administrative staff and so on. This is not always easy. It is notoriously difficult to predict the response to a public event. A considerable degree of judgement is needed to decide how big a venue to book for an event which will not be marketed for sometime after the booking becomes firm. This, and the other challenges for the organizer of public events, is discussed in greater detail in Chapter 9.

The number of delegates expected and the proposed programme will lead to other important specifications:

1. *The Main Hall or Meeting Room* What style of seating layout is required? There are several options:

- Classroom;
- Boardroom and hollow square;
- 'U' shaped;
- Theatre;
- Cabaret;
- Workshop;
- Political or Euro.

There are other layouts, for example 'T' shape, 'V' shape (or 'herringbone'), but these are not used very often.

The chosen layout will, to some extent, be dictated by the number of delegates and the type of event. The plenary sessions of a conference for several hundred or even thousands of people will probably have to be held in a large theatre, but there is considerable flexibility for the smaller meeting and it is worth thinking of the needs of both delegate and speaker before opting for a particular layout. Ask yourself questions like:

'Do the delegates need to write and take notes?' If they do, the classroom layout may be the most appropriate, or special chairs with writing rests may be needed.

'What audio-visual aids will be used?' The answer to this question can dictate the suitability or otherwise of many meeting rooms and conference hotels (see item 2 on page 33).

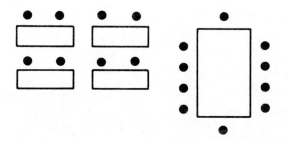

Classroom
Takes space but allows delegates to spread papers and take notes. Not suitable for large meetings.

Boardroom
Ideal for meetings involving discussion and decision taking. Suitable for groups up to about 30 people

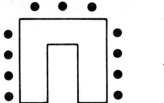

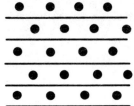

'U' shaped
Good for small training
meetings which involve
discussion between
delegates or where an
intimate atmosphere is
needed.

Theatre
Most suitable for large
numbers of delegates.
Ideally, seats should be
fixed to tiered or
sloping floor.

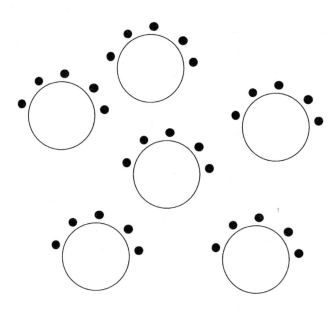

Cabaret/Workshop
Increasingly popular alternative to theatre or classroom layout for medium-
sized meetings. Especially liked by speakers at Human Resources events.

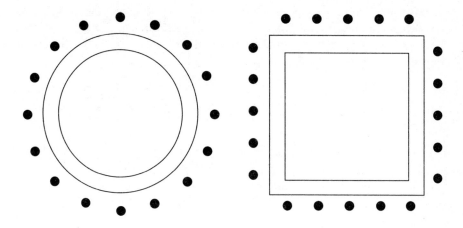

Political or Euro   *Closed square or Circle*
No seniority – delegates can be seated behind their representative.

'Is a more intimate layout needed – for example, a boardroom table for informal discussions? Is the 'U' shape more suitable?'

Even when the number leads to a theatre layout, thought must be given to the form of seating required. Will you demand fixed, tiered (or 'raked') seating, or will a flat floor suffice?

Once these options have been resolved, you can work out how large the meeting room needs to be. It is important to do this, since there seems to be no accepted standard for venues to follow when stating how many people a particular room will hold. However, there are maximum numbers set by health and safety and fire regulations, which the venue owner should know. Obviously, if the seating is fixed, the numbers are also fixed (subject to certain conditions which we will examine in Chapter 5), but where the floor is flat and the seating arrangements flexible, the capacities are less obvious. Table 2.1 gives a broad indication of the size of room you will need for different numbers of people seated in theatre and classroom layouts. This will help you to decide roughly how large a room you will need for your particular event.

2. *Audio-Visual (AV)* After the suitability and size of the conference facilities, this is arguably the most important aspect of the average event. It is also the most neglected. The prevailing attitude seems to be that a handful of colour slides and the odd video clip present no technical difficulty when dropped into a presentation. This is manifestly not so and, if

audio-visual aids are to be introduced, it is worthwhile going into considerable detail over this part of the requirement, since very few venues are properly equipped for even the most basic audio-visual work.

Table 2.1 *Size of room required for different numbers of people seated in theatre and classroom layout*

Number of people	Approximate area * (m^2) needed for		
	Classroom layout	Theatre layout	Reception/ tea/coffee
10	16	†	†
15	24	†	†
20	32	15	†
25	40	19	†
30	48	23	18
40	64	30	24
50	80	38	30
75	120	57	45
100	200	75	60
125	230	93	75
150	**	112	85
175	**	130	100
200	**	150	115
250	**	190	145
300	**	230***	175
400	**	300***	235
500	**	400***	300
1,000	**	745***	600
1,500	**	1,120***	900
2,000	**	1,500***	

*	See Table 2.2 for room size guide
**	Loose tables and chairs not recommended for these numbers; use tiered lecture theatres with writing facilities or theatre-style layout
***	Consider using theatre with fixed seating for these numbers
†	Even small numbers of people will be cramped if the room is too small

Note: Room capacities are reduced when other than simple audio-visual aids are to be used – see Chapter 5 (Table 5.1) for further details.

The surveys described in Chapter 1 reveal that 70% of all organizers either do not use audio-visual or provide it themselves. This emphasizes the importance of the attitude of the venue to AV; very few are properly equipped for even the most basic audio-visual work. If a venue demonstrates a lack of understanding of even simple AV, or if it does not have its own basic AV equipment, it may not be worth considering further. We return to this particular theme later in the chapter and AV in relation to the venue specification is discussed in detail in Chapter 5.

3. *Reception and Display Areas and Exhibitions*   Many conferences and meetings involve displays of equipment, charts, photographs and so on, and some are associated with larger exhibitions. These requirements are, of course, part of the specification, along with the reception facilities and areas for coffee, meals and so on. It has been estimated that only 20% of the total venue floor space is used for the formal proceedings of the typical conference. The remaining space is needed for reception, coffee and tea breaks, displays, syndicate rooms, eating and so on. Life will be miserable for everyone if insufficient space is allowed for these activities. One conference was all but ruined by inadequate reception and catering facilities at the venue. There was nowhere for delegates to put their coats and briefcases as they arrived and the lavatories were on a different floor. This might not have been so bad had they not had to queue up to be formally announced as they arrived in this cramped area. The chaos was unbelievable! But worse was to come. The conference room was 'L' shaped and coffee, tea and lunch were all served in the bottom leg of the 'L'. The day's proceedings were conducted to a background noise of the clattering of plates and tea cups, in spite of the genuine attempts of the staff to keep quiet.

Bearing this case in mind, it is well worth spending as much time and care over the specification and selection of these areas as of the meeting room itself.

It is not the aim of this book to deal with large exhibitions, but even small exhibitions and displays alongside a conference have requirements which must be taken into account. This subject is dealt with in detail in Chapter 7. Suffice to say here that a typical stand for a small exhibition will require about 100 square feet (9.3 – say 10 – square metres) of space. It will also need a power supply (the power consumption will depend upon the equipment to be displayed, but a 13 amp socket per stand is usually sufficient) and it may be necessary to specify the floor bearing strength, ceiling height, access and other services.

4. *Syndicate Rooms*   Separate break-down sessions are a feature of many events. For example, groups of delegates may wish to discuss specialized aspects of a particular subject, or the delegates may be split into a number of syndicates to consider a particular problem. Syndicate or discussion rooms or smaller theatres will be needed for such separate sub-sessions. The requirement for these must be specified and, as for the main theatre, the size worked out on the basis of the numbers of people who will use these rooms and the types of seating required. In addition, any special equipment or other materials must be specified – for example, desks, whiteboards or flip charts may be needed. Closed circuit television or role-play kits, telephones and other specialist equipment are needed in syndicate rooms for some events.

5. *Accommodation and Catering*   Meals and refreshments are an important part of the conference specification. We examine this subject in some depth in subsequent chapters but decisions on these items will dictate the space and the level of service which will be needed.

The number of rooms/delegate beds must be specified for residential conferences along with any sports and recreational facilities required. This part of the specification ties in with the style and standard of venue you want. The different needs of different groups of people were briefly mentioned in Chapter 1. It is also very much a function of the budget for the event. In drawing up your plan for food and accommodation, ask yourself:

◆ 'Will delegates share rooms?' (More popular than might be imagined, especially among younger delegates.)
◆ 'What is the balance between males and females? Will partners attend?'
◆ 'What sort of meals do we want?' (Buffet or sit down, hot or cold, etc.)
◆ 'Where and when will coffee and tea be wanted?'
◆ 'Do we need a bar?'

and so on. It will be much easier to hold a proper discussion with the venue staff if you have sorted out your ideas before you meet them.

6. *Security and Privacy*   As mentioned on page 28, any special needs must be known by the organizer. Valuable equipment or confidential conference proceedings must be protected and these considerations will affect the choice of venue. A good example of a secure venue is Leeds Castle in Kent. It is comparatively easy to insure and is accordingly a popular venue for top-level government conferences and other exclusive events. Security is discussed in greater detail in Chapter 13.

What support facilities will be needed?

Having broadly specified the size and type of meeting and display facilities needed, you should draw up a list of all the support accommodation and facilities the event will require. The following list is not in any way comprehensive, but is designed to show you the sort of detail into which it is necessary to go at this stage of the plan.

Office There can be few events where the organizer does not need a personal office. He or she will have to deal with crises, meet people and, occasionally, seek refuge from the crush. An office, close to the main meeting room and the reception area, is an important but frequently neglected part of the specification.

The office will need a telephone with Direct Dialling facility (or, in order to avoid the often exorbitant mark-up on the standard BT unit charge, it may be worth considering using a portable telephone).

Office Services Conference organizers, speakers and delegates all need office support during a conference. Speakers may wish to alter their papers or visuals at the last minute, delegates may have urgent letters to send and typing and photocopying services are always in demand. It is sometimes necessary to ask the venue to provide these services and this requirement must be included in the specification. Not all venues can cope, and staff and office equipment may have to be hired in specially. Even if a venue does claim to provide office or secretarial service, it is worth checking how comprehensive these are. Will they be available in the evenings? What sort of photocopier does the venue supply? Is it adequate for the task? What are the charges for its use? Will a PC be available and, if so, what software does it have? Do they provide adequate fax facilities? Will secretaries be able to take shorthand? All these aspects must be planned and checked in advance of the event.

Stage and Changing Facilities Many product launches involve stage shows, with dancers and other entertainments. These, too, must be accurately known in order that the right facilities can be found. Similarly, if sets are to be built or equipment shown on stage, these items must be included in the specification.

Rehearsal Room If several speakers are involved, it is wise to have a rehearsal room for them where they can check their computer graphics and load slides, work on their scripts and so on. This prevents their being a nuisance to the organizer and the projectionist and gives them somewhere to calm their troubled nerves!

Secure Storage Room/Space   For PCs, AV equipment, documents, hand-outs and so on.

Press Facilities   A suitable room and telephones must be provided if the press is expected to attend. In addition, special press facilities may be required in the conference hall, for example a press table, telephones and, for radio and television, space to install equipment, lighting and so on. Television, in particular, places considerable demands upon the venue and it is as well to involve the TV producers when choosing the venue.

Telephones   Not all venues have a large enough switchboard or suffi-cient spare extensions to cope with the demands of the conference orga-nizer. Information systems, such as the Internet, and computer terminals are often installed for conferences and they may need ISDN telephone lines. You must therefore work out the telephone facilities you will need before you visit the venue. It may be necessary to have special lines installed in which case British Telecom must be contacted to ensure that this will be possible.

Alternatively, it may make sense to hire portable telephones for the conference (eg Cellnet or Vodafone) – or use your own! These have the merit of being independent of the hotel/venue switchboard, and you avoid the often extortionate mark-up hotels, in particular, apply on tele-phones – anything from 300–600%!

Hand-held pocket telephones are a boon to the organizer.

Satellite Links   If you wish to install satellite links, this requirement should be part of your specification.

Simultaneous Translation   At some international events it is necessary to provide a simultaneous translation for foreign delegates. Interpreters are normally housed in special soundproof booths (one for each language) and headsets and selector controls are provided for each delegate. The latter may involve wiring to each set (although modern systems work on Infra Red signals) and, when simultaneous translation is to be given, the requirements for installing equipment and booths must be taken into account when considering the venue specification.

Leisure Facilities   Many conference organizers like to include leisure facilities (swimming pool, sauna, fitness centre and so on) in their venue specification even though, in reality, these are often hardly used by participants.

Car Parking   This is an often forgotten but important part of the specifi-cation. Many good venues in London are difficult to reach by car and, worse, have no parking facilities of their own or nearby. This situation is by no means unique to London and applies not only in the larger cities but even in some quite small towns. Even when a hotel has its own car park, it may not be possible to reserve places for conference delegates since hotels do not wish to deny parking space to other guests. Some hotels sub-let their car parks (for example, to NCP) and delegates may be charged for parking their cars. In this case it is worth negotiating a special contract with the car park company and, perhaps, including the cost of car parking in the conference budget.

VIP Parking/Valet Parking Especially good for executives and guest speakers.

Coaches and Loading Space If your event involves bringing delegates to the venue by coach (for example, from other hotels or from airports) you need to pay particular attention to this problem. Even two or three coaches take up a lot of space both when picking up and setting down passengers and when they are parked (you may not want to risk sending them off to park somewhere else – you may never see them again!)

By the same token, if a set is to be constructed or there is a lot of AV equipment and paperwork to unload, you need to ensure there is unloading and loading space close to the meeting rooms.

The list of things to include in the specification is already becoming a long one, and yet we have only talked in general terms about the typical needs for any event. The point is that a detailed specification, geared to the event in question, is a vital prerequisite for finding the right venue. Without this information, the subsequent search can be meaningless.

Porterage and Lifts Remember to check what porterage will be available and where the lifts are sited. Paper is very heavy – recently an Association had over 3,500 kilogrammes of handouts to take to a confer-ence. It was a problem in itself to get them into a hired lorry, then into the venue, stored and then distributed; but the final problem was that the delegates, many of whom came from overseas, were then subject to excess baggage charges. Again, distribution and access via the Internet will solve many of these problems.

The 'Ideal' Training Room For many conferences it is possible to create your own environment in the meeting room: this may involve building a set, importing special lighting and so on. This means the appearance of the room is not vital for these events. This is not quite the case for small training meetings. Little can be done to improve what is on offer at the venue. It is therefore advisable to have in one's mind an 'ideal' for your training room and confine your later research to trying to match this ideal. Figure 2.4 (page 41) illustrates the 'ideal' training room.

Going 'Green': Environmental issues

Few people can be unaware of the environmental lobby these days: concern for the environment touches every corner of our lives. Many people are deeply concerned about the environment. For example, delegates to one European management education venue complained vociferously about the plastic cups provided at the coffee vending machines. And many companies have very positive and demanding environmental policies.

It will therefore not surprise the reader to learn that green considerations are beginning to be applied to conferences and meetings. There is already an international conservation agency, Green Flag International, which works with the travel industry to stimulate environmental awareness, whilst the International Hotels and Environmental Initiative (IHIE) programme actively promotes the economic advantages of water conservation, recycling, donating food and collecting contributions for wildlife schemes. In one recent year, Inter-Continental Hotels saved US$5m (£3.3m) from its energy saving programme alone. The company has its own environmental operations manual based on the policies of 'reduce, reuse and recycle'. Other major hotel chains have similar policies: amongst IHIE members are Conrad International, Hilton International, Holiday Inn Worldwide, Inter-Continental, Sheraton, Marriott and Renaissance, to name just a few.

Organizers of incentives, in particular, need to be sensitive to environmental issues. Some incentive destinations, for example, the Seychelles, charge premiums which go towards funding conservation projects; others apply restrictions – for example on the numbers of visitors to sensitive areas like coral reefs. Surveys show that 10 per cent of travellers are prepared to pay an environmental premium and 80 per cent express concern about the environment. On these grounds alone, organizers should treat environmental issues seriously, otherwise they could end up by upsetting both their delegates and their destination countries.

Green Flag International produce a leaflet which offers a traveller's guide to green tourism. This can be adapted to the conference and incentive market and it is available in bulk for groups for a small printing charge.

You can also ask hotels about their local recycling projects and waste disposal. You can find out whether group handlers and car hire firms are using catalytic converters and lead free petrol in their coaches and cars – and so on.

These may seem to be trivial issues, but we have to start somewhere. And, if your delegates realize you are taking environmental issues seriously, the chances are they will be more supportive and appreciative.

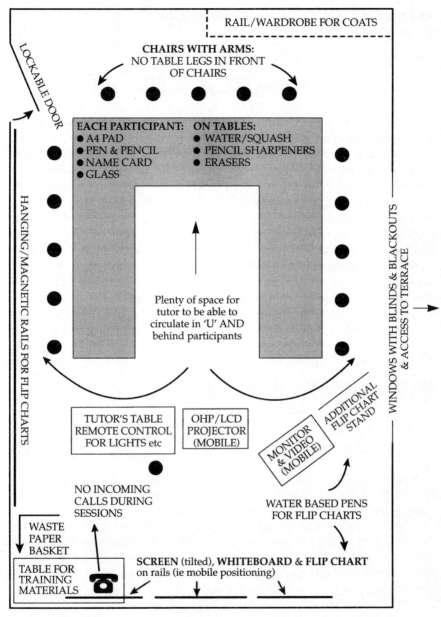

Figure 2.4 *The ideal training room*

Environmental issues may well therefore form a basic element of your specification.

DESK RESEARCH

Once you have a detailed specification you are ready to start looking for your venue and you will need luck, patience and perseverance in this task. Your first problem is to decide where to look. You will already have an idea of the area you want; the problem is to find what hotels there are in that area, whether there are any conference centres in the region and what other possibilities there are. Before embarking on a lengthy, costly and time-consuming search for the 'ideal' hotel or conference centre, it is worth looking at your own organization. Many companies have their own training centres, others have prestige boardrooms and conference facilities. Some organizations are highly autonomous and few executives in one division have any idea of what facilities are available in another. However, assuming that no suitable in-house facilities exist, how do you go about the task of finding your venue?

Sources of information

Your greatest problem – especially if you are a first time organizer – is where to look for information on venues in your target area. If the event is to be in your local area, you can reach for *Yellow Pages* or even use your own knowledge. But if you are planning to go to an area you do not know, how can you even begin to find out what venues are in the area?

Thanks to technology, help is to hand. There are several computerized venue databases available commercially, and many hotel chains promote their venues on the Internet.

Computerized venue directories take a lot of the drudgery out of your desk research. The principal benefit is being able to enter your search criteria – which can be any combination of dozens of criteria from event size to geographical location and from room capacity to leisure facilities. The systems produce instant shortlists of venues which you can then call to screen individually.

Viewpoint is a CD ROM based system which includes colour photographs of venues – often several pictures of each venue from exterior shots to pictures of bedrooms, meeting rooms and leisure facilities. Viewpoint have both a UK and worldwide directory which is updated twice yearly with the issue of new CD ROMs and on a monthly basis on the Internet.

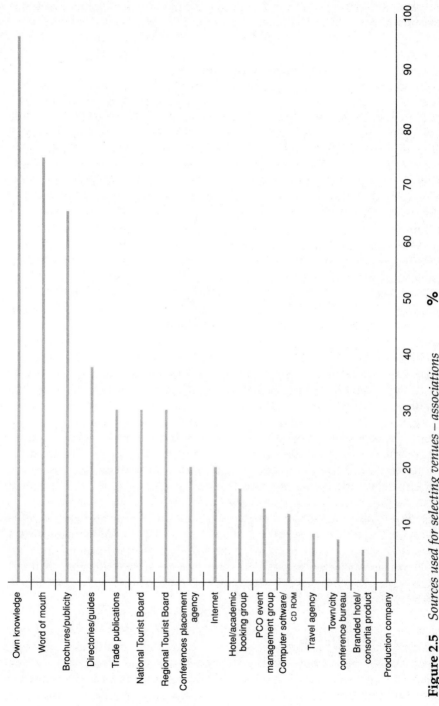

Figure 2.5 *Sources used for selecting venues – associations*

Another system, Venue Directory, offers similar search facilities but does not provide pictures of venues. However, it has what it calls a 'notebook' facility which allows you to add your own venues, or your own notes on venues you have used or visited.

Both systems operate on Windows format.

In addition to the above there are plenty of other sources of information. The major hotel chains have glossy information packs for their conference hotels, and there are a few independent publications, for example, the *Conference Blue Book* published by Miller Freeman Technical, the *OFMG* guide which has separate volumes for Europe and North America, and the *Worldwide Convention Centres Directory* which is sponsored by Phillips. The addresses for the first and third guides – which are usually offered free to genuine buyers – are given at the end of the book. The *OFMG* guide is published by Reed-Elsevier. A word of warning: these guides and databases are inevitably selective (venues pay to be included) and it is almost impossible to obtain all the information theoretically available. Even if the information could be assembled, there are further problems.

First, although there are hotel grading systems (for example, some guides use 'percentage' gradings, and the AA and RAC star-systems are widely used) these never cover the conference facilities. In fact, even the hotel star ratings are widely misunderstood: they actually refer to the facilities provided rather than to standards (although there is some correlation between the two, this is not always the case: some luxury country house hotels only rate three stars because they do not offer the facilities needed to merit higher star ratings).

Second, the facilities offered by many venues do not always match up to the promotional image. There is still a critical shortage of really good conference facilities in this country and the situation is not all that much better abroad. True, if you are trying to place an international conference for several hundreds of delegates you will have a good choice of prestige centres, but if your event is for around 200 people or 20 senior managers, the choice, although wider in terms of the number of potential venues, is in fact restricted because so few of them are really suitable for meetings at all.

Nevertheless, desk research and time spent on the telephone will not be wasted. An alternative to this 'do-it-yourself' approach might be to use a conference placement agency.

Placement agencies

Conference placement agencies (sometimes called venue finding services) are a bit like travel agents. They will undertake venue searches for you and provide you with a short-list of suitable and available venues from which you are invited to choose. Their services are truly free in that you are not charged for the searches made on your behalf, the cost of the operation being funded out of commission income from the venues where the business is eventually placed.

The advantages of using a conference placement agency are simple, but compelling:

◆ *You save time – and money.* The staff of a specialist agency are well used to the task of searching for venues and have access to a considerable bank of information based on research, knowledge and experience, and the opinions of previous clients. They also tend to be well informed about new venues as they come on the market and, because the agency staff tend to make a lot of facility visits, they have personal knowledge of a wide variety of venues. Better agencies have computerized data bases to help ensure an objective search. The 'occasional' organizer simply has neither the time nor the money to accumulate this sort of knowledge. The placement agency will probably know beforehand what venues have availability on the required dates and will therefore be better placed to come up with a short-list without wasting time on fruitless research.

◆ *Price.* The larger agencies have considerable purchasing power and are therefore often able to negotiate more competitive rates on your behalf – and know how to go about these negotiations. You will almost certainly end up with a more competitive price than you would if you negotiated direct with the venue.

◆ *'New' venues.* The better agencies have an almost uncanny ability to come up with real 'gems' – excellent venues that are ideal for your event – and of which, if you did not consult an agency, you would probably never have known.

The final choice of venue must still be yours – and visits to inspect those short-listed (with whom the agency will have made provisional bookings on your behalf) and to discuss the event with the venue staff are essential. It would be foolish indeed to accept the recommendation of a third party, even an agency, and to turn up on the day expecting everything to be in order … it has been known, but the better agencies would not let you be so casual! Inspection visits are discussed later in the chapter.

The eventual contract is usually between the user – you – and the venue, and not between the placement agency and the venue. In this respect, the agency acts as your agent and not as principal in the contract. This means that your *contracted* relationship – including liability to cancellation – is the same as if you had found the venue yourself.

Placement agencies are estimated to handle about 20 per cent of all conference bookings placed in hotels. In spite of this, some conference organizers are reluctant to use them, possibly because they fear they will lose control or that the agencies work for the venues rather than for their clients. What is more, as in any marketplace, some are better than others. Some are very good – some, being charitable, are not so good.

How can you find out how well a particular agency will serve you? One way is to ask a few probing questions:

♦ *'How can I be sure you will negotiate the best possible rate for me when you are operating on commission?'*
As we have seen, placement agencies earn their living from commission paid by venues on business they introduce. There are no standard commission rates, but it is no secret that the average commission runs out at 8–8½% on *pre-booked* accommodation, room hire, food and beverages.

However, commission rates vary widely (especially when particular venues are desperate for business and offer higher commission rates and other incentives) and some agencies will tend to steer you towards those venues which either pay a higher commission or are the more expensive – thereby maximizing their own income. If they do this, they can hardly claim to be doing their best for you.

So ask them what their policy is. And ask them what commission they stand to receive from the venues they recommend. If they will not tell you or admit percentages over 8–8½%, you can draw your own conclusions.

♦ *'Can you negotiate a discount for me?'*
It is not realistic to expect venues to discount their rates on small events in high season. But if you are placing a lot of business, or if you are holding your event 'out of season', you should *expect* the placement agency to negotiate a lower price for you. And, as indicated earlier, some agencies are able to command lower prices by virtue of the sheer volume of business they handle.

♦ *'Will you book me into a venue that does not pay commission?'*
Some venues do not pay commission to placement agencies and many agencies refuse to recommend these venues even if they would be best for their clients – either on suitability or cost. This is clearly not in the clients' interest.

Of course, in these circumstances, the agency is in a dilemma. If they do not receive commission, they lose income – and like any business they need to earn their living. One possible solution is for them to charge you a placement fee. The other is to accept the loss on that occasion in the hope that you are well satisfied and will use them again – possibly choosing a commission paying venue next time.

If an agency you speak to will not deal with venues which do not pay commission, do not deal with that agency.

♦ *'Wouldn't I do better to book direct?'*

Almost certainly not. You may think you will get a better rate by cutting out the placement agency, but you would be mistaken. If you book a flight, the cost is the same whether you book through a travel agent or direct with the airline (in fact, sometimes it is actually less expensive to use a travel agent). By the same token, hotels will not, as a general rule, reduce their rates if you approach them direct. It is not in their interest to do so, otherwise the industry would degenerate into a state of distrust, wheeler dealing and secret discounting. Everyone would lose in such a climate.

♦ *'Suppose I use a PCO working on a fee basis? Can I then pay net rates?'*

You can try, but most PCOs (professional conference organizers) receive commission on bookings placed through them and reduce their fees for organizing your event accordingly. PCOs who are members of the Association of British Professional Conference Organisers (ABPCO) are obliged to tell you if they take commission from suppliers when they quote their fees.

Many production and PR companies operate on the same basis although they, too, often use placement agencies to find venues for their clients, in which case the commission is paid to the placement agency and the question does not arise.

In short, placement agencies should work for you and do their utmost to find the best venue they can to suit your event. They should ensure you get the best deal, and they should help you by arranging inspection visits – sending someone along with you if you feel you need expert advice on the spot.

So, before you commit yourself to a particular agency, ask the above questions. If the replies you receive are evasive or unsatisfactory, use another agency.

WHAT SORT OF VENUE?

An early decision you will face is that of what sort of venue you should use. There are several types of venue, each with advantages and disadvantages.

Hotels

These are discussed first because the majority of conferences are held in hotels – not, it has to be said, because they are in some way the best type of venue but because, by volume rather than quality, they offer the greatest choice. Some are very good, some are very bad, most are just average. The major problem with hotels is that they are designed and run to provide visitors with food, drink and accommodation. Many hotels still regard the conference delegate in this light and few are prepared to provide all the extras the conference organizer invariably wants.

Many a hotel calls itself a 'conference centre' because it happens to have a large room which was once a ballroom and is now, thanks to the demise of the tea dance and formal ball, a rarely used white elephant.

The conference trade is seen as a useful and lucrative way of making these old rooms pay again but they are often offered with the minimum of facilities. As a result, the conference organizer is presented with a room which may not be the right shape or size, lacks the necessary extra adjacent space for displays, meals, receptions and the like, is next to a noisy kitchen, faces on to a busy main road, and, because it is a dual-use room, may be wanted for a disco or banquet in the evenings. One hotel in Yorkshire actually has a bar in full view behind the top table end of its conference room and one London hotel which still runs weekly tea dances has to insist that events on Fridays end early to make way for the dance.

This may seem harsh criticism, but it is undoubtedly true in many cases. That said, there are also some very good hotels, with excellent and modern conference facilities, the requisite equipment and staff who understand the needs of the conference organizer. These gems apart, it must be accepted that the hotel is usually a compromise conference venue. You can easily find hotels which offer excellent living accommodation and fine food. Many of them are small and private and ideal for the senior executives' meeting. Other are cosmopolitan and can cope with large numbers of conference visitors. However, in opting for these qualities you will almost certainly find that the meeting rooms are less than perfect. This is because these rooms are almost invariably 'multi-functional' which is to say that, in addition to meetings, they are used for many other purposes – everything from dinners to wedding receptions, and from exhibitions to antique fairs. Even the more modern meeting rooms may be claustrophobic, with low ceilings and no windows. Almost all will lack projection booths, built-in screens and tiered seating.

The conference organizer must decide whether he is prepared to accept this compromise. Is a hotel really the best place for a management course or a bare ballroom best for staging a product launch? True, the latter can be improved by constructing sets and a stage, but is it cost-effective to do so? Do you want your delegates to come into the conference through the hotel lobby, competing with the outgoing tourists? Or, as at a recent seminar held in a high-class hotel, do you want them to have to walk through the breakfast dining room to get to the meeting room? Is it acceptable to hold a major event, perhaps with video and slides, in a room with no projection box, inadequate blackout and no tiered seating?

In many cases, the answer to many of the above questions may be 'yes', or you may be prepared to accept some limitations in order to be at the right location, or to have the right accommodation and food. Or you might be able to use one of the rare excellent hotels which have everything you want. However, if you are unable to find a suitable hotel, what are the alternatives?

Universities

Universities have some of the finest lecture theatres in the country. Many are very modern and are equipped with the more common audio-visual aids. Some hold only a dozen or so people, others hundreds, and a few are even larger. Such theatres are excellent for conference use because they are properly equipped and have raked seating and other facilities. Accommodation is available, usually on site, and there is often space for an exhibition alongside the conference.

The university environment is, in many ways, ideal for a conference. The academic atmosphere, the availability of back-up (especially office support) and excellent campus amenities (everything from botanical gardens to museums and from galleries to first class sports facilities) are all attributes not easily found elsewhere.

Universities have not been slow to recognize that they are sitting on a valuable asset which, during the vacation periods, was not being used. Most now offer conference facilities during the summer and Easter vacations (and some offer them all the year round) and the rates are very reasonable. What is more, because they have accommodation for large numbers of students, universities can handle larger events on one site – something which is not possible if you are using hotels.

There are, of course, snags. University living accommodation is generally utilitarian. Few of the rooms have en-suite facilities, and tight budgets reduce the money available for regular redecoration. Further, many of the more modern universities (which, incidentally, often offer the better accommodation) are somewhat remote. That said, they are excellent venues for certain types of conference, especially professional and institutional events where delegates can identify with the academic atmosphere and are prepared to accept a somewhat lower standard of accommodation than that found in most hotels.

There are other disadvantages. It is not usually possible to use university accommodation in term-time. This is a major restriction for the commercial and industrial user since the university vacations coincide with the peak holiday periods, when business activity tends to slow down. However, other users who do not have these restrictions (for example organizers of professional and institutional conferences) will find the universities offer reasonably priced conference accommodation.

An increasing number of universities now have self-contained conference centres. These purpose-built centres, which are usually available round the year, offer accommodation of a higher standard than the usual student study-bedrooms. Most bedrooms have en suite bathrooms, colour television, direct-dial telephones and tea and coffee-making facilities.

A final disadvantage of university venues is the degree to which most are booked up, often two years in advance. If it is planned to use a university for a conference, it is therefore advisable to plan two or even three years ahead.

The British Universities Accommodation Consortium (BUAC) can give further information on the availability of university accommodation and the facilities offered in over 60 venues throughout the UK and Connect Venues (previously called HEAC) on accommodation at other educational establishments.

Business schools

Most business schools also accept 'outside bookings' from time to time to fill spare capacity (and to earn additional revenue).

Business school residential accommodation tends to be midway between universities and hotels. The lecture rooms are invariably excellent and are particularly suitable for training use. Cranfield School of Management has its own four star hotel, and other business schools such as the London Business School (in Regent's Park), Henley Management Centre and the Institute of Marketing (at Cookham) also offer equally good accommodation.

Conference centres

There is a growing number of purpose-built conference centres. Examples include the Wembley Conference Centre (2,700 seats), the Queen Elizabeth II Conference Centre (1,200 seats) and the Barbican (2,025 seats) in London and the conference centres at Harrogate (2,000 seats), Brighton (5,000 seats), the ICC Birmingham (3,000 seats), the Scottish Exhibition and Conference Centre (SECC), Glasgow (10,000 seats) and the Edinburgh International Conference Centre (EICC) (1,200 seats).

The choice of venues for larger conferences is far greater if you are prepared to go into continental Europe or further afield. Almost every major city in Europe, Asia and America has invested in a prestigious conference centre specifically in order to attract the major international events. Examples of excellent centres include the International Congress Centre (ICC) in Berlin, the specialist Ikituri Congress Centre Hotel in Finland, the Kyoto International Conference Hall in Japan and several first-class centres in the United States of America.

All these centres are excellent for the larger event and some have extra rooms which can be hired for smaller meetings. Many have adjacent exhibition space. Accommodation is not normally provided at these centres and delegates have to be bussed from hotels. Some are short of adjacent hotel accommodation (Wembley has only one hotel in the immediate vicinity and there are scarcely enough hotel beds in the whole of Berlin to support the ICC). However, the Loews Conference Hall in Monte Carlo is an exception: the hall is part of the hotel complex and there are several other first class hotels within easy walking distance, making Monte Carlo an ideal venue for the larger conference. The ICC Birmingham also has adjacent hotels. The purpose-built conference centres are ideal for the larger one-day event and for major conferences, where the many delegates can be housed in a variety of hotels. Because they are few in number, however, the major purpose-built venues tend to be booked many months, and sometimes many years, in advance.

There is another class of conference centre which is of particular interest to the organizer of the one-day seminar. This is the institutional and semi-private centre. Many of the professional bodies have their own theatres which can be hired for one-day events. In London, the list of such venues includes the CBI's excellent conference facilities at Centre Point (seating up to 350 in the Methven Theatre), the City Conference Centre (owned by the Institute of Marine Engineers and which seats 200), the Princess Anne Theatre at the British Academy of Film and Television Arts (213) at the top end of the scale and the majority of the professional bodies' theatres at the other end (so placed because they are usually less modern and generally do not have built-in projection boxes and other modern facilities). It is also possible to use some local authority buildings. Some council chambers are very fine (and it is possible to hire them if you ask) and a few local authorities, such as the Royal Borough of Kensington and Chelsea, have excellent town halls which can cater for both large and small events.

Specialist and unusual venues

In Chapter 1 we saw that the vast majority of meetings involve small numbers of people, often as few as 15 to 20. This is especially true of the residential management programme and 'think tank' for senior executives. Hotels are not always suitable for these but it is fortunate that a number of centres specialize in meeting this demand. There is a growing number of what can be termed specialist venues – country houses and similar rural establishments – which cater only for the residential executive conference trade. Some are very exclusive (and expensive), others are surprisingly inexpensive. Most of them are ideal for their market. They provide properly equipped meeting rooms, fine food and accommodation and, usually, the privacy and peace of a country house garden and park. Many also have swimming pools, squash and tennis courts and other recreational facilities. They vary in size. Some only take one group of around 20 at a time, others have around 80 beds and can accommodate three or four groups in separate meetings rooms. Venues in this category include Highgate House (near Northampton), the Chartered Institute of Marketing (Cookham), Hill House, Somerton (Oxfordshire), Middle Aston House (also Oxfordshire) and PricewaterhouseCoopers' Latimer House in Buckinghamshire, Lane End Conference Centre (High Wycombe) and Elvetham Hall (Hartley Wintney, near Basingstoke). There are many others.

Once again there is at least one snag which most of these specialist conference centres have in common: they are almost invariably booked up months, and sometimes a year or more, in advance. The order books of one which opened only very recently are already full 18 months ahead.

'Unusual venues' can be included in this category. Many of these are small hotels which cater for the conference trade for much of the year. Others are more exotic and include livery halls, castles (Leeds Castle in Kent has already been mentioned), ships (it is even possible to charter P&O's flagship, MV Oriana, for conferences, and one of the cross-channel car ferry operators offers full conference facilities with all the basic aids such as projectors, flip charts, lecterns, screens and microphones); cinemas and even night-clubs are often available (although one wonders what serious work would be done in the latter!).

The idea of hiring a ship for a conference may seem a little fanciful. In fact, it has many advantages. The pricing of cruise packages means that the buyer can have a clear idea of the cost, with few hidden extras. 'All inclusive' packages cover flights, food, accommodation, meeting facilities and on-board entertainment. Some companies even include bar drinks and excursions. Buyers are often surprised to learn that the final bill is not prohibitively expensive. The perceived cost of cruising is high but, when compared with conventional events, can be moderate.

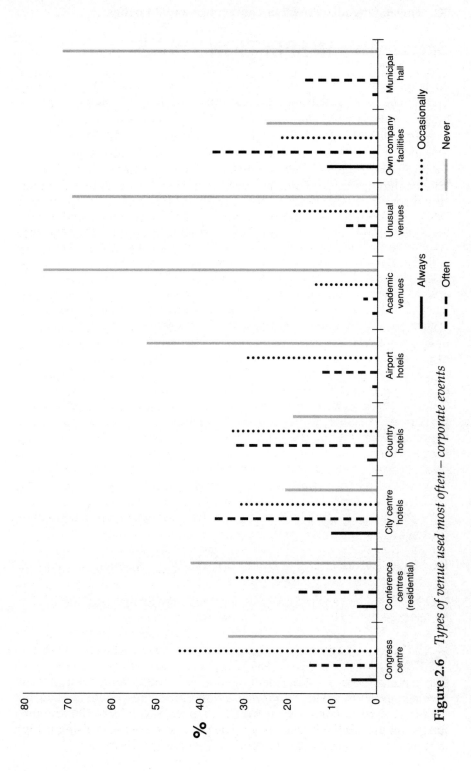

Figure 2.6 *Types of venue used most often – corporate events*

INSPECTION VISITS

An inspection visit to check out the venues on your short-list is essential. This can be time-consuming and tedious, especially if you have several venues on your short-list or if you are planning a road show. You may even be tempted to risk it and not do an inspection, especially for a small event.

Never, ever succumb to this temptation: to do so is to invite disaster (as the tale of the Sunday meeting at the start of this chapter demonstrates.) It is surprising how often people do not bother with this visit until they have committed themselves to the venue – or even fail to visit the venue at all. Such a lax approach is a sure recipe for disaster. How can anyone possibly know whether a venue is suitable unless they look at it? Even if someone recommends a particular place it must be checked out. One person's meat is another's poison and the venue which is suitable for one type of event may well not suit another. Trust no-one – not even your boss. It is one thing to stay at a pleasant hotel for a summer holiday, it is quite another to use it for a conference. Many senior executives are unaware of the pitfalls and problems already described and, even when you receive the strongest recommendation from your boss, or a colleague – or even from someone who has used a venue for his own event – you must still check the place out against your own specification.

An inspection visit is also the first part of setting up your team, which must include venue staff if you are to be successful. Throughout, your communications with the venue must be paramount. You may well ensure the success of the event, however big or small, by explaining his role to, say, the chef. If he is aware of the entire programme then he will be able to suggest a variety of menus and different types of meals to fit in with the daily activities.

Recently the co-author attended an international conference about conference management, and was served three consecutive lunches and dinners that were all buffets with similar dishes. Was that all northern Italy could produce? No, of course not, but the three chefs had no idea what the others were going to prepare!

All these mistakes have been made, and will continue to be made. We shall avoid this trap!

Contacting potential venues

If you are not using a placement agency, you will need to contact each venue yourself to arrange your inspection visits. This should be done by telephoning the conference sales office or, if the hotel does not have one, the banqueting manager.

Your first aim should be to discuss your requirements over the phone to make sure a visit is worthwhile: the conversation may reveal the venue is already booked, undergoing refurbishment – or that it is simply not suitable.

If possible, arrange to see the facilities when they are being used for another event. This will enable you to form a better impression of the capabilities of the venue and you may also be able to talk to the organizer of the event to find out what he thinks of the facilities and service. However, it is also necessary to gain access to the conference and public rooms when they are not in use in order to take detailed measurements and to carry out a thorough inspection.

As mentioned earlier, your initial telephone enquiry will establish whether the venue is likely to be available and whether it is, in fact, able to cope with your event. As already mentioned, the best venues are booked up well in advance. However, if your dates are not firmly fixed before you start to negotiate, it is often possible to find alternatives near to those you originally selected. Most conference organizers have occasionally persuaded clients to move the dates of their events in order that they could hold them in the most suitable places. This is yet another reason for planning well ahead to retain as much flexibility as possible. There is another good reason for being flexible. If you can hold your event at 'off peak' times of the year you may well save money. Most hotels and conference centres offer reduced rates during the traditionally quiet periods of the year in order to attract marginal business. In these days of pressure on budgets it is well worth considering moving the dates of an event in order to save money.

THE VISIT

A South Midlands hotel recently published a pleasing little brochure which claimed that the hotel was the 'ideal venue for senior management meetings'. There was a fine colour picture of the hotel, which was obviously an old house in an attractive rural setting. A conference organizer who was looking for such a venue for an important senior management meeting rang the hotel manager to arrange a visit.

He went with high hopes. Good hotels which offer the requisite standard of accommodation, food, meetings rooms and privacy are few and far between and he thought that he was about to discover a hitherto unknown gem. But his hopes were short-lived. As soon as he opened the front door he knew that his journey was wasted. A smell of stale cooking hung in the air and, after a long wait at the reception desk, a slovenly maid asked whether she could help. The conference organizer went through with his appointment with the manager out of courtesy, but knew it was a waste of time.

Or was it such a waste of time? Suppose he had accepted the brochure and telephoned assurances on trust and had made the booking unseen? The event would have been a disaster.

Armed with the result of your desk research, and the specification for your event, you should visit short-listed venues before making any further decisions. The following paragraphs describe how to conduct venue selection visits.

Be methodical and, if necessary, awkward

During your visits, be methodical and awkward. Insist on seeing every-thing and check everything against your specification. One conference centre manager used to be a professional conference organizer. She tells how she can always spot the organizer who knows what he is about and she says she would rather deal with the expert even though he is more difficult to satisfy. Some people never ask any questions and, she says, they are invariably the most troublesome later on.

Not that you necessarily have to be 'awkward' to have your way. A banqueting manager of a hotel on the Isle of Man recounts with some awe how a 'young lady' (to use his words) completed her inspection visit for a major event in just 30 minutes. 'She knew exactly what she wanted, had the authority to make changes to fit the layout of the hotel, and to negotiate, ' he said. 'If only everyone was so professional!'

Checklists

One way to ensure your approach is truly methodical is to prepare a checklist before you go and to work through it and complete it before you leave.

Two checklists designed and used by the author are reproduced at the end of this chapter.

- Checklist 1: Site/venue survey report;
- Checklist 2: Venue evaluation form.

The first is designed to gather factual data; the second is designed to record more subjective information.

It is not suggested that you use these forms; rather, you should design your own forms to suit your requirements. Nevertheless, the sample forms provide a useful model. They are very comprehensive and they are designed to be completed *on site*. This is important: if you are inspecting a number of venues you need to ensure you do not get the information muddled up. If you try to keep it in your head, you will almost certainly find your recollections less than perfect once you return home. And they are comprehensive because it can be a long way to go back if you have forgotten something!

Do not rely upon hotel brochures. They are not often very comprehensive and it is difficult to compare one venue with another if you rely on brochures which, by their very nature, tend to be individualistic in style, content, measurement units and so on. What is more, room capacities in particular tend to be over-estimated by hotel brochures – and by their sales staffs. They often fail to take the effect of room pillars into their calculation or to allow for the loss of space to accommodate the good viewing area (see Figure 5.1).

If the event involves the use of a production house or some other third party (for example, a training consultant), then a joint visit will almost certainly be required.

Don't drop your standards

The unsuitability of some so-called conference rooms has already been discussed. This theme is mentioned again here because it is so important. The organizer of any event owes it to the delegates to create the best possible atmosphere and conditions for the event in question. The venue is such an important part of the atmosphere that you cannot afford to compromise over standards, facilities and suitability. The problem is that venue staff, whether by accident or design, will only show you what they want you to see and what you insist on seeing. They will often entertain you to a fine lunch so that your subsequent inspection may well be coloured by the 'bonhomie' created by the wine and food, and a consequent feeling of commitment to the host. One organizer who uses the checklist described above always visits the venue incognito before making himself known to the staff. In this way he is sometimes able to find out a lot about the place which the management would prefer not to show him!

First impressions count

The smell of stale food which greeted a conference organizer at one hotel he went to check was described earlier in the chapter. Those first impressions indicated that the venue would be no use, and the subsequent inspection proved that those first impressions were right. If you are well received and shown round by a knowledgeable member of the staff, and if the hotel looks clean and well run, the chances are that it *is* as good as it looks. But if you are not expected, or have to wait for service, or if –

when you go into the conference rooms – you see dirty glasses and coffee cups left over from the last function, the chances are that the hotel is as badly run as your first impressions indicate. And remember, the delegates' first impressions when *they* first arrive are equally important. First impressions last and if the first impressions are unfavourable, then the whole event may be put in jeopardy.

Will it do?

Many people have difficulty in relating what they see to their specification, especially in hotels where the rooms may be laid out for another function or even when proper access to all the rooms may not be possible. The hotel or venue manager will be able to advise you on room capacities and so on, but, as already mentioned, you may find some are over-optimistic. The tables on pages 34 and 59 give a rough indication of the size of meeting room needed for various numbers of people and different types of room layout. Note that this is only an approximate guide. Any pillars and hanging lights which obstruct the view will reduce the capacity and, where all but the simplest audio-visual aids are to be used, it is necessary to make proper calculations to work out room capacities, sight lines, screen sizes and so on. We return to the audio-visual question in Chapter 5.

The ideal meeting room is proportioned 2:3 (width to length). Longer, narrow rooms tend to be claustrophobic; the shoe-box atmosphere destroys the intimacy of the gathering and people at the back have difficulty in seeing slides and overhead projector transparencies. Similarly, a room that is too wide means that the audience is too spread out for the speaker to address them without undue head movement and those on the outside ends of the seating rows have difficulty in seeing the screen. Table 2.2 gives a rough idea of the necessary room dimensions in the 2:3 proportion for the various areas given in Table 2.1 (page 34).

Not many rooms are in these ideal proportions and the figures are only intended to give you a rough idea of the sorts of dimensions involved. It is therefore neither necessary nor possible to follow them exactly, but the areas given in Table 2.1 are about right and certainly anything much smaller will be cramped. Ceiling heights must be adequate; below about four metres is too low and very high ceilings can spoil the intimacy of the smaller event. Indeed, too large a room can be a serious problem and the event can become impersonal and 'lost' if the room is much too large. There are ways of overcoming this if the seating is not fixed. For example, if the numbers are low, delegates can be seated classroom style in order to fill up the room – a useful device for the public seminar or programme where the response has been lower than anticipated.

Table 2.2   *Areas in Table 2.1 converted to approximate room dimensions (room proportions 2:3)*

Area (m²)	Dimensions	
	m × m	ft × ft
15	3.2 × 4.7	10½ × 15½
16	3.2 × 4.9	10½ × 16
18	3.5 × 5.2	11 × 17
19	3.6 × 5.3	11½ × 17½
23	3.9 × 5.9	13 × 19
24	4.0 × 6.0	13 × 19½
30	4.5 × 6.8	14½ × 22
32	4.6 × 6.9	15 × 22½
38	5.0 × 7.6	16½ × 25
40	5.2 × 7.7	17 × 25½
45	5.5 × 8.2	18 × 27
48	5.7 × 8.5	18½ × 28
57	6.2 × 9.2	20 × 30
66	6.3 × 9.5	21 × 31
75	7.1 × 10.6	23 × 35
80	7.3 × 11.0	24 × 36
85	7.5 × 11.3	25 × 37
93	7.9 × 12.0	26 × 39
100	8.2 × 12.2	27 × 40
112	8.6 × 13.0	29 × 43
115	9.0 × 13.0	29 × 43
120	9.0 × 13.0	29 × 44
130	9.0 × 14.0	31 × 46
145	10.0 × 15.0	32 × 49
150	10.0 × 15.0	33 × 50
175	11.0 × 16.0	36 × 52
190	11.0 × 17.0	37 × 55
200	12.0 × 17.0	38 × 59
230	12.0 × 19.0	41 × 61
235	13.0 × 19.0	41 × 62
300	14.0 × 21.0	46 × 70
400	16.0 × 25.0	54 × 80
600	20.0 × 30.0	65 × 100
745	22.0 × 33.0	75 × 110
900	25.0 × 37.0	80 × 120
1,120	37.0 × 41.0	90 × 135
1,200	28.0 × 43.0	95 × 140
1,500	32.0 × 47.0	105 × 160

Tables and chairs

Hotels tend to use standard banqueting tables for conferences: these are inevitably covered with baize cloth (usually green or brown) which might look pretty but hides the table legs. They then lay out the chairs (usually standard, armless banqueting chairs which measure 1ft 6 in square) at whatever spacing is needed to fit in the desired number of delegates.

This is all very well, but have you ever sat at such a table with the table legs right in front of you? It is uncomfortable, to say the least. Standard banqueting chairs are uncomfortable too – they are designed for short term use (even the longest banquet only lasts 2–3 hours – a conference day can last up to 10 hours and the wretched delegate ends up with back pains and a numb posterior after spending so long sitting on a banqueting chair). Ask for – indeed, *insist* on having – chairs with arms: most hotels do have them but prefer not to use them because they do not stack so easily and take up more space.

The standard banqueting table is 2ft 6 in (760mm) wide and either 4, 6 or 8ft (1220, 1830 or 2440mm) long: most are 6ft and can comfortably seat two people sice by side. Three is a crowd and you will end up with a 'leg problem' (above).

Allowing for space between each chair/table to enable delegates to get past to go to their seat, you should allow 5ft (1.5m) for each row.

Some venues have what are called 'half width' banqueting tables which are simply a narrow version of the standard table. These are useful for larger events since you save about one foot per row and so can fit more rows into the meeting room.

If you are not using tables, then you only need about 3ft (about 1m) per row. There are disadvantages: delegates have nowhere to put their papers and it is more difficult to take notes; they also feel more on top of each other; and fire regulations may dictate that chairs have to be fixed together.

Whatever layout you use, give careful consideration to where you place aisles. Most people put a wide aisle straight down the middle of the room. This means that you lose valuable seating space within the good viewing area (see Figure 5.1). A better alternative is to dispense with the central aisle and either feed delegates from the sides or have two small off-centre aisles (as in cinemas).

You will soon know whether the facilities are adequate if you use a good checklist during your inspection (and it *is* an inspection, not a social visit!). A more subjective judgement has to be made when assessing the atmosphere of the place, that is, in deciding whether the style and environment are suitable for the event in question and whether the food is satisfactory. The checklists provided later in this chapter help with both these aspects (see pages 69–81).

Pitfalls

There are, alas, many pitfalls – most of which you will discover by hard and bitter experience. Try to put yourself in the shoes of the delegate. Is it easy to find your way around? Where are the lavatories? Will they be adequate for the numbers involved? One venue was designed for male only use. The female lavatories were totally inadequate for the numbers attending a typical event – a constant problem for venue and users alike! Other questions you should consider include: Where are the kitchens? Will noise from these distract delegates? Can coffee cups be laid out quietly and can the organization serve the requisite number of coffees quickly enough? An aged retainer may be fine in the dining room but he can seldom be relied upon to cope with serving coffee to 150 delegates in the space of a few minutes. Find out whether extra staff are available. Where will delegates put their overcoats in winter, especially if the coats are all sopping wet? Several good venues fall down on this simple requirement.

Noise

Noise is the constant enemy of the conference organizer. Traffic noise is seldom completely insulated by even the best double glazing. If the meeting room you are shown looks out over the main road you must really make sure that the noise of the traffic is not intrusive. Check what increase in noise level there is at peak travel times and whether there are any roadworks scheduled at the time of your conference.

Kitchen and coffee-cup noises have already been mentioned. Make sure the venue staff realize that you set exacting standards in this respect.

It is amazing how often building work seems to be in progress during meetings. This work usually involves drilling and hammering which cannot be stopped without precipitating a walk-out or some other problem. Find out from the venue whether any work is scheduled at the time of your event. If it is, you may have to find somewhere else.

Aircraft noise can also be a problem, especially near the major airports. In most of the Heathrow hotels it is virtually impossible to hear the aircraft passing overhead – a tribute to the soundproofing and clever positioning. However, do not take these matters for granted. One course was held at a company headquarters which was under the flight path to Heathrow. The instructors had to break off every two minutes as noisy aircraft roared overhead – hardly the best learning environment!

Finally, if there are so-called soundproof partitions dividing the meeting room from other areas or meetings, are they really soundproof? More often than not they are inadequate, especially if audio-visual aids are to be used.

Other considerations

The list of questions and potential hazards is almost endless: Will sound reinforcement be needed? What audio-visual equipment is available and what has to be brought in? Do chandeliers and pillars obstruct the view? Check these and such things as the entrances (are they at the right end of the room?), fire exits, the comfort of the seats and the efficiency of the blackout, lighting controls and availability of special furniture and other items required. Is the heating system adequate – and what about the air conditioning? Does it work (have it demonstrated) and is it quiet enough? At one conference centre the heating system is so noisy that it cannot be used during formal sessions – to the discomfort of even the hardiest delegate.

It is worth checking even minor details: one conference organizer carries a 13 amp 'baby night light' plug with him and uses it to check that the sockets he wishes to use are 'live'.

Venue staff

When you are making your inspection, insist on meeting the person at the venue who will be responsible for co-ordinating the arrangements for your event. This may be the general manager of the hotel, the banqueting manager or someone with interdepartmental authority. It is unlikely to be the salesman. His responsibility will cease once the sale is made, and he is unlikely to have anything more to do with your event. Not long ago a 350-room overseas hotel was booked for nine nights and large-scale banqueting for three back-to-back corporate incentive meetings. It was the biggest revenue earner the hotel had ever hosted and it was booked 18 months previously. But on the day the organizers arrived the general manager went on holiday, leaving a very inexperienced assistant as his deputy. Unfortunately, too many hotels and even some conference venues still do not train staff on conference management, and few appoint conference managers to take complete responsibility for particular events. Venue managers are often ill-prepared for inspection visits. Few ask in advance whether the buyer has any specific requests – or ask for feedback after the visit.

It is extraordinary how often sales staff do not seem to be familiar with their own venues: tales abound of hosts fumbling in the dark to find light switches in meeting rooms, showing bedrooms that are furthest from the lifts and trying to open doors with the wrong keys. Such blunders do not inspire confidence in either the venue's efficiency or in its staff. The survey mentioned in Chapter 1 identified the problem only too clearly. Quotes taken directly from the reply slips include:

'Too many hotels and venues are still very unprofessional.'

'Lack of intelligent assistance from conference and banqueting personnel.'

'Lack of continuity... I need one contact name to coordinate or advise on banqueting, book rooms and AV facilities.'

'Finding a hotel that understands what a Training Manager needs is very difficult.'

Such comments confirm what has been said about venues for many years, and there are salutary lessons which many hotels in particular would do well to heed:

- Staff must understand that the detailed business needs of a conference organizer and his delegates are very different from those attending a banquet.
- Senior management must be available at all times or, alternatively, one person with interdepartmental authority must be put in charge and must always be available to the organizer. It is a simple task of management delegation to nominate one person as a contact-point throughout a conference, but few hotels offer this service.
- Audio-visual awareness, although certainly improved over recent years, is still not treated as a serious training requirement.

The general lack of understanding of conferences on behalf of staff can easily be remedied by proper and regular training. It is remarkable how few technical college and university hotel and catering courses rate knowledge and understanding of conferences alongside subjects such as Reception, the Kitchen and Accountancy.

You will therefore experience difficulty in finding someone at the venue who will have the necessary overall responsibility for your event. It is no use dealing with junior departmental staff. They will have no authority outside their own departments. You may well have to agree a number of things with a variety of different people. These agreements must be recorded on the checklist when they are made. Make a note of the person with whom the agreement is made and, after the visit, follow up with written confirmation. Remember that your event will be one of many for the venue staff. Once your visit is over, they will not normally have to worry about it until a few days beforehand. Staff turnover, particularly at hotels, is high. Information recorded on file will be available to new staff. Verbal agreements may be lost in the changeover.

Paradoxically, venues complain that many conference clients are just as bad. Venue managers say it is often impossible to know who is in charge of a particular event and that they receive conflicting instructions from different people. They also, often with complete justification, complain that organizers fail to give specific requirements, leave important decisions until too late and sometimes forget vital details. And, in spite of the advice on page 54, venue staff confirm all too many organizers never bother to inspect the venue before confirming their bookings: some do not even visit the venue before the day of their meeting.

The problem is one of communication (or lack of it), exacerbated by lack of knowledge on both sides. The wise conference organizer will therefore:

(1) give full, detailed instructions verbally and in writing;
(2) assume nothing will be provided unless it is requested; and
(3) check, check and check again and again.

Another important aspect of the negotiation procedure is the agreement on what is and is not included in the price. Some venues quote an 'all in' price and there are very few extras involved. However, most venues expect extra payment for AV equipment, projectionists, cloakroom attendants, facilities not directly part of the main conference area (for example, offices and changing rooms) and for the use of the facilities outside normal working hours.

Remember that most venues let rooms by sessions. For example, if you are using a room for a one-day event, you will be expected to clear the room by an agreed time (usually 5.30 pm) so that the room can be cleaned and re-set for an evening function. It has been known for venues to expect use of rooms in the evenings during residential programmes. Both parties must agree the rules at the time of booking to avoid such problems later on.

It is important, not only for budgeting purposes but also to avoid later disputes, to agree terms and in particular whether extra services, furniture or other facilities are to attract extra charges. It is also advisable to check that bar prices are not being set at special (high) rates for the event and to find out how much the hotel or venue charges for extras like the use of the telephone (often several times the normal rate), sports facilities and so on.

These discussions are important in another respect. They will help you to discover whether the venue staff are helpful, willing to understand your needs and problems and ready to respond to your event. Detailed discussions will also impress on the venue staff that you know what you want and that you are unlikely to accept low standards.

Further advice on dealing with hotels is given in Chapter 12.

Local information

Obtain as much local information as you can. Check sketch maps to see if they are accurate and easily understood (many are prepared by people who know the area so well that they assume knowledge that strangers will simply not have). It is advisable to walk round the area to find out whether the venue, car parks and so on are easy to find. Another way of gaining local information is to take a ride in a local taxi to find out the layout of the area and to draw upon the driver's knowledge. A visit to the local library and, for the larger event, the local authority is also worthwhile. The latter can be very useful and might even lead to a civic reception!

Seek a second opinion

It is difficult to be sure that you are right in all the opinions you form during your visit. Ask the venue staff to put you in touch with other users to seek their views and to draw upon their experience. It is also essential to get the person who is finally responsible for the event to check the venue before entering into any firm commitment. This can be very frustrating. You will often find what you believe to be excellent venues, only to have them rejected by senior executives on the most subjective grounds. One executive would not entertain using a town hall, not because it was unsuitable (it was just right for his event) but because he had strong opinions about local authority expenditure and was not prepared to have his company associated with any local authority building however good or bad it might be!

Failure

The importance of the venue inspection visit has been deliberately emphasized. The whole task of finding and approving a venue can be very time-consuming, frustrating and disappointing. You must, if possible, be prepared to compromise to some extent. It is seldom possible to find a venue which is perfect for your needs, but it is usually possible to find one that comes very close to answering them. If you can compromise over some of the details, you will have less trouble. Sometimes it is still not possible to find the right place – what then? As already mentioned, if you can be flexible over dates, it is certainly easier to get into the more popular venues. If this is not possible, you may have to contact one of the placement agencies. However, it is stressed that it is wise to use them right from the outset if you are in any doubt about your ability to find the 'right' venue. Many placement agencies justly complain that clients only come to them after failing to find somewhere themselves. This makes the placement agencies' task more difficult, especially if time is short, or if, as has been known, the client does not admit his failure and they spend fruitless hours contacting places he has already tried!

FACILITY VISITS

Conference organizers are often invited to go on facility visits. These are arranged by hotels, local authorities and some commercial companies. You should never refuse if you can spare the time because these can give you the opportunity of looking at venues without the pressure of a particular event in mind. Long after the facility visit it is often possible to narrow a choice down as a result of prior knowledge and few conference organizers visit a hotel on a facility visit with which they are not subsequently able to do business.

If you are planning a major event, it is sensible to contact the local tourist authority and request a hosted facility visit. You will seldom be refused, and you will be given overnight accommodation and be escorted round potential venues. If you are considering an overseas venue, free flights will probably also be offered.

VENUE CONTRACTS AND CANCELLATION FEES

Our industry is grateful to the Meetings Industry Association (MIA) for the sterling work it has done in producing its model Terms and Conditions for Conferences and Associated Events, but as always it is the case of 'buyers beware'.

Not only must you get specialist advice regarding the general terms and conditions but you should take a very careful look at the prepayment period, the required amounts and the cancellation policy (period brackets up to the event), with the corresponding penalties.

Many venues try to enforce a 100 per cent penalty but the MIA recommends a cancellation fee of 90 per cent for both bedrooms and meeting rooms and 65 per cent for food and beverages. However, in a recent article in *Meetings & Incentive Travel* magazine the managing editor produced a very straightforward alternative calculation of how you might negotiate a lower cancellation fee on room rates.

Taking a contract rate for hotel bedrooms at £100.00 he points out in the following illustration that VAT should not be charged on a cancellation charge as no supply has taken place, and consumables should be excluded as the hotel will not incur a 100 per cent loss on these items.

	£	£
Room rate	–	100.00
VAT element	15.00	–
Laundry	5.00	–
Bathroom toiletries	6.00	–
Electricity	1.00	–
Breakfast	8.00	35.00
Net amount payable as Cancellation fee	–	£65.00

In any event it may be wise to consider taking out insurance cover from a specialist event insurance company such as Insurex-Exposure, which has designed low-cost protection against no-shows or complete cancellation for less than £1.80 per delegate room night. In addition we suggest you take note of the *M&IT* Essential Checklist:

♦ If you receive terms and conditions after confirming the booking, they are legally invalid and can be ignored.
♦ Always ask for the cancellation policy to be amended to be more lenient.
♦ Make sure cancellation fees are net of VAT.
♦ Always ask for cancellation fees to reflect loss of profit, not loss of revenue.
♦ Make sure the contract terms and conditions are specific to your event.
♦ Make sure the booking lead time is not shorter than the first cancellation penalty deadline.
♦ In the event of a cancellation fee being invoked, always ask for proof that the venue has attempted to mitigate loss.
♦ In the event of a cancellation fee being invoked, always ask for proof that the venue has suffered loss by asking for room occupancy levels.
♦ At the time of cancellation, ask the venue how many rooms they have to sell and then ask them again on the day you should have arrived.

EXECUTIVE CHECKLIST

♦ Who is responsible for choosing venues for conferences and meetings in your organization?
♦ Does he or she work to a specification for each individual event? If so, does this specification include your requirements for everything both inside and outside the meeting room?

- Have you considered using a placement agency?
- Do you invariably visit potential venues before making your choice?
- Do you consider visiting the venue incognito before introducing yourself?
- Does your organization have a venue visit checklist and is it used for all venue visits?
- Does your checklist cover the following:
  - Will you need storage space?
  - Will you need a room where speakers can review their slides and prepare their presentations?
  - Are you planning exhibits? If so, what gross square footage will you need?
  - How many rooms are required for conference offices, press, VIPs and so on?
  - Is a room needed for guests, spouses or even children's hospitality?
- Do you check accommodation in detail?
  - The overall condition of sleeping rooms and furnishings.
  - Cleanliness of rooms and corridors (are old food trays left about?).
  - The sizes and standards of rooms, including VIP rooms, suites and standard rooms.
  - The size and lighting of the bathroom, and the toiletries (towels, flannels, shampoo, etc).
  - Room positions (front facing, rear facing, quiet locations).
  - Fire exits.
  - The number of lifts and response times during busy periods.
  - Room service.
  - Shoe cleaning facilities.
  - Are there designated no-smoking rooms?
  - What charge per unit is made for telephones?
  - Do the televisions work on all channels – and is the picture satisfactory?
- Do you seek the opinions of previous venue users?
- Do you confirm all agreements with venue staff in writing and note the names of venue staff with whom agreements are made?
- Does your organizer take advantage of facility visits?
- Have you considered the commercial terms and cancellation terms?
- Is the venue contract approved by the MIA?
- Do you need to take out special event insurance?

CHECKLIST 1: SITE/VENUE SURVEY REPORT

CHECKLIST 1: SITE/VENUE SURVEY REPORT	Completed by.................................. Date.............................

For.. Date...........................
    (Events)

NAME OF VENUE ....

FULL ADDRESS ....

....

....

....

....POSTCODE...............................

TELEPHONE NUMBER ....
(inc STD CODE)

FAX NUMBER ....
(inc STD CODE)

e-mail ....

GENERAL MANAGER	.... Mr/Mrs/ Initials Surname Direct Line Miss/Ms e-mail..................................
BANQUETING MANAGER	.... Mr/Mrs/ Initials Surname Direct Line Miss/Ms e-mail..................................
CONFERENCE CONTACT	.... Mr/Mrs/ Initials Surname Direct Line Miss/Ms e-mail..................................

HOTEL CHAIN GROUP
or PRIVATE OWNER
....

....

AA/RAC STAR RATING
....

AWARDS
....
(eg, Britain in Bloom, Michelin Stars, etc)

SITUATION
....
(ie, rural/town/village/city centre/seafront, etc)

GROUNDS .... (acres) WOODLAND [   ] PARKLAND [   ] LANDSCAPED

UNLANDSCAPED [   ] OTHER ....

TYPE OF BUILDING
....
(ie, modern/country house/Victorian/Grade 1 Listing, etc)

EXTENT RECENT RENOVATION/REFURBISHMENT ....

....

DEVELOPMENT PLANS OVER NEXT 12 MONTHS ....

....

LIKELIHOOD OF AN OVERRUN DURING ....
YOUR EVENT?

WHEELCHAIR ACCESSIBILITY?

TO RECEPTION   ☐   TO ALL RESTAURANTS   ☐

TO ALL BEDROOMS   ☐   TO MEETING ROOMS   ☐

TO BANQUETING ROOMS   ☐   TO LEISURE FACILITIES   ☐

NOTES
....

....

....

NEAREST MOTORWAY(S)	NUMBER	....	....	....	....
	JUNCTION	....	....	....	....
	MILES	....	....	....	....
NEAREST A ROAD(S) (if no motorways)	NUMBER	....	....	....	....
	MILES	....	....	....	....

DISTANCES	LONDON	.... MILES
	BIRMINGHAM	.... MILES
	GLASGOW	.... MILES

NEAREST LARGEST TOWN .... MILES
(Name)

NEAREST RAILWAY STATION .... MILES
(Name)

TRAINS TO LONDON   .... FAST ☐ CONNECT ☐
                       Hours   Minutes   SLOW ☐ DIRECT ☐

NEAREST AIRPORT   .... MILES
(Name)

NEAREST UNDERGROUND   .... MILES
(if relevant)   (Name)

LOCAL ATTRACTIONS   ....
                       ....
                       ....
                       ....

CAR PARKING   .... UNDER COVER ☐ OPEN ☐
                       (No. of spaces)

PUBLIC CAR PARKING   ....
                       (No. of spaces)   (distance from venue)

HELICOPTER LANDING   LAWNS ☐   PURPOSE-BUILT PAD ☐

MINIBUS/CHAUFFEURED   STATION ☐ AIRPORTS ☐ OTHER ☐
CARS FROM/TO

FIRE ALARM SYSTEMS

    TEST DAYS AND TIMES   ....

DOCTOR/NURSE ON CALL   YES [   ]   NO [   ]

DIETS

CAN HANDLE MEDICAL/PREFERRED DIETS?   YES [   ]   NO [   ]
(vegetarian, no nut oil, no milk, etc)

CAN HANDLE RELIGIOUS DIETS?   YES [   ]   NO [   ]
(Kosher, Muslim, etc)

NAMES OF RESTAURANTS

A LA CARTE	....	....	....	....
CARVERY	....	....	....	....
TABLE D'HOTE	....	....	....	....
SNACKS	....	....	....	....
COFFEE	....	....	....	....
ALCOHOLIC BEVERAGES	....	....	....	....
OPENING TIMES	....	....	....	....

LEISURE FACILITIES/ACTIVITIES
Tick relevant boxes, indicating with * if by arrangement only.

AMUSEMENT MACHINES	☐ Venue	☐ Nearby	HEALTH CLUB	☐ Venue	☐ Nearby
ARCHERY	☐ Venue	☐ Nearby	HORSE RIDING	☐ Venue	☐ Nearby
BADMINTON	☐ Venue	☐ Nearby	JACUZZI	☐ Venue	☐ Nearby
BALLOONING	☐ Venue	☐ Nearby	NIGHTCLUB	☐ Venue	☐ Nearby
BAR BILLIARDS	☐ Venue	☐ Nearby	POOL TABLE	☐ Venue	☐ Nearby
BEAUTICIAN	☐ Venue	☐ Nearby	RACING	☐ Venue	☐ Nearby
BILLIARDS	☐ Venue	☐ Nearby	SAUNA	☐ Venue	☐ Nearby
BOATING	☐ Venue	☐ Nearby	SHOOTING	☐ Venue	☐ Nearby
BOWLS	☐ Venue	☐ Nearby	SKI CENTRE	☐ Venue	☐ Nearby
CASINO	☐ Venue	☐ Nearby	SKITTLE ALLEY	☐ Venue	☐ Nearby
CHILDREN'S ROOM	☐ Venue	☐ Nearby	SNOOKER	☐ Venue	☐ Nearby
CINEMA	☐ Venue	☐ Nearby	SOLARIUM	☐ Venue	☐ Nearby
CLAY PIGEON	☐ Venue	☐ Nearby	SPA BATH	☐ Venue	☐ Nearby
CRICKET	☐ Venue	☐ Nearby	SQUASH	☐ Venue	☐ Nearby
CROQUET	☐ Venue	☐ Nearby	STEAM ROOM	☐ Venue	☐ Nearby
DARTS	☐ Venue	☐ Nearby	SWIMMING POOL		
			CHILDREN	☐ Venue	☐ Nearby
FISHING	☐ Venue	☐ Nearby	INDOOR	☐ Venue	☐ Nearby
			OUTDOOR	☐ Venue	☐ Nearby
GAMES ROOM	☐ Venue	☐ Nearby	PLUNGE	☐ Venue	☐ Nearby
GARDEN CHESS	☐ Venue	☐ Nearby	TABLE TENNIS	☐ Venue	☐ Nearby
GO KARTING	☐ Venue	☐ Nearby	TEN PIN BOWLING	☐ Venue	☐ Nearby
GOLF – 9 HOLE	☐ Venue	☐ Nearby	TENNIS COURTS		
18 HOLE	☐ Venue	☐ Nearby	ALL WEATHER	☐ Venue	☐ Nearby
CLOCK	☐ Venue	☐ Nearby	GRASS	☐ Venue	☐ Nearby
MINI	☐ Venue	☐ Nearby	INDOOR	☐ Venue	☐ Nearby
PUTTING GREEN	☐ Venue	☐ Nearby	OUTDOOR	☐ Venue	☐ Nearby
DRIVING RANGE ___ BAY	☐ Venue	☐ Nearby	TRAMPOLINING	☐ Venue	☐ Nearby
GYMNASIUM	☐ Venue	☐ Nearby	WATER SKI-ING	☐ Venue	☐ Nearby
MINI GYM	☐ Venue	☐ Nearby	WIND SURFING	☐ Venue	☐ Nearby
HAIRDRESSING	☐ Venue	☐ Nearby			

SHOPS IN VENUE ....   OTHER ....

....

....

ACCOMMODATION

NUMBER OF BEDROOMS .... SINGLE .... DOUBLE .... TWIN

.... EXECUTIVE .... SUITE .... TOTAL

BEDROOMS FOR DISABLED DELEGATES ....

BEDROOMS FOR NON-SMOKERS ....

SUITES

	Single	Twin	Double	Executive	Junior	Executive	Penthouse
EN SUITE							
BATHS AND SHOWERS							
BATHS ONLY							
SHOWERS ONLY							
SPA BATHS							

Please tick relevant boxes							
DIRECT DIAL PHONE							
E-MAIL SOCKETS/FAX							
SWITCHBOARD							
TV COLOUR							
VIDEO							
REMOTE CONTROL							
SATELLITE							
CABLE							
IN-HOUSE FILM							
RADIO							
TEA/COFFEE IN ROOM							
24-HOUR ROOM SERVICE							
TROUSER PRESS							
HAIRDRYER							
LAUNDRY							
MINI BAR							
INDIVIDUAL HEATING/ AIR CONDITIONING							
BATHROBE							

ATTITUDE/HELPFULNESS OF STAFF

	GOOD ☺			POOR ☹
RECEPTION	☐	☐	☐	☐
HOUSEKEEPING	☐	☐	☐	☐
CONFERENCE	☐	☐	☐	☐
RESTAURANT/BAR	☐	☐	☐	☐
MANAGEMENT	☐	☐	☐	☐

DECOR/FURNISHING/ATMOSPHERE

	GOOD ☺			POOR ☹
RECEPTION	☐	☐	☐	☐
LOUNGE	☐	☐	☐	☐
BARS	☐	☐	☐	☐
RESTAURANT	☐	☐	☐	☐
BEDROOMS	☐	☐	☐	☐
LEISURE FACILITIES	☐	☐	☐	☐

WOULD THE FOLLOWING BE 'AT HOME' IN THIS VENUE

	YES ☺			NO ☹
MANAGEMENT	☐	☐	☐	☐
DELEGATES	☐	☐	☐	☐
SPEAKERS	☐	☐	☐	☐

CONFERENCE ROOMS NOTE: FOR ROOMS WHICH DIVIDE, ENTER DATE FOR WHOLE ROOM AND EACH SECTION IN SEPARATE COLUMNS									
NAME OF ROOM									
AREA SQUARE METRES									
CAPACITY: U-SHAPE									
CLASSROOM									
BOARDROOM									
THEATRE									
BANQUET									
CEILING HEIGHT (Metres)									
ACCESS DOOR (H&W) Metres									
FLOOR LEVEL (Ground, 1, 2, etc)									
NATURAL DAYLIGHT (YES/NO)									

CONFERENCE ROOMS continued										
	NAME OF ROOM									
CHAIRS WITH ARMS										
TABLES FINISHED SURFACES										
AIR CONDITIONING										
ADJACENT FOYER										
PRIVATE BAR FACILITIES										
ADJACENT SYNDICATE ROOM(S)										
LOCKING OFFICE										
SOUNDPROOF PANELS										
DIRECT EXTERNAL ACCESS										
PENDASTRIP										
FIXED DATA PROJECTION										
FIXED SCREEN										
FULL PA SYSTEM										
SOPHISTICATED/BASIC AV (delete as appropriate)										
3-PHASE POWER										
BACK PROJECTION										
WORKING WALL										
TEACHING WALL										
CLOSED CIRCUIT TV										
BT LANDLINE										
STAGING										

OTHER:	FLIP CHARTS	☐	OHP	☐
	SCREENS	☐	35 mm KODAK CAROUSEL	☐
	EASELS	☐	VIDEO MONITOR	☐
	VIDEO CAMERA	☐	DATA PROJECTOR	☐

INCLUDED IN DELEGATE RATE ....

....

....

....

....

OFFICE:	SECRETARIAL	☐	PHOTOCOPYING	☐
	MESSAGES	☐		
	BUSINESS CENTRE	☐	HOURS OF BUSINESS .... TO ....

NUMBER OF SYNDICATE ROOMS .... NUMBER DEDICATED USE......................

SPEAKER REHEARSAL ROOM .... EXECUTIVE DISCUSSION/
                                        MEETING ROOM..

MAXIMUM EXHIBITION SPACE ....

DAILY DELEGATE RATE (inc VAT) ....

24-HOUR DELEGATE RATE (inc VAT) ....

RATES VALID UNTIL ....

AVAILABILITY OF CONFERENCE FACILITIES/ACCOMMODATION
IF NOT AVAILABLE ALL YEAR ROUND, INDICATE MONTHS NOT AVAILABLE

CHECKLIST 2: VENUE EVALUATION FORM

CHECKLIST 2:   Completed
VENUE SURVEY REPORT   by .... Date ....

NAME OF VENUE ....

When you complete this form, please try to convey as much as possible of the atmosphere and standard of the venue you have visited. Most purely factual information has been supplied by the venue: your report should be mainly descriptive, assessing the suitability of each room and describing its decor and ambience, and above all comprehensive.

ABOUT THE VENUE

HOW WOULD DELEGATES REACH THE VENUE FROM THE NEAREST MAIN ROAD OR MOTORWAY OR LARGE TOWN?

HOW EASILY DID YOU FIND THE VENUE?

WHAT WAS YOUR FIRST IMPRESSION OF THE BUILDINGS AND GROUNDS?

TICK IF PROVIDED/OK – CROSS IF NOT PROVIDED/UNSATISFACTORY

ROOM NAME						
ENVIRONMENT Decor (inc. floor covering)						
Furniture						
Ventilation						
Lighting controls/blackout						
Sound/noise						
Adjacent foyer						
Privacy						
Adjacent locking office						
Vision sight lines						
Doors/Access situation						
TECHNICAL Staging						
Interpreter's booths						
Fixed screen						
Sophisticated AV						
In-house dedicated operator						
Basic AV						
Sophisticated sound						
Basic sound						
Separate projection room 3-phase power/plenty of power points						
SUITABILITY Type of function/meeting						

OVERALL COMMENTS/ANYTHING UNUSUAL OR PARTICULARLY WORTH
RECOMMENDING?

OBTAINED/ORDERED: — BROCHURE

                                           — CONFERENCE PACK

                                           — BANQUETING MENUS

                                           — MAP

3

THE PROGRAMME AND SPEAKERS

A German diplomat was due to present the final paper at an international conference. It was a hot summer's day, and the organizers had been unwise enough to provide an excellent lunch... with wine. The delegates were naturally relaxed as they entered the auditorium and were in need of entertainment as much as anything else.

The session started well. The speaker entered the hall and, after discarding an ominously thick file of lecture notes, strode to the centre of the floor, looked up at the audience and said: 'In this presentation there will be no chokes. We have no *time* for ze chokes!' – and everyone roared with laughter. Their pleasure was short-lived. Two and a half tedious hours later, after an endless succession of complicated slides had been explained in excruciating detail, they realized that even the initial 'joke' had in fact been no joke at all. Few remembered anything of that afternoon apart from those unfortunate opening remarks. It was a typical example of poor programming and poor speaker selection.

THE PROGRAMME

The programme is, of course, the means by which the objectives for the event are met. The objectives should never be forgotten. They are, after all, the only reason for meeting. The objectives define the required information flows and other activities and thus dictate the length and content of the programme. But a programme which includes all that is theoretically needed to satisfy the objectives may still fail actually to meet those objectives if the presentation and scheduling are poor and the speakers are inadequate. This was the fault in the example described above.

Deciding the content is only part of your problem when you are constructing a conference programme. The way in which the information is presented and organized is equally important. This is true for any event. A good programme and good presentation are just as important for the minor training programme as they are for the major conference. When you are designing your programme you must try not to look at the task from your own point of view nor should you consider only the convenience of the chairman and speakers. Instead, look at it through the eyes of the unhappy delegate in row 26 who has a hangover, is worried about his monthly report and is irritated by the 'no smoking in the auditorium' rule. All will be wasted if your programme and the method of presentation fail to arrest his attention. Everything must be geared to keeping his mind totally attuned to your message. The pace and style of presentation must be changed as often as possible. Entertain and intrigue, amuse, surprise and, if necessary, shock your audience. Ensure that you select the best possible speakers and use your imagination when you plan the whole event, from the formal content of the working sessions to the social programme. There is plenty of scope for imagination in even the small meeting or seminar and the cost is often not so much a matter of money as of imagination and thought at the planning stage.

Remember, too, what the delegate expects of the event as a whole (Chapter 1). He wants to be comfortable, to enjoy himself, to meet other people, to learn, to discuss matters of interest and so on. Our programme must meet all these needs.

Framework

The first task is constructing a programme is to create a framework from the themes and objectives. This will identify the main subjects and activities, and the number and type of sessions needed to cover the required ground. The need for visits, displays, video and so on will also begin to emerge at this stage.

The grouping of delegates and the types of session are important decisions. There are two main options open to you:

1. *Formal and plenary sessions.* These involve the whole conference group. They are sometimes also called 'total group sessions'.

2. *Workshops and syndicate sessions.*   These are used as the generic terms for workshops, syndicate discussions, breakdown/breakout groups, study groups, special interest groups and the like. They involve smaller groups of the main conference body numbering from as few as five to ten people to much larger sub-groups. These are formed to discuss specific topics, to work on particular problems, to come up with agreed findings or recommendations, to exchange ideas, apply new information and to practise skills. There are many types of work-group; the exact type of group will depend upon what the session is intended to achieve.

There are, of course, other types of conference activity ranging from pure entertainment (particularly on an incentive – see Chapter 8) to Adventure Based Learning (ABEL as it is called in management circles). The types of session and the types of activity need careful thought and planning.

What type of session and what activities?

Some subject matter, such as new information, resolutions and new theories, policies and principles, will usually be more effective if presented to the total group. Official actions, such as voting, action on committee reports and similar activities, are also best handled as total group sessions and talks by key personalities and featured speakers easily fall into the general session.

Many other activities are more suited to the smaller group. The dividing line is not always obvious. If the material to be covered includes recommendations for a future course of action or possible ways of handling a complex problem, you must decide whether this can best be dealt with in one session with the total group or be explored in small groups in which more delegates can take an active part in the deliberations and hence share 'ownership' of the outcome. Indeed, the key to the decision is usually delegate participation. Good discussions involving everyone in the group can seldom be achieved if the number of people exceeds about 20. Probably the best size for a small group is around six to ten.

Content and participation are not the only criteria to apply when deciding the best type of session. Research has shown that delegates find some types of session and presentation methods more acceptable than others. Thus many think that programmed learning (which involves following prepared texts and examples), case studies and discussions are much better ways of acquiring factual knowledge than formal lectures and videos, while role play and discussion groups are thought better than lectures and programmed instruction for achieving attitude change. Indeed, it has been shown that the formal presentation ranks poorly in terms of knowledge retention, problem solving, interpersonal skills and participant acceptability. However, there are occasions when an expert speaker giving a formal presentation is very effective.

Using case studies One manufacturing company recently decided to build its annual sales conference round a major case study. Every salesman was issued with a bulky document which described the problems of a Scandinavian company which manufactured steel and other products for the building industry. The salesmen were invited to study the document beforehand and in syndicate sessions during the conference. Syndicates were invited to give presentations to the assembled sales force on their analyses and recommendations for the future. There was some resistance at first ('Too much reading to do...' and 'I don't see the point of all this' were typical of the comments heard during the early stages of the conference). However, as the sales team became immersed in the case study, they realized that the situations described were broadly similar to those of their own company and that there were many lessons to be learnt (indeed, one delegate said the case study was a thinly disguised description of their own company – which, in fact, was not true).

The whole structure of the event was so different from the traditional conferences of previous years, and the message so apposite, that there is no doubt that this experiment was a lasting success.

Adventure Based Learning A particular product of the fashion for 'team building', ABEL is seen as a means to achieving that end. It is not without its dangers – physically and conceptually. To quote one executive, 'The attitude seems to be, "We've a free half-day during the annual conference – why not throw in a team building exercise?" '

Good adventure based activities can indeed build confidence, morale and improve team performance. However, the activities tend to be very physical and competitive. Losers and those who do not like physical activities can be demotivated rather than motivated. The dangers lie in trying to mix personal and team development together, in making individuals do something they do not want to – such as abseiling or rock climbing if they do not have a head for heights, or white water canoeing if they cannot swim.

STRUCTURING PROGRAMMES FOR LARGER CONFERENCES

A problem with large conferences is that discussion during plenary sessions is almost impossible. One way round this is to organize the event round a series of plenary sessions and workshops during which plenary speakers are made accessible for those who are interested in pursuing a subject in greater depth.

A programme structured in this way may look as follows:

Plenary session	Speaker A	30–40 mins

Plenary session	Speaker B	30–40 mins

Break

Workshops – Session 1	Speaker A	Speaker B	Special interest workshop: Speaker P	Special interest workshop: Speaker Q	45 mins

– Session 1	Speaker A	Speaker B	Special interest workshop: Speaker P	Special interest workshop: Speaker Q	45 mins

Lunch

... and so on.

By repeating the workshops (Workshops sessions 1 and 2), delegates can in the above example, attend 2 out of 4. The special interest workshops are added to:

1.   add new, minority interest subjects to the event; and
2.   prevent the main speaker workshops becoming too crowded.

If there is an exhibition alongside the conference, this can be open during workshop sessions to provide an additional activity. Arranging exhibitions alongside conferences is covered in detail in Chapter 7.

This programme pattern is demanding administratively but is popular with delegates who have a wider choice than is usual.

The very large technical, medical and professional conferences often run dozens of workshops simultaneously to enable delegates to pursue topics of their particular interest. These workshops are not usually repeated. Poster sessions may also be scheduled in the programme – see 'Calls for Papers' (page 106).

PLANNING SESSION TIMINGS

The *timing* of each session is particularly important. Once you have decided the types of session you will have to slot them into the programme. Some will naturally follow others, but there is always some degree of flexibility. Some activities, especially those which demand prior thought or preparation by the participant, are best undertaken after a break. Others are unsuitable for inclusion early in the day. For example, a keynote speech delivered first on the programme, before the delegates are ready to listen, can impair the whole event and a summary given at the end of a long, hard day may well fall on deaf ears. It is important to think about the audience's attitude to each subject, the fatigue factor, the relationship to other subjects on the programme, the resources needed for the sessions and the methods and types of session chosen. Answers to the following questions will help you to decide how to schedule sessions:

◆   Where will this subject best fit into the programme – what does it follow or precede?
◆   How interested will the audience be?
◆   How important is the subject to the organization – and the audience?
◆   How familiar is the audience with the subject matter?
◆   What are audience attitudes towards the subject – is it hot news, controversial or something delegates really *need* to know?

♦ How much participation is anticipated – or wanted? Will participation facilitate 'ownership' of conclusions reached by the group?

♦ Would this be better handled in the total group or in smaller groups? Why?

♦ If in small groups, should these be composed of individuals from similar backgrounds or should groups be mixed? Why?

♦ What resources will be needed for this session? Will a formal presentation do or should you aim to entertain and impress delegates?

♦ Do you need to exhibit equipment and samples?

♦ Can you enhance interest by introducing case studies or case histories?

♦ What audio-visual material do you need?

♦ Do the participants need to prepare themselves for the session?

♦ Is the session best included in the morning or afternoon?

The last question raises the subject of the *length* of both the session and of the programme day. There are no hard and fast rules, but it is in this context that the programme planner really must try to put himself into the shoes of the delegate. There is always a temptation to overcrowd the day. The prevailing attitude often seems to be 'Now we've got them here they can earn their keep'… but remember the poor fellow in row 26 with all his problems.

The programme day sets the whole pace of the event and it must be a policy decision to lay down the start and end times. Administrative considerations apart, the decision will, to a great extent, depend upon the objectives and type of event. Some conferences are intentionally relaxed affairs so that delegates have plenty of time in which to meet socially and to encourage informal exchanges (sometimes the most valuable part of the event). Other meetings are intentionally hard-working with ambitious objectives. But a conference that lasts from 9 am to 5.30 pm each day is a real test of stamina. An event which mixes plenary and breakdown sessions in fact requires delegates to sit down and concentrate for most of the day. Even office-bound people spend a surprising amount of their time on their feet and moving about. They therefore find a long conference day very tiring.

Some organizers, particularly of internal training programmes, like to work participants until late in the evening. This can be counter-productive if all you do is to extend the day with more and more plenary and syndicate sessions. However, if the group or sub-groups are given a task to do overnight (eg, prepare a presentation), then the time will be used to good effect. Indeed, working long hours to a tight deadline can be a very effective team building exercise.

Remember that however well the information is presented and however varied the types of session and speaker, the average delegate will ultimately remember only a tiny fraction of the material covered. Nevertheless, more subtle objectives can be achieved in a long and busy programme. Examples might be attitude change, team building or commitment to a new policy or idea.

Start time: first day   Deciding when to start is difficult: too early, and delegates will arrive late – disrupting proceedings and missing out on the opening session(s); too late and everyone is left hanging about.

Events in London seem to start at either 9 am or 9.30 am. Provincial events often start later, for example with registration and coffee from 10 to 10.30 am.

There is an added complication for residential events: bedrooms may not be ready for occupancy until mid or even late morning. Arrangements have to be made to store baggage and time allowed later in the day for delegates to register and take over their bedrooms.

Some residential meetings start the evening before, perhaps with a reception and a buffet, and even a formal session. This also enables registration to be completed, saving valuable time later.

A novel idea, no doubt imported, is to start at 8 am and offer a running breakfast for early arrivals. This gives them something to do and a chance to talk to the other delegates.

Breaks   Whatever timings you decide on, do vary the pace. Do not make any session last too long. Allow time for a break during which delegates can stretch their legs, go to the lavatory and use the telephone for urgent business. Coffee, tea and meal breaks are an important part of the programme. Sufficient time must be allowed for everyone to obtain and consume their refreshments, and even the type of meal served has a direct effect on the delegates' subsequent attention span and ability to concentrate. Wherever you can, mix the types of session so that there is movement from the main hall to group rooms and back – but do allow enough time for any delegate movement. It always takes longer than you would expect, especially if the move-ment is between buildings, between floors of one building or to and from transport.

Session length   The length of each session is important. Our attention span is limited. In a 40-minute presentation or lecture, we are only likely to assimilate permanently the gist of the content of the first 10 minutes or so and the final summary. No wonder so many speakers are remem-bered for their jokes – usually at the expense of the subject matter to hand! You might wonder why we bother with the centre portion? This served to add to the credibility of the message and to reinforce delegate attitudes. Nevertheless, as a general rule no session should last more than 40 to 50 minutes without at least a short break and some people advocate sessions of no longer than 30 minutes.

Another consideration is whether or not time is to be allowed for questions and discussion after a formal presentation. Delegates prefer to ask questions at the end of each session rather than at the end of the day. This is an important point: the organizers of many one-day seminars tend to leave the 'discussion' session until the end of the day when people are more interested in going home than in asking questions.

METHODS OF PRESENTATION

The way in which material is to be presented is another question the programme planner must face. This is particularly important for the total group sessions. The decision depends upon the nature of the material and the situation in which it is to be presented. There is no right way to present any subject, but most large meeting presentations fall into one of the following categories:

Speaker unassisted   This is the straight lecture or talk, with no visual aids. It is most appropriate for the good speaker relating personal experience or opinion, the inspirational talk and some kinds of information giving. A lot depends upon the quality of the speaker. Many people have experienced lectures which have held them spellbound, but all too often the unassisted speaker fails to reach these heights.

Speaker with visuals   Most speakers prefer to use some form of visual aid, usually slides (or, more likely, LCD projection) or overhead projector transparencies, to help them explain technical or complex matters.

Demonstration   This is used to show objects, processes and procedures. Situation demonstrations are sometimes used to illustrate behaviour – for example, leading a discussion or handling an interview.

Dramatic action   Skits are sometimes used to drive home specific points. They are often intentionally humorous and should therefore be used with care since they can sometimes offend and even backfire, having the opposite effect to that intended. Such skits should, in any case, be short and they are usually performed in association with a talk or presentation.

Panel, symposium, workshop debate or forum   These are used to present different points of view of the subject, to encourage audience participation and to cover topics outside the formal agenda or proceedings.

Role play This is an effective training technique. Participants are given different roles to play in a set situation – for example a sales interview or negotiation. The principal benefit of role play is the process of reading into the role – and the understanding this affords. A useful variation is to use actors or briefed outsiders (even customers) for 'the other side'. Because these people are not known to the 'players' the role play is more realistic. Some agencies specialize in providing actors for role plays.

Poster session Used at major technical conferences, the author is available at a poster board display of an abstract or summary of his paper to answer questions and to discuss technical detail with interested delegates.

Video, multimedia and television These methods of presentation are dealt with in detail in Chapters 5 and 6.

To a great extent the choice is a *production* decision. This word seems to put many people off. It conjures up images of complex screen presentations or scantily clad models waving the 'product' in the air. These techniques should not be rejected out of hand – in the right context they are an excellent way of putting the message across. In any case, every meeting is 'produced'. The selection of the venue is certainly a production decision, because one of the very first impressions of the conference is that made by the place at which it is being held. The layout of the meeting room, the positioning of the microphone and lecterns and the order of speakers are all production decisions which affect how well the aim of the event is achieved.

AUDIENCE PARTICIPATION

Adequate opportunities should always be provided for audience participation. The social interaction of the conference or meeting is one of the most important benefits to delegate and organization alike and today's conference delegate not only wants but also expects opportunities for audience participation. One way of doing this has already been described – through dividing delegates into sub-groups and small working parties in which everyone has a chance to take part. Leaders of these groups need to be skilled in discussion management so that the sessions are rewarding to all participants.

Audience participation is much more difficult to arrange in the larger, total group sessions. Question periods are frequently used but are also frequently misused and often fail to achieve their objectives. There are many reasons for this failure – for example, inadequate time or poor scheduling. It is a brave person who rises to ask a question just before lunch when everyone wants to get to the bar. People usually ask questions because:

1. They need clarification or amplification of a particular point.
2. They do not see the application to their own situation.
3. They disagree with the point made.
4. They are trying to open up the discussion.

Many good questions are never even asked because people are too shy to raise them in so large a group, and, if questions are not screened for relevance, well organized presentations of ideas can be ruined by an unstructured discussion during the question period. This is why public political meetings can be very exciting and why some staged press conferences and panel discussions can be so dull. Even the technique of the 'planted' question should be used with care – if the session is unlikely to generate questions, why embarrass either audience or speaker by programming a question time?

The audience must be forewarned of the opportunity when a question time is programmed. If a speaker unexpectedly asks for questions at the end of the session, the only responses are likely to relate to the last part of the speech, since the audience does not have time to think back to its earlier parts. This can lead to emphasis on minor issues at the expense of the more important aspects of the subject matter. Thus, if the audience is warned beforehand that questions will be welcomed, and if adequate time is allowed at the end of the presentation before the question and answer session begins, the response is likely to be much better than if the questions follow on without a break.

If you are inviting questions from a large audience it is worth using an audience response system (see Chapters 6 and 14).

Rest, recreation and visits

The longer residential conference might include rest and recreation in the programme. Delegates are often a long way from home and may not be familiar with the district – or even the country. One of their reasons for attending might be to take advantage of the travel opportunity. Similarly, the social element of some conferences, especially in the incentive field, is of prime importance to the delegates. Even the more 'serious' or academic delegate needs rest from the business in hand and will usually appreciate opportunities for relaxation.

The organizer of the residential event should therefore endeavour to provide opportunities for a variety of activities such as walking, swimming, tennis, table-tennis and squash, so as to cater for all tastes and levels of athletic enthusiasm. These requirements affect the venue choice (see Chapter 2).

Guided tours and visits to local attractions are often a vital part of the conference programme (and, incidentally, often a very satisfactory profit centre for the organizers) and visits associated with the business of the event can be very worthwhile. Delegates to a conference with a strong social bias might be taken to see a slum area or a new housing project, a shocking example of a mental hospital, or the latest experiment in providing care for homeless families. Their dedication to their task may well be sharpened by the disturbing examples and their enthusiasm quickened by the utopian ones.

If you are organizing a large, international conference with a one-week programme, it is worth considering a whole free day or, failing that, a free half-day to enable foreign visitors to do their sightseeing, go shopping and conduct private business. A free day such as this will reduce 'absenteeism' during the rest of the event and relieve some of the pressure on everyone – especially the organizer and venue.

Balance must be maintained. If an isolated venue has been chosen deliberately in order to avoid distractions from the business in hand, it would not make sense to go out of your way to restore the distractions with visits and extra-mural activity!

There are several types of event where most, if not all, the programme takes place outside of any meeting room. Of these, Adventure Based Learning (ABEL) has already been discussed; the 'Incentive' is considered in Chapter 8 ('Organizing events overseas'); two others – Team Building and Corporate Hospitality – deserve special mention here:

Team Building   How often have you arrived at an annual sales industry conference and felt that sinking feeling that you are in for days of drab corporate presentations? And when it is all over, how often do you really feel invigorated by the experience, and enthusiastic about the months to come?

If you recognize this in your own company, then perhaps it is time to suggest a change of tack. More forward-thinking businesses have realized that corporate events are only worth the investment if they make a measurable difference, and that staff expect more than the usual rhetoric. As a result the events management industry is changing its spots, like any other industry where customer expectations have changed. As well as this, budgets have become tighter since the last recession in the UK and clients have much higher expectations of what they should get for their money.

In striving to maximize employees' performance in the broadest sense, companies are also looking to keep a lid on the rising costs of training and motivational programmes. As a result, managers are realizing the benefit of integrating motivation and team building into sales conferences and product launches. In this way they can lead their staff up steep learning curves relating to new products and services, while creating a better environment for improved team working and all in the context of an experience that will not be remembered for turgid presentations by marketing and sales managers.

While the basic sales conference was innovative in its day, a broader and more creative brief can bring a fresh perspective to how people work. IMS Health, for example, used an event in Cyprus to launch a new approach to how it worked as a company. The whole event had a theme – to communicate and reinforce the new ethos – combining team-building exercises focusing on collaborative working with the introduction of a new, long-term incentive programme and presentations on marketing and sales issues.

An inspirational event is a powerful platform for communicating with employees, and by building in people-skills elements, forward-thinking businesses not only benefit from increased staff performance, but are saving money.

Corporate Hospitality   Although not in fact strictly a conference or meeting, many of the organizational disciplines apply equally to this activity. Corporate hospitality is a way of informing through entertainment, a way of communicating a sales message without being overbearing, and of improving relationships between clients and colleagues.

Gone are the days of extravagant jollies when everyone had a lot of fun, probably drank far too much, and went home none the wiser about their hosts. (One financial services company invited some of its customers to a concert, which was followed by a lavish reception. At the end of the evening the chairman gave a short address, not to sell his company, but to promote the CDs and tapes of the chamber orchestra! There is, it is said, no such thing as a free lunch and there is little doubt that the guests would not have been in any way offended by a short 'sales' talk – indeed, most were probably surprised not to receive one, and not to go away at least with a pack of literature.)

A well organized event mixes happy existing clients with potential customers (what better way to put your message across than to have one of your clients do it for you?), and participation days – golf, clay pigeon shooting… even driving tanks and hot air ballooning – are becoming more and more popular. Many of the older 'standards' retain a certain cachet – Henley, Wimbledon, the FA Cup Final and so on. But as a buyer, beware of the black market – only deal with reputable suppliers, for example members of the Corporate Hospitality Association (CHA).

There are plenty of dos and don'ts in Corporate Hospitality. Here are some of them:

- Decide your objectives.
- Select your guests carefully.
- Choose an event that will interest you and your clients.
- Ensure you have sufficient hosts to look after your guests (maximum 1:5).
- Arrive before your guests… and leave after them.
- Ensure your staff are fully briefed… and make sure they do not drink too much.
- Plan the business content.
- Follow up afterwards – did your guests enjoy their day and get home safely?

BREAKS FOR FOOD AND DRINK

As already mentioned, these can be a vital ingredient of the programme and can even dictate the success or otherwise of the event. The timing of meals and coffee and tea breaks, the types of food and drink served and the efficiency of the service all affect the delegates' moods, enjoyment and comfort. If they are rushed, have to wait a long time to be served or cannot have what they want, their interest in the overall proceedings will be reduced. Too much is as bad as too little. The first session after lunch is not called 'the graveyard shift' for nothing. If they are allowed to over-indulge, the delegates, somnolent and slightly sozzled, will snooze their way through even the most arresting session. There is a strong case for not serving anything more than a glass or two of wine with the food at lunchtime. Indeed, it has become fashionable not to serve delegates alcohol in the middle of the day. This controls expense and delegate behaviour and simplifies administration without unduly spoiling delegate enjoyment There is usually plenty of time for social drinking during the evenings of residential conferences and delegates to routine day-long programmes do not normally expect heavy meals and too much to drink.

Movement Breaks It is common practice to arrange exhibitions and display equipment which is relevant to the event and to have information on display boards. These displays are often in the foyer or an adjacent hall. Breaks can be used to give delegates a chance to view these displays and exhibits. Chapter 7 gives further advice on this topic.

It is sensible to plan coffee, lunch or tea during a break when delegates are scheduled to move from the main hall to syndicate/work rooms or back. This gives them time to find their way and makes the time the movement takes less critical. Many delegates will use even the shortest break to make a telephone call or go to the lavatory and these activities inevitably prolong the movement breaks. By serving coffee or tea at these times you are recognizing this and will remove some of the pressure from both delegate and organizer. What is more, if a session overruns, the slack created by the planned break helps mitigate against subsequent disruption to the programme timings.

Length of breaks   How long should you allow for meals and coffee and tea breaks?

– *Buffet lunch.*   A buffet lunch takes less time than a sit-down meal *provided* the service is good and there are sufficient serving points. For large events, you need at least one serving point for every 50 delegates, and the movement of people needs to be managed. For some reason, people often seem to be slow at cottoning on to the fact that there are several serving points which inevitably means there is a long queue at one point whilst others are idle. Such problems cause delays. That said, a well managed three-course buffet should not last more than an hour, *including* allowing delegates to have sufficient time for personal administration.
– *'Sit-down' meals.*   These take longer – how long depends upon the menu, the level of service and a number of other factors. It is sensible to have a cold starter already on the table – this means delegates can begin to eat as soon as they are seated (a hot starter cannot be served until everyone is sitting down). Assuming delegates are seated at round tables of 10–12, and assuming a ratio of 1½ –2 waiters/waitresses per table, the main course and wines can be served quite quickly, especially if traditional silver service (where everything is brought on a large platter and is served at the table) is replaced by pre-plated food (which is not only quicker to serve but can look a lot better). A three-course meal will take between 1¼ and 1½ hours, a four-course meal rather longer.
– *Coffee and tea breaks.*   Allow 30 minutes (15 minutes for very small groups) – and insist that there are adequate serving points and that milk, sugar and biscuits are served from separate self-help points (to prevent congestion and delays). Remember – coffee breaks are also used by delegates to make telephone calls and to go to the lavatory – these activities all add to the time required (especially in venues where there are inadequate toilet facilities or insufficient public telephones).

- *Timings when there is an exhibition.*   When you have an exhibition alongside your conference, you must allow more time to give delegates a chance to look round the exhibition (and to give exhibitors a fair exposure to the delegates). It is worth holding tea and coffee breaks in the exhibition hall. Further advice on this subject can be found in Chapter 7.

Working meals   These can be very effective during smaller meetings. A waiter-served sit-down meal can be turned into a discussion session. The discussions are best conducted over coffee and, possibly, liqueurs when the participants are relaxed and are not disturbed by serving activities. Discussion can be in small table groups or, if the meeting is not large (say up to 20 people), round one table. Each table needs a discussion leader and it is normal to expect a report back during the ensuing formal session. Some organizers ensure at least one of the main speakers is seated at each table to give delegates a further chance to talk to them.

Meals and refreshment breaks are therefore important elements of the conference plan. You must decide what types of meal will be provided: self-serve buffet or sit-down with waiter service, hot or cold, with or without alcoholic refreshment (and, if with, bar service or controlled quantities of wine with the meal), etc. All these considerations are affected by the type of event, the type of delegate, the budget and the capabilities of the venue. Special diets must be catered for and alternative dishes provided for those whose religious beliefs make this necessary.

There is a body of opinion which believes that, in larger conferences, meals should be 'voluntary' (ie, should only be available to those who pre-book). This of course prevents you from having working meals, but it formally recognizes the reality of the situation where a significant proportion of delegates prefer to make their own arrangements. Catering is considered in greater detail in Chapter 12.

Gala dinners

An end of conference social function – for example, a gala dinner – is worth considering in any programme. It can provide a memorable highlight. An otherwise very ordinary annual conference of one association was lifted by an excellent dinner-dance on the last evening which will long be remembered by those fortunate enough to have been there.

Although such functions are almost invariably held on the last evening of a residential conference, there is a school of thought which says this is the worst possible night for such an event. Delegates inevitably stay up late (and often drink too much) and then have to wake up early the next morning to clear their rooms. A mid-conference dinner is said to be easier on the delegates, and it helps them get to know each other socially earlier in the event.

Cabaret

It is not uncommon to stage a cabaret at the gala dinner (above). As with nearly every other aspect of the programme, there are problems and pitfalls for the unwary. You will be fortunate if you succeed in pleasing everybody: 'one man's meat is another man's poison', and this is certainly true in terms of people's tastes in light entertainment.

There are some entertainers who succeed in pleasing everyone – some conjurers, a few singers and comedians – and you would be wise to opt for these rather than the latest pop group. Beware the risqué comedian, especially when you have mixed company. And it is worth noting in this respect that some comedians are very much 'bluer' when performing in private as opposed to on stage or TV. Careful vetting and pre-briefing are essential.

VIP speakers

Residential training programmes often end with a course dinner at which a VIP (typically the chief executive or a senior manager) is invited to give an address. Sometimes – in fact almost always – an informal 'off the record' question and answer session over coffee/liqueurs is far more useful than an address.

Ceremony

Many people enjoy ceremony. A formal opening and/or closing cere-mony is well worthwhile at the larger conference, especially if the dele-gates all belong to the association or have some other common bond.

Opening reception   It is common practice to hold a reception either the night before the conference opens or, more commonly, at the end of the first day. These receptions help the process of intermingling, making it easier for delegates to meet one another.

ACCOMPANYING PERSONS

Once upon a time delegates were apparently all male and some of them occasionally took their wives to conferences. Today, to avoid any accusation of sex discrimination (and to recognize the 'real world'), we talk about 'accompanying person' and 'partners' to define wives, men friends, ladies and husbands. The decision to invite accompanying persons must not be taken lightly. One group from an American company had arrived in London on a very expensive incentive/conference trip. They had come to England on the QEII, were staying at one of the top five-star hotels and were due to return home by Concorde. The wives had come too... and the event was a near disaster. While the men were conferring in London, their wives were left to fend for themselves. None of them had been to England before and they had no ideal what to do or how to organize their stay. The group was only small, and it would not have taken the company much time, effort or additional expense to have laid on a special daytime schedule for the ladies. As it was, they were bored and unhappy and could not wait to get home.

The point is that, if there are accompanying persons, they must have a programme and be looked after as well as the conference delegates themselves. A few companies even include partners in some of the formal conference activities. Parallel sessions to brief spouses on their partners' company and jobs can be invaluable, although you may end up arranging two conferences instead of one!

But, beware! These days the sexes do not split neatly into male delegates and female 'accompanying persons'. Any social programme must provide for male as well as female partners. Some conferences have even provided creches for the children of delegates or accompanying persons.

THE SPEAKERS

We see and hear good speakers almost every day – the news readers and presenters of television and radio and the professional entertainers. These people, through training and practice, seem able to speak in public easily and effectively (although Harold Macmillan admitted to being terrified before making any major speech in the House of Commons). Most of us are less fortunate and find speaking in public an ordeal to be avoided at all costs. Most experts, be they leading scientists or industrial executives, like us, are not natural public speakers. Conversely, most good public speakers are not experts in the required subject areas. The few who are good at both are in great demand and are often over-exposed.

It is therefore not always easy to find suitable speakers. Some may be dictated by circumstances. The company or association chairman may insist on delivering the keynote speech (just pray he is a good public speaker!) and some speakers may be naturals for particular sessions. But the organizer is usually left with the task of finding at least some speakers.

It is a task that takes time and patience. First, you must know exactly what you are seeking. Prepare a short brief summarizing the objectives of the event itself, indicating the number and type of people expected to attend and stating the exact requirement for the session in question. This will clear your mind and help you deal with questions when you first approach someone.

Speaker attributes

Speakers must have good knowledge of their subject. This might seem self-evident, but professional speakers have been known to deliver papers which were written for them by someone else. Although, in every case, the delivery was faultless, the performances lacked conviction because the speakers did not know enough about their subject matter to speak with authority, nor could they take questions afterwards. It is usually necessary to compromise and, if the choice is between the real expert who is a disaster on the platform and the lesser expert who is an excellent public speaker, it is normally better to choose the latter unless the former is such a well known figure that people will be prepared to listen in spite of his failings.

It is also worthwhile being adventurous. At one event a worker from the shop floor held 150 senior executives spellbound during a seminar on industrial relations. The speaker received a long ovation for an honest insight into aspects of the subject which few of the audience ever considered and of which, with less imaginative programming, they would have remained in ignorance.

Finally, it is important to find a speaker who will relate to the audience and vice versa. It is necessary to find out about the style and personality of prospective speakers to ensure that they will be acceptable in the planned forum. A studious dissertation on 'marketing' to a group of successful salesmen during an annual incentive event could be as great a disaster as inviting a flamboyant salesman to address an academic audience intent on a theoretical analysis of a particular subject.

Whom to approach

It is impossible to give other than general advice on this matter, but the following paragraphs will help you to identify the main sources of potential speakers and to handle the approach itself.

The principal sources of speakers are:

- internal personnel;
- professionals in the field;
- academic experts;
- 'personalities';
- politicians;
- 'big names'.

Internal personnel   These should not be overlooked. Of course – as already mentioned – you may be forced to use some internal speakers such as the company or association chairman to give a keynote address. But even where you have the choice of going outside to find your speakers, do make sure you do not overlook suitable experts in your own organization. Any personnel or marketing manager worth his salt should be able to give a competent talk on his subject and, since he comes from within, he can ensure what he says is relevant to the organization – all too often, external speakers fail to make their content specific to the audience in front of them.

Internal speakers have to be well briefed, but beware of *over*-briefing. This is particularly true when you invite senior executives to open a course or particular session: they invariably ask for a brief and simply parrot back what the brief says. Again, any senior executive worth his salt should *know* what to say. The message will be much better if it comes 'from the heart'.

Professionals in the field   There are experts in every subject you can think of – the problem is finding them. The best thing to do if you do not know who they are is to seek expert advice. Experts in the field in question will almost certainly know who the other experts are, who is 'up and coming' (these are the ones who will have something new or topical to say), whether they are good at public speaking and whether they might be willing to take part. Professional bodies, academic institutions (business schools and universities) and the training departments of the larger companies are all sources of this sort of information.

Academic experts   It is often better to opt for an academic expert in the subject rather than a practitioner. There are several reasons for this: they tend to be more up to date; they are usually used to speaking in public (not that this necessarily means they are good at it) and they are more likely to take a wider view. As with professional practitioners, you should approach the business schools and universities for suitable 'names'. Academics tend to charge more than practitioners (but not more than consultants whose fees are usually similar to those charged by academics), and you do have to 'manage' them – in particular, it is essential to ensure they come with decent AV aids (most of them seem to rely on handwritten OHP slides and the whiteboard).

'Personalities' from the world of entertainment are often used as conference speakers and/or presenters, but you need to take care: at one high-profile association conference a series of well-known figures from the entertainment world were engaged to give a series of presentations on subjects ranging from speaking in public to marketing and PR (public relations). The event was a near disaster. To be sure, all spoke with confidence – indeed, they were word perfect and hardly glanced at their scripts. But they lacked credibility: it was clear their scripts had been written for them and all they were doing was 'delivering'. TV and stage celebrities are just that – they are, in reality, famous for being something other than themselves. They 'act out' their scripts and, in the acting mode they are credible. But in the presentation mode they are not.

This is not to say that personalities do not have their place in some conference programmes. Used appropriately, they can lift the proceedings to new heights.

Personalities (ie, celebrities) can be used for a number of purposes:

- as after dinner/after luncheon speakers;
- as linkmen, introducing sessions and acting as a bridge between sessions or to introduce cabaret;
- as chairmen of question and answer sessions;
- in an investigating role (interviewers);
- as role players (for example, as interviewees);
- as speakers/presenters in their own right.

We discuss each of these in turn below.

The *after dinner/after luncheon speech* is almost an art form in itself – one at which only a few are really good. There are few things worse than the poor after dinner speech: at best it can be mildly disappointing – at worst it can be an unmitigated disaster. You need to give some thought to what sort of speaker you want – a straight entertainer (possibly a comedian); a well-known personality (from business, politics, the sporting world and so on) or someone who has something to say that is germane to the event. Unfortunately, the better after dinner speakers tend to be over-exposed (they also tend to be expensive and difficult to get on account of their busy schedules). There are agencies that specialize in after dinner speakers and it is probably best to seek their advice; they will probably know of someone who would not only be ideal but would not be prone to the pitfalls already mentioned.

Personalities, especially those from television, make excellent *linkmen* – not least because for so many, this is their stock in trade. Whether it is worth paying a lot of money to get someone well-known to do something which a good chairman should be able to do rather better (see Chapter 14) is open to question. Personalities are, however, very good at introducing cabaret (and so they should be since this is sheer entertainment and they are simply doing what they always do).

Rather, it may be better to use a personality to *chair question and answer sessions* or, better, in an *investigative role* (ie, as interviewers). This is something the best are very good at – and their use in this way can add a great deal of credibility to the event. At one conference, the chairman of BBC's *Question Time* ran an in-house Question Time where the panel was made up of leading company figures and the audience was made up of people from all parts of the company. The session was the highlight of the conference.

Actors can be engaged to undertake *role plays*. As previously mentioned, role play is a very effective training 'tool' and the use of actors – who are unknown to the in-house 'players' can make the role play very realistic. However, the actors have to be well-briefed otherwise they will not be credible.

We have already mentioned the dangers of using celebrities as *presenters* to deliver scripts they have not written themselves and which are beyond their normal purview. However, some celebrities can be used as speakers in their own right – ie, when they are talking about something they know about. Some presenters are very knowledgeable in their fields (especially the sports commentators); others are celebrities because of their success in their particular fields. These people can be excellent when their subject matter – or what they have to say – is apposite to the event. However, many are 'big names' in their own right – (see page 104).

Problems with personalities.   The cost apart (the question of fees is discussed in a later paragraph) there are other problems associated with using personalities. Even with the most careful briefing they can tend to go their own way, exhibiting a degree of independence which may be good entertainment but may not be good for the event. A senior politician may be able to withstand an onslaught of hostile questions or being the target of offensive humour, but the company chairman may not and the experience could do him and his reputation more harm than good. Another problem can be caused by a difference in perception as to what you are paying for. Some personalities appear, do their contracted bit and leave at once: the organizers of a major charity event were dismayed when – having delivered her lecture – a famous figure departed immediately rather than stay on for the formal dinner which people had paid large sums to attend. If you expect such people to mingle with your delegates or stay for a meal or coffee break make sure this is agreed beforehand, otherwise you may end up feeling 'cheated'.

Finally, like it or not, personalities respond to being pampered. The organizer of one international conference in Monaco arranged for his personality to be flown from Nice airport by helicopter: the dividend came in the form of a longer and better 'performance' than might otherwise have been forthcoming.

Politicians   It is common to use a leading politician to give the keynote speech at important conferences – for example, the Minister for Health at the annual conference of the British Medical Association or the Minister of Agriculture at the annual gathering of the National Farmers Union.

These speeches can be important occasions since they allow the minister to promote government policy to his 'public', and it enables delegates to hear – and often question – the minister at first hand.

There are dangers in engaging politicians:

- They may be of a different political persuasion to some (even all) of the audience and may therefore antagonize them.
- A 'political' speech may be inappropriate to the event.
- The politician may cancel at short notice because of an unexpected political event of greater priority than appearing at your conference.
- You will probably be given a 'topped and tailed' version of a standard political speech so that overall what is said may be only partially appropriate (and may not be very 'new').

That said, the appearance of a senior cabinet minister or an appropriate member of the Opposition may give your event a great deal of additional status, especially if you have an international audience.

Elder statesmen can often be 'better' than practising politicians: they are freed from the constraints of office and can therefore speak more frankly. What they have to say can be fascinating. At one international conference a retired, internationally known statesman held the audience spellbound with his insight into the political attitudes of each member state of the EC.

Politicians, especially elder statesmen, can be expensive. People like Lady Thatcher command huge fees for a single appearance. Lesser figures can be comparatively inexpensive and, of course, some politicians will appear for nothing if they believe you are offering them a high-profile public platform for them to express their views.

'Big names'   These deserve a paragraph of their own even though some have been mentioned above. Big names include politicians, leading sports personalities (especially those who specialize in speaking on subjects such as 'leadership' and 'motivation'), well-known

businessmen, high-profile churchmen (for example, Rabbi Lionel Blue), academic 'gurus' and top entertainers.

They are, almost without exception, very expensive. It is difficult to put a price to a single appearance – anything from a few thousand pounds for a single lecture right up to £50,000 or more.

In spite of the cost, the 'right' big name can 'make' the event. One internationally known US academic guru knows that just having his name on the speakers' list adds 10 per cent or more to the eventual number of registrations: he charges a fee commensurate to the added value he brings – plus all expenses (first class air fare or, preferably Concorde) and he picks and chooses the events he graces with his presence. (As he told one hapless conference organizer who was trying to persuade him to speak at a particular event – an elaborate international congress involving dozens of speakers – 'You can't buy me at *any* price. However, I might reconsider if you hold the event in the winter rather than the summer – I could do with a shopping trip to London just before Christmas!')

The approach

Having identified the speakers you want, you of course have to invite them to come along to your event.

Personalities and many 'big names' use agents and a good starting point is therefore a reputable agent. A booking fee may have to be paid but in return the agent will establish communication (not always easy: 'big names' in particular go to great lengths to protect their personal privacy); they will also ensure the contract is correctly drawn up.

Speaker agencies have access to all the 'big' names (and also to the lesser known specialist speakers) not only in the UK but worldwide.

The better agencies are choosy about whom they take onto their books. They avoid the 'professional speaker' who writes a standard spiel to be repeated at conferences round the world. As one agency says, 'Those who are not prepared to do what we ask, we drop. Our speakers command fees of anything from £1,000 to £100,000 for a single session – but they deliver. They will not speak on anything that can be read in a newspaper – there will be no generalities.'

The first step in the process, once the brief has been agreed, is a meeting between client and speaker. Speeches are customized and fine tuned to ensure they are exactly what the client wants. The need to brief speakers cannot be overemphasized. We return to this subject below (page 108). Finally, clients are debriefed afterwards to ensure their objectives were met.

Conference producers (see Chapter 5) are also used to contacting and engaging speakers (especially personalities and 'big names'). They will usually in fact deal with the agent but, being used to the task, will be able to relieve you of the work – and will do it better.

However, many speakers (and potential speakers) do not have agents and these you have to approach yourself. The initial approach should, if possible, be by telephone. This gives you the chance to explain, persuade and respond to queries. A follow-up written invitation can be sent once the speaker has indicated he or she is willing to help.

Payment   The question of fees usually crops up at an early stage (and, as we have already seen, some speakers can be very expensive).

When discussing the matter on the telephone always start by offering to pay the speaker's expenses and, where appropriate, offer hotel accommodation. Then ask what fee is expected: if it is more than you can afford, be honest and start negotiating.

Not all speakers expect a fee: the publicity or kudos gained by appearing is sufficient for some. For others, a case of wine may be a better form of remuneration than a fee. Still others are not allowed to accept payment as part of their terms of employment.

The amount expected by the others depends upon factors such as their public standing, the value of their time and their own financial aspirations. Most speakers are very modest in their aspirations and leave it to you to suggest a figure.

It is not possible to give much guidance on actual costs. A fee of £50–£100 for a single session may suffice someone from industry, while some leading academics command fees of several thousand – sometimes tens of thousands of pounds for a similar programme slot.

An after dinner speaker can start at about £650 plus expenses and VAT up to £15,000 and more for an international name. The fees for top entertainers vary so widely that it is impossible to quote meaningful figures.

Sometimes even top speakers will appear for nothing if they believe the event is 'worthwhile' in some way. Perhaps we should take a course in negotiating skills beforehand.

Cancellation fees will almost certainly be due if the event is cancelled. Insurance should be taken out to protect against the liability associated with unforeseen cancellation, either of the event or by the celebrity speaker – see Chapter 4.

CALLS FOR PAPERS

It is common practice to make a public call for papers for technical, medical and association conferences (or, to put it crudely, to advertise for speakers). Conferences are seen by academics and researchers as ways of making their work (and, it has to be said, themselves) known, and such is the demand for platform time at some events that speakers actually pay for the privilege of presenting a paper.

The call for papers is sent out, in either letter or brochure form, well in advance of the event. The call may also be placed in leading industrial, professional and academic journals. Individuals or institutions are invited to submit abstracts, usually no more than 250 words, before a strict deadline. The call must give full details of the conference (dates, venue, title, theme, programme structure and so on) and also specify how the abstract should be written, including house rules for titles, authors' names (eg surname followed by initials and so on).

An organizing committee is usually appointed to review abstracts and decide which should be accepted. The clerical burden of handling the abstracts, sending confirmation and rejection letters to authors and supporting the conference committee can be considerable.

Abstracts have to be sorted into categories and should be indexed and, once selected, authors have to be briefed by letter confirming the date, time, location, session title and chairman, the manner and length of presentation, rules for AV support and the layout/house style of the actual paper and so on. It is not uncommon for organizers to accept submissions on disk or via e-mail: this enables them to alter the typeface and layout to the common 'house style'. Many professional conference organizers use a computer to handle the abstracts for large conferences. Bearing in mind there can be anything between 500 and 1,000 abstracts to sort by author and title, it is not surprising that they use computers.

The abstracts are usually included in the conference programme, and titles and authors are given in the conference brochure.

Paper/abstract presentation methods

Papers may be presented as plenary session lectures, at workshops or even at abstract review sessions. The latter may restrict the author to five or ten minutes, with a shorter period for questions.

Poster sessions are often included in major conferences. Successful authors are allocated space on one of a series of notice boards: charts, graphs, tables and a brief summary are displayed and the author stands by his display at times specified in the programme to discuss his paper with interested parties and to answer questions. Although the poster technique is relatively new and is not universally popular with either authors or audiences, research from America suggests that in fact it is a very effective method of presenting a lot of papers. One reason for it being so effective is that, in contrast to the lecture and plenary question and answer session, the author is exposed to a few delegates at a time, enabling an intimate and free exchange of views.

Poster sessions need careful management. Poster boards should be situated in a central and easily accessible area. They can be combined with an exhibition to attract delegates to both activities.

The Committee should decide on the maximum number of abstracts they wish to accept as poster presentations and how long the posters will remain in place (one day, half a day, for the whole event and so on). The event organizer should advise the Committee in making these decisions: space limitations will clearly influence whether or not posters have to be changed during the event.

Authors should be allocated a board (typically one metre wide) and posters should be grouped by topic. Each board should bear an identifying number so that posters can be easily located. The organizer should provide fixings to enable the author to fix his poster and any illustrations neatly and easily. It may be necessary to provide additional lighting.

Authors should be advised as to the best size and format for display material – which may include text, photographs, drawings, graphs and so on. They should also be told when to be at their board to answer questions – and time must be allowed in the programme for this activity. Programme time may also be given for posters to be reviewed either in a plenary session or in a workshop.

BRIEFING SPEAKERS

Speakers should be carefully briefed. It is best to adopt the principle that they must be told everything they need to know, from where and when they are speaking, to how to get there and what they are expected to cover in their session(s). Synopses should be exchanged between all interested speakers at an early stage and, if formal papers are wanted for publication, make sure they are aware of the deadline and the size and layout of their contribution. The last is an important point. It is not easy to edit material submitted by speakers and you will save a great deal of time if copy you receive is in the right format. You may be able to persuade them to submit camera-ready copy (ie copy that is ready to go to the printers) to avoid the additional work of re-keying the copy before printing. However, if you have an optical scanner the latter task is, of course, eliminated.

If the press is to be present at the event in question the speakers should be warned. This will give them a chance to modify their talks if some of their material is private or confidential or, indeed, to decline to speak if they have particular objections. Some speakers welcome the presence of the press since it gives them a chance to obtain extra publicity.

Speakers' meetings

Some organizers like to assemble all their speakers for a personal discussion during the planning stage. This is sometimes necessary for larger and more complex events. However, the majority of speakers are busy enough and may not be willing to give up time for such a discussion. If you are concerned about tying up the different sessions it is worth visiting speakers to establish contact on a personal level and to iron out any difficulties they may have. A dinner for all speakers the evening before the conference – or even a series of such dinners during the event – is a useful alternative to the individual briefing if a meeting is not possible during the planning stage.

You will need biographical notes on your speakers. The programme chairman will need them when he introduces each speaker and it is good practice to give brief details in the conference programme.

Many speakers need help with their audio-visual aids and this should be offered. Even if they do not seek help, it is advisable to obtain copies of their audio-visual aids in order to check that they are of an acceptable standard (if they are not you may have a diplomatic problem persuading the speakers to accept smarter versions).

Finally, try to persuade any speaker who has some distance to come to arrive the previous day, especially if he is due on early in the morning. One speaker gave the organizer of a one-day seminar in London a few anxious moments when he arrived with only a few minutes to spare. He was a good performer and he got away with it, but the organizer's nerves were stretched – especially as he knew the speaker was travelling up from Cardiff and there was snow in the West!

The natural reaction when – as in the example at the beginning of this chapter – a speaker goes down badly with the audience, is to blame the speaker. Assuming he has done his best (not always the case – but usually so) then what has gone wrong?

Few blame the conference organizers: but it could be argued that the meeting planner who allows a poor speaker onto the platform is culpable – the speaker should never have been selected. By the same token, if an experienced speaker fails to hold the audience either he was a bad choice for the audience in question, or – more likely – he was badly briefed: in both instances the conference organizer must take the blame.

One experienced speaker lists amongst his pet 'hates' which are guaranteed to spoil his performance:

1. Not briefing him about the organization, the event or the size and expectations of the audience. ('People assume I know it all', he says.)
2. Failing to send proper administrative instructions ('I need the same information as the delegates').

3. Not providing an opportunity to rehearse – or even to see the conference room before his session.
4. Altering the programme at short notice – either bringing his session forward or delaying it – both exceedingly unsettling for the speaker.
5. Failure to tell him the media will be present.
6. Using the wrong name – or wrong pronunciation – when introducing him; giving incorrect information about him; introducing the session subject incorrectly ('There is nothing like being introduced as a speaker "who will entertain you" when you are prepared to give a serious dissertation!', he declares).
7. Pre-empting the session by revealing its content in the introduction.

A final pet hate is an unwillingness to be open about fees and expenses. He says he hates having to raise the subject when he is approached to speak at a conference. Even worse is being expected to speak 'as a favour' (ie for no fee).

To quote another well-known personality who regularly speaks at conferences: 'I don't like being parachuted in and out. I prefer to go along early, have coffee and chat to the delegates so that we understand each other. Question time is the most important part of any session, then everyone feels they have had their money's worth.

'I have been known to get it wrong – discover that I have misunderstood the reason for the conference. If that happens, I'll say "Sorry – I've brought the wrong speech" and think out a new approach on my feet. I am paid an awful lot of money to speak and it is right that I do my homework first.'

The moral is clear: not only do you need to find good speakers who are appropriate for your event and your audience – you must also brief them properly if you want to get the best out of them.

Reserve speakers

Speakers, like anyone else, are prone to sudden illness, unexpected business commitments, bereavement and other difficulties which can make them cancel an engagement at short notice. The conference organizer should always have reserve speakers in mind and should actually appoint and brief the reserves for key speakers.

SIMULTANEOUS TRANSLATION

A decision on whether or not to provide translation for an international event – or for an event where you have foreign speaking speakers – is fundamental to the event itself. It has implications for the actual programme since the process of translation alters the character of the proceedings, can slow the programme down, and affects the briefing of speakers.

The easy option is to opt for English as the sole language. But it may not be a wise decision: 70 per cent of the delegates whose mother tongue is not English may *claim* to have a working knowledge of the language – but the degree to which they understand (and are understood) will vary. And what about the other 30 per cent who do not speak or understand English? They may be in the minority but they are just as important as their fellow delegates. If they realize that they will not be able to follow the proceedings, let alone ask questions or express opinions, they will either refuse to come or, if they do, they will probably skip the meeting and go shopping instead.

It is for these reasons that you should provide conference translators if you are holding an international meeting. And if you do so decide, you will need professional translators and all the associated translation equipment – translators' booths, headsets and so on.

So how are you going to find these translators? Rather than trying to recruit and organize them yourself, it will save you time and money if you engage the help of professional consultant translators who will be able to guide you through the complex decisions to be made. The consultant translator will provide advice and a cost estimate, recruit the staff and liaise between you and the team until the completion of the meeting.

Ideally, you should obtain a clear idea of the translation arrangements and costs at an early stage in the preparation of your event. For example, there are different forms of conference translation and the choice you make can affect the selection of a venue. If the meeting is a small group discussing business matters or drafting a document, it would probably be appropriate to have whispering or consecutive translation. The translator either whispers simultaneously to one or two delegates or takes notes and, following the statement, conveys the message in the other language.

If, however, you are holding a large conference and there are to be several conference languages, you will obtain the best results by opting for simultaneous translation. The translators sit in sound-proof booths, listening to speeches through headphones and translating directly to the delegates in their own language. Special sound equipment is needed for this form of translation and ISO (International Standards Organization) standards exist for both the built-in systems to be found in some conference centres and the mobile equipment which is available from specialist suppliers. If you are using mobile equipment, remember that not all meeting rooms will be able to accommodate the booths you may require.

Professional translators study the subject of the meeting beforehand and prepare the relevant terminologies. You can help them by sending all available background documents, papers to be presented, agendas, and so on, as far in advance of the conference as possible.

At the start of the conference, delegates need to be informed as to how the translation functions, with speakers being briefed on such things as speed of delivery. Throughout the meeting, one person should be appointed to provide the translators with last-minute papers, changes in timing, and so on.

The International Association of Conference Interpreters offers the following 'golden rules' on translation at conferences:

♦ Make your meeting truly international by making it multilingual.
♦ Ask a professional consultant translator for advice and quotes.
♦ Discuss types of translation and equipment required before finalizing the venue.
♦ Always use equipment which conforms with ISO standards.
♦ Insist on professional translators. Do not sacrifice quality for the sake of false economies.
♦ Once you are certain of your requirements, sign the contracts with the individual translators to ensure their availability.
♦ As far ahead as possible before the meeting, send all available conference documents to the translators.
♦ Keep your sessions to 3–3½ hours. Remember the effect of stress and fatigue on the translators, as well as the delegates' attention span.
♦ At the start of the meeting delegates and speakers should be fully briefed on the use of translation (see below).
♦ Throughout the conference, appoint a representative to liaise with the translators' head of team.

Briefing speakers The International Association of Conference Interpreters produces a set of guidelines for speakers: these are reproduced at the end of the chapter and can be adapted for your particular event.

Some other points speakers should consider when using translators are:

♦ avoid little-known words (such as 'efficacy') and also ambigous words (eg, 'correct' which can mean 'to cure'; 'to scold'; and 'to make conform to a standard') which can leave room for misinterpretation;
♦ explain the major idea in two or three different ways, as the point may be lost if covered only once;
♦ avoid long sentences, double negatives, or the use of negative sentences when a positive form could be used (eg 'this is the worst

example' or 'this is a bad example rather than 'this is not the best of examples');

- try to be expressive and use gestures to support your verbal messages;
- do not be put off if part of the audience reacts (eg laughs at a joke) some moments after the main body – there is a natural lag when translating into some languages, particularly those which are particularly 'wordy'.

Briefing delegates   It is vital that delegates are taught how to operate the headsets so that they can 'tune in' to the appropriate translation – an obvious point but one which is frequently overlooked.

EXECUTIVE CHECKLIST

- Do you base the content of the programme on the event objectives?
- Do your programmes satisfy those objectives?
- Do you draw up a programme framework to decide the number of sessions and the objectives of each session?
- Do you arrange the types of session to suit the content?
- Do you vary the pace of the event and the types of session?
- Do you design breaks to fit the programme? Do you allow adequate time for delegates to move, eat and relax?
- Do you serve appropriate meals and limit alcoholic refreshments?
- Do you provide for rest and recreation during residential conferences and schedule appropriate visits as part of the formal programme?
- Do you make sure accompanying persons have their own organized programme?
- How do you select speakers? Do you try to find the very best public speakers in the subject area? Do you seek a second opinion?
- Are your speakers properly briefed? Do you ensure that synopses are exchanged between speakers?
- Do you appoint reserve speakers?
- Do you provide simultaneous translation for your international events?

TRANSLATING: SUGGESTED GUIDELINES FOR SPEAKERS

The organizers of this conference have provided professional interpretation so that delegates of different languages and cultures can understand each other. The quality of interpretation depends on good co-operation between speakers and interpreters. The interpreters are your allies in bringing your message across to the audience. *You* can help them by following these simple guidelines.

1. If you have a *written text or notes of your speech*, even if you do not intend to read it out, hand it to the secretariat for the interpreters, so that they can become familiar with your subject and terminology. Interpreters do not read a speech, they interpret its meaning. So you may freely stray from your text or add to it as you speak. AIIC interpreters are bound by professional secrecy, so your document is quite safe. If you wish, it can be returned to you after your statement.
2. If your paper is *very technical* you may wish to give the interpreters any technical vocabulary that you have, or papers on the same subject in other languages. You may also ask the secretariat to organize a briefing with the interpreters. They like to meet their speakers. They are interested in you and your message.
3. If you want to show a *film, slides or transparencies*, make sure that the interpreters get the script or a copy of the transparencies. The booths are often situated far from the screen and it will help your interpreters to have the projected text in from of them.
4. Speak at a *normal pace,* ie, about 3 minutes per page of 40 lines. Try to resist the natural tendency when reading to speak much faster than normal. Otherwise your audience will lose you, your message will not get across.
5. Before you speak, switch on your *microphone* or make sure it is switched on by the technician. Please do not knock on the microphone or blow into it to test it – this is painful to the interpreters' ears. To try whether it is on, just say a few word, such as 'Good afternoon' or 'Thank you Mr Chairman'.
6. Do not speak too close to the microphone, as this creates interference. Also, don't leave your receiver set close to the microphone when you speak, as this causes feed-back whistling.
7. If you *move away from your seat*, eg, to point at a slide or transparency projection, please use a neck or lapel microphone. Without a microphone the interpreters cannot hear you, however loudly you speak.

8. If you are speaking from the rostrum or a lectern and want to reply to questions from the floor, please make sure you have a receiver set with you so that you can listen to the questions as they are interpreted.

Thank you! We wish you a good conference!

Your Interpreter Team

Reproduced by permission of AIIC
(International Association of Conference Interpreters)

4

THE BUDGET

We all have to be budget conscious these days and conferences and meetings, like any other business activity, should be organized within a planned budget.

The need to have a budget for events organized on a commercial basis is self-evident, be it a public seminar designed to make a profit or an association conference which, whilst not necessarily intended to make a profit, equally must not make a loss.

The need for a strict budget for internal events is, in some ways, less evident. However, if firm discipline and financial control are not exercised, costs can easily escalate out of control.

The budget is therefore an essential element in the disciplined control of expenditure for any event, large or small, public or in-company. The company which hides its conference expenses in general overheads is just as improvident as the person who contemplates arranging a public event without having a clear idea of the financial implications involved.

The first part of this chapter discusses the mechanics of preparing a budget, pricing policies and the cash flow forecast. Other financial matters such as economizing on the budget and a number of practical considerations are dealt with separately in the second part of the chapter.

THE BUDGET

The budget is the basis of the financial plan. In this chapter we consider the forecast budget, which is a statement of *projected* income and expenditure for a particular event or series of events. We begin with costs since these apply to all types of event, internal and external.

How much will the event cost?

The first step in drawing up a forecast budget is to work out how much the event will cost – the projected expenditure. These costs can then be compared with projected income or allocated funds so that, if there is a discrepancy, subsequent adjustments can be made to reduce the chance of overspending or, in the case of the public event, making a loss.

Forecast costs can be broken down into: *fixed costs* (those costs which will be incurred irrespective of how many delegates attend the event) and variable costs (these costs which vary according to the number of people attending).

Fixed costs

Things which have to be paid for no matter how many delegates eventually attend include:

- charges for the hire of venue facilities;
- speakers' fees, and their travel and accommodation expenses;
- marketing costs:
    brochure – artwork, typesetting and printing;
    mail-out – postage, letters, envelopes, etc;
    press release;
    advertising;
    press conferences and other publicity expenses.
  Note: even internal events have to bear 'internal marketing' costs – a factor often conveniently forgotten.
- administrative costs (or conference organizer's fees);
- AV costs: preparation and/or hire costs of video, multimedia material and computer graphics, OHP transparencies, audio-visual and sound equipment hire/purchase;
- hire charges: furniture, office equipment, interpreters' booths/simultaneous translation equipment, lecterns, lights, etc;
- printing: speakers' papers/conference report, programmes, badges, etc;
- exhibition costs: shell scheme for stands, publicity;
- services: telephone, interpreters, extra staff at venue;
- signposting, stage set, flowers;
- transport;
- insurance;

- ◆ legal and audit fees;
- ◆ interest charges to service loans and overdrafts;
- ◆ contingencies.

Some of these items merit further explanation:

1. *Administrative costs*   Of all forecast costs, these are the most difficult to estimate accurately, especially as they normally include a large element of overhead costs which may not necessarily be charged to the conference budget. For example, the staff of many associations and professional bodies regularly arrange annual conferences and other meetings. These duties are considered to be part of their jobs and are recognized as being an element in the organization's annual overheads. The salaries and wages of permanent staff are therefore paid for by members' subscriptions and income other than that from conferences and meetings. It is argued that the conferences and meetings are part of the service provided for the organization as a whole and that a delegate attending an event should therefore only contribute towards the actual additional expenditure of the meeting concerned. This sort of accounting procedure is a policy matter for the organization concerned, but few such organizations are aware of the size of the overhead cost absorbed by conferences and meetings. If they took the trouble to find out, their rather generous policies might be changed.

However, even if the staffing costs are excluded, there is other real expenditure involved in administering conferences and meetings. What, for example, about non-salary overheads? Telephone bills, in particular, soon mount up and stationery, postage and out-of-office expenses (travel, entertaining, accommodation and so on) are all examples of expenditure which can and should be attributed to the conference budget, but which are often treated as a general overhead.

Few associations and professional bodies systematically apportion these expenses but, if they are not so apportioned, conference budgets and, consequently, the price charged to delegates, can be artificially low. Indeed, if the administrative costs are not accurately calculated and if these are not included in the budget, the event which is apparently making a profit might in fact be losing considerable sums of money. Should the few (the conference delegates) be subsidized by the many (the members)?

Commercial companies which employ (misemploy?) executives who have other regular responsibilities to arrange conferences and meetings are often equally ignorant of the true cost of arranging their meetings. Invoiced expenditure like transport, accommodation, entertainment and production only represents the tip of the iceberg. The person selected to organize a company event is frequently a sales or marketing manager with an already full workload.

The additional work involved is considerable. It has been estimated that, in organizing a sales convention for 200 people, an executive will:

- personally sign over 150 letters;
- make over 100 telephone calls;
- receive over 100 telephone calls;
- send 25 or more faxes and/or e-mail messages;
- make five lengthy journeys;
- negotiate 5 to 10 contracts for meeting space, food and so on;
- personally check up to 50 pieces of work that someone else should have checked;
- receive, have to check and query, up to 25 invoices.

He will, in addition, have to spend time researching venues and facilities, and presumably, if he has not handled such an event previously, take a great deal of time in locating the services and suppliers that he will inevitably need. For each hour he spends in contemplating any of the above functions (and the above list is by no means a total appraisal of the workload) he will lose an hour from his normal job function.

Other staff and facilities also become involved – secretaries to word-process letters, the printing department, other managers, the workshop, the photographic and computing departments – all expensive facilities which should be itemized in the budget.

There is no precise way of translating the cost of all this executive and secretarial time and of the overheads and other facilities into a cash sum, but £20,000 or more would not be an unreasonable estimate. Smaller meetings are, of course, less expensive to arrange, but the reduction in cost is not *pro rata* and the administrative costs of arranging a meeting for 50 people may not be much less than those involved in arranging a meeting for 200.

The *real* cost of a company conference can, however, be much greater. A national distributor of consumer goods regularly brought its salesmen to London for a two-day convention. No one had ever questioned this corporate tradition. Then a new managing director asked a firm of consultants to draw up a realistic balance sheet. The consultants counted up the direct and indirect costs and calculated the business lost as a result of the entire sales force being out of action for up to 72 hours. The result was a seven figure sum and there was no indication that sales performance improved after the event. Their report was never seen outside the managing director's office, but the company never again held that kind of national jamboree.

Any organization which artificially reduces the apparent cost of its conferences by meeting the staff and overhead costs from a central budget as opposed to apportioning them to the conference budget should at least be aware of the cost of the policy to the organization.

2. *Conference organizers' fees and expenses*   When a professional conference organizer is engaged, his, or more usually her, fees and expenses replace most of the administrative costs considered above. Indeed, it is usually possible to demonstrate that it is cheaper to sub-contract the task of arranging a conference to a professional organizer than to handle the work internally on a 'do-it-yourself' basis. This is because the professional, being experienced in the field and equipped with the administrative support the task requires, is able to do the work more efficiently than the manager who, in trying to do his own job in addition to the (to him) unfamiliar task of arranging a conference, does neither as well as he would wish. Relieved of the task of dealing with the company conference, executives are able to carry on with their normal work before the event and, because they are not involved in the administrative problems, are left free to participate in and enjoy the actual event. The benefits of using a professional are not only financial! That said, there are pitfalls to avoid in choosing which professional to employ: this subject is discussed in depth in Chapter 15.

3. *Contingencies*   No matter how accurate the budget and how good the cost control, there will be unexpected expenditure. Visuals are needed at short notice, prices increase, changes are made to programmes, documentation, speaker lists and the like. It is prudent to allow 10% of the total budget for the unexpected.

Variable costs

The principal variable costs for each delegate include:

- Meals, coffee, tea and refreshments. Some venues charge an inclusive fee per delegate to include an element of room hire charges. This increases the variable cost per delegate but reduces the room hire element or fixed costs. It is worth remembering that, if you book 24-hour rates, hotels should not charge for room hire for a private evening function.
- Accommodation (if not paid for separately by delegates).
- Any entertainment or functions.
- Conference kit (badges, folders and so on – see Chapter 11).
- Document costs (post, secretarial cost of registration, invoicing and so on).

Hotel rates and charges are discussed in detail in Chapter 12 (Dealing with Hotels).

Total cost

The total cost of the event can be expressed graphically by adding the fixed and variable costs (see Figure 4.3, page 123). The final budget depends on the number of delegates who attend the actual event. The organizer of the in-house conference will know, to within a few delegates, how many people will be attending. His total budget can therefore be accurately predicted and he can bid for funds accordingly, his only problem being reducing costs if forecast expenditure exceeds the budgeted figure. The organizer of the public event is less fortunate. He has to work out how many delegates he can expect and what to charge before he can decide whether the venture is financially feasible.

However, the following two charts show the 'daily rate' spend of both associations and corporate bodies in 1999.

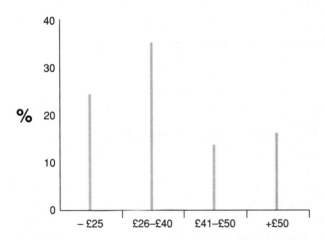

Figure 4.1   *Average budgeted daily rate – association events*

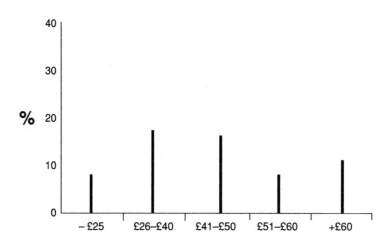

Figure 4.2 *Average budgeted daily rate – corporate events*

WHAT INCOME WILL THERE BE?

The principal sources of income are:

1. Delegates' fees – see below.
2. Grants, sponsorships and trade contributions. These may represent savings on either fixed or variable costs.
3. Advertising – revenue from advertising in the conference programme.
4. Sales of conference papers.
5. Exhibition revenue.

Pricing policies for delegates' fees

The price to be charged for an event should be considered in two ways, by calculation and from the delegates' standpoint:

1. *Calculation* The following formula can be used to calculate the minimum possible delegate registration fee:

$$\text{Delegate registration fee} = \frac{\text{Net fixed costs}}{\text{Number of delegates}} + \text{Variable cost per delegate}$$

The *net fixed costs* are the fixed costs less any contribution from advertising, exhibition income, sponsorship and so on.

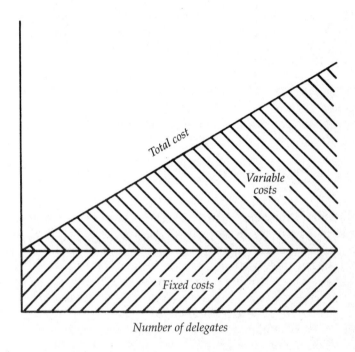

Number of delegates

Figure 4.3 *Total cost*

The problem is to decide how many delegates might attend. Sometimes there is accumulated experience which helps in forecasting this figure. The numbers attending regular association events are often constant and the response to certain public seminars and programmes is often consistent. Where no prior experience is available an estimate must be made to establish the *break even figure* for the event. The break even figure is the number of delegates needed to cover the fixed costs. Above this figure the event makes a profit and below it a loss is incurred.

Notes:

a. Allowance must be made for any discount schemes for encouraging early registration.
b. Income from social programmes is often treated as a separate profit centre and is not included in the conference budget.
c. Profit usually increases sharply with numbers, especially if a low break even point is set or the registration fee is intentionally set at a high level.

It is normal to reduce the estimated number of delegates by one third when deciding the break even figure. This gives a margin of safety in case of an unexpected shortfall and compensates for natural over-optimism when estimating anticipated attendance.

The break even number of delegates (that is, two thirds of the anticipated attendance) should be used as the 'number of delegates' variable in the above formula.

The profit for any number of delegates above the break even point can be calculated by using the formula:

$$\text{Contribution per delegate above break even} = \text{(Registration fee)} - \text{(Variable cost per delegate)}$$

2. *The Market Orientated Approach*   The above calculations produce a delegate fee which, while theoretically sound, may bear little or no relation to the commercial value of the event. If, in planning the event, we are extravagant, the calculated cost may turn out to be too high. In this case we have to re-examine the budget to see what savings can be made to bring the delegate cost down to a figure which the market will bear, or we can look for other sources of income.

In reality, the calculated figure is usually well below what the market will bear. This is because:

♦ The benefit to the delegate who attends the event has commercial or market value which is not related to the calculated figure.
♦ There is a considerable risk involved in staging a public event. The sheer size of the investment involved in setting up and promoting the event is important, since with limited funds there is a degree of *opportunity cost* surrounding the investment. Would an alternative investment offer a greater return? Because of this risk it is usual to set a low break even figure so that, in the event of success, a good return is made on the investment.

It is therefore advisable to adopt a market orientated approach when pricing an event. This is discussed further in Chapter 9.

Expenditure

	£
1. Hire of conference centre, including:	35,000
a. Simple AV eqpt and operators	
b. Services (telephone, cloaks, etc)	
c. Delegates' lunch, tea and coffee	
2. Printing, artwork and design:	
a. Exhibition brochure	1,500
b. Event brochure	19,500
c. Preprints of papers	12,000
d. Final programme, delegate lists and exhibition catalogue	4,000
3. Postage (exhibition brochure and some event brochures)	4,000
4. Provision, erection, dismantling shell stands, spotlights, electrical connection, hire of furniture, fire extinguishers, etc	10,000
5. Cleaning contract (exhibition area)	1,000
6. Stage presentation	2,000
7. Administration costs	17,240
8. Insurance	3,000
9. Interest and misc expenditure	5,000
10. Contingencies (10%)	11,420
Total expenditure	£125,660

Income

	£
500 delegates @ £170	85,000
50 exhibition units (at average price of £750 each	37,500
Advertisements in exhibition catalogue	3,000
Total income	125,500
Expenditure	125,660
Nominal loss at break even point	160

Notes:

1. VAT is not included in these figures
2. Many venues charge day/24 hour delegate rates which include room hire etc: in this example day delegate rate is £35.00 (500 × 2 days @ £35 = £35,000)
3. Profits increase dramatically at higher attendances:

Number	Profit £
600	6,400
700	12,800
1,000	32,000

Figure 4.4 *Example of draft budget for a conference and exhibition at break even point (500 full-time delegates)*

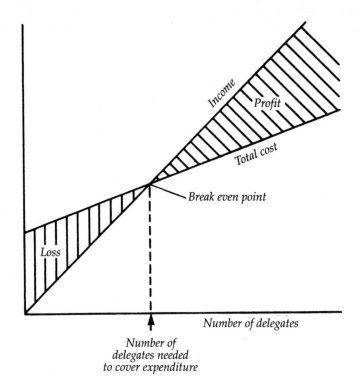

Figure 4.5   *Break even point*

EXAMPLE BUDGET FORECAST

An example of a draft budget for an event is given on page 125. The figures given are based on an actual conference and exhibition and illustrate the sort of detail involved. A second example, for an in-company event for 50 delegates is given on page 127.

CASH FLOW

Much of the expenditure for a public event takes place before any income is available. Early outlay includes marketing costs, venue deposits, insurance premiums, interest charges on loans, and administrative charges. Delegate income will not be available until fairly late in the planning cycle, although it is sometimes possible to improve the cash

Sample budget: Two night residential meeting for 50 delegates, with gala dinner on second evening. Prices *excluding* VAT.

24-hour rate × two nights @ £150 × 50	£15,000
Video projector and monitor (2 days @ £125)	250
Four syndicate rooms (including one included in 24-hour package @ £150 per room	450
Soft drinks/mineral water with lunches @ £5 pp	500
½ bottle wine pp for two dinners @ £7 pp × 2	700
Upgrade cost of menu for gala dinner @ £5 pp	250
Pre-dinner drinks @ £5 pp	250
Liqueurs @ £4.50 pp	225
Flowers for dinner table	80
Signing etc	100
Fax/phone	150
Contingencies (10%)	1,796
	£19,751

Note: cost of speakers, administration, AV aids etc not included.

flow by offering discounts for early registration. We therefore need a cash flow forecast to estimate the expenditure and income during the planning and preparatory phase and the shortfall at various stages over the period.

The cash flow forecast for the six quarterly periods leading up to the event in our example budget is given on page 129. The figures in the 'total' line represent the total expenditure in the quarter covered, and the figures in the 'income' line are the quarterly income figures. In this example, delegate registration fees are shown to be received in quarters 3–6; the exhibition income is primarily scheduled in the final two quarters. The figures in the bottom line are the net cumulative totals of income and expenditure and represent the *deficit* at each stage of the run-up period. The greatest deficit (£40,040 in the second quarter) would have to be covered by a bank loan, overdraft or some other source. Note that VAT has been excluded from this figure: taking VAT into account may increase the negative cash flow in the early quarters.

Again, the figures for a smaller event are correspondingly lower, but the method of forecasting the cash flow is the same and there is invariably a shortfall until the income becomes available.

Covering the cash flow shortfall

High interest rates have been a regular feature of our economy for a number of years. Even if a bank loan or overdraft can be negotiated, the interest charges can be substantial. It is advisable to find other sources of cash to reduce your borrowing. Sources might be:

♦ grants from government, the EC or industry;
♦ low interest loans (available through the British Tourist Authority for some international conferences);
♦ central funds of the organization;
♦ surpluses from previous events;
♦ local authority sources.

Sponsorship

Sponsorship has, in the past, been a rapidly growing business and hence a readily tapped source of funds, provided – and this proviso is important – that the event is suitable for sponsorship. Sponsors are not entirely altruistic: they provide funds in return for exposure of a name, or a product, to either a wide audience or a group of potential buyers. That said, some association conferences, especially those in the medical field, can sometimes attract sponsorship, the money coming from drug and pharmaceutical companies. However, the laws governing exhibiting by drug and pharmaceutical companies have been tightened up in recent years. Sponsorship and exhibition costs can no longer be offset against tax, and the 'pot of gold' is no longer what it used to be.

Even quite small events may be able to find sponsors, especially those in the travel and computer sectors. Airlines and tourist boards some-times sponsor receptions or specific meals which may not alleviate pre-event cash flow problems but will make the cost of attending less expensive, thereby attracting more delegates.

Budgetary control

The forecast budget and the cash flow statement are not only tools for calculating delegate fees, overdraft requirements and anticipated profits. They are also invaluable for monitoring and controlling expenditure. Regular checks show where estimates are being exceeded and give an early warning of problems. The discipline of keeping within a fixed budget and cash flow helps the profitability of any enterprise.

Quarterly Periods	1	2	3	4	5	6
Expenditure (£000s)						
Venue charges	2.50					32.50
Print		21.00			12.00	4.00
Post		3.00			1.00	
Shell scheme				5.00		5.00
Cleaning contract					1.00	
Stage presentation					2.00	
Administration costs	2.87	2.87	2.87	2.87	2.87	2.89
Insurance	3.00					
Interest and misc		1.00	1.00	1.00	1.00	1.00
Contingencies (10% overall)	1.90	1.90	1.90	1.90	1.90	1.92
Total	10.27	29.77	5.77	10.77	21.77	47.31
Income			25.50	25.00	38.00	37.00
Cash flow (Cumulative)	(10.27)	(40.04)	(20.31)	(6.08)	10.15	(0.16)

Note: VAT excluded from figures; although this increases negative cash flow in early months, VAT refunds in early quarters, interest earned from delegates fees paid in advance and careful scheduling of payments to creditors means that the cash flow effect of VAT is neutral.

Figure 4.6 *Outline cash flow at break even point*

Inflation

Europe is currently blessed with low inflation and correspondingly low interest rates. It was not always thus, nor may the present situation last. For example, who, in 1979, when the inflation rate in Britain had fallen from 20+ to around 8 per cent, could have anticipated that, within 12 months, it would again have risen to more than 20 per cent only to fall again to around 3 per cent a few years later? Given these uncertainties, how can we draw up a budget for an event which may be two years ahead?

In drawing up the forecast budget we can only work on the basis of what we *know* – that is, on today's prices. Adjustments for inflation can only be made later. In this context, it is advisable to agree future prices with as many suppliers as possible and to leave the final decision on the delegate fee until as late as possible. Clearly, an estimate of future inflation has to be made at some point. Most people err on the pessimistic side and, if anything, allow for greater rates than subsequently occur. If all businesses do this, it is no wonder that inflation continues to be a problem!

Value Added Tax (VAT)

The total cash flow for some small events may not exceed the annual limit above which VAT registration is required. The cash flow for most will be far above this figure and VAT registration is obligatory. Voluntary registration is permitted in the former case and the Customs and Excise Authorities will always advise on when registration is required.

If you are not required to register for VAT, it pays you to scrutinize incoming invoices with care. For example, printing is VAT zero rated in most instances and VAT should not be charged on this item by sub-contractors such as professional conference organizers (nor on postages paid in advance).

For VAT registered conferences VAT is neither difficult to administer nor is it particularly demanding in terms of time and resources. VAT must be charged at current rates on all income and must be paid on all but exempted purchases. The balance is, of course, remitted to HM Customs and Excise but, since returns (and hence payments) are made quarterly, VAT held pending payment can mitigate the cash flow problem.

When quoting delegate fees it is normal practice to show the net fee and the VAT as separate figures and as a total. Many delegates to public events are funded by their companies in which case the VAT their companies pay is recoverable. The net fee therefore represents the true cost to the VAT registered business purchaser and there is no merit in quoting only the inclusive figure on publicity material directed at business users since it makes the event seem more expensive than it actually is. Conversely, if potential delegates will be paying out of their own pockets and cannot claim back the VAT, then the gross figure should be clearly stated so that delegates can immediately be aware of the full cost. As in a restaurant, nothing is more annoying than finding out that the quoted price is well below the actual final bill because VAT and various extras were excluded.

There are some pitfalls in accounting and charging for VAT which are causing concern in industry:

◆ 'Harmonization' of various fiscal rules and regulations within the EC means that the rules on VAT and taxation are the subject of seemingly endless discussion and change.
◆ Although not aimed at the conference industry, the Tour Operators' Margin Scheme (TOMS), introduced in 1988, precludes the reclamation of VAT on tours and related activities. This affects conferences with a high entertainment content (banquets, tours and so on). The best advice is to seek professional help from an accountant who knows the rules if TOMS applies to your event.
◆ If you are holding events overseas you can reclaim cross-frontier VAT. VAT rates vary from country to country (standard rates in Europe vary between 12% and 25%), and so does expenditure upon which VAT is refundable. It usually pays to seek the advice of a VAT specialist when reclaiming input VAT from overseas.

If you are in any doubt about your interpretation of these changes or, indeed over any UK VAT matter, your VAT office should be able to advise you. It is better to consult them at the planning stage than to be faced with an unexpected liability after the event. Alternatively, it may be worth seeking the advice of a professional conference organizer who is used to dealing with these matters.

Insurance

One of the two principal speakers at a technical seminar died about a month before the event. A few days before the seminar, the second speaker became ill and could not appear. Because these speakers were both specialists in a technical subject, replacements could not be found and the event had to be cancelled. These disasters took place after an expensive publicity campaign and venue cancellation charges were also liable. Fortunately, the organizers had taken out insurance to protect themselves against eventualities of this kind and they were able to claim on their policy and avoid any loss.

The organizers of this event were among the more prudent. It is a fact that only about 1 in 10 of all conferences and meetings are insured to protect the organizers against the risks associated with such events. There are several reasons for this: organizers just do not think of it; if they do, they believe their existing policies provide the necessary cover; many people are unaware of the risks to which they are exposed.

The risks can be considerable. The loss of speakers mentioned earlier is but one. Happenings which have nothing to do with the event can be equally disastrous. Strikes at venues or in transport systems are obvious examples, but even wars and *coups d'etat* have been known to disrupt conferences. The Gulf War halted travel from the United States in particular literally overnight resulting in a large number of cancellations of whole events as well as individual registrations to particular events. National disasters can have a profound effect: when Princess Grace of Monaco was tragically killed in a car accident, Prince Rainier declared a period of mourning which included a ban on all public performances and music. A major product launch at a Monaco venue had to be cancelled at 24-hours' notice.

These cases clearly demonstrate the wisdom of insuring any event against risks such as abandonment due to non-appearance of speakers, strikes at the venue or in transport services, failure to vacate the venue at the end of a meeting (eg due to a set not being dismantled in time) and so on. Public and employee liability insurance is also always needed and should be taken out if the regular venue or company policies do not cover conferences and meetings.

Specialist insurers who offer custom-made policies for the conference industry provide comprehensive cover to protect the major risks to almost any event. Cover is available on a worldwide basis and premiums, which are very reasonable, depend on factors such as the estimated expenditure and income, the location of the venue, the dates of the event and the time of year.

The principal risks covered by the typical policy include:

◆ cancellation;
◆ failure to vacate;
◆ non-appearance of principal speakers or entertainers;
◆ loss or damage to property;
◆ damage to venue;
◆ legal and contractual liabilities;
◆ travel insurance for delegates.

Protection against cancellation due to events beyond your control is particularly valuable. The insurance covers cancellation due to transport strikes, bomb scares, power failure, non-availability of the venue, non-appearance of key speakers and so on. However, some risks cannot be covered. Cancellation due to failure to reach the break even number of delegates will cause losses which cannot be recovered by insuring against such an eventuality. The reason is obvious – one could make quite a good living arranging events, insuring the total anticipated cash flow and then cancelling due to 'poor response' to (non-existent?) marketing effort!

Nevertheless, taking out protection against more normal risks which can be covered is not only prudent, it is, in the case of some risks, essential.

It is important to take out insurance as early as possible and to be realistic in your estimate of the costs to be covered (the budgeting exercise described earlier in the chapter will assist in this respect). It is also important to cover all the risks – failure to vacate may seem a remote possibility but what if you are stuck in an overseas venue due to fog and another group is ready to move in? (You may think the airline is responsible for providing accommodation – and meeting the cost – in a case such as this. However, if you are using a charter aircraft, the company may not be responsible for delays due to weather.)

When things do go wrong, contact the broker immediately: many people only think of doing so after the event which can mean they underclaim or fail to realize what support was available at the time of the crisis.

International events

Care has to be taken to avoid currency losses when delegates are paying in foreign currencies. International money transfers can attract bank charges and any foreign currency price quoted must allow for these extra charges. Currency fluctuations sometimes make it difficult to predict what the rates of exchange will be at any one particular time. Such fluctuations can work out to be an advantage, but losses are equally likely. One company gets over this problem by quoting any event in 'company international units'. The rate of exchange is given at the time of invoicing. In this way, the company ensures that it always receives payment at an up-to-date exchange rate. Others price things in euros (but this does not entirely eliminate the risk of exchange losses). It is possible to give details of the bank account, branch and sorting code and specify that overseas payments must be made direct to the specified account in a specified currency. This tends to be more reliable than payment by cheque and also prevents losses due to currency fluctuations.

Payment by credit card   It is now the rule rather than the exception for conference organizers to accept payment by credit card. Being able to accept credit card payment offers a number of advantages:

- the money received will always be the correct amount;
- it will be in the required currency;
- it is possible to accept details by fax or over the phone;
- payments from abroad are simplified: once the card details have been provided no further chasing up is needed;
- if changes have to be made, for example refunds or additional payment (eg, for social events), these can be applied without recourse to a further request for another cash or cheque payment;
- credit card payments can be taken on site during the event.

There are snags. The commission rates charged by the credit card companies are quite high (typically 2%–5%). However, in the UK you can now legally make a surcharge to recover this additional cost. Not all conference organizers like to do this – they point out that being able to pay by credit card is an incentive to delegates and encourages them to book earlier and to sign up for more functions. Why then, the argument goes, penalize them with a surcharge?

Another potential snag – unless you have the on-line facility – is the time it takes to obtain authorization by telephone. Telephone authorization costs time and money, especially as the credit card companies will only accept two authorizations at a time (although they do make concessions to some professional conference organizers). Bearing in mind that typically 50 per cent of all payments are made by credit card, the authorization tasks can be very considerable for an event of over 1,000 delegates. If you are handling significant numbers of credit card transactions you should opt for an on-line authorization facility. This eliminates the above problem.

In short, credit card payment is an extremely useful means of collecting in the fees for larger events, especially those with a strong contingent from overseas.

ECONOMIZING ON YOUR BUDGET

We are all aware that, by shopping round and bargaining, most things we buy can be bought more cheaply than if we simply accept the first price we are quoted. Some people become almost fanatical over saving money on everything they buy. Significant savings can be made in family budgets with a little perseverance and effort. Much the same is true of conference budgets. The potential for making savings is considerable and the scale of some savings can be quite dramatic.

The venue

In Chapter 2 we discussed how the choice of venue reflects the style of the event. This is also reflected in the budget. The geographical location of the venue will also affect costs. The leading hotels in London are rated as some of the most expensive in the world but even in London good bargains can be found if you widen your field of choice. Even more dramatic savings can be made by going to the provinces. The inclusive daily full-board conference rate at a five star hotel in Bournemouth is less than the nightly room rate (exclusive of breakfast and service charges) of all the five star hotels in London. Similar variations in price can be found in the residential management centres and facilities at the more expensive are often no better than those in the cheaper centres.

Some companies have actually saved money by holding meetings overseas. We all know that package holidays in the Mediterranean sun can be cheaper than the overall cost of travelling to and staying at a seaside hotel in this country. As with holidays, so with conferences.

(Organizing conferences overseas is discussed in detail in Chapter 8.)

The timing of the event will also have a significant impact on the budget. Most hotels offer reduced rates during the off-season periods and, if the organization can be flexible over the timing of its event, considerable savings are possible.

It therefore pays to be as flexible as possible over dates and geographical location when choosing your venue. It also pays to *negotiate* prices. Indeed, in times of recession – when hotel occupancy rates decline – the conference organizer is in a very strong negotiating position. Even at reduced rates, it is much better for a hotel to have its rooms filled rather than empty. This helps cover overheads and, even if the rates given are so low as not to make a significant contribution, the delegates will spend on drink and services and generate at least some marginal income.

Some companies and commercial conference organizers are significant buyers of hotel accommodation in their own right and there is no reason why they should not negotiate special prices, especially if they are buying direct. 'If you don't ask, you don't get.'

Transport

The transport costs of a conference can account for up to 40 per cent of the total budget. Of course, if you hold your conference in a provincial hotel the savings in accommodation costs might be negated by the extra cost of travelling to the venue, further increasing the proportion of the travel cost. But this is not necessarily so. Group travel by luxury coach can be much cheaper than individual travel and some of the rail operating companies offer savings on regular rail fares for groups.

Large savings can be made when you are holding an event overseas by choosing the most economical air fares. The structure of air fares is constantly changing and the conference organizer is advised to contact a travel agent, preferably one specializing in group travel, for up-to-date advice.

Services

Careful budgeting and sensible purchasing policy can lead to equally significant savings in the many support services used for the event. Printing, AV, food, drink and so on can be unduly expensive if you are not careful. Printing, in particular, is a field where estimates vary greatly. Similarly, visuals prepared overnight by a London audio-visual company can cost ten times as much as those made well in advance of the event.

Food and wine costs can be reduced by judicious choice of menus, eating foods in season and offering the cheaper wines. It is said that the majority of people cannot tell red wine from white when they are blind-folded. If this is so, why waste money on the expensive wines at conference functions? The subject of food and drink costs is discussed in greater detail in Chapter 12.

That said, it is as well to realize that 'you get what you pay for'. The backstreet jobbing printer may be cheap but his quality of work will sometimes be inferior to that of an established printer. Similarly, it is often better to use the London AV houses in preference to the local company when top quality, quick response and an understanding of the user's needs and requirements is essential. As with so much else, it is a policy matter which, in turn, is dependent upon the financial resources of the organization.

Unplanned expenditure

However careful we are when we prepare our forecast budget, there will always be expenditure we had not thought of beforehand. Experience tells us that we need to include a figure of about 10 per cent of the budget total to cover such contingencies. However, if the original estimating has been poor, or if plans are changed, unplanned expenditure can rise dramatically. Senior executives who change plans, scripts, AV aids and timings at the last moment should be made aware of the *cost* of each change they make. Revising slides overnight and altering seating lists, programmes and other material at short notice can be hideously expensive. Control and consistency are essential.

Every change in the plans costs money!

Euphoria

The company chairman who, on the spur of the moment, orders cocktails all round or extra wine at dinner can wreck the budget at a stroke. How to prevent this sort of thing happening is another matter. One executive ensures that the extra expenditure is charged to the personal account of whoever makes the order. In this way the reason for the subsequent over-expenditure is understood even if it is not appreciated.

Novel sources of income

Any novel source of income to defray the cost of the event should be considered. Some companies give free programme advertisements in return for low interest or interest-free loans to reduce early borrowing. Others sell delegates lists to mailing houses. Mailing lists, such as the list of delegates attending a specialist international conference, can be commercially attractive to other organizations wishing to reach that particular specialized market segment. However, care has to be taken not to breach either the terms of the UK Data Protection Act or European laws on data protection when using electronically held data for such purposes.

IN CONCLUSION

Budgets and cash flows are everybody's responsibility. The organization which fails to control its finances is heading for trouble. Budgets should also be comprehensive.

The salary cost alone of every employee adds up to 1p per minute worked per £1,000 of his or her annual salary. Overheads mean that a person's real cost to the company is two or three times as much. Discussing the holiday, our health and the weather before getting down to business on a long distance telephone call at peak charge times can cost several pounds! Is it realistic to ignore these very real administrative costs in your budget?

Conferences and meetings should be treated in as business-like a manner as any other activity. Public events should be regarded as profit centres or as necessary and recognized calls on expenditure. Other events should be treated as expenditure which can be justified. Whether your meeting is in-company or public every penny spent eventually has to be recovered and is ultimately reflected in a balance sheet. Conferences and meetings are seldom seen in this light. They should be.

EXECUTIVE CHECKLIST

◆ Do you really know what your meetings cost?
◆ Do you draw up a budget and cash flow forecast for your conferences and meetings?
◆ Are all overhead costs and adminstrative expenses included in your budgets?
◆ Do you insure your events against unforeseen cancellation, public liability and other relevant risks?
◆ Do you allow for inflation? How?
◆ Do you allow 10% for unforeseen expenditure?
◆ Do you base the break even figure for the public event on two thirds of the anticipated number of delegates?
◆ Do you adopt a market orientated approach to pricing policies?
◆ Do you explore the possibility of raising income in addition to that from delegate fees, for example from sponsorship?
◆ How can you economize on your conference budgets?
◆ How can you cover negative cash flow without drawing on bank loans and other funds which attract heavy interest rates?

5

PRESENTATION AND PRODUCTION

'You are ruining my presentation.' The speaker had departed from his prepared script and was addressing these despairing remarks to the projection box after a succession of visuals had been miscued. Although he was not a professional speaker, he really had no excuse. The theatre had every modern audio-visual aid and he was speaking from a script. The presentation would not have collapsed if it had been properly planned and rehearsed.

Not that the professionals always get it right. One professional was heard to apologize because the slide he was showing could not be read from the back of the hall (and that during a presentation extolling the virtues of Audio-Visual (AV) as an aid to good presentation!) and on another occasion delegates booed a speaker off the stage after his AV show had failed not once but three times.

But examples of breathtaking excellence have also been witnessed. An artist with a passion for the seashore put together a short two-projector slide-tape mood sequence which was stunning, and some of the shows created for product launches, in particular, are exciting displays of artistic and technical brilliance.

Good presentation and production begins at the earliest stage of the planning procedure. If you want a professional, effective event, presentation and production must be considered even before the venue is chosen. The theme of choosing the venue has been dealt with in Chapters 1 and 2, but some of the specific specialist requirements which have to be taken into account for the more sophisticated audio-visual work are considered later in this chapter. But even if no visual aids are to be used, or only a simple overhead projector (OHP) is needed, it would be wrong to suppose that any room which is large enough and meets the basic requirements will do. A simple rule to follow is 'Look good, be good'. Few meetings or conference rooms are good enough as they stand. The bare, unadorned rooms will remain ordinary and unimpressive unless the organizers make an effort. Flowers, display boards, custom-made signs, staging and decent hired furniture can all be used to make a venue look better. If the hall does not have a stage of built-in screens, then, instead of putting up a simple screen on a stand, consider constructing a small stage and putting in a kit with a proper screen and lectern or even constructing a proper set. Enhancements such as these stop the room looking bare and create a professional image.

SMALL BUSINESS MEETINGS

Meetings are often held in company boardrooms and offices. A delegate arrived for one such meeting to be greeted by a blank stare from the receptionist. No, she didn't know about the meeting but she supposed it would be in the conference room – could he find his way there? The delegate eventually found the room in question. It smelt of stale cigarette smoke and the ashtrays were unemptied. After a few minutes some other people arrived. After a rather foolish silence they broke the ice and introduced themselves. Eventually an executive of the host company arrived (well after the appointed start-time) and they sat down to do business ... just as the coffee arrived. There was no agenda, and no blotters, writing paper or pencils were provided. Once the business of the day was under way the meeting went well, but none of the outsiders can have been very impressed by the host organization.

The appearance of company offices and meeting rooms and the way strangers are received are important. Conference rooms in many firms seem to be designed to give the wrong message: blue walls, poor lighting, uncomfortable seats and tables that rock are commonplace: some rooms look like working libraries, stacked high with books, papers and full ashtrays. Others are galleries of dull executive portraits, or lunch rooms with the smell – and even remnants – of unfinished meals in evidence. These things detract from the corporate image and leave outside visitors wondering about the company's management style, its goals and even its self-respect. First impressions *do* count and last. It is therefore worth taking a little trouble to make sure that even the smallest business meeting is properly stage-managed. The room should be clean and businesslike. Simple matters need attention: provide name plates around the table, a blotter, paper and pencil for each delegate, and water and glasses. There should be an agenda and, if it is a large meeting, a delegate list and seating plan. Visitors should be received and escorted to the meeting room where coffee or tea should be served before the meeting begins.

LARGER EVENTS

The image conjured up in many people's minds by the word 'conference' is often still the traditional one of an audience sitting in rows in a priceless example of our architectural heritage watching someone read a speech they cannot hear. All too often, delegates who have paid large sums of money are forced to listen as experts appointed by the organizers deliver lengthy, simplistic and questionable papers, verbatim copies of which are included in their conference folders. Traditionally, lecturers have primarily been concerned with educating an audience. They have relied heavily on the personality and delivery of the speaker – often with disastrous results.

The use of visual aids has historically been confined to the whiteboard – or even the chalkboard – and, possibly, the overhead projector, the latter with hastily prepared handwritten slides.

The approach *might* just be acceptable in a university or higher education college setting where highly motivated students eagerly pick up pearls of wisdom dropped by the expert, but it is certainly not acceptable when the audience is there to be motivated, persuaded or even just informed. Thus conferences concerned with persuasion – sales conferences and many in-house and inter-company meetings – need something more. Delegates to these *expect* slick presentations and audio-visual spectaculars, and programmes at this kind of conference – anything from the launch of a new model car to a dealer network or a sales force presentation of a new soap powder – are complex, lavish and expensive. Companies believe the expense is justified. One life insurance company took the main hall at the Wembley Conference Centre for a major production for its sales force. Morale was boosted to such an extent that the six-figure cost of the event was repaid by an immediate increase in revenue. A large printing company spent about £100,000 on a five-stop tour of Britain launching a new range of offset litho printing machines. Its return came in the form of over £1 million worth of orders before any other promotion was carried out.

Only the best information conferences are following suit and lecturing still predominates in all too many commercial conferences and seminars.

Some speakers often turn up with just a few notes and speak extempore; others read their paper out loud without giving any thought to the difference between the written and spoken word. When audio-visual aids are used, the result is often amateurish. However, delegates to these events also have higher expectations than hitherto. It is therefore safe to argue that any event has to be better presented than ever before. Even if the speaker does not plan to use AV aids, if your audience is greater than, say, 500, you should consider using a large screen video projection of the speaker's head so that everyone can see the facial expression of the speaker. The need for these and for well presented information is recognized by many of the more enlightened universities and professional bodies – a fact reflected in the modern lecture theatres and multi-media equipment to be found on their premises.

Good and bad AV

What are the properties which make audio-visual techniques so important?

Good audio-visual can lift an otherwise mundane session. It can reinforce a particular message, set moods, illustrate, explain, enlighten, persuade and entertain. Poor AV can do little good and much positive harm. How often have you been forced to watch out-of-date or irrelevant training films or videos projected out of focus, on a makeshift screen in a poorly darkened room, unable to see the screen because it is obscured by the heads of the people in front of you? How often have you been unable to read what is on the screen because the writing is too small or because there is too much to read? And how often have you seen slides shown the wrong way round, upside down, out of focus or dirty with dust and thumb marks? And how many overhead transparencies you see are readable, well produced and truly relevant?

We see good graphics and presentation on our television screens every day. We would not tolerate poor standards from the broadcasting companies. Why, then, accept poor standards elsewhere?

Cost is often given as one reason. Indeed, some AV programmes cost a great deal, but others are inexpensive. The seashore sequence mentioned earlier cost only a few pounds to put together from the artist's library of slides. Even if you do not have access to existing slides it is possible to produce good ones at very reasonable cost. Many other effective production methods and aids can be very simple and are well within the scope of even a small meeting. One company chairman used a video clip of part of a football match to illustrate the need for and importance of teamwork – the effect was dramatic, and the cost (only a few pounds) negligible. At the other end of the scale, the life insurance and printing company examples above show that it can be well worth investing in more expensive productions. The average presentation falls between these extremes but, whatever the complexity, all have one common characteristic: the use of audio-visual aids demands a great deal of planning and forethought by all concerned.

The rest of this chapter is concerned with the main factors which should be considered when planning the use of audio-visual techniques at public and in-house events. More sophisticated AV and new techniques of presentation and production are discussed in detail in the next chapter.

In both chapters, the word 'visual' is used quite liberally: it should be taken to apply to any projected image, be it from an OHP transparency, a slide or from a PC.

VENUES

When other than the simplest AV aids are to be used, the room or hall selected must satisfy a number of criteria and, as mentioned in Chapter 2, these criteria must be taken into account when selecting the venue. The real troubles begin here.

There are very few conference centres designed and equipped to handle all the modern audio-visual aids and even some of the better ones have severe limitations. One venue in London seats around 200 people in a well equipped theatre, but less than half that number can be accommodated for a buffet luncheon. Many venues which can accommodate such numbers lack even basic facilities for audio-visual aids. Hotels generally present difficulties. Projection equipment cannot be located in soundproof boxes for a start. Some hotels have inadequate blackout arrangements. At others the ceilings are too low and very few have raked floors and comfortable seating. Room acoustics are sometimes poor – especially when room dividers are used to separate two simultaneous conferences. If live television is to be employed, the aerial systems in many hotels will be found to be unsatisfactory, although many leading hotels have recently installed antennae capable of picking up transmissions from Intelsat (International Satellite organization communications satellites).

The situation is not unique to London. At least in that city there is a wide choice of hotels and other conference venues. However, in many European cities it is frequently easier to find a grand venue for over a thousand people than an acceptable one for a mere two to three hundred.

Room facilities

It may therefore be impossible to find the ideal room for the event you have in mind. The eventual choice may be a compromise and it might be necessary to modify the chosen room to improve its suitability. This means installing screens, projectors and loudspeakers and, possibly, improving blackout standards. In any case, the chosen room should:

1. *Be large enough* for the greatest number of viewers expected. Table 2.1 on page 34 gives the seating capacities of various sizes of room for different layouts. However, the need to fit the whole audience into a good viewing area will usually reduce the actual capacity of the room. Furthermore, some projection techniques take up a lot of space, also reducing seating capacities. See 'Good Viewing Area' opposite for further details.

2. *Be capable of being blacked out*   This presents severe problems at many venues. Translucent shades and venetian blinds seldom make a room dark enough, especially on sunny days. Good thick curtains or purpose-built blinds are needed and, if these are not available, temporary blackout arrangements must be made. If full blackout is impossible, special screens and a number of other techniques can be employed to permit daylight viewing. Professional advice should be sought on these techniques.

3. *Provide needed illumination*   A low level of illumination during projection is needed to permit note-taking and to maintain a social atmosphere. Ideally, dimming devices should be available to control light levels but, if they are not fitted, it should be possible to use a proportion of the normal fitted lights. In either case, light should not shine directly onto the screen.

4. *Provide adequate electrical control*   Room lights should preferably be controlled from a point near the projector or the speaker's lectern. Alternatively, arrangements must be made for someone to turn the lights off as soon as an image appears on the screen. The electrical supply for the projector must remain live when the room lights are turned off. The light controls in a so-called conference room of one of the United Kingdom's best known hotels are so placed that, to operate them, someone has to go down on their knees and reach inside a cupboard which is situated on the wall right by the entrance!

5. *Provide good ventilation*   The ventilation should be independent of the room darkening device. If smoking is permitted, a generous supply of

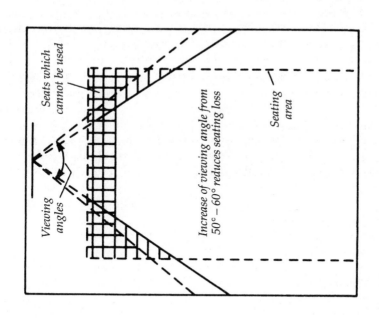

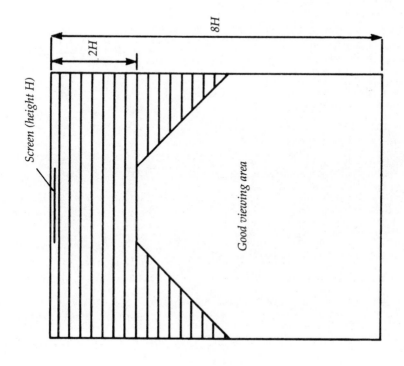

Figure 5.1 *Effect of viewing angles on room capacity*

fresh air will be needed. The air-conditioning outlets of one otherwise excellent London conference room are behind the fitted curtains. Blackout is complete when the curtains are drawn but the air-conditioning is rendered useless.

6. *Be acoustically good*   Most rooms are satisfactory. Check reverberation with a small handclap. A sharp, ringing echo indicates poor acoustics although an over-live room will always reverberate less when filled with people. Any loud noises or clearly audible speech coming from outside the room should be controlled or eliminated. The waiting staff at hotels have a habit of carrying on their own conferences off-stage during the formal proceedings! Low level background noise does little or no harm.

7. *Have a sufficiently high ceiling*   It should be possible to raise the screen so that all members of the audience can see. A stepped or raked (ie, sloping) floor is ideal. See 'Screen and Image Height' below.

Good viewing area

The screen is usually the weakest feature in a projection chain. The proportion of light reflected back from the screen is generally around 85 per cent and, although some specialist screens have a better performance close to the axis of the projector, in every case the brightness of the image falls away as the viewer moves from the axis of projection. The audience must also be neither too close to the screen not too far away from it. Provided slides and film conform to the commonly accepted standards described later in this chapter, projected material will be legible to everyone who is not closer than two times (2H) and not further away than eight times (8H) the height (H) of the projected image (see Figure 5.2). The good viewing area is therefore restricted in the manner indicated in Figure 5.1 on page 145.

It is possible to match the projector lens and brightness to the chosen size of screen, but the good viewing area is dictated by the shape of the room and the type and size of the screen chosen.

Viewing angles depend on the type of screen used:

1. *Matt screens*   These are the most commonly available screens and include most collapsible and retractable models. Viewers should be no more than 30° to the side of the projection axis.

2. *Beaded screens*   These give a very bright image for viewers seated within 25° of the projection beam but the image rapidly falls away outside this area.

Many conference rooms have ceilings that are too low. This makes them very claustrophobic. Some rooms are not high enough to accommodate a screen big enough for every delegate to see properly. Use the simple criteria on this page to make sure your room and screen heights are sufficient. Note: the projected image must fill the screen.

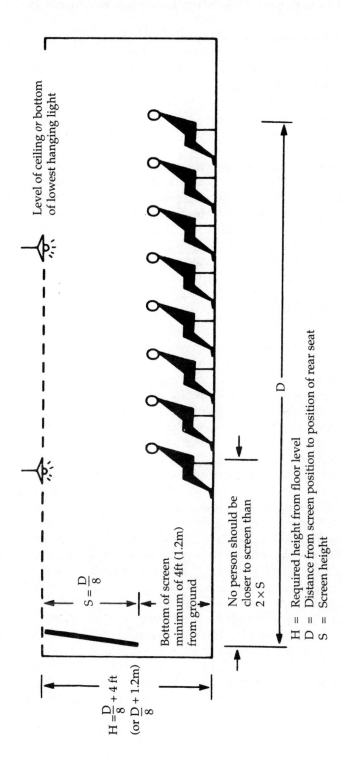

Level of ceiling *or* bottom of lowest hanging light

$S = \dfrac{D}{8}$

Bottom of screen minimum of 4ft (1.2m) from ground

$H = \dfrac{D}{8} + 4$ ft

(or $\dfrac{D}{8} + 1.2$m)

No person should be closer to screen than $2 \times S$

D

H = Required height from floor level
D = Distance from screen position to position of rear seat
S = Screen height

Figure 5.2 *How high should the room be?*

3. *Rear or back projection*   This is discussed below.

4. *High gain aluminium screens*   These have a sheet of specially grained aluminium foil laminated onto a special, non-collapsible frame. The screen reflects the projected light into a 60° arc and, because the image is very bright, daylight viewing is possible. Professional advice should be obtained on the use of these and other specialist types of screen.

The effect viewing angles have on room capacity is illustrated in Figure 5.1, and the table on page 149 gives the approximate theatre seating capacities for different room sizes where allowance is made for the loss of seats outside the good viewing area. The seating capacity can be calculated accurately by making a template to scale and placing this over a seating plan of the hall. This will give a direct indication of the seats which fall outside the good viewing area.

Rear projection

Rear (or 'back') projection is often used at major events, especially if a set is to be constructed. Special translucent screens are used in back projection. Alternatively, you can go to the expense of installing special screens with lined (ie 'pinstriped') surfaces that baffle any light falling upon them. These screens have a narrow viewing angle. Rear projection has its own advantages and disadvantages.

A person or object in front (that is, on the viewer's side) of a rear projected image does not interfere with the projection beam. This makes rear projection useful where close examination of the screen is necessary or where equipment or people are to appear on stage in front of the screen. Rear projection also enables the projectors to be hidden from view, a particularly useful feature if the room does not have a projection box.

The technique can also have disadvantages. With conventional projection, the space over the heads of viewers is usually used for the projection beam. With rear projection, the projection beam is wholly or partially on the opposite side of the screen. Consequently, space for the beam must be provided behind the screen. To reduce the space needed for rear projection, short focal length lenses are common used. Alternatively, mirrors can be used to 'fold' the projection beam. Either method will reduce image brightness and quality and up to one-third of the floor space can be taken by the projectors and associated equipment when rear projection is used.

Table 5.1   *Seating guide: Theatre-style seating for different room sizes*

Room Ratio 1:1			Room Ratio 4:3			Room Ratio 3:2			Room Ratio 2:1			Room Ratio 3:1		
Room Size– ft	Viewing Angle*		Room Size– ft	Viewing Angle*		Room Size– ft	Viewing Angle*		Room Size– ft	Viewing Angle*		Room Size– ft	Viewing Angle*	
	50°	60°		50°	60°		50°	60°		50°	60°		50°	60°
L x W	Seating Capacity		L x W	Seating Capacity		L x W	Seating Capacity		L x W	Seating Capacity		L x W	Seating Capacity	
16x16	10	11	16x12	8	8	16x11	6	6	16x8	–	–	16x5	–	–
20x20	18	21	20x15	15	16	20x13	13	13	20x10	7	7	20x7	–	–
24x24	28	33	24x18	24	26	24x16	22	23	24x12	14	14	24x8	5	5
28x28	41	48	28x21	36	39	28x19	33	34	28x14	22	23	28x9	9	9
32x32	56	66	32x24	50	55	32x21	46	48	32x16	33	33	32x11	16	16
36x36	73	87	36x27	66	73	36x24	61	65	36x18	45	46	36x12	23	23
40x40	93	111	40x30	85	93	40x27	78	84	40x20	59	60	40x13	32	32
44x44	115	137	44x33	106	116	44x29	98	105	44x22	74	77	44x15	42	42
48x48	139	167	48x36	129	141	48x32	119	128	48x24	92	95	48x16	52	53
52x52	166	199	52x39	154	169	52x35	143	154	52x26	111	115	52x17	66	66
56x56	195	234	56x42	181	200	56x37	169	182	56x28	132	137	56x19	80	80
60x60	226	272	60x45	211	233	60x40	197	212	60x30	155	161	60x20	96	96
64x64	259	313	64x48	243	269	64x43	227	245	64x32	180	187	64x21	112	112
68x68	295	356	68x51	277	307	68x45	259	280	68x34	206	214	68x23	131	131
72x72	334	402	72x54	313	347	72x48	293	318	72x36	234	244	72x24	150	150
76x76	374	452	76x57	352	390	76x51	330	357	76x38	264	275	76x25	171	171
80x80	417	504	80x60	393	436	80x53	368	399	80x40	296	309	80x27	193	193
84x84	462	558	84x63	436	484	84x56	409	444	84x42	330	344	84x28	216	216

(For conference-style seating, use one-half the seating capacity shown)

Screen and image height

For visual effect, it is sometimes desirable to project an image somewhat larger than the legibility standards specify, but the dimensions of 8H and 2H given above are the absolute minimum. The screen and image height should therefore be one-eighth of the distance from the back row of seats to the screen position. The bottom edge of the screen should be at least four feet (1.2 metres) above the floor to avoid the screen image being obstructed by the audience. Hanging lights must be above the top edge of the screen to prevent the projection beam or the reflected screen image being obstructed.

Many venues which do not have built-in screens and projection equipment lack the necessary ceiling height. When vetting a venue at the selection stage, the required ceiling height can be roughly calculated by using the following formula:

Required height from ground to ceiling or up to bottom of suspended lights $= \dfrac{\text{(Distance from screen to position of rear seat)}}{8}$ + 4ft or 1.2m (depending on whether you are working in metric or imperial measurements)

(See Figure 5.2, page 147)

Multimedia presentations

Multimedia presentations are becoming increasingly common. A two-image format can be used to good effect in a presentation to compare two different products, graphs and so on or to show a close-up next to a general view. Multimedia presentations often show images side by side. The positioning of screens and projectors requires even greater care for multi-image shows and expert advice is normally needed to ensure that the best possible viewing area is achieved.

Projector location

All too few venues have built-in projection rooms but organizers should avoid having free-standing projectors in the meeting room. They are noisy and cast stray light, and there is always a danger that a delegate will knock the projector stand out of line or trip over a mains cable. Back projection should be considered if there is no projection booth or a special projector cover can be hired to mask at least some of the noise and light.

The projector lens should be on a line extended at right angles vertically and horizontally from the centre of the screen surface. Projectors must be positioned high enough so that their beams clear obstructions such as the heads of viewers and also overhead projectors placed at the front of the hall. Excessive upward or downward projection angles cause a wedge or 'keystone' image unless the screen is tilted. A keystone image can only be avoided when an overhead projector is used at the front of the room if the screen is tilted forward, but few venues and not all makes of portable screen have the necessary forward tilt facility (and even when they do, the facility is seldom actually used!).

The distance from projector to screen is determined by the focal length of the projector lens and the image size needed.

Zoom lenses are available for many modern projectors and these ease the problem of matching the variables to obtain an image which fills the screen. If zoom lenses are not available it may be necessary to hire or purchase alternative projectors or lenses. Most photographic dealers can advise on the focal lengths needed for particular situations, or professional advice can be sought from a production company.

The image brightness must also be checked and the necessary projector lens/lamp combination selected to ensure a bright enough image. This is particularly important when data projectors are being used. Larger LCD and CRT projectors are usually suspended from the roof in permanent installations. Professional advice may be needed on this matter.

Sound

This chapter is about *audio*-visual aids and yet most of it is concerned with *visuals*. Sound is often the poor relation – but you neglect it at your peril. Put it this way – no matter how good the visuals, if you cannot hear what is being said you are completely lost (have you ever tried watching TV with the sound turned down – it is impossible to work out what is being said unless you can lip-read or there are sub-titles).

The spoken word In all but the smallest meetings, some form of sound reinforcement is needed to amplify what is being said. The ability to hear the amplified voice depends upon:

1. the quality and suitability of the amplification system (microphones, amplifiers and speakers); and
2. the speaker's use of the microphone.

Taking the second point first, it is a fact that the great majority of occasional public speakers (by which we mean company executives and also training personnel – even lecturers) are not used to microphones. If you are using sound amplification, it is necessary to brief speakers on the techniques they should use and on the pitfalls and dangers – and you should rehearse them to boost their confidence, to check sound levels and to ensure they get it right.

The most common pitfalls are speaking too loudly and too quickly. If you have a good amplification system, it should not be necessary for the speaker to raise his voice – a firm but conversational level voice should suffice. It is necessary to speak a little more slowly – but not so slowly as to sound boring. Hence the need to rehearse.

The other most common pitfall is moving away from the microphone, for example, turning one's back on the audience (and the microphone) to point to something on the screen – and continuing to speak. The words are, of course, lost.

If your speaker does want to move about, use a halter or lapel microphone on a long lead – but do remind the speaker to take it off before he leaves the podium! Better still, use radio microphone systems. These are usually more expensive but do away with the need for leads and cables everywhere.

Music and video/film sound   Sound engineers seem to love really loud music – especially the music which accompanies slide and multi-media shows. Insist that sound is kept to reasonable levels.

Amplification systems   There are so many good systems available these days that there can be no excuse for inadequate sound, feedback (the whistle when the microphone and speakers interfere with each other) and all the other 'village fête' fiascos. It pays to hire in good equipment – hotel amplification systems, in particular, are rarely satisfactory.

Positioning loudspeakers   Loudspeakers should be placed near the screen and high enough to be seen by everyone. If speakers are placed on the floor the sound is muffled and only the people at the front will be able to hear properly.

Proper tone control adjustment can do much to increase sound intelligibility. Muffled or poor quality sound is usually caused by too much bass. Tone controls should be set near or at maximum treble. These settings do not give a very pleasing reproduction of music, but they do reduce reverberation and make speech more understandable.

Extra speakers may be needed if the room acoustics are very poor. These can be placed in a corner or put part-way down the room.

PLANNING AV AIDS

Audio-visual for conferences and meetings falls into two distinct categories:

◆ *Speaker support*, by which we mean relatively simple AV aids used on anything ranging from training programmes to visuals in support of formal presentations.
◆ *Production:* the more sophisticated show associated, in particular, with product launches. These use multimedia, live entertainers and all sorts of special effects – usually with spectacular results.

Speaker support

The production and actual use of AV aids need careful forethought and planning. If you are invited (or nominated!) to speak at a conference or meeting, you need to know how to plan, produce and use some good AV aids.

And if you are responsible for supporting someone who has to give a presentation, or are organizing a programme in which speakers will be using AV aids, you, too, need a working knowledge of the subject so that you can influence and police the quality of material which is used.

By and large, speaker support is primarily concerned with *visuals* as opposed to full AV (although, of course, this is not exclusively so). For simplicity, we use the term 'AV' to cover the whole spectrum of speaker support material.

AV aids should be used to complement and enhance the presentation. Most speakers will soon identify places where they need to use AV aids as they prepare their scripts. Some information can only be presented visually. A good example of this is used by a speaker who regularly gives talks on the subject of using AV. He begins by telling the audience about a jug he uses – describing its vivid colours and the birds and flowers and grasses with which it is decorated. At this stage, the audience is at best puzzled. Apart from wondering about the speaker's taste, no-one can have any idea what the jug looks like. Then he produces it – and immediately those close enough to see it know exactly what it looks like (they may still question his taste but at least they are doing so on an informed basis!).

However, if the audience is large, most will still not be able to see the jug and so are none the wiser. He therefore then shows a photographic slide of the jug – but, of course, has to black the room out (turning the lights off – pulling curtains across windows and so on) so that people can see the image. Now everyone is, quite literally, in the picture.

As a final demonstration, he uses a video clip with the jug rotating so that the whole pattern can be seen, and, by adding a caption of the make and pattern – and the volume/dimensions – the information transfer is complete.

The above example provides an excellent insight into how visual aids can help the process of communication. They also illustrate the need for preparation: having the visual aids made; having the correct projection equipment set up and ready for use; using a room which can be blacked out ... and so on.

In preparing his script, the speaker must decide what AV aids are needed and what they should be: photographic; text; video and so on.

The choice will be influenced by the type of presentation and the size of the audience as well as the information to be imparted by the AV material. There is a range of AV aids which can be used either alone or in combination:

- basic visual aids – flip chart and whiteboard;
- overhead transparencies (sometimes called vufoils);
- slides – photographs, text or diagrammatic;
- video, film and CCTV/business television;
- computer data and graphics projection;
- sound alone;
- multimedia.

Mixing these media together can help keep the audience on the edge of their seats and helps stimulate and maintain interest. However, it is best not to be too ambitious in speaker support: remember, you are planning AV aids, not a show!

Each type of aid has its characteristics and its particular strengths, weaknesses and pitfalls. These are discussed below.

Flip charts

One of the most widely used of the basic AV aids, the flipchart is to be seen in almost every training room – and certainly in every hotel meeting room (if only because hotels seldom provide whiteboards – see page 156).

Most people use the flip chart as a large notepad to capture or present ideas during discussion and informal presentations. Trainers, in particular, like to keep each completed sheet in view so that the walls soon become covered with sheets of notes. If you are using flip charts in this way, (1) ensure you purchase perforated pads so that sheets can easily be torn off and (2) make sure there is provision to fix the flip charts to the walls. Purpose built training rooms have either 'grab' rails or metal rails and magnetic 'buttons' for hanging flip charts. These rails are seldom available in hotel meeting rooms, in which case you will need an ample supply of Blu-Tack.

Pens   Make sure the pens you provide are suitable for flip charts: the type you need are water soluble. The other types of pen – dry and permanent markets – are not suitable for using on flip charts. Dry markers are designed to be used on whiteboards and, unlike water soluble pens (which make strong, bold lines and letters), dry markers soon run out when used on paper. Permanent markers have no place in the meeting room: they smell; they dry out quickly (especially if the cap is left off); worse – if used on whiteboards they will leave a 'permanent' mark which, whilst removable with special cleaners, leaves the surface damaged once removed.

Many people pre-prepare flip charts for their presentations. Nowadays, you can enlarge A4 note paper to flip chart size using special copiers such as the Fujix Poster Printer 100. The 'output' is on paper similar to fax paper, and you can buy different papers to give colour prints: black, blue, red and so on.

3M has solved the 'hanging' problem by producing a flip chart version of its Post-it Notes. The manufacturers claim you can fix the flip charts to any surface – and remove them – without risk of damage. The pads come with a carrying handle and universal flip chart stand holes (to cater for the different spacing between holes according to the brand of manufacture).

Most flip chart pads are available as either plain white paper or ruled in boxes in feint blue: the latter are particularly useful if you are making pre-prepared flip charts, or wish to draw graphs or bar charts.

The flip chart pad does have its drawbacks. It has a 'low tech' image and is not suitable for formal presentations.

Other points to remember if you are using flip charts:

◆ In hotels, check the pads provided to make sure there is no old copy left by previous users somewhere in the pad.
◆ Ensure venue staff are instructed *not* to remove used sheets during cleaning – especially those displayed on walls.

◆ If your flip charts contain confidential material, take them away with you for secure disposal. Also, check the pads you leave behind to make sure you have taken all your material with you.

Make sure you remove all papers from all your meeting rooms. Delegates sometimes leave their notes behind and speakers fail to take away their flip charts – and what a fund of information can be found on a flip chart stand!

Not long ago two large international computer companies were running consecutive meetings in a large hotel in the UK. The planners in the two companies had both done their homework and the venue was aware of the extreme sensitivity and competitive nature of the businesses. However, the first company left their company's product development plans behind on a flip chart and a delegate's briefing folder on a desk! True, the venue's management was at fault for not checking the room but it was a quick change around and when such important matters are at stake the message is: 'do not rely on anyone else – make sure you carry out security checks yourself'.

The whiteboard

This has all but replaced the dusty chalkboard in schools, colleges and training centres. It is rare to find whiteboards in hotel meeting rooms (mainly because these are multi-function rooms, and whiteboards – and flip chart rails (see above) – are not compatible with the decor required for receptions and formal dinners).

Ensure you provide dry-marker pens – and make sure there are no permanent markers in the room (see the explanation under 'pens' above).

The whiteboard has gone 'high tech' in that it is possible to buy boards which electronically capture what is written on them and reproduce this on an A4 sheet at a touch of a button – clearly very useful if a record is needed.

The whiteboard is mainly an educational and training AV aid, and is clearly only suitable for use in comparatively small meetings.

The overhead projector (OHP)

The ubiquitous OHP was originally designed to replace the school chalkboard. The theory was that, with the image on the projector in front of him, the teacher could refer to it – and even write on a blank acetate – without turning his back on the class, secure in the knowledge that what he could see in front of him was being projected on the screen behind him. Some OHPs have rolls of acetate so that, when the copy is no longer required or more screen space is needed, the acetate roll on the projector can be scrolled on.

In fact, it was the whiteboard which replaced the chalkboard, and the OHP became a popular presentation aid.

There are sound reasons for the popularity of the OHP. It is genuinely user friendly even for the most timid 'technophobe'. It can be used equally effectively for presenting to small and medium groups to people. And it throws an image bright enough to cope with high ambient levels (obviating the need for room black-out and facilitating note taking … and alertness!). Finally, overhead transparencies can be produced by a wide variety of means – even by hand – and some of these are particularly cheap, quick and easy.

How it works   OHP technology is intrinsically simple. Light is transmitted through large (commonly A4) transparencies and focused by a lens system to give a big, bright image on screen. Image size is controlled by the focal length of the lens assembly (this is fixed to an arm above the working surface and can be moved up and down for fine focusing), and the distance of the OHP from the screen.

There are two types of OHP technology – transmissive and reflective.

With transmissive OHPs the light source is sited in the base of the unit and its output is evenly distributed across the work surface by condenser lenses. Just below the work surface itself is a fresnel lens, a flat-cut convex lens for focusing the light towards the lens head.

Whilst the transmissive OHP is recognizable by its quite bulky, box-like base, the *reflective* type is very compact, having a very slim base. This makes it eminently suitable for portable presentations, being lightweight and foldable.

The light source is most often a tungsten-halogen or quartz bulb set. Lamps are commonly 24 volt 250 watt but high-power projectors use 36 volt 400 watt bulbs. There are also increasing numbers of projectors offered with powerful metal halide lamp systems.

If an LCD panel is to be used with an OHP, two points should be remembered. These can only be used with a transmissive OHP, as the panel itself sits on the working surface and light has to pass through it. They also require a 400 watt or metal halide lamp system to give their best.

OHP pitfalls   The OHP is not without its pitfalls. It has a 'low tech' image and it is not really suitable for formal presentations (except where it is used with an LCD panel which is, in reality, a different form of projection: see Chapter 6.) Further, the arm and lens, which stand above the working surface, can be obtrusive and spoil the sight lines for some delegates. Some OHPs have noisy cooling fans which keep operating even when the projector lamp is turned off.

A further distraction stems from the way OHPs tend to be used by presenters. Some like to turn the projector on and off as they change transparencies; others do not bother, and the whole change process is very visible. The former is the more 'professional' approach but can, paradoxically, be a distraction.

OHPs tend to be placed quite near to the screen so that the keystone effect mentioned on page 151 is particularly pronounced. It is essential to use screens with a tilt facility to avoid this effect when using an OHP.

Finally, some users do not use the OHP to best effect. Here are a few 'tricks of the trade':

◆ 'What you see is what you get' (WYSIWYG – pronounced in the business, 'wissy-wig'!): when the transparency is on the working surface what you see will be on the screen (provided the projector is properly set up and focused). *Therefore*, if it is upside-down or reading back to front when you look at what is on the working surface, it will be the same on the screen – why, therefore, do so many seemingly intelligent people always get it wrong and/or look at the screen when they put on their first transparency?

◆ The reveal technique (item 4 on page 162) is very easy to use with an OHP. The brightness of the image means that if you use an ordinary sheet of white paper to cover part of the transparency you can still read what is covered up (but it will not appear on the screen).

◆ If you want to point to something it is not necessary to turn to the screen – use a pen or pencil and point to the word/item on the transparency on the working surface. The shadow of the 'pointer' will be on screen.

Preparation of OHP transparencies   This is discussed later in the chapter.

The 35mm slide projector

The 35mm slide has, for many years, been the most common speaker support aid for formal presentations. Its greatest strength is its ability to provide images – very big images if necessary – of unbeatable quality.

Although projectors with straight slide magazines can be used for straightforward speaker support, the automatic projector with a rotary slide tray has become the standard for business presentations. This type of projector was invented by Kodak (as the Carousel) and has been widely imitated since. The standard tray holds 80 slides (although larger capacities are available).

Slide projectors can be used singly but it is more professional to use two in conjunction with what is called a 'dissolve unit'. This permits the operator to fade out one image and fade in the next at the same time – a better alternative to the 'on'–'off'–'on' change achieved using a single projector.

There are control systems designed for large numbers of projectors and simultaneous multimedia work, but these are the province of the production company rather than of speaker support.

Modern projectors have an autofocus facility. Although glass-mounted slides will remain in focus during projection, slides in glassless plastic and cardboard mounts can 'pop' because of the heat of the projector and so go out of focus. The 'AF' facility corrects this.

A wide choice of lenses, including zoom, is available for slide projection and the better quality products will keep the image sharp right into the corners.

What are the disadvantages of the 35mm slide?   The main problem of the 35mm slide is the effort needed to produce it. In the past, text slides had to be made from artwork which would be photographed using a rostrum camera. Each slide then had to be developed and mounted. It was a laborious and slow process, and late changes were difficult if not impossible (an overnight change could cost £50 or more for a single slide!). Because a key requirement for slide projection when using dissolve – especially in build-up sequences – is perfect registration, the set-up of multiple projector shows is also slow and laborious (even when only two projectors are being used). Computerized graphics and the use of Polaroid film helped overcome – at least partially – these difficulties.

Another disadvantage is that, in general, you need a darkened or nearly darkened room for slide projection.

Finally, unless you are using back projection, any movement – for example, the speaker moving about – in front of the screen causes a shadow on the image.

Is the slide obsolescent?   There are those that argue that with the advent of PC graphics and ever-improving data projection (see Chapter 6) the 35mm slide as a presentation aid is obsolescent. Whilst many users have indeed abandoned the 35mm slide, it still offers unrivalled image quality (surpassing even HDTV – High Definition television), especially for pictorial photographs. It is therefore premature to write off the slide as a speaker support aid, but its use will still continue to decline.

Video

Video has an established role to play in presentations. Moving images of products, locations and people talking convey a different kind of information to that provided by charts, word slides or even still pictures. It is good at communicating emotion, a sense of time or place and concerns about issues, rather than outlining a factual argument.

Historically, video has been difficult to use in the presentations environment. Making video is a very different process to the production of a stills presentation. And showing video required VCRs and monitors or more sophisticated projectors. It is therefore hardly surprising that all but the most sophisticated speakers decided they could do without.

However, new video production technology is making it easier to originate material that can be easily incorporated into a presentation. This is discussed in the next chapter.

Of course, you do not have to create your own material. Film and video libraries are a particularly rich source, and archive documentary, newsreel and entertainment films should not be neglected (remember the soccer video clip mentioned earlier in the chapter). A particular company or commercial video may contain a useful sequence, but speakers should not fall into the trap of using all of an existing piece of material. It will certainly have been produced with different objectives and different audiences in mind. A good technician can isolate the shortest sequences and these, in particular, can do much to lift a presentation from an amateurish, mundane level to a polished level of professionalism. Short clips from videos are particularly easy to isolate and, incidentally, to show (thanks to remote controls).

Copyright   Whenever existing material is used, it is essential to obtain permission to use copyright material. Failure to do so can, at best, cause undesirable publicity and, at worst, can lead to prosecution and awards of damages to the owner of the copyright. An Irish bank settled out of court for an undisclosed sum of over £10,000 when threatened with legal action when a video company discovered the bank had illegally copied and used training videos which it had hired from the company.

Permission to use copyright material is normally not difficult to obtain. Sometimes, as in the case of the training video, you will have to pay a royalty, hire or buy a copy of the material. In other cases, as for example, with Table 5.1 on page 149, permission will be given provided the source is acknowledged.

Equal care must be taken when using audio material, although in many cases, if the venue is registered with the Performing Rights Society, there should be no undue problem over using prerecorded tapes and records.

Computer graphics, multimedia and so on

As already mentioned, multimedia is in the province of the production company rather than that of speaker support. Computer graphics, on the other hand, is very relevant to speaker support as well as to the production company. Both of these are discussed in the next chapter.

Preparing AV aids

The actual AV aids you or your speakers use will depend upon the purpose. They may be:

◆ a picture or sequence of pictures;
◆ words on the screen;
◆ symbols;
◆ charts or diagrams;
◆ action sequences.

Whatever the choice, the visual must be *legible*.

Legibility

For many years, Kodak ran a campaign to improve the quality of lecture slides. The company produced a range of information sheets on the subject of preparing slides for presentations and the advice these contain applies equally to computer generated material. To quote from one Kodak information sheet, 'Let's stamp out awful lecture slides':

> The primary consideration is legibility – remember the people sitting at the back. Most errors in slide-making stem from the mistaken idea that legibility in one form means legibility in another. Our reading experience is acquired mainly from printed pages read at a distance of about 12 to 18 inches. In a lecture theatre the slide may be projected onto a six-foot wide screen and the rear seats may be 70 feet away. Reading a slide projected on the screen at that distance is like reading the first page of this chapter at a distance of 12 feet – the titles are distinguishable but the text is lost.
>   Always plan for maximum legibility. When in doubt, go for boldness and clarity even if it means less information on the slides – you can always make a second containing the extra information required.

Legibility can be achieved by following these tips:

1. *Keep copy to a minimum*   It is only necessary to put key words onto the screen. All too often speakers display short essays, especially if they are using overhead transparencies. What is the point? Should the speaker stand silent while the audience reads the visual (assuming those at the back *can* actually read it)? Or should he read it aloud, insulting and annoying the audience as he does so? Or should he continue with his script – perhaps saying something entirely different? It he does so, what should the audience do – ignore him and read the visual, or listen and ignore what is on the screen? Visuals should be used to supplement the talk, not to repeat visually what is to be said aloud.

2. *Keep copy simple*   When a lot of information has to be shown – for example, a table or unavoidably lengthy passage, the copy should be simplified as much as possible and split into several slides. No single visual should contain more than 15 to 20 words or 25 to 30 figures. Consider alternative ways of presenting the information – for example a picture or graphically (see below). Titles should be used to supplement, not duplicate data.

3. *Only use 'landscape' format*   When using slides, the 'landscape' (ie horizontal) picture format can be projected to fill the standard screen. 'Portrait' (ie vertical) pictures overlap the top and bottom of the screen and look unprofessional. Although the focal length of the projector can be adjusted to accommodate both, you are left with blank areas on the screen. The best advice is to use only the landscape format.

4. *Disclose information progressively*   This technique is particularly suitable for listed information. Instead of displaying the whole list at once it is better to add one line at a time – that is, one line to each slide in a series – until the list is complete. This has several advantages. It is easier for the audience to assimilate one thought at a time as it is added to the preceding idea. The system also prevents the audience from reading ahead of the speaker and the apparent pace of the presentation is stepped up since the same visual is not kept on the screen for very long. Fortunately, PC programs such as PowerPoint and Freelance Graphics have made it very easy to produce this sort of material: see also Chapter 6.

5. *Produce special artwork*   Illustrations from books or engineering and technical drawings and diagrams are seldom suitable for showing on the screen. This is because, in the original form, they are drawn carefully and in detail. Such detail is unlikely to be legible when projected on to the screen.

Simplified versions should be prepared with bold lettering and the use of colour and diagrammatic blocks in place of complicated detail. Computer graphics have revolutionized the production of visuals: see Chapter 6.

6. *Use pictures*   The old cliché that a picture is worth a thousands words is very true. Pictures should only show what is essential. Unless background is important, the camera should be taken in as close as possible to show the important details clearly. Masking and enlargement techniques can be used to cut out unwanted detail.

It is a simple matter to make slides of pictures in books or to take stills from film and TV pictures. As with film, such illustrations can add much to a presentation at a very reasonable cost (but beware of copyright restrictions). For example, a picture of New York when an overseas office in that city is mentioned, or of an aircraft when a particular trip is highlighted, can add interest to the presentation. Old photographs can be used to raise a quick laugh and lighten a serious passage. Many speakers use slides of varying depths of pornography with the same intention, but this technique is highly questionable. A picture of a lovely nude may stimulate the audience – but, if it is totally unrelated to the matter in hand it will in fact hinder rather than help the flow of information. What is more, many people are offended by the use (some would say 'exploitation') of the female form in this manner.

7. *Use graphs and diagrams* in preference to tables. Data can usually be absorbed more quickly in simple graphical, bar chart or 'apple pie' form. Figures should be rounded and captions kept to a minimum. For graphs, make curves reasonably prominent. Axes and grid lines should be clearly visible but relatively inconspicuous.

8. *Use bold lettering*   As we have seen earlier, there is always a temptation to put too much copy on each visual. Using bold lettering helps overcome this temptation. The advent of the PC and programs such as PowerPoint and Freelance Graphics has made it much easier to follow the basic rules if only because of the cost of producing a large number of visuals (in order to keep copy to a minimum on each one) is negligible. Beware of using desktop publishing (DTP) for artwork, especially for OHP transparencies. When projected the resolution may not be as good as you want and the letters may look ragged.

9. *Simplify maps*   It is often necessary to show a map. A simple outline map should be used rather than a picture taken from an atlas. Outline maps can be purchased from suppliers of educational stationery and, when produced in reversed text (see point 10 below), can look very effective.

10. *Use reversed text techniques*   The appearance of slides and OHP transparencies containing words and line drawings (such as maps and simple organizational diagrams) is considerably enhanced if the text is in white on a dense black background. In this technique, known as 'reverse text', the slide is actually the negative of a high contrast film used to photograph black artwork and lettering on a normal white background. The technique has a number of advantages:

- Legibility is improved.
- Dust and dirt marks are less discernible.
- Large, bright, white areas on the screen are eliminated.
- The copy can be seen in a partially lit room.

The ability to show the slides in a partially lit room is particularly useful. Delegates can take notes and the lights do not have to be repeatedly dimmed and raised between slides at times when the screen is left blank.

11. *Vary the pace*   Visuals should only be left on the screen while they are actually needed. Blanks or the company/organizational logo can be used in between visuals, and no visual should be left on the screen after the subject has been discussed.

12. *Use duplicate images* if it is necessary to refer to the same visual more than once in the presentation.

13. *Plan ahead*   AV materials take time to prepare. Work out what is wanted well beforehand and avoid late changes. This will make it easier to produce good material and will avoid the very high price premiums associated with rushed jobs.

14. *Use colour sparingly*   It is perhaps unfortunate that PC graphics enable us to use colour so freely: it is tempting to use lots of colour to 'liven up' our slides, but in reality too much colour can be a distraction. The best advice is to use colour sparingly as a means of highlighting or emphasizing certain points.

Artwork

Some tips on artwork have been given in the preceding paragraphs. The most common (and best) way of creating slides is by using computer graphics. However, if you are forced to use conventional artwork, then you need access to someone who can produce good work. If your organization has a drawing office you are fortunate. If outside help is needed, freelance artists and designers are usually able to produce excellent artwork. However, for really professional work it is, of course, sensible to use a professional company which specializes in artwork and slide production.

Overhead projector transparencies (vufoils)

The pre-prepared OHP transparency presents its own challenges. Pre-prepared OHP slides are more appropriate for formal presentations; they are also used to a great extent in training. As much care should be put into preparing these as with the graphics for 35mm slides or computer data projection material. Unfortunately, the OHP slide area is roughly the same as an A4 sheet of paper and it is all too easy to copy typescript straight onto the transparency using the office photocopier. As a result the projected letters are far too small to be read and too much copy is fitted on to the slide.

Legibility depends on the size of the projected image of the letter and not the size of the image on the slide. Thus, typewritten copy is acceptable on a 35mm slide and not on an OHP transparency. To illustrate this point, a letter 1/8 inch (35mm) high projected on to a 48 inch (1.2 metre) high screen will be legible at a distance of 222 feet (68 metres) from the screen when projected from a standard 35mm slide but, when projected from an OHP, will only be legible from a maximum of 20 feet (6 metres).

The best guide to follow when preparing OHP slides is to keep the amount of copy down to the same level as that recommended for slides (see point 2 above), and to use desktop publishing software to achieve legible characters on the screen.

Slide production

Many organizations have computer sections which can produce computer graphic slides (provided they have the necessary hardware and software). Failing this, you may have to use a local computer bureau. If you need your slides to be registered (ie, each projected image is positioned in the same place on the screen – important where you have a series of slides which reveal information progressively), then you need the help of a professional AV house. They have the expertise, facilities and the resources needed to produce good work. They understand the complexities of the business and, when time is short, have the ability to produce visuals very quickly – an important consideration if scripts and facts are likely to alter right up to the presentation day.

Slide production using computer graphics is discussed in the next chapter.

Final preparations

When you have written your script and assembled all your AV material you are ready to rehearse your presentation. Rehearsal is essential so that you are familiar with the sequence and timing of your AV aids. This will give you confidence on the day and enable you to brief projection staff properly.

Several days before the event you should let the programme chairman or organizer know the size and type of slide mounting you are using, the types of other AV aids (film – optical or magnetic tracking, OHP, video and so on) and whether you need computer data projection. Ideally, you should load your slides into your own trays and carry these with you but if the projector provided is of a different make you must ask the organizer to provide magazines for you. You will need to know whether front or rear projection is being used in order to know which way round the slides should be loaded.

Slides should be sequence numbered and thumb-spotted in the lower left-hand corner when read correctly on hand viewing. This simplifies loading and sorting.

Clean your slides – dusty slides or thumb marks spoil the image.

Carry your slides and PC disks with you in your hand baggage on your trip to the venue, especially if you are travelling by air. Nothing is worse than arriving to give a presentation in, say, London and finding your baggage and visuals are still on the plane to Honolulu!

Arrive at the venue in good time in order to meet and brief the venue AV technicians, load slide trays, test PCs, projectors, video and other aids. If time permits, have a full rehearsal. This is often possible the night before and, by rehearsing properly in this way, you reduce the chances of a nonsense next day and boost both your own confidence and that of the projectionist. A rehearsal is *essential* if you are using Autocue.

Ask for a projector or PC with a remote control or, if this is not possible, prearrange a *silent* signal to the projectionist to call for changes. Agree script markings if changes are cued to the spoken word.

Never try to give your AV material to the AV technician when he is busy with another presentation. Projection staff cannot deal with one speaker and simultaneously follow a live session. But, as any projectionist will tell you, each speaker demands instant individual attention.

Always run through slides and other material and check they are in the right sequence, and that slides are the right way up, are clean and have not slipped in their mounts.

Production

The more sophisticated productions and shows mentioned earlier in the chapter are beyond the purview of the average speaker – and the average conference organizer. However, many companies spend (… invest?) huge sums of money on complex shows and productions – in particular for new product launches. To illustrate this last point, as mentioned previously, one manufacturer of agricultural tractors spent in excess of £1 million on the launch shows for dealers of a new model of tractor.

Shows like these can involve dancing girls, multimedia shows, dry-ice 'smoke' lasers, complicated sets, multi-directional sound and every other trick of the trade to capture the imagination of the audience.

If you are planning a complex show of this sort, you will almost certainly wish to engage a specialist production company. In doing so, it is best to be clear about the division of responsibilities for complex shows of this type:

1. *The client.* This, basically, is you – the person appointed by his company to mastermind the event. You will have superiors and internal advisers and helpers and, no doubt, a committee or working party to whom you must report, present proposals and from whom your authority to deal with the production company will stem. In the eyes of the production company, you will *represent* your organization although, of course, in the final analysis, your company is the true client. But producers and organizers (see below) need a prime point of contact: hence the term 'client'.
2. *The producer.* He produces the actual show and is the person who is, in effect, the production house counterpart to the client. In addition to producing the show, the producer will become heavily involved in the choice of venue. Indeed, he may make the initial recommendation.
3. *The organizer* is responsible for the detailed organization of the event *apart from* the show itself. The organizer may be the client (or someone else from another part of the client's organization); it may be someone from the production company; or it may be a PCO (professional conference organizer); it may even be a travel agent, at least in respect of travel and ground handling for events held overseas (see Chapter 8).

Production houses vary in size and in what they will undertake. Some specialize in, say, audio-visual presentation or in live shows; others offer a comprehensive service and can, in effect, relieve you of almost everything.

It would be somewhat pretentious to say the typical production house is split into separate divisions for audio-visual (slides and multimedia), scriptwriting (speeches, sketches, linking and so on), video production, music (composition, orchestration and recording), choreography, set and lighting design, sound, special effects, costume, casting (guest speakers, personalities, artistes, cabaret and linkmen) and conference organization (dealing with venues, catering, travel, print and so on), but the larger production houses certainly offer all these services as well as the in-house facilities and workshops needed to set up and stage the show.

The relationship between production houses and clients has changed in recent years. Instead of coming in to stage a one-off show, production houses tend to have longer-term relationships – anything up to three years or more. These more enduring relationships mean that events can be themed in line with longer-term marketing and corporate objectives. This, in turn, tends to take the production house beyond its original brief into the role of communication consultants. To quote one production house managing director, 'We concentrate on how we can add to our clients' communications. Rather than just respond to requests we actively participate in their daily business.'

This is not surprising. It takes a considerable material investment between client and production house to stage a show. During the process, the production house has to learn a great deal about their clients and, with their experience in communication, are often able to give valuable advice. The benefits are not all one way: most production houses offer significant savings in rates in return for longer-term contracts.

Events   There are, of course, many types of event which fall outside the field of 'conferences' and 'production' – for example, incentives, exhibitions … even parties and trade fairs. Furthermore, as we have seen elsewhere, you sometimes have to create your own environment inside a venue – for example, themes for gala dinners, or to transform a bare room into an acceptable environment. You may even wish to build your own temporary venue.

When you undertake tasks like these, you may well employ a production house. However, some organizers prefer to handle everything 'in-house' – although they rely on a host of subcontractors to supply everything from lighting hire to marquees, and from mobile toilets to furniture and electrical power.

Corporate Event Services is an indispensable source of information on supplies of services to the industry: published yearly, it is comprehensive and well laid out. For address details refer to the Appendix at the end of the book.

Corporate video Many companies invest in video presentations (the 'trade' name is corporate video) for a multitude of purposes from staff training to explaining pension schemes or presenting the annual report, as well as incorporating videos into shows of the type already described. It is usual to employ a specialist video producer to make stand-alone videos; those which are part of a complex show may be produced by the production house.

Selecting professionals is discussed in Chapter 15. Once selected, it is essential to brief the producer. According to the chairman of one of the leading production companies, many companies still make two basic mistakes when making and using AV material.

The most common mistake is the inadequate brief. If the company fails to sort out what the programme or production is intended to convey or how the material is to be used, it is unlikely to be able to brief the production house properly. Clear objectives are essential.

Another common mistake is to assume that a video or sophisticated show prepared by a professional production company will somehow relieve you of all responsibility. AV programmes should never be a substitute for other, basic communication methods; they are certainly no panacea for bad communication.

'All singing, all dancing' productions are really only suitable for the larger promotional and persuasion events. They cost a lot to stage and would, in any case, seldom be appropriate for events with a high information content or for smaller groups. However, it is worth considering having something more modest specially made. For example, an opening AV sequence to set a theme may well be a good investment. One company which runs seminars on office technology had a six-minute presentation made for just this purpose. A simple two-projector slide show set the theme in a lighthearted manner and also gently raised the issues which were to be highlighted during the later sessions. The benefits of this short sequence are hard to measure in financial terms but the cost, spread over about 20 events, was modest and the show was always well received.

Shows of this kind are very versatile. Visuals can be replaced to bring shows up to date and the effects which can be created with the simplest of visuals can be stunning. Movement can be simulated and superimposed images can create very dramatic effects at comparatively low cost. Indeed, it is in this field that the 35mm slide still has a role to play now and in the future (in spite of all the new technologies). There are those who believe, with some justification, that the computer controlled multi-image slide show, with a high quality, synchronized soundtrack, is still the most dramatic presentation tool. Exploiting the ability of slides to produce images of great size and quality, multiple projectors in 'rigs' of 6, 9, 12, 18 (the more common configurations – but 30 and many more have been successfully employed) are used with very large screens. Sequences and combinations of images can be programmed to create a dramatic experience. With powerful sound – and sometimes other effects like dry ice and lasers – the emotional power of the multi-projector show can be considerable.

Such sequences can easily be transposed on to video or disk to facilitate distribution and showing the material in a variety of dispersed locations.

If the role of individual speakers is particularly important – for example, a chairman's keynote speech, or a session to promote a new incentive scheme – a short visual programme using slides, PC graphics or simple multimedia or special five-minute video, costing a few thousand pounds, may be money well spent.

Investing in any AV material is like entering a minefield. There is, as we have seen, a bewildering range of techniques available. But how cost-effective is AV? A company spending £20,000 to £25,000 on a video reaching 30,000 employees has a *per capita* outlay of only 50 pence, but how many companies have 30,000 employees? How, when and where should presentations be made for maximum impact, and what is the cost of each presentation? What investment in hardware (computers, projectors, screens and so on) is necessary?

A final word of caution: money should only be spent on audio-visual if such expenditure is cost-effective. There is no direct measure of the cost-effectiveness of one visual or even of a full presentation. However, if audio-visual aids are not used and, as a result, delegates fail to understand or respond to the programme, then the event may fail to achieve its objectives. Does it make sense to risk squandering the entire budget for the sake of saving on audio-visual aids?

EXECUTIVE CHECKLIST

- Do you make sure even small business meetings are properly stage-managed?
- Do you use rooms which are adequate for the audio-visual aids you intend to use?
- Do you match the room, screen and projector to obtain a satisfactory image, and seat the audience within the good viewing area?
- Do you position loudspeakers correctly and keep projectors out of sight?
- Do you choose the most suitable AV aid for each situation?
- Do you, when producing and using visuals:
  1. keep copy to a minimum (no more than 15 to 20 words or 25 to 30 figures on each visual)?

2. only use 'landscape' format?
3. keep copy simple; use several simple visuals rather than one complicated one?
4. disclose information progressively?
5. produce special artwork (rather than copy from existing diagrams, illustrations and technical drawings)?
6. use pictures, graphs and charts in preference to words?
7. use bold lettering?
8. use dark background and reverse text slides?
9. read out what the visual says?
10. leave a slide on the screen after discussing its subject?
11. check your slides are legible from the back row?

- Do you consider using video clips and archive material?
- Do you always clear copyright on your material?
- Do you warn organizers of the kind of AV material to be used?
- Do you seek professional help?

6

MODERN TECHNIQUES IN PRESENTATION AND PRODUCTION

The speaker who follows the advice contained in the previous chapter will be supported by AV aids which look good. They will achieve the aim of enhancing the presentation and will help put the message across to the audience. Surely that is enough? Isn't it better to rely on the tried and tested rather than to venture into the unknown; surely, the new and ever changing technologies are the purview of the expert and the production house?

The answers to these questions is a firm no. New technologies and new ideas provide a constantly changing pattern to everyday life. The conference industry has not been slow to adopt these technologies. We ignore them at our peril. Rather, we should embrace them with the enthusiasm they merit.

In this chapter we examine modern techniques in presentation and production. You might (rightly) think that, by definition, some of the material will be out of date before the printing ink is dry, so quickly are existing technologies being improved – or ever superseded. That said, technology does not change everything – it just improves ways of doing things, and there are certain aspects which will prove to be enduring.

Of course, it can be argued that all of these new developments are really only providing means of doing existing things better than before.

But the dividing line between 'doing things better than before' and using technology to do what was not previously thought possible is blurred. It would be easy to confine our use of new technology to the former. But to do so would be to bury our heads in the sand. We need to understand, and use, modern presentation and production techniques to enhance the communication process – and to benefit from the savings in time and money so often associated with new technologies.

It is upon these that this chapter concentrates – with the indulgence of a brief glimpse into the future to illustrate the still better things to come.

Technical jargon   There is, inevitably, a whole new language associated with new technology, and with the production of shows. Professionals use it as a matter of course; the Glossary of Terms at the end of this book will help you understand what they are talking about.

A TECHNOLOGICAL REVOLUTION: ELECTRONIC PRESENTATION

Historically, graphics for presentation visuals were originated on the drawing board. The advent of the computer brought dramatic changes, but even only a few years ago graphics for slides, overhead transparencies – and even colour prints – could only be produced on high end systems that had the capacity to handle the vast amounts of data and environments such as PostScript (for a definition of PostScript see the Glossary at the end of the book).

Today, all this has changed: presentation graphics are the province of the desktop computer, with its low cost peripherals such as scanners, projectors and colour printers. It is no exaggeration to say that the ability to produce graphics for visuals – often called 'Electronic Presentation' – on the Personal Computer (PC) has revolutionized the world of presentation and production.

What PC?

When the first edition of this book was published in 1981, word processing was the only PC application and computers were beginning to replace electronic typewriters. Now, as we see throughout this edition, their uses are many and varied. Now you will not find meetings executives working in their office, at a potential venue or on-site during a meeting without their PC loaded with specialist software and an e-mail connection.

Software

The choice is wide. The most popular software packages are not always the easiest to use (just as Apple Macs have always been easier to learn and use than other PCs but sell in lesser quantities). But the 'popular' packages have the benefit of compatibility with industry standards.

Popular charting and graphics packages include Harvard Graphics, Lotus Freelance and Microsoft PowerPoint, to name but a few. The distinction between these packages and multimedia and video software is becoming blurred.

In choosing software, you must first ascertain your basic needs, for example:

- the output required:
  - slides;
  - overhead transparencies;
  - electronic output (eg to LCD panels);
- graphics, text and so on required;
- whether you wish to link your graphics software with other office systems (for example – to link Microsoft Excel spreadsheets with PowerPoint).

Most software packages have 'outliners': these are text entry systems that enable you to enter your visual data in word processing or spreadsheet fashion, the software then following your pre-determined templates to automatically format the visuals.

Developing a style

Once you have your system up and running the real problems start. Every Tom, Dick and Harriet likes to think of him or herself as a designer, and soon you'll have 20 variations of presentation style on your hands. The simple truth is that presentations require clarity of design, with simple, clean colours and images. So it's best to develop a corporate style and instigate rules for image creation and presentation (following the legibility rules explained in Chapter 5). Fortunately, the computer can help you do this via the built-in template features of most software.

These templates can be created by either a competent system manager or a bureau, and can be 'locked'. This will mean, for example, that your company logo will only appear in one colour, in one place, and that only specified type styles are chosen, according to certain rules.

Using such a management system means you will achieve consistency as well as style.

Outputting systems

35mm slides   For the reasons explained in the previous chapter, the 35mm slide is still a very effective speaker support visual. 35mm slides offer the highest resolution (from 2,000 to 16,000 lines per slide) and are imaged on film recorders. This can be done through a bureau (at a cost of between £5 and £10) or by buying your own film recorder (in which case you will have to bear the cost of film processing). Where very fast turnaround is required, Polaroid offer some excellent packages which produce a slide in a few minutes, albeit at the cost of a slight loss in critical quality.

The major advantage of using bureau-imaged slides is that they are returned in register mounts, meaning that constant elements in a dissolve show or a 'reveal' will not hop around the screen.

Colour printers are used to produce OHP transparencies (and, indeed, hard colour copies). Printers are available in a wide range of technologies, qualities and costs. Thermal transfer, inkjet, bubble jet, laser and dye sublimation are just some of the available technologies. Dye sublimitation printers offer the smoothest quality for photographic images and produce excellent transparencies – but they are expensive. The other technologies will produce satisfactory overheads – especially when coupled with PostScript drivers: as always, you get what you pay for in terms of quality versus price.

Bureaux   One option mentioned earlier is to use a bureau. Many now offer template creation services, user training in graphics preparation, and, of course, imaging of slides, OHP transparencies and full presentation creation services.

Projection   However, most users are turning towards projecting their computer generated visuals: this is discussed later in the chapter.

Video

Video has come of age. Most of us feel comfortable with it: we use video recorders at home; many of us have camcorders; and, of course, television is part of everyday life.

Video has an established role to play in presentations. Moving images of products, places and people talking convey a different kind of information to charts and still images. It is good at communicating emotion, humour, a sense of time or place, and concerns about issues, especially when TV style documentary is used, rather than simply outlining a factual argument.

However, until hitherto, video has had its limitations:

♦ It was difficult to integrate into a presentation and additional special equipment (VCRs and monitors) were not readily available.
♦ Making video was – and is – a very different process to the production of stills: and it is costly.
♦ Readymade materials is often not entirely relevant – and isolating parts of a video was not easy.

It is principally for these reasons that, historically, video has not been used extensively in presentations (although it is used a lot in training).

However, new video production technology is making it easier to originate material and to incorporate it into presentations. Cameras are much easier to use, and the same computer that is used to create computer graphics can be used to edit digitized video. New technologies are making it easier to show video: data projectors can be used to show it, or it can be run from a computer's hard disk or from a CD (see the section on projection below). The development of video compression (effectively reducing computer file sizes by not holding information about bits of the picture that do not change from frame to frame) and high speed transfer of information within computers mean that it is becoming easier to make multimedia presentations which include moving images and audio as well as stills. Special effects, such as tumbling, wrap round and morphing (an example of which is a sequence which rapidly 'ages' a face from youth to old age in an apparently seamless progression) are easy to incorporate. All these techniques have opened the doors to 'multimedia'.

Multimedia

Multimedia has been mentioned many times in this and the preceding chapter. What do we mean by the word?

In the world of conferences and presentations, multimedia is the storage and use of a combination of media – eg sound, text, graphics, video and still pictures – from a computer drive.

The computer therefore becomes the machine that enables the presentation to be made interactive (in this context this means being able to access and display any information at will). An appropriate computer is an obvious requirement (one that is fast enough to do the job), so is an appropriate display device – a monitor, projector or LCD panel.

These elements aside, presentation-specific multimedia/interactive technology can be divided into two classes of product – those that are integral to the computer, and external drives. Running even short video clips from the desktop or laptop computer requires massive file sizes and creates speed problems, so most multimedia systems use some form of 'plug-in' format (ie external drives).

The leading multimedia software packages are Microsoft's *Video for Windows* (VfW) and Apple's *Quick Time*. Both use compression techniques (see above).

Photo CD   Although recording CDs are now available, Kodak's Photo CD provides the best means of incorporating still photographs into multimedia. A single CD ROM can contain up to 80 35mm slide images in digitized form and you can have new pictures added to existing CD ROMs (provided there is space!).

Digital cameras   A range of digital 'still' cameras is now available which, instead of recording images on film (which then has to be processed), stores them digitally. These cameras have a built-in screen to review pictures after they have been taken, and if not wanted, they can be erased and over-recorded. The digital file can be downloaded onto PCs for use as stand-alone pictures or for incorporation into multimedia programs.

PROJECTING COMPUTER DATA AND VIDEO AND MULTIMEDIA MATERIAL

It is only in recent years that acceptable standards have been reached in computer data and video projection (and by 'acceptable' we mean acceptable in terms of image quality, reliability and cost). The greatest technical problem has been the difficulty in projecting an image of sufficient quality. The quality of the image depends upon a number of factors: brightness, resolution and size.

Manufacturers have pursued two different technologies in their search to overcome these problems – CRT (cathode-ray tube) and Digital Data Projectors.

CRT

We all familiar with CRT displays – it is these we see on our televisions and PCs. The CRT technology of television and the PC monitor is 'old' (at least in terms of computing technology). The CRT is heavy and bulky: it is essentially a piece of glass blown up like a balloon, with all the air evacuated from it. Over 30,000 volts are applied on an electrode which fires a beam of electrons straight towards the user: these electrons hit phosphors on the inside of the screen so hard it makes them glow. As one industry commentator says, 'If you told a Martian that we expect people to sit in front of these things eight hours a day, he probably wouldn't believe you.'

Data projectors

When they were first launched the majority of the portable data projectors were video only. Now, as you will see from the chart, data projectors have become the most popular piece of AV equipment for meetings and conferences.

	99	98/97	96	95
1	PC data projector	Flip chart	OHP	OHP
2	OHP	OHP	Video/monitor	Flip chart
3	Flip chart	PC data projector	PC data projector	Slide projector
4	Video/monitor	Slide projector	Flip chart	Video/monitor
5	Slide projector	Vide/monitor	Slide projector	PC data projector

Figure 6.1   *Most used items of audio-visual equipment*

These projectors have superb quality. They can handle graphics up to VGA standard directly and are well suited to multimedia presentations as they are able to accept several sources simultaneously. Portable data projectors are very simple to use.

In fact, one of the major benefits of this kind of technology is its simplicity – presenters can appear technically competent and knowledgeable without ever really having to know how the equipment operates.

A typical presentation might take place thus:

- Place projector on table and plug into power.
- Plug in video source (eg VRT) or computer connection to the projector.

- Erect a projection screen at a suitable throw distance.
- Dim lights and adjust image for colour, contrast and focus.
- Adjust volume.
- Press 'play' or activate computer to begin presentation.

It's a process that's as quick as setting up an overhead projector or a flip chart.

The sheer convenience of a data projector lends itself to several application areas – training, for example, where on-site presentations of high quality can be given with portable systems. Multimedia presentations are simple too, with remote control switching between video and data. It is also often used in places where it is unwise to leave an expensive projector lying around, ie sports clubs and hotels. Portable systems can be stowed away when not in use.

In summary, portable data projectors have become the primary source of speaker support in our industry because they:

- provide bright images;
- can fill a screen up to 10ft wide;
- accept data to VGA standard;
- are very fast to set up – 'plug and play';
- are very easy to use;
- are transportable;
- are largely maintenance free.

Sound   The audio features of data projectors are frequently ignored. Many have some form of built-in speaker and loop-through for linking to a larger sound system. Some even have a microphone socket built in so the presenter can use the panel as a PA input and speaker. The volume of most built-in speakers is inadequate, however, for anything but the smallest audience.

What are the snags?   All technology has its snags and users of PCs will be aware of these – especially of the importance of compatability of systems (see, in particular, the comments on graphics standards above).

There are other potential problems. If you ignore the basic rules of legibility (see previous chapter), or overuse/misuse colour, your visuals will lose their impact (this is true for all computer graphics presentations).

'Pixelation' is obtrusive at large projections, and not all data projectors are ideal for projecting video (if you mainly want to project video rather than graphics, opt for an OCD projector).

CRT projectors

Also expensive, the CRT projector offers the highest resolution of any video/data projector – in practically any number of colours.

The CRT projector incorporates three small TV-type tubes (between seven and nine inches diagonal) – one for the red, one the blue and one the green element of the video or data image. These act like torches and produce very bright images which are focused onto the screen through three lenses (hence the typical three-lens front appearance of the CRT projector).

The brightness of the final image depends upon the brightness of the tubes themselves: this is the limiting factor for CRT projection brightness. If the tubes are 'pushed' too hard, the definition suffers. It is this limitation which has been the main driving force behind the development of the Super LCD projectors (which give a very bright image): it is for this reason that LCD technology is gently superseding the CRT.

CRT projectors are heavy and sensitive to movement. They are therefore best used in permanent installations (usually roof mounted), or in conferences where a solid mounting is available and there is plenty of time to set up the projector and align the lenses. All CRT projectors will suffer from 'drift' in time (where the tubes' alignment goes out of register). This can usually be corrected by the operator using a remote control. Some systems such as Barco have an automatic self-registering facility, called 'magic eye'.

CRT projectors are therefore well suited to boardroom installations, presentation suites and 'high tech' conference rooms.

Pictures of between 6ft (1.8m) and 30ft (9.2m) wide can be achieved with CRT projectors (depending on the brightness of the model). All projectors can handle the main video TV standards (PAL, SECAM and NTSC). Projectors are designed to handle computer data and graphics. Some CRT projectors have built-in TV tuners.

If you are using the CRT projector for multimedia (mixing computer and video in the same presentation) you can have a projector that can store the set-up parameters in memory, switching instantly between inputs during the presentation.

Improving video definition

The image offered by a video source is not particularly high-definition – unless of course, you use an HDTV system. Using an input source such as Betacam, U-matic or Laserdisc can provide better-looking images, but will not change the basic nature of the picture – 625 lines which, blown up over 10ft wide, can be distinct and intrusive. One way to artificially smooth out the image is to use a line doubler. This device reconstructs the video image, interpolating extra lines and giving the appearance of a sharper image.

The alternative is to use a scan converter: a device that up- or downgrades a signal to match another device – for example, you can project images from a 64kHz workstation on a 32kHz projector by converting its signal to 32kHz. This will preserve the colour capability that would be lost by simple stepping down the workstation's graphics rate, but this is at the cost of some image clarity. Note that, at present, there are no High Definition TV (HDTV) projectors on the market.

(Note: thus far, we have not discussed horizontal scan rates: these are explained in the Glossary. Suffice to say here – and this applies to all types of projector – that in addition to having compatible graphics standards, you need compatible scan rates. The computer outputs its screen image at a particular scan rate – say 64kHz. If your projector's scan rate is different, the scan converter overcomes the difference.)

Rear projection   CRT projectors are well suited to back projection. Called Retro Systems, special CRT projectors for rear projection are transportable. They use a CRT projector with a folded light path and a 40 or 60 inch screen. They are not much bigger than a large-screen TV or monitor, and their main advantages are that they need no set-up adjustment, they can be wheeled around from one room to another and, being rear-projected, they retain their brightness in well-illuminated environments.

Videowall

The videowall, as its name implies, is a wall of CRT TV screens.

In its simplest form, the videowall is no more than a big image display device. A single incoming video signal is passed through an electronic 'splitter' which feeds part of the signal to each individual screen in the wall (or 'array'). To the viewer, the overall image looks like a normal picture covered by a grid (rather like looking through a window).

However, many believe the videowall medium comes into its own as a multi-image system. More sophisticated control systems allow a wide range of special effects such as switches from multi to single image, changes in magnification, frame freezes and transitional effects.

It was in the latter configuration that videowall made its public debut at trade shows and exhibitions. Reasonably compact, especially if built into the stand, videowall provided the first effective means of showing moving and multi-image effects in an exhibition environment (mainly on account of the brightness of the TV screen even in high ambient light conditions).

Videowalls are usually arranged with equal numbers of screens horizontally or vertically (eg 3×3, 6×6 and so on). The reason for this is that the subsequent large image retains the normal television aspect ratio. However, displays in other aspect ratios are possible and, indeed, are often used in exhibitions and for advertising displays (for example in airport arrival lounges and in reception areas of company headquarter buildings). But these 'non-standard' arrays do require special production methods and so tend to be more expensive.

The display unit may be made up of video monitors (as described above), or video projectors can be used. Monitors are less expensive and, although quite heavy (a 32-screen display weighs about one tonne), take up less space than projectors (which have to be mounted in special cubes with high gain rear projection screens). Although projectors take up more floorspace, they have the advantage of a very small gap between image sections. They therefore produce a more pleasing overall effect. As ever, the choice between systems tends to be a compromise.

Videowalls are used in conferences as big image display devices, usually for speaker magnification (as seen, for example at party political conferences). The array can be built into the set, capitalizing on the advantages of requiring minimal space. They give a reasonable image without the hall lights being dimmed and even under the glare of television lighting (as in the case of the political conferences).

Videowall can be particularly useful for multi-venue roadshows. The equipment is easier and quicker to set up than a multi-image slide show, and overall the system is less prone to failure. Black and Decker used a 32-screen videowall for a product launch roadshow which was seen by over 7,000 salesmen and distributors all over Europe. The same exercise with a multi-projector show would have been fraught with technical difficulties, would have taken longer and would have cost a great deal more.

The videowall technique is still relatively expensive. Not only is there the cost of the equipment – and of the associated technical support – programming the wall is also expensive. A 10-minute show could take five or more days to program, at a per diem cost of £1,500 or more.

Videowall – in spite of its cost – is here to stay, and prices may come down in time. Whether the average user would wish to copy one British equipment distributor who used a 108-screen wall to demonstrate the medium is open to question. However, it is already an established technique, especially in exhibitions.

Live TV

Traditionally, all AV material used at conferences and meetings, whether it was on slide, film or video, had to be pre-recorded. An increasing number of users have recognized that 'live' video can have a much greater impact on the audience and can be a more flexible and effective communication aid.

The many possible applications which can be used alone or in combination with the others include:

1. A live picture of a speaker projected onto a large screen so that the audience can observe facial expression and so on (this technique is now standard practice at the major party political conferences). For very large meetings, the live picture can be relayed to overflow halls. This technique has been used at places like the NEC Birmingham at the AGMs of the new public utilities companies.
2. The speaker's support visuals can be shown on the same screen, along with pre-recorded video.
3. As we have seen, new information and data can be fed into the computer for instant projection onto the screen, making it possible to respond to new statistics or ideas generated, for example, during a discussion ('live modelling' to use the jargon of the experts).
4. At conventions where speakers want large numbers to view small objects or demonstrations of fine detail, live TV coupled with a large screen can overcome the problem. An obvious application is at medical conferences where experiments, and even operations, can be followed by audiences of several hundred people.
5. Images of distant speakers (for example, of someone overseas), or delegates as they ask questions, can be projected onto the screen. (This technique has been used to good effect at the CBI annual conference.) See also 'Business television' below.

The possibilities are almost endless.

A recent product launch for a new detergent was an excellent demonstration of the imaginative use of video. The event was held 'in the round' with the audience on tiered seating round a central stage area above which six video screens were suspended. Clever lighting permitted activity on the set without spoiling the TV image, and many of the techniques already described were used. Observers of the event claim that the immediacy of live TV had a dramatic effect. It seems that the delegates, knowing the event was live and not pre-recorded, were caught up in the feeling that the whole event was always on a knife edge. Instead of sitting back and merely watching, an interactive loop was established in which the audience consciously listened, observed and understood the proceedings and were able to participate to the full.

The two-hour show, which was followed up by dinner in an adjacent marquee and a cabaret evening back in the 'theatre', used video to present the product relaunch story through the use of a well-known TV journalist. The journalist, acting on behalf of the retailers, customers and the salesforce audience itself, interviewed executives in the best truth-searching style. The interviews were mostly live and unscripted (although they had been structured in rehearsal). Similarly, presentations were made live to the camera and even chemical tests and experiments were demonstrated live to the audience.

Technically and conceptually the event was a *tour de force*. The producer had to consult the architects of the hall before suspending the 2½ ton load of six TV projectors, screens and the lighting rig from the roof. The whole concept was new and the producer readily admits that the enthusiasm and commitment of the board of the company made the show possible. The producer also stresses that such an ambitious approach will not suit everyone; he says that only a few companies can afford such a complex show. However, cost does not preclude experimenting with live video as an alternative to slides and multi-screens as a way of arresting, and keeping, the attention of the audience.

Interactive video

Interactive video is the term used to describe video which responds to an external input from a viewer or operator. The most familiar use of interactive video is computer-based training where the screen, image and information respond to the learner's inputs. The video disc is now opening up interactive video for use as an AV aid. Video disc systems store images (and associated sound) on a disc similar in size to a long playing record. The image is read by laser and the reproduction is of the highest quality.

Video discs can be used to store individual pictures which can be accessed and held on screen indefinitely (unlike video tape where the frame hold is inherently unstable). The capacity of a video disc is quite astonishing; a single side can store four million words, or the equivalent of 656 trays of slides, each containing 80 pictures. Alternatively, the disc can be used to display over half an hour of moving sequences with a dual track audio system which can produce, for example, either stereo sound or simultaneous commentaries in two different languages.

A significant advantage of video disc is that individual frames can be accessed quickly and accurately; it is even possible to 'zoom in' on a particular detail of a selected frame. A video disc can therefore be linked to a control system which can be programmed to select pictures at random from the disc library (a process which is very slow and laborious when using slides in carousel trays). The clear advantage of such a system is the ability to save time by watching only the material relevant to the viewer's needs.

One system under development in America enables a pictorial map of, say, a town to be stored on disc and the operator can control access so that the screen displays the scene as though a camera is moving down the street. If the operator turns right, or left, the image responds accordingly – a sort of 3-D televised map.

Audience response systems

An American import, this equipment allows a presenter to tailor his script, test audience attention, find out subjects which are of particular interest to the audience, and even stimulate interest through competitions, polls and quizzes. Response systems consist of a keypad for each member of the audience linked to a computer which drives a graphics generator. The analysed results of the audience inputs can be projected onto various types of screen.

Audience response systems can be used to record and instantaneously analyse delegates' votes at AGMs and other meetings where votes have to be taken.

The screen image of the results can be tailored to suit the needs of the event. Viewers of TV shows in Britain like *You've been framed!* are very familiar with response systems like these, and with another crude form of audience response system: viewers are asked to 'phone in their answers to particular questions, and the results are displayed on the screen in horizontal bar chart form.

Audience response systems are also a useful aid to conference chairmen, enabling them to control questions from the floor – see Chapter 14.

TELECONFERENCING

There are, the saying goes, many ways of cooking an egg. By the same token, there are many ways by which groups can receive and exchange information. It is for this reason (as we saw in Chapter 1) that before we rush into arranging a conference or meeting it is prudent to consider whether we even need to gather people together in this way. Can the objectives be met by other means, for example through newsletters, corporate videos or site visits? Of course, these methods all have limitations which may lead you to the conclusion that, in spite of the cost in terms of time and money, a meeting is necessary. But there is another possibility to consider: 'teleconferencing'.

Thanks to advances in technology, teleconferencing offers viable alternatives to many types of business meeting. The term 'teleconferencing' covers three different activities, each serving different purposes:

- *Audio conferencing*, where individuals and small groups of people at two or more locations are linked into what effectively becomes the same telephone line, using nothing more complicated than the phone on their desks.
- *Video conferencing*, which enables individuals and small groups at two or more locations to see and hear each other, face-to-face, over live video links.
- *Business television*, which you can use to broadcast your own live or pre-recorded material from a central location to audiences of any size at any number of locations, using satellite and microwave links.

Which you use depends upon what you want to achieve. All offer significant advantages over gathering people together at one location:

- *Savings in time and money.*   There is no travel involved in getting to and from a meeting venue saving time (and time is money) and the direct costs of travel, hotels and so on. These savings can be substantial.
- *Speedier response.*   It can take very little time to set up a teleconference: there is no need to find a venue and, as we have seen above, no travel is necessary. These savings mean that urgent matters can be resolved more quickly: speedier responses can be invaluable, especially in a competitive business environment.
- *Meetings are easier to arrange.*   It is invariably easier to find time for a short teleconference than to set up a meeting for people from several different locations since the latter makes such a large 'hole' in people's diaries. In addition, little administrative work is required, there being no venues to find, no accommodation to book, no joining instructions to send... and so on.
- *Effective use of people.*   Apart from avoiding wasting time in travelling to meetings, it is often possible to call in experts who would not normally be available for meetings away from their normal base but who *could* be spared (or spare the time) for a short teleconference.
- *Increasing personal productivity.*   Provided the time saved (above paragraphs) is put to good use, teleconferencing can lead to increases in personal productivity.
- *Avoiding stress and fatigue.*   There is a lot of stress and fatigue associated with travelling to and attending conferences and meetings – everything from being caught up in traffic jams to the frustration of late trains and cancelled flights, jet lag, fatigue after long car journeys, the domestic stress of being away from home, loss of sleep and even over-indulging during residential events. All this is avoided when you use teleconferencing.

Bearing in mind these advantages, it is hardly surprising that a wide variety of organizations regularly use teleconferencing.

Audio conferencing

You can hire BT's Conference Call bureau service on an 'as required' basis (for example for a regular monthly sales conference or for one-off discussions) or, if you are a very regular user of audio conferencing, you can buy the necessary equipment.

Video conferencing

Given the advantages of video conferencing, it is hardly surprising that there has been dramatic growth in its use in recent years. This growth has been fuelled by better and cheaper technology. In the early days of video conferencing it was strictly for the multinationals who had the necessary hundreds of thousands of pounds to invest in systems which required expensive, dedicated transmission lines.

All this has changed. The current generation of video conferencing equipment is comparatively inexpensive and it operates on ISDN lines (the digital network that covers 98 per cent of the UK and which provides compatible international video and computer links).

The video conferencing market divides into two segments:

♦ Group systems designed to transmit larger meetings which involve several people in several locations.
♦ Desktop systems which are principally used on a one-to-one basis.

The development of the latter was accelerated by the arrival of the PC with its multimedia capability, enabling it to combine video communication and data transmission. Systems offered by BT, Picture Tel and others consist of a small camera, which sits on top of the screen, some extra hardware and software, and a special phone.

Users can see the person to whom they are talking on all or a portion of the screen; they can exchange files and work together on applications as they confer.

BT and a host of other suppliers offer a range of equipment for group video conferencing to meet a variety of user needs. You can rent video conference centres if your demand is insufficient to warrant a dedicated system.

The Civil Service is Britain's largest single user of video conferencing. The DE group, which is an amalgamation of the previous Department of Employment, the Training Commission, the Employment Service, and the Health and Safety Executive, has established nine purpose-built 'video-conferencing studios' at a cost of around £80,000 per studio.

The DE group began using video conferencing back in the late 1980s by renting a system from British Telecom. In addition to video conferencing facilities, the studios were equipped with fax and data links.

The network is in use 90 per cent of the time between 8 am and 6 pm, usually with two link-ups of two studios operating simultaneously. Surprisingly, travel costs have not declined (which implies a certain lack of control). However, proponents argue there are other benefits in terms of increased management effectiveness and the quicker completion of projects.

The group found that staff were particularly keen to use the system and showed little of the resistance usually associated with new technology. After first use, 67 per cent of users wanted to use the facility again, this figure rising to 80 per cent after the second.

The majority of the meetings concern policy development, strategy, and planning with around 140 meetings a month and lasting an average 1½ hours.

Other Government department users included the Welsh Office, which used a London–Cardiff link for several years, and the Inland Revenue, which also has a studio network and which, unlike the DE group, has cut travel costs between some centres by as much as 50 per cent. The DSS has a London–Newcastle–Blackpool link.

One is tempted to ask why the Government leads the field in building such networks? The main reason is the way in which Government offices – and their managers – are separated by long distances which, in part, stems from a deliberate policy of decentralization and moving offices to areas of high unemployment.

This is not to say that commercial organizations have been slow to adopt video conferencing, especially the larger companies which have similar problems of dispersed management. For example, Ford, BP, British Gas, STC, the Royal Bank of Scotland, Barclays Bank and IBM are all significant users.

The commercial value of video conferencing is well illustrated by the following example from the Ford Motor Company. The company's UK Dinitron engineering facility, together with their main European manufacturing plant in Cologne and their worldwide HQ in Detroit have been using video conferencing for several years. On one occasion, they were experiencing production problems with silencers for the XR2 which was produced in Valencia. Using video conferencing, design and production engineers from several countries throughout Europe discussed the problem. Images of the part concerned were projected live during the discussion and the problem was soon resolved. Without this facility, the group members would have had to have travelled to a central meeting point at great cost in time and money.

Ford do not confine their use of video conferencing. The company claims that video conferencing was a key factor in saving a year in the development of the Mondeo.

Smaller organizations are increasingly turning to video conferencing to improve internal communications and save time and money. For example, an insurance broking business with offices at six sites around the country invested about £40,000 in video communications equipment. They use BT desktop systems for board meetings, management meetings, presentations and training. The company cites the usual benefits of video conferencing (savings in time and travel costs), but also stresses other benefits, in particular the importance of the visual image and the ability to observe body language and facial expression.

When all is said and done, however, no one claims that video conferencing will replace the 'traditional' conference. In reality, the medium is being used to improve regular inter-office communication rather than to replace meetings – which is fortunate for the conference organizer to whom this book is directed!

Business television

Unlike video conferencing, business television is a one-way video link (although a return sound channel is often established when the medium is used 'live').

Business television is ideal for one-off events such a sales conferences, product launches or annual general meetings where you may wish to transmit either live or prerecorded material from a central location to dispersed venues. A particular application is to use a video link to allow a distant speaker to address a conference. Some speakers are often too busy or simply too far away to attend a conference but can find the time to address the gathering using business television, and even to answer questions put to them by way of a reverse sound only link.

Another use of business television is in permanent private networks which are used for staff training, broadcasting company news to staff or for selling to customers.

If you think business television is 'not for me', you may be mistaken. New communication satellites and technological advances are making teleconference links more reliable, and cheaper. Some venues in London, for example the Intercontinental Hotel and Barbican Conference Centre, have installed the necessary aerial systems to link up with the transatlantic satellites, and similar facilities are available in a limited number of venues throughout Europe. Forté Hotels also installed a business television network linking a number of their hotels.

In the US, Holiday Inn hotels link their properties coast-to-coast and regularly transmit group communications programmes covering everything from the latest promotional material to mundane subjects such as bedmaking for trainee housekeepers.

OTHER DEVELOPMENTS

After the sophisticated technologies described above, some of the other aids may seem almost prosaic. They nevertheless deserve mention.

Television prompts

Although not new, the value of television prompt systems (such as Autocue) as a presentation aid is still not widely appreciated.

Autocue were first in the field when they developed the system now in most common use, especially by the television companies. The near word perfect newsreader who seems to stare glassy eyed at the camera as he or she reads the news with hardly a glance at the script on the table is, in fact, reading from a reflected image of the script which is projected from a monitor onto a glass plate in front of the camera. The plate is invisible to the camera. A hidden operator scrolls the script, which is typed onto a roll of paper, in front of the lens of a second camera and reverse image is relayed to the monitor for projection onto the glass plate.

Autocue is regularly used at larger conferences. In a large auditorium, the glass plate is virtually invisible to the audience, and the speaker can read his script without looking down. Politicians regularly use Autocue when they deliver major speeches. They compare very favourably with those politicians who still prefer paper notes and stand hunched over the lectern, obviously looking down and reading instead of (apparently) looking the audience in the eye.

It is possible – for the brave – to use a phonetically spelt speech in a language with which the speaker is not familiar. It is said that one executive speaking to a Chinese audience with the aid of Autocue became so confident that he was tempted to ask for questions. Few would be so bold, but Autocue can make better speakers of us all and it is an invaluable aid in the sophisticated production where timing, cues and content have to be perfected.

That said, Autocue and similar aids are not for the 'ad-libber' – the speaker who either wanders from the prepared script or prefers to speak to a series of headings rather than a prepared script. The operator who controls the projection of the script onto the screen has to know exactly where the speaker has reached and the roll onto which the script is typed is moved forward accordingly. There are only a few lines on the screen at any one time and, if the speaker ad-libs or departs from the prepared script, the operator has no option but to stop rolling the script forward. If the speaker is undisciplined and chooses to pick up what he was saying in a different sequence, the operator will be 'lost' and there is little chance of the right words ever appearing in front of the speaker.

The other point is that, however well-written the script (ie, using natural, 'spoken' language rather than the English of the written word), some people simply cannot read aloud well. Such speakers are usually better 'ad-libbing' from a series of headings and notes and Autocue is not for them.

Movement

Occasionally – very occasionally – a gifted speaker will hold an audience spellbound. Often speaking without notes or supporting AV aids, these people have a rare ability which few can emulate. Most of us have to use every trick available to arrest – and keep – attention. Some speakers assume the generous use of slides will help, but the example of the German in Chapter 3 using hundreds of complicated slides belies this assumption.

Movement can be used with considerable success to overcome audience boredom and inattention. This does not mean that the speaker has to leap about the stage like a demented pop star. But some movement is essential. If a speaker wears a neck or 'tie pin' microphone he is able to move away from the lectern – perhaps to point to a slide or even to move amongst the audience. A once favoured technique was the use of two speakers, one either side of the stage to 'Box and Cox' the script. This has the advantage of maintaining interest as well as enabling more imaginative scripting.

But movement of apparently inanimate objects can be even more arresting. For example, the stage can be raised, lowered or revolved, and different and contrasting backdrops, sets and lighting effects can be used to maintain audience interest or even to change the mood and anticipation of the audience.

In product launches, the product itself has been raised, lowered, dropped, slung over the audience's heads and even showered upon them from an exploding cannon in the centre of the stage (crisps!). In one particular instance, it was suspended below a helicopter which circled a ferry on which delegates had been invited for what would otherwise have been a standard day out on a lake.

In an attempt to achieve the greatest possible impact, many different methods have been used to reveal products at product launches, and devices such as hydraulic lifts, turntables, fork lift trucks, cranes and reversible scenery are standard tools of the production trade. One successful and startling variation of this particular theme involved taking the audience to the product. A specially constructed raked auditorium was winched along a track, carrying its human load to the static 'reveal', passing through a succession of dramatic sets on the way.

Robotics

Robots can provide a suitable and amusing link between speaker and audience. They can be radio controlled, pre-programmed or actually manned.

As a gimmick and an 'attention grabber' they work well, but it is difficult to see how they can be employed in a meaningful role in any serious conference. However, a robot was used by one US university to give the inaugural lecture, but this particular example could be said to be 'over the top'. Like the inappropriate slide of a nude, or the inappropriate joke, there is always the danger that the audience will leave with the memory of the gimmick, having forgotten the serious message.

Aniform

Similar to robots, but in certain circumstances somewhat more effective, is the use of Aniform, a trade name for cartoon characters which respond to audiences, identifying individuals, asking questions and even conducting conversations.

An operator manipulates a model and provides the voice responses; a TV camera is used to relay the image to a screen or TV monitor. The secret of this effect is that the operator remains out of sight but can see the audience, either directly through a peephole or via a TV monitor. He can therefore respond to what is happening in the auditorium. This presentation is extremely effective in stopping and holding visitors at a stand in exhibitions and can be used as an introduction to speakers and even to provide continuity and to conduct question and answer sessions at certain types of conference. However, it is very difficult to sustain, once the novelty has worn off.

Talking head

This is a three-dimensional, visual effect which is more commonly seen at product launches and exhibitions.

A pre-filmed face is projected on to a sculpted head. The result can be uncannily realistic; the head can be of any character – even the managing director. It can be of almost any size and an accompanying body can be set up to enhance the illusion. However, as with the other gimmicks described previously, the talking head should only be used sparingly, and then only in events where such gimmicks are acceptable.

Mirrors

The size and shape of a stage – or even a conference room – can sometimes be modified by the use of mirrors – a trick the stage illusionist has known about for a long time.

Smoke and pyrotechnics

Another conjurors' trick is that of masking the sleight-of-hand with a pall of smoke. Explosions, wreaths of dry ice vapour and sparklers have all been used separately and in concert to add dramatic atmosphere, especially in product launches. Would be users of such techniques should be warned: chemically-produced effects must be properly controlled for safety, and should be professionally directed in order to achieve maximum impact.

Lasers

When lasers were first introduced into the meetings business some years ago, the laser had not advanced beyond its early pattern-producing form. Laser technology is advancing rapidly thanks, to a large extent, to the American 'star wars' research programme.

Lasers can now be used to present excellent graphical displays. Until recently, laser generated graphics of, for example, logos or script, had to be continuously joined up by a fly-line. Today, lasers can project moving graphical displays onto almost any surface. The quality is similar to that achieved with computer video graphics. Laser displays can be projected 'live' to the audience and can be integrated into static slide shows. When used in the more sophisticated (ie, more expensive) shows, lasers can produce stunning effects.

Fibre optics

Fibre optics – the science of 'bending' light along a series of minute fibre glass filaments – already has its place in the telecommunications industry. Fibre optics are also used in the more sophisticated venues to transmit video and other material from one part of a building to another, thereby eliminating the need for bulky cables.

Although fibre optics are not yet in common use in the production business, the transmission of light has always been a fundamental of presentations, and there is every reason to suppose that the application of fibre optics will find its place in future product launches.

Computer controlled systems

The extent to which computers are used to control lighting, sound and visual effects is not fully appreciated by the layman. The lighting schedule for a major show can be exceedingly complex. Computers can be programmed to control and sequence lighting effects precisely. Sound effects can be similarly controlled. One microcomputer controlled audio system produced by a Finnish company eliminates the possibility of human error during a sound effect scheme in a reveal (production launch) or 'high tech' conference. Up to 1,000 cues can be put onto memory, a single diskette providing the key to a wide range of dynamic audio effects.

Infrared control systems

Major international conference centres often have sophisticated computer controlled sound and voting systems ('s-i systems'). The Finlandia Hall in Helsinki uses a German infrared s-i system which links delegates' individual microphones to a central computer. Interpreters' equipment, also linked to the computer, allows the chairman of the session to see on his monitor a list of those delegates who wish to speak generated by delegates using either magnetic or infrared coded badges to indicate they want to ask a question. When the chairman calls the delegate (through the control system), the computer automatically sorts out the languages involved and alerts the appropriate interpreter.

SIMPLE IMPROVEMENTS

Much of the foregoing has described equipments and techniques which are more suited to the major event, especially the so called 'production'. There is a range of simple improvements which can be used to enhance even the most modest presentation.

Hand-held laser pointers can be used instead of a long cue (which is usually invisible to the audience) or, worse, the hand. The bright spot of red light focuses the eye and compels attention. One laser pointer now freely available has a range of 150ft in bright light – and over 1km at night!

Flip charts and whiteboards As briefly mentioned in the previous chapter, even the humble flip chart and whiteboard have been enhanced by technology.

One problem many users experience – that of keeping a record of what is written on a flip chart or whiteboard – has been solved by the introduction of a machine which can produce A4 copies of whatever is written on the whiteboard. These can be kept as a permanent record and, of course, can be copied for wider distribution. This device is particularly useful for recording the ideas generated during a 'think tank' or planning discussion where formal minutes often miss details which are essential to the overall rationale of the discussions.

Another machine works in the reverse way: it can be used to create flip chart size copies from A4 originals. The enlargement copy is made by a process similar to that which produces the hard copy from a normal fax: indeed, the paper is of similar weight and texture to fax paper. However, several colours of text are possible, for example blue and red as well as black. The ability to produce flip charts from A4 originals provides a useful additional professional aid for use in training and for small presentations. Indeed, the pre-prepared flip chart is now a viable alternative to the OHP which, as many users know, has inherent disadvantages when used for formal presentations.

Three final innovations which will be welcomed by many flip chart users:

- Sasco now produce a 'Dual Easel' which enables you to have two A1 pads side by side. The ability to use two pads side by side will be welcomed by the many users who find one pad limits their style.
- A very simple and long overdue improvement is the introduction of flip charts with perforations along the top of the pad to make it easy to remove sheets without tearing them. Why didn't someone think of it before (or did they do so but fail to promote the idea effectively)?
- 3M have introduced a 'Post-it Notes' version of the flip chart (this is described in detail on page 155).

DISSEMINATION TO WIDER AUDIENCES

The UK chapter of a worldwide association attracts 16,000 delegates to its annual conference... it is difficult to decide who to feel sorry for – the delegates or the organizers! Few would wish to go to the effort – and expense – of assembling so large an audience. However, it is often necessary to repeat events for the benefit of subsequent audiences – itself a costly and sometimes inconvenient process which ties down speakers and can involve travel and a great deal of time.

It is therefore sometimes worth transferring the original presentations or show onto film or, as is more usual, onto video tape for subsequent showings to new audiences. Even complete shows which use video, slides and other aids can be simultaneously recorded on one tape – a technique which is particularly useful for recording multi-screen shows which, if shown in their original form, would involve transporting and setting up large numbers of projectors for every showing.

There is one problem to overcome. Many modern shows are presented at low light levels – a euphemism for darkness illuminated with pools of dramatic light. These do not transfer to video very well and hence can look disappointing, negating all the intended good!

The National Westminster Bank recently adopted a different method when it was decided to put 60,000 staff from its domestic banking division through a one-day seminar. Seven temporary (but semi-permanent in construction and appearance) conference centres were set up in locations ranging from Knebworth House and the Hurlingham Club to Chiddingstone Castle and several similar venues in the North. The conference centres were especially designed for the purpose; each had a main hall with tiered seating for 120 round a platform behind which was concealed a display of future branch equipment, computers and so on. There was a facility to show a specially commissioned video on screens suspended from the ceiling and the group could split into four syndicates/workshops and work in separate breakdown rooms grouped round the main hall.

The bank's own staff, specially trained and briefed, ran the days assisted by technicians from the production company. The day was professionally orchestrated, ending with a mini 'production' with dry ice 'smoke', flashing lights and music at the 'reveal' when the equipment was unveiled for inspection by the attendees.

Sometimes a less ambitious record will suffice – for example, a simple audio cassette of a particular presentation. Several firms provide a recording service and produce duplicate cassette tapes for sale immediately afterwards. There is a strong market for such tapes: they are apparently most often played on car cassettes – on long journeys (or in traffic jams) – perhaps a welcome relief to unremitting pop or the bland utterances of the star programme presenters!

A GLIMPSE INTO THE FUTURE

It would be a brave (or foolish) prophet who tried to predict future developments in presentation and production. Clearly multimedia will develop and more and more sophisticated (and, paradoxically, simpler) ways of doing things will emerge. And, as with all developing technologies, prices will fall.

The Internet

The Internet is, of course, already with us; it is growing rapidly – and a bit like Topsy. The final pattern of its commercial use is only emerging slowly. Nevertheless, event organizers should investigate as suppliers from the travel industry move into 'e-commerce'.

Already hotel chains, carriers, transport providers and tourist authorities from Spain to Japan, and Bali to Philadelphia are on the World Wide Web. Many providers include information targeted at the groups market, enabling organizers to move quickly through the laborious decision making process of event management.

The Internet as an information source is the future. Where some lead, others follow. As discussed in Chapter 11, some organizers are already making conference papers available on the Internet. How long will it be before it becomes commonplace to register for events on the Internet, receive joining instructions, maps and so on?.... As always, we are limited more by our imaginations rather than by the technologies already available to us.

Holography

Holography was, at one time, seen to have great potential: perhaps it still has. Holography is a technique which captures a three-dimensional image on a two-dimensional plane. The technique is still young but examples can be seen at a number of science and art galleries. But until holograms can be projected (or produced in a size which can be seen at distance) their value to the conference business will be marginal.

It has been said that, in the foreseeable future, it will be possible to project holographic three-dimensional images of almost any object. Theoretically, at least, it will be possible to sit down at a table with holographs of people who are on the other side of the world: the idea of a conference of holographic images is, to say the least, bizarre – but who knows?

However, the 'future watchers' are now more excited by another new development which, they claim, has a far greater potential – that of Virtual Reality.

Virtual Reality

Virtual Reality has emerged from the field in computer science known as human computer interface (HCI). The aim of HCI is to create what is described as a harmonious interface between man and machine so that what we want a computer to do is achieved effortlessly. Early HCI work was aimed at making computers easier to use. Computer programs are now better designed using sound (for example, voice activation/voice recognition), graphics and text to steer people through even the most complex applications. 'Windowing' is a good example of the use of user friendly graphics and text with a simple mouse control to drive very complicated desktop publishing programs.

Virtual Reality, however, represents a quantum leap forward in HCI applications. Virtual Reality is, in effect, a world generated by computer which responds realistically to the physical movements of the operator.

The effect is achieved by the operator – or 'traveller' as he is called in the relevant technical jargon – wearing a special helmet which places two tiny computer screens in front of each eye. Each screen displays a slightly different view of the scene to give the illusion of stereoscopic vision. Sensors attached to the traveller relay every movement to the computer which adjusts the projected scene accordingly. Look up and you will see the sky; look down and you will see the ground. Move forward and you will move through the scene – you can climb steps, run, stop – even fall off a computer-generated cliff. Whatever you do, the images change appropriately.

At present, the computer-generated scenes are relatively crude (although they are improving all the time and will eventually be sufficiently well defined to be totally realistic).

At this stage, the imagination begins to run riot. In a book on the subject, one scientist speculates on the possibility of people wearing sensitized body suits taking part in simulated orgies (not, it has to be said, the best publicity for a science which has such enormous potential).

Virtual Reality is already in commercial use in games arcades (the 'Cyberspace' experience as the buffs call it). It is also used in military battlefield simulation.

Some people are already predicting that within 10 years, we will have Virtual Reality rooms in our homes from which we will be able to shop, and where we will be able to choose holidays ('previewing' the hotels and beaches) and, of course, play sophisticated games.

So, it is not unreasonable to foresee intercontinental Virtual Reality meetings where delegates interact in a very convincing manner. Of course such ideas are very futuristic but they cannot be dismissed out of hand – who was it who said 'Well informed people know that it is impossible to transmit the voice over wire and that if it were possible to do so the thing would be of no practical value'? Someone forgot to tell Alexander Graham Bell.

Back to actual reality

But, lest our minds run away with us, let us return to the more prosaic world of the conference organizer – the real world in which we embrace any new technology if it enhances the communication process or facilitates the running of the event and is cost effective. The use of technology for its own sake is seldom either effective or worthwhile. It is our job, in our consultancy role, to restrain the wilder excesses of the over-enthusiastic – and to encourage the use of new technologies and new techniques when they are appropriate.

EXECUTIVE CHECKLIST

- Does your organization use electronic presentation technology? If not, why not?
- Have you tried video projection instead of conventional monitors when showing videos?
- When you have large audiences, have you considered using video to project an image of the speaker's head?
- Have you considered using live TV?
- Do you save time and money by using teleconferencing?
- Have you tried out a television prompt such as Autocue?
- Are your presentations static and boring, or do you use movement and novelties to maintain audience interest?
- Do you record your conferences and/or presentations for dissemination to new audiences in your organization?
- Do you use a laser light pointer?
- Do your AV aids enhance the communication between you and your audience?
- Are your AV aids as modern, varied and effective as they could be – and should be?

7

EXHIBITIONS AT CONFERENCES

The practice of holding exhibitions or trade shows alongside conferences has grown significantly in recent years. In the UK all the annual party political conferences incorporate exhibitions to attract attendance from the major corporate companies. The exhibition at the annual IPD (Institute of Personnel and Development) conference seems to grow bigger and better each year. In one case, at the annual Education, Training and Personnel Development Conference the exhibition now attracts 16 times more visitors than delegates to the conference. The exhibition has thus become the main activity and the conference is of secondary importance (but is still an integral part of the event).

More and more conferences and meetings now have secondary exhibitions, and these are not confined to commercial events like those already described. Many association and medical conferences include exhibitions in their programmes and even many small conferences have modest exhibitions. For example, one-day seminars often have supporting equipment displays and others have bookstalls which show the latest publications relevant to the events and sell books to delegates.

WHY HOLD AN EXHIBITION?

There are two main reasons for electing to arrange an exhibition or trade show alongside your conferences:

- To make the events more interesting to your delegates, ie to provide more information than would otherwise be available.
- To make money.

An additional bonus to be derived from having an associated exhibition is that exhibitors themselves often help attract additional delegates to the event. This is because exhibitors have a vested interest in making the event a success, and because they often have access to people in the subject field, they will promote your event on your behalf. Some conference delegate lists are made up of up to 50 per cent of people 'invited' to the event by the exhibitors. It is therefore worth considering offering exhibitors discounted registration fees for delegates they introduce to encourage them to work on increasing numbers on your behalf.

Adding interest

In a perfect world, this would be the only reason for holding an exhibition alongside your conference. Bearing in mind everything we do should be geared towards achieving the aim of the event and towards the delegate, if an exhibition or trade fair facilitates these processes, then we should include one in our programme.

Exhibitions can be invaluable to the delegate. They can give him the opportunity of seeing equipment, possibly to view the latest developments in technology and possibly to see processes in operation. None of these can be achieved so well in the formal presentation or lecture, however good the audio visual support.

Exhibitions are also invaluable sources of information. Delegates can compare the offerings of various suppliers, check prices, obtain technical information, and discuss their particular needs with representatives of the manufacturers.

Finally, delegates may be able to purchase books or even goods from exhibitors, possibly to obtain material which has been discussed during the conference.

The very presence of exhibitors at an event can be a benefit in itself. It is common practice to allow exhibitors to attend conference sessions and their knowledge and additional expertise in specialist fields can greatly enrich a workshop or question and answer session.

Exhibitions can therefore 'add value' to the event, being seen by the delegate as something offering benefits over and above the basic conference. This can be an important consideration for the 'open event'. But beware of over-doing it. As a general rule, admission to exhibitions held in their own right is free but even if an admission charge is made, those who go do so in the knowledge that they will be 'sold to'. This is not the case when delegates pay to attend a conference and some people resent being 'sold to' under these circumstances: 'I didn't pay to come here to be sold to.'

Note that exhibitions are not confined to public events. Some 'in-house' conferences also attract exhibitors who are anxious to make contacts within the organization.

Making money

The other reason for holding exhibitions with conferences is to make money. Exhibition income has become a major part of the budget of a large conference. The income from an exhibition which commands top-end-of-the-market exhibitor fees may make the difference between an event being financially viable or not. Association and medical confer-ences, in particular, often use exhibition income to keep the cost of atten-dance to an affordable level for individuals who do not have their fees paid by their employers.

It would be foolish to think that having an exhibition alongside your conference is a licence to print money. Exhibitors at conferences tend to regard themselves as second class citizens, the exhibition being seen as peripheral to the main event. We return to this theme later in the chapter; suffice to say here that it is, as a general rule, harder to sell stand space at an exhibition alongside a conference than it is for a stand-alone exhibition.

WHAT'S IN IT FOR THE EXHIBITORS?

Exhibitors will only come to your conference if they believe it will be worth their while.

An exhibition is a marketplace in which potential buyers come to the seller. It is, or rather should be, a low-cost selling opportunity created by meeting, face-to-face, people who are interested in the exhibitors' products or services. There are other benefits: exhibitors have the opportunity of evaluating their competitors' products and their promotional activities – possibly to see a new competitive product for the first time. And, of course, the exhibitor can talk to visitors – often to obtain feedback on what new products or technologies the market is seeking.

Exhibitors will only come to your event if they think the potential audience you can send to their stands will be the 'right audience' (ie decision makers and not 'freeloaders') and that the cost is reasonable. Remember, you will be competing for a slice of the organization's promotional budget; you will also be competing against established exhibitions which offer much larger audiences (although, as we shall see later, this can be a double-edged benefit). So what are the benefits of exhibiting at a conference?

First, there are the benefits which apply to any exhibition:

◆ *The buyer comes to the seller*   Retailing apart, no other promotional activity acts in this manner. Compared with having a salesman on the road, the exhibition can be significantly cheaper in terms of cost per useful contact. What is more, the exhibitor has the added advantage of being on what is, in effect, his own 'territory' as opposed to going into the prospect's office where the prospect has the psychological advantage.

◆ *Access to decision makers*   Research has shown that the better exhibitions attractive the decision makers. One survey of a leading trade exhibition showed that 84% of all visitors had some influence on purchase decisions. By comparison, travelling salesmen never have a similar opportunity to reach so many decision makers.

◆ *New prospects attend*   Exhibitions are ideal places to meet new prospects. Firstly, because visitors see exhibitions as an easy and cost-effective way of finding out what is available in the market, and secondly because many visitors are new to their jobs and go specifically to learn and to make contacts.

◆ *Contact is face-to-face*   This affords the chance to tailor the sales message to the individual, answer questions, overcome objections and close the sale.

◆ *Access to 'hard to see' buyers*   Many professional buyers are hard to reach. At an exhibition there are no appointments to be made, no secretaries to convince – suddenly the inaccessible buyer is accessible.

◆ *Exhibition visitors are 'receptive'*   As mentioned earlier, exhibition visitors expect to be 'sold to'. The visitor, by virtue of being there, has given time to tour the stands. This is not the case when the salesman visits his office where the appointment can be seen as an intrusion. What is more, exhibition visitors also tend to be 'captive' – there are no telephones ringing, no heads round office doors with urgent requests and no pressures on the buyer's time.

◆ *The exhibition stand is a 'stage'*   The stand is a temporary showcase for the company and the product: and it is staffed. The overall effect can be high profile visibility for both. What is more, because it is possible to put several people on the stand, all the information visitors seek can be provided there and then. (Salesmen 'on the road' often have to refer back to their companies when asked technical questions.)

Second, there can be particular advantages of exhibitions at conferences:

♦ *The audience is even more valuable*   Although, as we have seen, exhibition visitors tend to be well targeted, there will always be some – even many – 'freeloaders'. A conference audience, although smaller in numbers, will tend to be of better quality. Since conferences are usually geared towards very specific market niches, any exhibitor whose products or services are of interest to that audience is bound to do better than he would showing to a larger but more general market. A publisher took a stand at an exhibition at a one-day seminar on management development. Although only 150 people attended the conference, the exhibitor was well pleased. To quote the post-exhibition appraisal: 'There is no other way we could have reached this particular group of managers. They had plenty of time to see our books and we won some excellent orders on the spot'.

  This raises the inevitable question, how big does a conference have to be before an exhibition becomes a viable proposition? There is no definitive answer. One of five exhibitors at a conference for only 50 people was delighted with the results. At a bigger event, he felt he would have been lost in the crowd. At the other end of the scale, some exhibitions have become so large and so important that exhibitors queue up for stands because these conferences attract more delegates than the average trade show in those particular fields.

  The answer is inevitably a function of cost *vis-à-vis* the value of the audience and, to a lesser extent, the prestige of the event (the exhibitors at the party political conferences go simply to be seen to be there).

♦ *The exhibition is not so overtly 'commercial'*   Delegates often see exhibitors at conferences as being less overtly commercial than those they see in normal exhibitions. They feel more comfortable as a result, thinking they will not be subjected to a 'hard sell'. In the case of the publisher at the management development conference, the 'stand' was in fact no more than a table covered with a cloth, with a very simple display panel. Delegates felt very comfortable in this 'low-key' atmosphere.

♦ *Stands are often inexpensive*   It is very expensive to take stands at some of the major exhibitions. Stands at conference exhibitions tend to be considerably cheaper and, bearing in mind the nature of the audience, they offer excellent value for money.

  It is not possible to suggest prices: these depend on many factors including the industry, the type of audience, the value of the market and so on. At the bottom of the scale, stands have been let for as little as £50 for two days; at the other end of the scale, stands are just as expensive as those at the major exhibitions.

◆ *Intrinsic benefits* There are less obvious benefits associated with exhibiting at some conferences. By taking stands, exhibitors become associated with the ideals of the conference, perhaps demonstrating some degree of social commitment to a particular cause. Exhibitors may also see their presence as doing no more than keeping themselves in the public eye – not unlike, on a lesser scale, the exhibitors who show at the party political conferences 'just to be seen to be there'.

ARE THERE ANY DRAWBACKS FOR THE EXHIBITOR?

There are inevitably disadvantages to conference exhibitions from the exhibitor's point of view:

◆ Low numbers of delegates/visitors.
◆ Low exposure to delegates.
◆ The 'long day' factor.

Low numbers

Paradoxically in view of the earlier remarks about the value of the smaller audience at the typical conference, many exhibitors see low numbers as a serious disadvantage. While they acknowledge that the 'football crowds' at larger exhibitions are often a waste of time, very small numbers make it prohibitively expensive to put in and staff a stand, especially since, in contrast to the normal exhibition, the times at which delegates have access to the exhibition are restricted to breaks between conference sessions.

The problem of low numbers of delegates can be solved by throwing the exhibition open to non-conference visitors. This has the clear advantage of increasing the number of visitors but adds to the problem of promoting the exhibition, adding to the promotional cost of the conference itself. As a general rule, the exhibition would have to be promoted independently, ie the conference would be promoted to the appropriate target audience, the exhibition being highlighted in the promotional literature, and the exhibition would be promoted as a stand-alone event to a much wider market.

Admitting the general public also complicates the administration of the event. It is not unusual for a conference exhibition which is also opened to the general public literally to 'take over' and either become more important than the conference or, like the IPM conference at Harrogate, become a 'permanent' (ie annual) event in its own right.

Low numbers of delegates in the exhibition area can bring other problems: the number of exhibitor personnel can exceed the number of visitors, and the exhibition space can seem empty and quiet. One exhibitor gets round the latter problem by playing what is called 'white noise' over the public address system. This is a recording of the hum of conversation and noise of a larger, busy exhibition: provided the volume is kept at a low level, the effect can be to make the exhibition sound busier than it is in reality.

Low exposure to delegates

This is a major problem. Having paid to exhibit, it is not unnatural that the exhibitors should expect value for money which means in particular that they would expect good exposure to the delegates. However, many delegates attend the conference for its own sake and tend to view any attached exhibition as a voluntary 'side show'. Some never even bother to go round the exhibition.

Further, conference delegates can only visit the exhibition in breaks between conference sessions. This results in what one exhibitor recently described as 'six hours tedium and two hours frenetic activity'. Exhibition stand staff find it very difficult to keep gearing themselves up for these short bursts of activity and prefer the more even and continuous pace of a normal exhibition.

It is standard practice to hold Registration and to serve tea and coffee in the exhibition hall (only practical if the exhibition hall is close to the meetings rooms – not always the case due to venue layout restrictions) and similarly also serve a buffet lunch in the exhibition area. But this is only half the answer. Many people do not like mixing a stand-up buffet, which is 'difficult' enough in terms of coping with a plate of food, a glass of wine and so on with walking round stands and talking business.

It is therefore preferable to build the exhibition into the programme and earmark set time for visiting the exhibition at various stages of the conference. This could easily be accomplished in the sort of mixed plenary session and workshop programme described on page 87. Exhibition open times could be substituted for some of the 'lesser' subject workshops, giving delegates to the conference the chance of either attending a workshop or going to the exhibition. Poster sessions (see page 91) can be held in the exhibition hall to encourage delegates to go into the exhibition.

Another ploy to stimulate attendance is to stage promotions and prizes for delegates to win by going round the exhibition.

The long day

The 'long day' problem is similar to that of limited exposure already described. If the exhibition times are geared to the conference timetable, the day is inevitably long. Normal exhibitions tend to have a shorter day than the average conference and any extension to the open hours causes problems, not least that of fatigue: manning an exhibition stand is physically demanding and the longer the day, even with fewer visitors, the greater the drain on individual reserves.

This problem can best be solved by only opening the exhibition at certain times, say first thing in the morning until the afternoon tea break. The traditional evening session is often poorly attended, so little is lost.

ENHANCING THE 'PACKAGE'

It is clear from the above that it will not always be easy to attract exhibitors to your conference in spite of all the advantages your event offers. You need to do all you can to enhance the 'package' you offer exhibitors to make it worth their while to attend. Typical enhancements include:

- attendance at sessions included in fee;
- list of delegates;
- chance to speak at conference;
- special meals/accommodation package.

Attendance at sessions

Provided exhibitors are not allowed to dominate the audience by virtue of their numbers, it is a good idea to offer exhibitors free places at the conference itself. This is often popular with exhibitors: it gives them a chance to learn, to contribute to the discussion in question and answer sessions and to make new contacts away from their stands. It also helps solve the problem of what to do while the conference is in session and there are no visitors in the exhibition hall.

List of delegates (by name, company address, telephone and fax numbers, and appointment)

This is very valuable to the exhibitor. It saves him having to note down the name and address of every visitor, saving valuable time. It also takes some of the 'hard sell' pressure off the exhibitors. Knowing they can follow up after the event, exhibitors can be more relaxed than if they know they cannot make a subsequent follow-up and have to close the sale there and then.

Chance to speak at conference

If, and only if, you know your exhibitors have something to contribute to the proceedings, they can be given the opportunity of speaking at your conference. However, this must be controlled otherwise the speakers will deliver their standard sales pitch: remember, people do not like going to a conference to be 'sold to'.

Hotel meals package

It may be possible to offer exhibitors the chance of joining meals thereby providing an additional opportunity for them to mix with delegates. It also helps to keep exhibition stand staff 'on site' – there is a danger otherwise that stands will be empty during the important lunch session because the staff are away having their own meals! By the same token, it is often possible to include hotel accommodation in the exhibitors' package, but care must be taken to prevent their taking so many rooms that you do not have enough left for your delegates.

HOW TO ORGANIZE YOUR EXHIBITION

This chapter is not a detailed guide to organizing exhibitions: that would be a subject for a separate book in its own right. However, there are guidelines which you can follow to ease the task.

Like arranging a conference, organizing an exhibition is a demanding, but not a difficult administrative task. A small exhibition of a few stands, or even a few display tables, is within the capability of anyone who is able to cope with a conference of any significance.

Even a fairly small exhibition of up to 20 or 30 stands can be handled by a competent team (the stand 'shell scheme' apart – see below) but if you are contemplating something larger, say 50 or more stands, then you should consider professional help.

That said, as with any professional help, you must work out what help you need and then find the appropriate supplier.

Professional exhibition organizers

It would be a mistake to assume that the answer to all your problems lies in finding a professional exhibition organizer. Unlike the professional conference organizer (PCO), whose task is primarily administrative (ie to handle all the administrative load of the conference), the exhibition organizer's task is to promote exhibitions (ie to attract visitors).

True, they will, on your behalf, handle all the other arrangements (for a fee), but in reality they sub-contract out all the physical work such as shell schemes, power and so on.

Thus, if you have a ready-made, captive audience for your conference, for example a professional body or trade association, and you are not contemplating opening up the exhibition to the wider public, you will not need a professional exhibition organizer.

If you do decide to seek the services of a professional exhibition organizer, it is best to employ one with a proven track record in organizing exhibitions, preferably in fields close to your own (someone well versed in computer exhibitions may not be able to handle the promotion of an exhibition of heavy engineering machinery).

There are plenty of organizers from which to choose. Some are either owned by the exhibition venues (and clearly serve their master's interests – all right if these do not conflict with your own). Others belong to trade associations who may or may not be truly representative of their industry. Journals and magazines have, in recent years, become involved in organizing exhibitions: some act as sponsors and sub-contract the actual task, others have in-house capabilities. Finally, there are the commercial firms who make a living out of organizing exhibitions.

There are several associations which will put you in touch with a number of their members who would be capable of handling your exhibition; their addresses are included in the 'Useful Addresses' section at the end of the book.

DIY

If you decide to 'do-it-yourself', you will need to use specialist contractors for many of the physical tasks (eg setting up and dismantling the shell scheme, power supplies, carpeting, signing, decor, on site labour, furniture, security staff, and so on). The British Exhibition Contractors Association (BECA) will supply lists of members who conform to industry standards (including the various union rules – a pitfall for the unwary but not the problem it is sometimes said to be, provided you use BECA members).

Remember, however, that sub-contracting is never cheap so you should only sub-contract what you have to. In particular, if the venue is *truly* capable of providing the support you need at an 'all in' price, or indeed at reasonable cost, use those services rather than an outside agency.

Attracting exhibitors

First time round, this will not be an easy task. For this reason alone it is worth, initially, being modest in your aspirations and putting a realistic, and low, limit on the number of stands you will accept. This has two advantages:

(1) it makes the marketing task of attracting exhibitors less demanding; and
(2) it keeps the administrative task within your resources.

If the number is allowed to grow like Topsy, you may end up with an exhibition which is beyond the capabilities of your organization.

The actual marketing task is similar to any other and the general principles in Chapters 9 and 10 apply. If in doubt, an exhibition organizer should be contracted to sell the exhibition space.

PITFALLS TO AVOID

As ever, there are plenty of pitfalls, many of which have already been described. There are others.

Exhibitions place particular demands on venues. Depending on what is being shown, they need facilities (power, water, gas and so on), special access, set-up and break down time and, above all, space.

Most venues with a bit of space – and a banqueting suite or an old ballroom certainly provide space – would claim to be able to take exhibitions, just as they would claim to be able to cater for conferences. This is not so unless your exhibition is little more than a village bazaar – a series of stand-alone display tables.

Shell scheme

Any exhibition of quality is based on 'stands' and these can be specially constructed for the event, either by the organizer or by the exhibitors. This is the expensive course of action, applicable to the major trade shows and events like the Motor Show or Ideal Home Exhibition. The more normal practice is to set up a shell scheme, providing each exhibitor with a basic stand into which he can move furniture, displays and so on.

Each stand needs power for lighting, and many exhibitors expect telephone lines and even facilities like compressed air, gas and three-phase power.

You must therefore check the venue against your specification – and never accept the venue's plan unless it is an established and recognized exhibition venue. Even then, it is wise to check the height of the hall, and of the access (including goods lift dimensions and weight capacities), shape, power points, pillars, floor loadings and so on. Clearly, if you use sub-contractors, they will help with this and it must be remembered that the needs of the exhibition may override those of the conference in deciding the venue. One point already mentioned is that the exhibition space must be as close as possible to the meetings rooms. The number of visitors to the exhibition will be inversely proportional to the distance from the main conference area – too far and you will have an empty exhibition and a host of dissatisfied exhibitors.

Test the market

Before deciding whether to hold an exhibition alongside your conference, test the market. What competition will you face? What sort of prices can you charge for stands? It may be worth discussing your plans with one or two would-be exhibitors and offering them a free or reduced rate stand in response to help with answers to some of these questions.

Avoid cuckoos

There is a danger, already discussed, of your exhibition being too successful and 'taking over' from your conference, just like the cuckoo in the nest. Is this really what you want? You may make a lot of money, but what about the original intention behind the conference itself? Your exhibition should never prejudice your conference – it should only be used to *enhance* the conference, not destroy it.

One way of avoiding this problem is to put a strict limit on the number of stands. If your event is popular with exhibitors, you will then be in the fortunate position of not having to sell the exhibition space at all – they will come to you. Indeed, with luck, you will find your event has a higher market value because demand exceeds supply. This means you will be able to raise your prices accordingly, increasing income without increasing the administrative burden.

Theft

No, not theft during the exhibition, although security is a major headache at exhibitions (someone once said, 'if it can be moved it will be' – it is said a car was stolen from a motor show one year, but that is another story!). What may happen, if your exhibition is successful, is that an alert competitor (more often than not an exhibition organizer) will steal your idea and set up an exhibition in direct competition with your own – probably at a 'better' time of year. If this is successful, you may find they then organize a conference alongside their exhibition – and you may eventually be left with nothing.

'MINOR' PITFALLS

Exhibitions take more time to set up and to break down afterwards than it takes to set up the conference itself. Carpets may have to be laid, shell schemes installed, and then time allowed for other service contractors – and for exhibitors themselves – to 'set up shop'. All this takes time and you will need day and night access to the venue site during the set-up period – and afterwards for break down. This time costs money. Some venues allow lower charges for set-up periods – others charge the full rate for the whole period.

Many venues seem incapable of providing food and refreshments for contractors' workmen round the clock. One exhibition was actually late opening because the venue could not cater for hungry and thirsty crews at night and the workforce decamped to the nearest all-night transport cafe several miles down the road. Most venues will, of course, make special provision for 24-hour service – at a price. But you have to remember to ask for it!

Because of the nature of exhibitions associated with conferences – short bursts of activity followed by long periods of inactivity – and because conference delegates tend to drift away early especially on the last day, it is necessary to plan the exhibition timings very carefully. You do not want your delegates to witness the exhibition being dismantled before their eyes because exhibitors have decided the last afternoon is a 'waste of time'. On the other hand, there is little point in keeping exhibitors hanging around to no useful purpose, waiting for visitors who will never arrive.

The only answer to this problem is to specify the exhibition timings, but it is probably sensible to make it clear to delegates that the exhibition will close before the end of the conference. Provided the break down does not disrupt the conference (eg noise), and provided it is not visible to the conference delegates, then everyone will be satisfied.

By the same token, it is good practice to open the exhibition before the conference begins. This allows delegates to 'settle in' and view the exhibition before the first conference session, covering the ambiguity caused by an extended coffee and registration session during which delegates have little to do if they have arrived early.

Exhibitor registration

Exhibitor personnel should be registered in a similar way to conference delegates; they should have distinctive badges, perhaps in a different colour, or over-printed 'Exhibitor'. Exhibitors seldom know in advance who will be on their stands, so a permanent on-site exhibitor registration facility is needed. This should be in operation during set-up and remain open throughout the event.

Exhibitors, contractors and stand staff should always wear badges for identification and access and the number of complimentary registrations must be specified, especially if staff meals are part of the exhibitor package – if not, you will end up feeding an army.

The registration desk(s) should have the equipment and staff to cope with the anticipated number of registrations – see the section on registration procedures in Chapter 11 for further details.

Set and enforce house rules

It is sensible to specify what exhibitors can and cannot do. Failure to regulate their activities may lead to some stands being rebuilt so as to dominate the rest of the exhibition, or you will find exhibition staff roaming round the whole of the conference area accosting and harassing delegates to attract attention to their stand. Matters such as this should be covered in the exhibitors' manual: a comprehensive briefing document, often incorporating the exhibition contract, which should cover matters such as:

- rules for eligibility and selection of exhibitors;
- how spaces will be allocated;
- standards for the design, construction, decor and safety of exhibits;
- specification of shell scheme (including dimensions, power points, spotlights, furniture (if provided) and so on);
- restrictions on sound, lighting and other attention-getting devices;
- all other rules and regulations, including venue fire and safety requirements;
- schedule of fees and charges; the policy for advance deposits and full payment, cancellation charges and conditions, invoicing, settlement procedures, and so on;

- a summary of exhibitors' responsibilities and liabilities; cancellation clauses; insurance requirements;
- other information relevant to the venue, access, timings for set-up and break down, administration, exhibition opening times, registration procedures on site, security, and so on.

The list is almost endless but the better the instructions and information, the more smoothly the event will run.

IN CONCLUSION

The decision to add an exhibition alongside your conference should not be taken lightly. If you are fortunate enough to have an audience of decision makers or influencers who would be interested in seeing the latest developments in their industry, you may well be able to enhance your conference with an exhibition – and also boost your income, with all the attendant benefits.

However, the administrative task becomes very much more complicated once you embark on anything other than a minor, low-key exhibition and you run the risk of the exhibition taking over the whole event, to the detriment of the conference.

EXECUTIVE CHECKLIST

- To what extent would an exhibition enhance your conference?
- Is your audience 'attractive' to potential exhibitors?
- Will the extra funds an exhibition provides cover the additional administrative burden?
- How will you test the market to determine the viability of your proposed exhibition?
- What outside help will you need (a) to attract exhibitors, (b) to attract visitors and (c) to set up the actual exhibition?
- Is the exhibition area close enough to the meeting rooms?
- How will you ensure delegates actually visit the exhibition? Will you build exhibition viewing time into the formal programme?
- Do you check every detail of the venue exhibition space?
- Do you draw up a comprehensive exhibitors' manual and contract?
- Are you sure an exhibition really will be worthwhile?
- How will you find out details of potential exhibitors?
- Where can the exhibition be situated to ensure flow of conference delegates?
- Can tea and coffee breaks be served in the exhibition area?
- What other attractions can be held alongside the exhibition?

8

ORGANIZING EVENTS OVERSEAS

A major European association holds two members' conferences every year: both events attract around 600 delegates and 400 partners – and both events are invariably held overseas. The association has never hosted either event in its 'own' country in spite of the much greater administrative task arising from organizing two major events in two separate countries within six weeks of each other.

This example is by no means unique: an increasing number of corporate and association conferences are held overseas and many organizers never hold meetings at home. Why is this so? What are the advantages of going overseas – and what are the disadvantages?

This chapter discusses overseas conferences and meetings.

WHO GOES ABROAD?

The overseas conference market divides into three groups, the first two of which, from an organization and travel point of view, are broadly similar:

- ◆ corporate meetings – in particular, incentives;
- ◆ association conferences (home-based groups meeting overseas); and
- ◆ national chapters of international bodies travelling to join an overseas conference of their organization.

Corporate events

There is no 'typical' overseas corporate conference, even within one company. In a single year, one major UK retailing company arranged a variety of events abroad:

1. *Store directors' conference:* this event, attended by about 200 store directors and more senior executives, discussed corporate policy and future plans.
2. *Pre-retirement seminars:* two groups of about 70 long-serving personnel were taken overseas for pre-retirement briefings. The seminars were designed to prepare staff – many of whom had served in the company's department stores for 30 years or more – for retirement and to provide a memorable 'thank you'.
3. *Incentives:* two groups of 30 were taken to exotic locations to reward sales performance. Many companies offer similar incentives to reward good performance and as an encouragement for the future.

In addition, the company arranged a number of smaller events overseas, including a 'think tank' for top executives in an exclusive and luxurious hotel in Venice.

When the Americas Cup series was held in Freemantle, Australia, Perth was a popular venue during the period of the preliminary elimination rounds and the actual races, whilst Spain became a popular destination when it hosted the World Fair and Olympic Games. These are but a few examples of the wide variety of corporate conferences and meetings held in locations as far apart as Tokyo and Amsterdam, Hawaii and Majorca.

The point is that corporate meetings range from the pure incentive to the straight working conference and any combination in between (even the most lavish incentive will often contain some 'serious' elements – if only to salve the conscience of senior management).

Associations and professional bodies

These are regular international travellers: the medical and legal profession, in particular, hold a wide variety of meetings overseas. The BMA, Law Society, Electrical Contractors' Association and even travel agents often meet abroad, The International Equestrian Federation with their President, Prince Philip, held their annual conference on a Nile cruise ship which set sail from Luxor in southern Egypt. The Association of British Travel Agents won widespread and (for the Association) unwelcome publicity recently when a conference the Association had arranged for its members was double booked at the hotel venue. If the travel professionals cannot get it right, it was said, who can? We return to the problem of 'double booking' later in this chapter but suffice to say here that perhaps they should have sub-contracted the task of organizing the event to a professional organizer!

National chapters

Major international meetings are a vital source of professional and commercial information and also provide a forum for an informal and formal exchange of new ideas. Almost every international professional body holds an annual or biennial conference and large delegations attend from many countries. It is usual for these delegates to travel as a group and such movements form a significant proportion of overseas conference business.

WHY GO ABROAD?

The jet-setting business traveller will tell you that these days one hotel is very much like another, be it in London, New York or Tokyo, and he will claim that overseas travel is a boring, necessary evil, to be endured rather than enjoyed, and to be avoided whenever possible.

It would be a mistake to assume that this is the prevalent attitude. Even today, overseas travel is, for most people, a rare and stimulating experience: something to anticipate with pleasure and to enjoy to the full. Overseas travel means different things to different people; sun, foreign food, new sights and sounds, a different language, drink, shopping, education, culture – the list is almost endless. In short, most people *like* going abroad – be it for pleasure or for business, and this is the main reason who so many conferences and meetings are held overseas. Just as the mountaineer climbs a peak 'because it is there', some go abroad just because the destination is abroad – and different.

But this is not the only reason why conferences are held overseas. It can be cheaper to go abroad rather than meet at home, and the overseas event is often offered as an incentive or a reward. Some conferences are bound to be abroad for the majority of delegates: an international conference, by definition, attracts participants from many countries – often from several continents.

While the 'incentive' is a mainstay of the UK outward bound conference market, not all overseas events are 'incentives': on the contrary, a surprising number of association and corporate conferences have intensive and full working programmes (although almost all involve an element of sight-seeing, and many corporate conferences balance incentive activities with a proportion of serious business – the balance can be 90 per cent business:10 per cent incentive to as little as only 10 per cent business).

Another important factor which influences the decision is the wider choice of suitable venues overseas. There is a shortage of large, modern, first-class hotels in the UK, especially if the specification includes sports facilities such as an indoor swimming pool, squash courts, tennis courts and nearby golf. There is a wider choice overseas. The growth of the package-holiday business has brought a corresponding development of a large number of excellent hotels which meet the most demanding specification (even down to a high proportion of single rooms – most UK hotels only have a small number of single rooms but, as we saw in Chapter 2, many people do not like sharing rooms and, unlike in North America and the Far East where you pay the same rate for one, two or three occupants per room, many UK hotels charge a supplement for single occupancy of double rooms). Most large overseas hotels are easily accessible from a variety of international airports. Further, because most major conferences take place outside the peak holiday seasons, they tend to be readily available and comparatively cheap.

WHERE?

Where are all these overseas conferences held? The clever answer would be: 'almost anywhere', and, indeed, this would be true. But there are 'popular' destinations for the traveller from the UK:

Paris and Amsterdam top the list by a wide margin. The reasons for this popularity are not difficult to find. Both cities are highly accessible from the UK, being served by several flights a day from all major – and many minor – airports. In international terms, they are close-to-hand with flight times of well under one hour. What is more, the Channel Tunnel and Eurostar have added to the competition and compare very favourably with air travel on both price and travel time. These factors mean that, wherever the starting point, the journey will be easy; travel time will be minimized and, because of the large number of available flights, the most convenient departure and arrival times can be selected. One group of over 350 delegates was assembled in Amsterdam from 14 departure points as far apart as Glasgow and Exeter within a space of a couple of hours using four airlines with no more than 30 on any one aircraft.

Accessibility is not the only reason for the popularity of Amsterdam and Paris. Both are excellent tourist centres with plenty to see and do outside the conference hall. There are likely to be fewer language problems. English is the second language of Holland; most of us can muster at least a degree of conversational French. Another important consideration is the ability for delegates to 'add' on a few extra days, either before or after their conferences, at very reasonable rates. Finally, where cost is a major consideration, Amsterdam and Paris score heavily, mainly on account of the short – and correspondingly relatively cheap – flight. Amsterdam, in particular, is seen by many as a 'budget' venue.

Italy is well up the list, with Venice, Florence and Rome all very popular 'cultural' destinations for incentive, corporate and association meetings.

East coast of America   Overcapacity, especially in the off-season (which, paradoxically, is the 'on season' for conference activity), has led to a big reduction in real terms of transatlantic air fares (and the published tariffs are very negotiable). This has made Florida and the east coast of the US popular destinations. It is at present no more expensive to send a group to Florida than it is to go to Italy for the same length of event and this, along with the attraction of the US, accounts for the increased interest in this part of the world as an incentive and overseas conference destination.

Spain is the next most popular destination (mainly on account of the Balearic Isles: a very high proportion of the Spanish conference business from the UK goes to Majorca). Once again, cost is a major factor with higher air fares often offset to a considerable degree by reduced hotel costs (with, it should be noted, no reduction in standards; indeed, many hotels in Southern Europe offer superior food, drink and accommodation at considerably cheaper rates than those charged by their Northern European competitors). The greater chance of fine, warm weather, more pleasant surroundings (most hotels in Paris and Amsterdam are in heavily built up areas) and better recreational facilities are also factors which make Majorca, in particular, so attractive.

Athens is also high on the list: this city has a romantic lure which the reality of concrete and smog belies, but some of the more popular conference hotels are very fine and the ruins of the Acropolis and the archaeology of the nearby Delphi, the sun, the islands, and the surprisingly large number of flights to Athens all combine to make the city an attractive venue. Athens is also a natural choice for an event attended by delegates from Europe and the Middle or Far East. The city is situated on the main air routes, approximately 'half-way there' from either direction, and is considered to be safer politically (and, it must be said, physically) than many Middle Eastern countries.

Exotic Destinations   The organizer of incentives casts his net far and wide in search of somewhere new and exciting. Almost every exotic destination has been used and long haul venues are particularly popular (and well within the reach of many incentive budgets). The most popular incentive destinations (in order of popularity) are the US, particularly Florida and the East Coast (see above), Spain (also discussed above), Hong Kong, the Caribbean, Cyprus and Portugal. South Africa is an up and coming destination, with Sun City a popular choice. Cruising is also a popular incentive activity and even Moscow has sometimes hosted incentives although in reality the States of the former Soviet Union offer a more appropriate destination for international conferences and trade fairs.

The more exotic destinations are usually well beyond the purse of the conventional meeting, although not, it has to be said, for major international conferences organized out of, say, the US. Viewed from there, many of these exotic destinations are highly accessible and reasonably priced: the convenience of groups attending from Europe can be a minor factor when set against the wishes of larger groups from the US. Thus, many far flung cities from the Americas to the Far East are venues for major international conferences and national chapters often have to face long – and often relatively expensive – journeys in order to participate.

It is the long-haul, wide-bodied jet which made the Far East a practical proposition for conference groups from Britain. For example, Tokyo can be reached in 11½ hours non-stop from London. What is more, bearing in mind that Japan is a very expensive country, long-haul conference 'packages' can be excellent value for money. The cheapest standard air fare London–Tokyo return is around £1,150 with a minimum stay of 14 days in Japan (a more flexible fare which allows return at any time costs about £225 more). A seven-day package for a group (leaving day one, five nights accommodation, returning day seven) with some sightseeing and all meals and accommodation can cost as little as £2,300).

The organizer is, in fact, spoilt for choice. The major destinations are marketed aggressively – in particular, Hong Kong, Australia and Singapore are heavily promoted, often offering attractive packages in special promotions for incentive groups. Even China is getting in on the act. Now that it has opened up again to foreign visitors after the Tiananmen Square massacre it is an inexpensive and increasingly popular destination and Beijing and Xian, in particular, have plenty of hotels of top international standard.

One wonders whether, in the search for something 'new', some of the excellent destinations nearer to home are overlooked: why go all the way to the Far East when, in Europe, we have places like Venice and Monte Carlo and a host of other places which can be just as enjoyable, less expensive and – being closer to home – less exhausting in terms of travel and jet lag.

Are incentives different?

There are other factors which affect the choice of incentive destinations in particular. For example, the company's perception of a destination and the way it will be perceived by potential winners of the trip are an important part of the selection process. Buyers of pure incentives want destinations to sound fun and possibly exotic – this is why destinations such as Paris, Monte Carlo and New York are popular incentive destinations.

Paradoxically, exotic sounding destinations are not necessarily the most expensive as they also tend to be popular tourist destinations and so benefit from low air fares and plentiful and inexpensive hotel accommodation.

Perception can also act as a deterrent. Buyers tend to be worried about politics, and by recent events. Not everyone is happy to use destinations fresh from political turmoil – hence Israel, Russia and South Africa are viewed with some suspicion, as is Florida (but for different reasons: a few well publicized muggings and murders causing the concern).

Another factor in selecting the 'right' destination is the need to match the city or country to the group profile. What is 'old hat' for some may be the trip of a lifetime for others. Thus, the pharmaceutical, automotive and financial services industries, which have been operating incentives for sales staff for many years, tend to be the most adventurous when choosing destinations: it is these industries which are more likely to send groups to South Africa, Malaysia or even trekking in Nepal. Buyers new to incentive travel or those rewarding staff other than salesmen are more likely to be drawn to the tried and tested destinations which offer value for money, good access, and where there is less risk of things going wrong. Cyprus, Spain, Holland and France feature high on the list for these buyers.

But even those who opt for the exotic in reality want to play safe. It is an old cliché, 'When in Rome, do as the Romans do'. In fact, we like to take our national cultural 'print' with us, which is perhaps why hotels the world over tend to offer American/European environments and cuisine, and why few venture into the real world of the exotic destinations they choose. The reasons for this are not merely cultural: firms cannot risk the health and safety of their key staff in areas of poverty, disease, poor food and poor infrastructure.

That said, buyers of incentive travel expect packed programmes for their incentives. And this leads to another paradox: provided they know they will have a good time, many do not seem to mind where they go!

You might be tempted to ask whether all this expenditure on incentives is justified. Do they work? The short answer is 'yes'. The qualified answer is yes, provided they are used properly. Salespeople, in particular, respond to goals and if the reward is a well publicized and spectacular incentive, there is no doubt that they respond to the challenge. As one organizer puts it, 'People on the trip last year would sell their grandmother to win a place this year!' For people in the company in question, the incentives are so successful that they have become a way of life for the winners. There is little sympathy for the losers – those whose performance is not good enough to win a place. To quote one salesperson: 'There would have to be something wrong with me if I didn't win. There is a bit of bad feeling when people have missed the target by a small margin. But it is tough – their chance is the same as mine. They've had the same training and they've got the same equipment. It's their fault – perhaps they shouldn't have gone shopping instead of working. It's the ones who work who are successful.'

And that, in many ways, is what incentives are all about.

One final word on incentives. Participants have mixed feelings about whether spouses/partners should accompany them. Including partners can be seen as a thank you to spouses in particular who provide behind the scenes support and encouragement to their often frantically pressurized partners. However, partners sometimes feel left out as the company teams party, crack 'in' jokes and talk shop. By the same token, some participants are inhibited by the presence of their partners. As one organizer explains, 'People who are usually wild become very quiet when accompanied by their spouses!' As always, the decision depends upon the group, the objectives, the destination... and on the budget.

How big is the typical group?

There are no set norms; one London-based group travel specialist has handled groups from as few as eight up to 1,400. The average works out at around 70–100.

How long is the typical event?

Overseas events in Europe tend to last three days: delegates travel to arrive in the late afternoon or evening and stay three nights. Surprisingly, most overseas events take place over a weekend. There are two reasons for this:

◆   Hotels (like those in the United Kingdom) tend to be occupied by business travellers for much of the week, but there is little local demand for Friday, Saturday and Sunday nights. The incoming group is therefore valuable marginal business which means that competitive rates can be offered for rooms which would otherwise have been empty – or have been filled with less profitable weekend break holiday business. Better air fares are often available at weekends, making the whole economic package very attractive.

◆ In selecting weekends, the delegates lose less time from work. For the private delegate, this minimizes the time he may have to take off, perhaps out of his holiday and, for the corporate group, the company in effect holds the event, be it an incentive or a working conference, in the employees' own time.

More distant events, for example in China and the Far East, tend to be longer, the norm being around one week.

Is cost a critical factor?

Cost is usually, but not always, a factor in planning overseas events. However, cost is seldom a *critical* factor (except for UK delegates to international meetings who, because they pay their own fares, invariably look for the best deal). Many buyers adopt a budget-based approach: they fix a budget at an early stage and tailor the event accordingly. Budget considerations will usually dictate a destination such as, for example, Amsterdam as opposed to Hawaii and, as we have already seen, it is the incentive that usually commands the higher budget.

Once the budget has been agreed, the appropriate 'package' can be worked out between the organizer, his travel agent and other interested parties. If, once detailed planning is under way, it is apparent that the original budget was a little too low, it is usually possible for the sponsor to accept a small increase in the interest of having the best possible package (although this is not true for association meetings where the cheaper package will almost invariably be selected). Once the final budget is agreed, further changes should not be necessary.

All this is not to say that the costs of individual elements of the budget are treated in a manner different from usual business practice: good housekeeping and striking the best deal possible is as essential a process in planning an overseas conference as it is in any business purchase. The competitive prices available abroad *vis-à-vis* those available at home have been mentioned several times in this chapter and it is often the savings over prices at home which make the overseas event a feasible proposition in the first place. Similarly, the discount air fares available for group travel are an essential element of the budget, and hence an important factor which influences the initial decision to take a conference out of the country.

With whom does the decision rest?

Corporate events   It is rare for the actual sponsor of the corporate event to decide the destination. As a general rule, it is the personnel director or a senior administrative executive who sanctions the overseas conference. Thus, the sales or marketing executive may initiate the idea of taking a particular conference abroad, and he will inevitably be involved in planning the content of the event, but the final authority for the overall budget, and the actual decision to go overseas, may rest with someone who will not be involved in the event itself. (It is worth noting here that sometimes going overseas is vetoed even when it is manifestly less expensive than holding the event at home. As one managing director of a very successful – and profitable company – remarked: 'How can I sanction an overseas incentive when I am about to close a factory with the loss of over 1,000 jobs?')

Association events   In the case of an association or professional body, the decision is normally one of consensus, often at the end of protracted consideration in committee. Internal – and external – political considerations will often be paramount. The cachet associated with hosting a large international conference is considerable, both to the host nation organizing committee (often a semi-independent, or even autonomous, professional body) and to the host nation government – not to mention the venue town or city. There is often an intensive lobbying process designed to influence the decision. A US firm runs a computerized database which lists every major international conference, giving all previous venues (by host country and town or city) and, where known, future destinations (venues are often selected several years in advance). This information is invaluable to national tourist boards and convention bureaux in their attempts to woo prestigious (and lucrative) international conferences.

Planning timings

The long lead-time in planning association events has already been discussed. Typically, an association will decide on a venue two or more years in advance. There is always a degree of risk associated with this type of conference: the final numbers are seldom known more than a few months beforehand since the decision to attend is usually made by individuals who have to consider whether it is worth spending their own money on the conference. Most delegates prefer to leave this decision until as late as possible and may wait until the firm programme, speakers and list of papers are published. Venues and organizers therefore face a degree of risk and uncertainty for much of the planning period and late cancellations or lower than anticipated numbers are not uncommon. Sometimes the reverse is the case and numbers far exceed the original estimates.

These problems do not affect either the venue or the organizer of the typical corporate event. Although the planning time is considerably shorter (it is rarely greater than six months), numbers are firm and the risk of cancellation is low once the decision is taken.

What are the 'popular' times of year?

It used to be a fact that the 'high season' for overseas conferences was in March, April and May and in September, October and November (although November was less popular). Organizers tended to avoid the summer because it is the peak holiday season. The only significant exception to this rule is that the UK hosts a large number of incoming international conferences during the summer months. These are held in university accommodation which can accommodate large numbers in students' bedrooms which have been vacated for the summer. Universities also have fine lecture halls which are ideal for the larger professional and academic conferences.

The seasonal pattern has changed in recent years, again thanks to over-capacity on most international routes caused by the ubiquitous wide-bodied jumbo jets. Nowadays, the season seems to last all the year round. In particular, exotic destinations and the sun, coupled with inexpensive packages and non-stop long-haul flights, have extended the busy season through the whole of the winter.

What are the organizational problems?

This book seeks to show how to organize successful conferences and meetings: the detailed work involved in planning and running a particular event is much the same wherever the event is held. When it is to be organized overseas, the planner is faced with a range of extra tasks and problems which are associated with transporting the group to and from the venue and making arrangements with the venue itself. These are basically *travel* matters of the sort handled by travel agents as a matter of routine: airline bookings, tickets, couriers, transfers, ground handling arrangements and close liaison with overseas hotels.

The conference organizer is therefore well advised to appoint a travel agent to handle all travel and overseas administrative matters. Although a local travel agent will probably claim to be able to undertake this task, it is advisable to appoint a specialist in group travel. In the UK, the Guild of Business Travel Agents has some 40 members, many of which have group travel departments (although only some specialize in conference travel). Another trade group, which specializes in incentive travel, is ITMA (The Incentive Travel and Meetings Association). Its full members (about 30 firms) all hold Air Travel Organisers Licence bonds (ATOL) and additional financial security in line with the EC Directive on Package Travel. There are other travel agents outside the Guild and ITMA who, although smaller, are equally good at handling conference business, but it is as well to check their credentials.

These experts have all the knowledge, resources and skills to handle every conceivable overseas conference. They provide couriers to accompany delegates and to look after the group while it is abroad and they undertake all the detailed planning in the host country, including hotel rooming, ground travel and transfers and arrangements at the venue. They will advise you of the 'best' times of year for each destination, help you avoid local bank holidays and festivals and other major events; they will know the countries you plan to visit – and they will have key contacts; they will ensure you do not offend local religious, ethnic or political sensibilities and advise you what hotels to use; and they will even make sure the 'local' food will be acceptable to your delegates. For the inexperienced corporate or association executive, this work is full of pitfalls and, indeed, is almost certainly beyond his resources. In short, the golden rule is: appoint a specialized travel agent for all overseas events.

There is seldom any extra cost involved. All travel agents live off commissions which are not available to the layman. Further, travel agents can usually negotiate better deals with airlines and hotels, often by virtue of the large amount of business they place. If the travel agent does need a fee for this work, this will be made clear from the outset and can be built into the budget with the confidence of knowing that there will be no hidden extra costs at a later stage.

Production houses sometimes undertake the organization task for the whole event. There are reasons for this: the production (perhaps for the gala dinner or the keynote address) can be the major part of the overall organizational task (and of the budget: the cost of presentation for one 5-day/4-night conference for 500 delegates in Athens was greater than the remaining cost of the event!). It is for this reason that production houses like to take everything under their wing in order to maintain control, cut duplicated effort and conflicts of interest.

Choosing a travel agency   Having made sure companies on your short-list are financially sound (which, in effect means excluding any without ATOL), it is sensible to ask two or three agencies to pitch for your business. However, you must be clear in your mind what criteria you will apply when making your final choice. Buying merely on price is foolhardy: anything outstandingly inexpensive will be so for a reason. You will either end up being saddled with a massive extra bill, or you will receive inferior service and an inferior package.

You should give your short-listed agencies as much information as you can about your company, the participants, your reasons for running the event and your history of incentive travel. And, of course, they need your budget, your dates – and give them time to prepare their proposals. The better your brief, the better should be the pitches you receive.

When the proposals come in, look at what is included in the package. Make a list of everything, from printed luggage labels to welcome drinks and gifts in rooms on arrival – and of course the overall package itself.

The final choice is bound to include some subjectivity: if you like the people and the proposal, you may well do best to go with that agency rather than one which is a little less expensive but does not have the right 'chemistry'.

WHAT ARE THE SNAGS?

It would be idle to pretend that there are no snags or disadvantages in taking conferences overseas, or that there are no pitfalls for the unwary.

The principal problems come under one (or more) of the following headings:

1. Weather.
2. Disruption because of strikes.
3. Co-ordination problems.
4. Security.
5. Political problems and local custom and practice.
6. International and local wars.
7. Natural disasters (floods, earthquakes, etc).

Weather

Since many overseas conferences are held in the winter, there is always the risk of disruption – and even cancellation – due to bad weather. Fog is, of course, the main problem since most overseas travel is by air. Airline schedules are invariably thrown into chaos by fog, and the effects can carry over for a day or two after the fog has dispersed. At best, the outward or return journey may be delayed; at worst, the event may have to be abandoned – something the wise organizer will insure against (see page 233).

Delays can be frustrating – and expensive. If the outward journey is delayed, the whole programme may be affected, with dire results. The problem is no less severe if delegates from only one destination are delayed, since their late arrival will still disrupt proceedings. Even the late arrival of one individual can be a disaster if he or she is a key contributor. One management training course had to be abandoned because the professor who had been engaged to run the programme spent an uncomfortable few days fog-bound in Germany while his pupils, who had been drawn together from fog-free Britain, Scandinavia, France and Italy, spent three days of enforced idleness in the pleasant surroundings of Monaco at its 'winter's best'.

Fog can be equally disruptive at the end of an event: it may be impossible for a group to leave because an incoming aircraft is delayed. Failure to vacate, for whatever reason, can be serious if there is an incoming group expecting to take over the hotel. This problem has often resulted in friction and acrimonious debate between venues and the incoming and outgoing groups.

In the worst extreme, an event may have to be cancelled due to weather problems. This is a risk which always faces the organizer of the overseas conference.

Outside the winter months, disruption caused by weather is rare – but there is little relief: the airways in Europe are literally clogged with traffic. As a result both charter and scheduled flights are often subject to delay. Although seldom catastrophic, these delays can be irritating for passengers and take the gilt off the gingerbread if they last more than a few hours.

Strikes

Although less of a problem than they were a few years ago, strikes, especially those involving airline pilots and staff, and air traffic controllers, can have disruptive effects similar to those of fog described above. Less disastrous, although just as inconvenient for the individual, is the strike by baggage handlers which can cause all sorts of delays and annoyance. It is unfortunate that such strikes are commonplace, as most seasoned travellers are uncomfortably aware.

Co-ordination

The reader will, by now, be well aware that the overseas conference needs a lot more planning and co-ordination than the event at home. The bigger the event, the more complex the task of the co-ordinator, especially for conferences where delegates are to be assembled from a variety of starting points. This does not mean that the overseas event is not worth the extra work and hassle. On the contrary, if the organizer and his travel agent have done their work properly, the delegate will enjoy the event – blissfully unaware of the detailed planning and organization behind the scenes. That said, the prospective organizer should at least be aware of the magnitude of the task being tackled, and he should assemble the necessary resources to handle the extra work involved.

Security

In these troubled times, security has to be a major consideration even if the risks are perceived as opposed to real. There was a dramatic reduction in conference traffic from the US to Europe at the time of the Gulf War – and it took a long time for confidence to return.

In some countries, the threat is very real and it would be unwise to contemplate a destination where the risk is such that delegates would feel ill at ease. The rule must be: if in doubt, do not go to that country. There is always the risk of the unexpected and, as bombings in London demonstrate, even the most stable democracies can have their problems.

Personal precautions   All the risks – mainly to property – with which most travellers are familiar (even Mr Gorbachev had his gold watch stolen from his hotel room in Germany) apply equally to individual members of groups. Indeed in some respects they are greater since sub-groups of delegates often venture into night clubs and bars which they would not frequent on family holidays.

Credit cards   Particular care has to be taken with credit cards. 'Cloning' cards either electronically or from carbons – and from stolen originals – is big business in some countries. These risks apply to individual and corporate cards alike.

PITFALLS AND PROBLEMS

There are plenty of potential pitfalls and problems, many of which can be avoided.

Health

Contrary to the popular assumption, it is possible to drink tap water south of the English Channel without risking typhoid or some other dire disease. Nevertheless, there are precautions to be taken when visiting some countries. Smallpox has been eradicated, but various injections and inoculations are advised before visiting many tropical countries.

Many overseas travellers – conference delegates included – *do* fall ill, usually with stomach and bowel disorders. Most of these illnesses are self-inflicted and occur within the first 48 hours of arrival: unwise eating and drinking, taking ice in drinks – or even drinking local tap water, and foolhardy exposure to the sun are the root causes of 99 per cent of all health problems experienced by the overseas traveller. The solution lies in self-discipline and moderation, and in effective pre-journey briefing.

Climate and the effects of high altitudes can cause problems for the unwary; so can air-conditioning (many people who are not used to air-conditioning experience chest problems after a few days). Advice on the clothing to take and the possible effects of temperature, humidity and weather should be given in written briefings issued well in advance.

Many company groups take their own doctors with them: often a wise (and financially sound) precaution. Travel insurance, with adequate medical cover and repatriation arrangements, is a must. One member of an incentive group in India was unfortunate enough to be bitten on his heel by a cobra. He was given excellent treatment by a local doctor but the hospital was a grim experience. He shared a ward with a leper and a madman and was more than grateful for the speedy 'Medivac' to the UK.

Within Europe, most countries have varying levels of reciprocal arrangements with our own NHS to provide medical cover to qualifying visitors. However, the rules are often not understood and organizers are well advised to obtain, and study, the requisite leaflet on the subject, E111, which can be obtained from local Department of Health offices.

Jet-lag affects some more than others. One seasoned and frequent traveller admits he needs one day 'recovery time' for every two hours of time change. And he says people who claim they need less recovery time in fact rarely perform well until they have passed the time his formula suggests. If the destination is in a time-zone more than three or fours ahead or behind the departure point, most delegates will therefore suffer some of the effects of jet-lag. The programme should allow for this. One group which went to Dubai from the UK (a time difference of plus four hours) overcame the jet-lag difficulty by keeping to UK timings throughout their conference. The locals thought the group idle (since it started so late in the day which, in any case, begins earlier than is the norm in Britain), but the group made up by working the afternoon when many locals take a long break.

Group travel: safety considerations

A major international company considered holding a conference and incentive for its top 20 sales executives in Egypt but abandoned the idea when it was discovered that it was not possible to assemble the group in one day without having four or more executives on one flight. As Manchester United football team discovered to its cost in the tragic crash at Munich Airport in 1958, if too many key personnel travel on one aircraft, an accident can result in their loss. But, surprisingly, the lesson had not been learnt nearly 40 years later when all the delegates from Northern Ireland flying to a conference in Scotland were killed when their RAF Chinook helicopter crashed on the Mull of Kintyre. Ten members of the RUC, nine Army intelligence officers and six MI5 officers perished along with the RAF crew of four. The accident, which did irreparable harm to the security services in Northern Ireland, exposed the folly of allowing so many key personnel to fly in one aircraft – a lesson still not learnt by far too many companies who still have no corporate 'rules' in this regard.

Perhaps a more important consideration is the wording of the company insurance policy which may well dictate how many people may fly together. This factor may well restrict the number of potential venues.

Passport problems

Some countries will not accept delegates from certain other black-listed states. For example, Israelis are not admitted to many Middle Eastern countries. One conference had to switch venues at very short notice when it was discovered that Israel was sending a delegation. Fortunately, a country with a more relaxed attitude to that of the original host was found a month beforehand and the conference was able to proceed.

All passports should be checked before any overseas conference to ensure there are no offending visas. Fortunately, most airlines double-check before departure since they have to repatriate offending would-be visitors, but it is obviously better to avoid the embarrassment of such late problems by checking this detail well beforehand.

Short stay visitors to the US have not had to have a visa since July 1988 *provided* they are in possession of a valid return ticket when they arrive in America (and provided they travel with an airline which participates in the scheme – practically all now do so).

Freight

It is not unusual to send freight – by air or sea – containing papers and even technical equipment for an overseas conference. Documentation and customs clearance at the receiving end can cause seemingly endless problems and delays. A consignment of material to one Middle Eastern country was opened by customs and found to contain material which referred to Israel. The whole consignment was seized and vital papers for the conference were lost.

Many organizers also overlook possible problems when they bring freight back into the UK after their events. Problems over documentation and customs clearance can apply on the return journey, especially if you bring back less than you took out. A recent consignment of technical equipment for a conference in La Palma had a trouble-free outward journey but was delayed for several days on the return to the UK for exactly this reason. Meticulous attention to detail when preparing freight documentation is essential.

Technical problems

Voltages, electrical plugs and sockets and even television systems and standards differ from country to country. A speaker hoping to use a British VHS video-tape in the US will be frustrated: the standard is PAL and it is little use taking playback equipment unless arrangements are made for a special 240V supply (the US mains is run at 110V).

Contracts with venues

Contract laws vary widely from country to country and it is essential to check liability; this is something a specialist travel agent should be able to undertake and on which he should give expert advice.

Value Added Tax

The rules vary from country to country and it is well worth taking the trouble to find out what VAT (if any) you can reclaim on overseas expenditure (and, indeed, what you can purchase free of local duties). For example, as mentioned in Chapter 4, it is possible to reclaim VAT on at least some expenditure in many EC countries.

VAT on the non-tour element of group travel, mentioned in Chapter 4, causes endless problems to the tour operators. The group budget is normally only marginally affected, but organizers should check the position of their events with their travel agents.

Currency

Many countries still have very strict currency controls. It is usually not a problem to move money out of the UK to almost any destination overseas, but the reverse may not be true. The organizer of an event involving delegates from countries with currency restrictions should insist on advance payment, preferably in a specified currency (for example, US dollars): payment in a restricted national currency may be an embarrassment if that currency cannot subsequently be changed into another.

In spite of the plans for a Single European Currency, we live in an era of widely fluctuating exchange rates. It is possible to enter into forward contracts at fixed rates to gain protection against unexpected extra costs arising from changes in exchange rates. Since most events are arranged well in advance, and since no-one can predict what will happen in the volatile currency markets, 'buying forward' can provide protection and peace of mind. The major banks all operate these schemes.

Special diets

Special diets are not always readily available overseas and must therefore be ordered well in advance. The same applies on long-haul flights. The airline must be advised of special dietary needs so that they can make the necessary provisions.

Insurance

You will have observed that there are extra risks associated with overseas events. Failure to vacate (ie, not being able to vacate the venue by the agreed time – perhaps due to flight delays), or double booking (where the incoming group finds the destination hotel fully booked and occupied) can lead to considerable unforeseen additional expenditure. Some risks can be completely unpredictable: when Princess Grace of Monaco was killed (see Chapter 4) all music and dancing was banned in Monaco; an expensive product launch involving dealers from all over Europe had to be cancelled at less than 24 hours' notice. As we saw in Chapter 4, few companies even consider the additional risks associated with conferences. By the same token whilst most of us are aware of the need for health cover when we travel overseas, few think about the commercial risks of delay, cancellation and abandonment of overseas conferences.

Fortunately, it is relatively easy to insure against these risks. Several brokers offer policies specifically designed to protect organizers against loss due to the hazards described above. This cover is inexpensive and a number of organizations have been spared serious losses by insuring their overseas conferences.

Medical cover

It is essential to ensure the group has adequate insurance to cover medical expenses incurred overseas (see also the comments under 'Health' on pages 229 and 230).

A FEW TIPS

Inspection visits

The organizer of an overseas event should always insist on an inspection visit even if he has appointed a specialist travel agent. This visit is normally included as part of the agent's standard charges, which means that it is not an extra charge on the organizer's budget. The importance of the inspection visit has already been emphasized in Chapter 2. An overseas inspection visit is every bit as important as the visit for a home-based event. The rules and methodology outlined in Chapter 2 hold just as well for overseas inspection visits, except that there is more to check, plan and discuss: time is invariably limited and, once back at home, there is no going back for a second check or to find out some overlooked detail!

Because some standards in overseas venues fall short of those required by UK and EC laws, conference organizers need to pay extra attention to a number of matters which they might take for granted at home:

1. *Hygiene*   Anyone organizing a conference abroad should inspect kitchens and be particularly aware of basic points such as the fact that ice could be made from non-potable water, buffets attract flies if left uncovered – and quickly deteriorate if not refrigerated. You should therefore inspect the way food is stored, how and where it is prepared and how it is transported. You should notify venues of your specific requirements to eliminate – or at least reduce – the risks of food poisoning.
2. *Fire*   Regulations can be lax in some countries, and enforcement weak or non-existent. Points to check include:

◆ All exits should be lit and fire exits should not be locked, should be unimpeded by rubbish, stored furniture, exhibition stands and so on.

◆ Liaise with local fire authorities (they may have powers to issue immediate prohibition of any meeting they consider dangerous).

◆ Be aware that disabled delegates can cause separate problems, as can the elderly and children.

◆ Trained stewards and staff are essential.

◆ Fire doors should be kept closed (and should not be locked (*qv*)).

◆ You must not accept more delegate registrations than the capacity of the venue or meeting room. It is necessary to have a separate 'satellite' area with closed circuit television rather than make do by restricting or blocking aisles with extra chairs.

◆ It is the organizer's responsibility to display temporary fire exit signs if existing fire exit signs are obscured by stage sets, etc.

◆ Organizers should not bring hazardous material into a venue, and all temporary lighting and other electrical circuits must be thoroughly tested for safety (most fires are started by faulty electrical wiring).

◆ If you are organizing an exhibition, you must provide separate storage rooms for boxes and packing materials. You must also provide extra fire extinguishers.

◆ It is imperative that you read venue contracts, especially the terms for liability (see below).

3. *Liability* The need for organizers to ensure they have adequate insurance to cover against an event being cancelled, failure to vacate and so on is stressed elsewhere in the book. As contract law and liability varies from country to country, it is necessary to seek the advice of an insurance specialist.

The importance of reading venue contracts has already been stressed. What if the venue has no contract? In the UK the organizers would normally be held liable under Common or Civil Law for any loss, damage or bodily injury caused by the venue's own negligence, both of their staff and probably their sub-contractors as well. The situation may be similar or even worse overseas (for example, you could face unlimited fines, detention and confiscation of goods). Again, it is prudent to seek the advice of a specialist insurer: the addresses of three specialist brokers are given at the end of the book.

Co-ordinating the departure

The need for a good briefing prior to an overseas conference has already been mentioned. The following paragraphs provide further advice on how to keep the departing group together (and happy) and how to simplify essential procedures.

If possible, the group should be assembled at a convenient hotel the evening before the departure (or, for an afternoon departure, the morning of departure day). This is clearly not always possible, especially when several departure airports are involved, although the advice which follows can be applied equally well to a number of dispersed groups.

Having assembled the group, it is possible to do several things:

◆ Individuals can be 'checked-in' and issued with their airline tickets as they arrive.
◆ The group can be given a comprehensive verbal briefing in order to ensure everyone knows where to be, and when; what is expected of them and what to expect (right down to when tips are expected and how much, and delicate matters about how women should – or should not – dress in public). In addition, last minute advice on clothing for the journeys can be offered, queries can be answered and fears allayed.
◆ Baggage can be taken away to be taken to the airport as a single load. This relieves individuals of the worry and physical inconvenience of lugging bags around prior to departure (although, for security reasons, individuals have to identify and check in their own bags at the airport). By the same token, at the destination luggage can be taken in bulk to the hotels and placed in delegates' rooms. An 'alpha-numerical' bag labelling scheme can greatly simplify baggage handling – see below.
◆ Boarding passes can be issued to individuals as they alight from their coaches.
◆ Individuals identify their own suitcases and check them in – note that, if the group is large, it is usually possible to arrange special check-in desks for the group.
◆ It is worth considering taking bulk orders for duty-free goods to save individuals having to worry about this chore. One very organized company took all the orders well before the event, shipped the bulk goods out to the destination and issued individual orders at the end of the trip!

Baggage labels   One tour operator gives each individual a set of baggage labels marked with that person's unique alpha-numeric code: the letter indicates the hotel at the destination and the number of the individual person. This makes it possible to line up cases and bags in numerical order at the departure airport, making identification much easier, and to sort bags into hotel 'lots' at the arrival destination (even where local porters cannot read Anglo-Saxon names).

Airline security   We are all familiar with the higher levels of security necessary to prevent terrorist attacks and bombings. The procedures described above will satisfy the security requirements of most airports and airlines.

Keep the group together

This is easier said than done, especially if there is a delay at the departure airport. One group suffered a four-hour delay at Heathrow Airport. Crowded at the best of times, the terminal was little short of bedlam. The desperate courier actually missed the flight because he was searching for wayward members of the party. He eventually tracked them down in one of the bars, very tipsy and quite oblivious to the last calls for their flight.

'Welcome' touches

Some organizers use in-flight time for additional briefings and even for part of the event programme. Clearly this is only possible when the whole aircraft is occupied by the group, but even if the group is only part of the total passenger load, a 'special' welcome message from the pilot can create a favourable impression.

An interesting variation to the verbal in-flight briefing was used by an oil company: the tour operator produced a special eight-page in-flight newspaper for the event which included information about the conference, the hotel, planned social activities, some useful Portuguese phrases (the event was in Portugal) and a travel quiz. It also contained instructions to help speed the group through the arrival airport and on to their coaches (where, incidentally, they filled in the hotel registration forms to save more time). The idea of using a paper in this way was to prevent boredom on the flight and develop enthusiasm for the conference. The informative sections – giving well-presented company information – also had the effect of saving time at the annual conference, where such information would usually be communicated.

It is usually possible to ease the arrival and make the group feel very welcome at the entry airport. Bulk clearance and handling of baggage has already been suggested. Another welcome touch is to have a large sign, possibly with the appropriate logo, to welcome delegates. A special information desk should be set up and coaches should be clearly identified with the name of the group and/or event and the destination hotel.

Similarly, at the hotel, a separate check-in should be arranged and a welcome folder, gift and possibly fruit or flowers can be placed in the delegate's bedroom. These little details are easy to arrange and can be inexpensive; they do a great deal to make delegates feel welcome.

Hotel check-out

It is usual to expect delegates to settle accounts for extras (for example, drinks, telephone calls and so on) before departure. This can create problems if the number of delegates is large. One successful conference ended on a sour note when the problem had not been anticipated and departing guests were kept waiting to check out – some missed coaches to the airport and hence flights home. Others departed without paying, leaving the hotel and organizer to haggle over the responsibility for unpaid extras. Most of the delegates blamed the hotel for the debacle. In fact the organizer was to blame for failing to warn the hotel in advance. The hotel could then have geared itself up and, possibly, have arranged an express check-out (using credit card slips – a system favoured by many of the larger hotels).

Speakers and VIPs

Speakers and VIPs should always be given separate treatment. They should be individually met on arrival and taken on by car to their hotel rather than by coach. One organizer of a major international event at Monaco arranged helicopters to whisk VIPs and speakers direct from the tarmac at Nice airport to the Monaco heliport, saving the long and tedious road journey. One visiting speaker, a leading American politician, was most impressed by this reception: 'Better than anything I have had in the States,' he declared, 'and the view of the coast is something I will always remember.'

That remark, in essence, captures the whole concept of the overseas conference. Whatever the event, wherever it is held, and for however large or small a group, it should be a pleasant and memorable experience for every delegate. This means, more than ever, meticulous planning, imagination, and a fine attention to detail by the conference organizer. If it is worth doing, it is worth doing well!

EXECUTIVE CHECKLIST

- ◆ Have you ever considered arranging an event overseas?
- ◆ Did you know it could be cheaper to hold a conference overseas?
- ◆ Did you know that there is a wider choice of first-class hotels with sports and recreational facilities overseas?

- Do you adopt a budget-based approach to planning overseas conferences?
- Who authorizes overseas group travel in your organization and what criteria dictate the decision?
- Do you appoint a specialist group travel agency for your overseas events? If not – why not?
- Do you have an alternative plan in case weather or strikes delay or prevent your overseas event?
- Do you brief your group(s) before departure? Do you assemble them beforehand for check-in and briefing? Could you use an alpha-numeric baggage labelling system?
- Do you legislate against passport problems?
- Do you insure against the extra risks associated with overseas group travel?

9

ORGANIZING CONFERENCES FOR PROFIT

RISK

You may have noticed how many public, or commercial, events are promoted these days: conferences on every conceivable topic from architecture and the environment to global warming and women in management, seminars, on a bewildering variety of subjects, one-day and residential programmes for management, professional people, salesmen and accountants... the list is endless. One must assume that all these public events are successful and profitable – or are they?

Any hotel manager will tell you a different story – of organizers who, full of optimism, book facilities for large numbers of people and who, at short notice, drastically reduce numbers or even cancel their events due to poor support. These organizers are not deliberately over-optimistic. It costs a great deal to promote even a small public event. No one would set out to do so unless he thought the response would be good enough not only to cover the set-up costs but also to make a reasonable profit.

What goes wrong? There is, of course, no simple answer. Some events are very successful. Association conferences can make substantial profits and there are plenty of well established firms in the business of promoting public events. It is, however, a very competitive market. In any competitive situation there are winners and losers, and the losers tend to be the less strong, the less well established and the less professional. The trouble is that most of us at some time or other think we have a worthwhile subject for a conference or seminar. A quick, back-of-the envelope calculation demonstrates that, if successful, the event would make a lot of money and we are tempted to proceed with the arrangements without first preparing a proper marketing plan. This requires much more than a few thoughts and a sketchy budget. Before even deciding whether or not to proceed, careful analysis, research and planning is needed to try to find out whether the proposition is viable. In this chapter we examine some of the factors which should be considered before deciding whether to stage a public event. (Throughout the chapter, the words 'public event' are used to describe any event which is organized on a commercial basis and which the delegates pay to attend – including association and trade conferences as well as those which are 'sold' on the open market).

Public events are big business. They range from huge international congresses to small one-day seminars. The medical profession, in particular, has a wide choice of national and international meetings (there is even a specialist magazine for the medical meetings business in the United States) and association events often attract delegates by the thousand. A number of specialist companies arrange everything from large conferences to small educational events. One British company arranges about a dozen large conferences and nearly 600 other seminars and training sessions, briefings and workshops every year and has a turnover of well over £5 million.

Some professional bodies and associations have their own conference staff; others form ad hoc committees to run specific events on a do-it-yourself basis. But professional conference organizers are often called in, either for a fee or in partnership with the sponsor to arrange many of the larger events.

But whatever the event, and whoever does the actual organizing, all face a risk when they decide to organize an event on a commercial basis. This chapter is aimed at anyone who organizes events which delegates pay to attend. Some associations do not consciously organize conferences for profit – indeed, some subsidize their annual conferences and other training activities as part of the service to their members. Nevertheless, unlike the organizer of the 'in-house' event, they, along with those with purely profit orientated motives, are operating in a commercial environment and must therefore adopt a very different approach to their task.

Financial risks   The financial rewards can be considerable, but considerable risks are involved. The main costs of running a 'venture' conference break down into the following principal elements:

1. The organizer's overhead costs.
2. Selling costs.
3. The event running costs.
4. Speakers' fees and expenses.

If an event has to be cancelled due to lack of support, the first two, which are committed at an early date, represent lost expenditure. Apart from cancellation charges, the last two costs are committed later and can often be saved if any early decision is taken to cancel due to poor response.

A typical one-day event for 100 or so delegates can cost between £15,000 and £20,000 to promote. This figure includes 10,000 to 15,000 mailshots at about 35p each (although mail-outs of 40,000 or more are not uncommon), some display advertising, the cost of PR, and some telephone follow-up. The 'normal' success rate is well under 1 per cent for events publicized on the open market. Associations achieve better success rates from their members but, even so, the cost of promoting any event is considerable.

Larger, international events are much more expensive to promote: the promotional budget for a three-day event for 500 people could be as high as £50,000.

However, whatever the event, once the administrative, selling and speakers' costs have been covered, the contribution per delegate is considerable. The marginal cost per delegate is not high and the large proportion of the fees of each delegate above break-even point is clear profit. A successful conference for 100 or so delegates can make a gross profit in the region of £20,000. Larger events generate greater profits and even conferences run on a 'no profit' basis can make considerable surpluses if attendance is well up on expectations. A recent association conference, which was not intended to make any profit, actually made over £20,000 for just this reason.

But the stakes are high. In the worst case, having spent £10,000 to £15,000 promoting an event, no-one registers and the investment is totally lost. Conference organizers spend a great deal of time planning and researching ideas for conferences, but, to quote one professional organizer: 'No-one I know can predict just how many delegates will come to a particular conference. It is a large risk business. To attract the right number of participants, you must have the right subject at the right time covered in the right way.'

This chapter is about reducing the risks. You can never eliminate risk – there is no such thing as certain success – but you can reduce the risks to sensible levels. The organizer of the in-company or in-house event is very fortunate because he can easily forecast the number of people who will attend, the figures being dependent upon an organizational policy decision. The organizer of the public event has no such prior knowledge. The success of his event depends entirely on the efficacy of his marketing campaign. He has to invest a lot of time and money to attract people with no certainty of success. Before he can know how many delegates he will have – and hence the administrative and practical problems involved – he must mount a marketing campaign. This involves promoting and selling a viable 'product' in a competitive market.

THE PRODUCT

In general terms, people will only buy a product – be it soap powder, a car, a book or, indeed, a place on a seminar – if they think the product will satisfy their needs. It is useful to think of a conference or seminar as a 'product' because, by thinking in this way, we can adopt an entirely different approach to the marketing problem. There is a wide choice of most services and manufactured products which people can buy and in this respect the public event is very similar. We may think our particular product is unique, special and attractive, but the public will view it as yet another item competing for their time and money. They have to decide whether to invest in our event, another one, or perhaps in something entirely different. The purchase decision is complex but, in general, people compare relevant products on the market and choose the one which, in their view, is most likely to give them what they want at a price they are prepared to pay.

If, then, we plan to sell an event, we must look at what we are offering from the customer's point of view. What will make him want to attend? The customer will consider many factors – for example, where the conference is being held, the cost and the date of the event. However, it is the content of the event which will first attract the customer's interest. If this is good enough he will go to considerable lengths to attend. It is very common for one-day events to attract people from overseas and larger, international conferences are often of vital importance to delegates who congregate from all over the world, incurring expenses and inconvenience which are tolerated because of the quality of the 'product'.

Who are your customers?

It is, then, essential to create a product which meets the wants of those you wish to attract. This is not as easy as it sounds. Right from the start you will have an outline event in mind, but your ideas may not be firm. By deciding who might want to attend you can build a programme to meet their wants. Who are 'they'? Who are your potential customers? An association or professional body will know who its members are and how to contact them. If you are selling an event on the open market, it is not so easy to identify the people you are likely to attract. However, if you scrutinize the market you usually find that the members of that market fall into natural groups or segments within which customers exhibit the same broad characteristics. These segments form separate markets in themselves and can often be of a considerable size. Looking at markets in this way is termed *market segmentation*.

A number of meetings organizers have found that if they can identify a viable sub-market or market segment they can cater exclusively for the needs of that segment and gain a degree of dominance that would probably not be possible in the whole meetings market. Several professional organizers arrange meetings for the medical profession. Others concentrate mainly on large, international conferences, and still others specialize in segments ranging from incentive programmes to sales meetings and from management seminars to product launches. By specializing in this way, the organizers are able to understand their chosen market segments. This enables them to achieve a close matching of customers' needs and the 'product' or service offered.

If segmentation of our markets has these positive advantages how may we actually identify such groupings of customers? Two approaches to segmentation suggest themselves:

1. Market segmentation through an analysis of the characteristics or attributes of the customer.
2. Market segmentation through an analysis of the responses or behaviour of the customer.

Customer Characteristics or Attributes   This form of segmentation poses the question 'What sort of characteristics?' There are many ways of looking at customer differences – age, sex, profession, industrial grouping, etc. Some of these groupings are clearly of greater significance to the conference organizer than others. Professional groupings are particularly relevant, as are management job functions (personnel, accountancy, production and so on). Americans and the British have a penchant for forming professional bodies and associations which along with company and commercial groupings, at least in theory, divide much of the population into readily identifiable market segments which can be exploited by the meetings organizer.

Customer Behaviour and Responses   It is also possible to examine the benefits that the customer is seeking from a meeting and to use these as a basis for segmentation. This is called *benefit segmentation*. This approach is particularly useful in programmes and events which have a high information content. Seminars on desktop publishing, computing and other technical developments are common and offer the benefits of new knowledge. More general short programmes on public speaking, report writing, selling techniques and so on are also popular. Each represents a benefit which can provide the basis for marketing strategies.

Criteria for segmentation

The means whereby we distinguish between customer groups must be appropriate to the market situation. In other words, why segment a market on the basis of say, age if this attribute has no relationship to potential purchasing behaviour? This is the advantage of endeavouring to identify the benefits the customer is seeking from his purchase. Once we know the nature of these benefits and the particular combinations that the market seeks, then we are able to position our 'product' offering to those customers who are most likely to be attracted by it.

Clearly, for a strategy of market segmentation to be successful, there are a number of requirements that must be met:

1. As we have noted, the criteria used to differentiate between customer groups – market segments – must be relevant to the purchase situation.
2. The segment should be of sufficient potential to ensure that an adequate return can be made on any marketing investment made within it. This is very important. For example, some segments are very large but people within them do not generally attend seminars. It is particularly difficult to attract local government employees and civil servants to public events and one designed to attract such a segment may therefore fail. Similarly, some segments are too small and too dispersed to be worth trying to attract.
3. An identified market segment can only be exploited if it can be reached at an acceptable cost.
4. For a segment to be viable in its own right it is necessary that it should be distinguishable from other segments but, at the same time, people within the segment must have a high degree of similarity as regards the criteria adopted for segmentation.

Satisfying the need

There is a danger, in trying to create your 'product', of attempting to make it all things to all people. This is usually a recipe for disaster: it is also the aspect which attracts most criticism in the marketplace.

People will generally only sign up for an event if they think it will contain something of use to them. They will consider it a waste of their time if their expectations are not met. The most common criticism of public events is that they are too general for the audience. This is particularly true of conferences and seminars which promise a full insight into a 'hot' topic and present an agenda with speakers from a variety of companies and agencies. Such events almost invariably 'fail to deliver'. To quote one disappointed delegate after one recent event, 'After a day and 10 speakers, I had heard six or seven pieces of pure puffery – half hour expositions about how marvellous the speaker's own company was and virtually nothing on the subject matter'. He blamed the organizers whom, he said, were interested only in profit and allowed the speakers' PR departments free rein. To quote another delegate to the same event, 'I resent paying to be sold to'.

On the other hand, the good commercial event can be invaluable. Delegates to an event devoted to political developments in environmental policies in Europe were almost lyrical in their praise for the seminar. One delegate said of the day, 'It covered all environmental legislation over the last couple of years and what was likely to come up. For any company in our field that sort of information is dynamite and really worth knowing. The day was a bargain.'

Sadly, excellent public events of this calibre are still the exception rather than the rule. That said, association and trade conferences are viewed in a different light. Arranged by the industry for the industry, the content is almost invariably apposite, topical and useful.

The lesson is clear. If you can attract the right audience to the right conference, you will be successful. You need to give specialist information that will satisfy your audience ('specialist', it should be noted, does not necessarily mean your programme has to be deeply technical or complicated. Rather, the content must be tailored to suit the audience: the subject matter must be relevant and new – at least to potential customers in the chosen market segment. For example, subjects such as 'Effective Public Speaking' or 'Accountancy for non-Accountants' are typical short event subjects which are repeated time and time again. Clearly, these are not 'new' subjects, but they continue to attract participants because there is a constant 'supply' of new people entering the market segment as their careers progress. On the other hand, some subjects or conference themes cannot be repeated. Thus the content of an annual association conference will be radically different each year since it is necessary to attract substantially the same people year in, year out).

A final note of caution. If, in an attempt to increase our potential market, we dilute the degree of specialization to attract people from other fields, we run the risk of creating an event which appeals to no-one: the specialist is bored and the generalist is out of his depth.

Your delegates will judge the event as a whole: the venue, the credibility of the speakers, the audio visual and many other things are brought into the equation.

We therefore need to think about the event as a whole. For example, an exhibition alongside a conference (or vice versa, a conference held in conjunction with an exhibition) can do much to enhance the overall 'product' offering. Exhibitions (see Chapter 7) can also generate valuable additional income. Remember, if your target audience is highly segmented then your audience is a 'product' to someone else who also wishes to sell to that group of people.

The term 'product', then, covers much more than the content. The whole 'package' – subject, speakers, location, dates, and even the audience itself – makes up the 'product' perceived by the potential customer.

Speakers

Speakers are considered in some detail in Chapter 3. However, the quality and reputation of speakers engaged for public events is even more important than is the case for in-house events. Speakers should have established reputations in the chosen subject area. If they are well-known figures, the 'attractiveness' of the event is much enhanced, especially if some of the speakers are known to have controversial or unusual views.

It must also be apparent that the speakers have a contribution to make to the event. This is not always easy to ensure. A leading trade unionist was engaged to speak at a conference for personnel managers. The theme of the event was the trade unions' response to the introduction of new working practices. His talk contained nothing which was new or which would not have been known to any practising personnel manager. As a result, many delegates were disappointed. While this may not have affected the original commercial viability of the event in question, it did harm the organizers' reputation, and the credibility of events they subsequently promoted to that market segment was diminished.

It is therefore essential to vet what your speakers are going to say to ensure that the content is appropriate to the audience and that they are not going to promote themselves or their organizations: remember the delegate who complained that he did not like going to conferences to be 'sold to'.

Venue

The location and type of venue is also part of the 'product'. Venue selection is discussed fully in Chapter 2. However, the organizer of the public event has further factors to consider. The location of most public events is dictated by considerations such as accessibility, acceptability to the delegate and his organization, and of course, price. Acceptability is an important consideration. Some companies may be reluctant to send delegates to a training programme in a five-star hotel or in an overseas venue, whatever the price advantages (in Chapter 2, we saw that some provincial top quality hotels are much cheaper than lesser hotels in capital cities and that it is sometimes cheaper to hold events overseas in spite of the extra travel costs involved). The reluctance stems from unwillingness to be seen to be sending employees on what may look like pleasant jaunts rather than useful educational courses. On the other hand, the attractiveness of the country, city and hotels is an essential ingredient of the international event and of many association conferences. It is for this reason that most leading conference cities make great efforts to promote themselves and attract the large, prestigious international conferences.

The great majority of public events in Britain tend to be held in London and the major conference towns. That said, the organizer should not automatically discount provincial centres. The north of the country is starved of good seminars and conferences and an event specifically located in the region may well attract delegates who would not be prepared to travel to London.

The audience

Right at the beginning of the book, we saw that people go to conferences for all sorts of reasons: to learn something, to enjoy themselves, for stimulation and reassurance – and peer group approval, as a reward, and to *network, make contacts* and *do business.*

These last factors are crucially important at most trade and association conferences; they can also be a significant factor in the decision to attend a commercial event. Events with the reputation for a good delegate list – for example, the annual conference of the Institute of Personnel and Development (IPD) – almost sell themselves.

Delegates who attend a large number of conferences often complain about the quality of participants. The finance director of one of the UK clearing banks stormed out of a one-day seminar complaining that the other delegates were dull and uninspiring. He had decided to attend because the content was topical and the brochure claimed the seminar was 'relevant to finance directors'. Expecting to make useful, high level contacts and discuss matters of mutual concern, he had been dismayed to find a total dearth of senior executives.

The answer is to screen registrations and reject those which are unsuitable. But few (if any) commercial organizers do this, preferring to build up numbers (and hence the eventual profit). It takes commercial courage and a high degree of integrity to turn unsuitable business away, but it could pay dividends in the end.

It is worth reminding ourselves at this juncture that the programme must allow time for delegates to intermingle. This means that the formal sessions in a one-day seminar have to be restricted. It is quite difficult to achieve a balance between offering sufficient formal input and time for informal discussion. A buffet style lunch helps since it allows delegates to move about during the meal.

Timing

There are several factors to take into account in deciding when to hold a planned event. The most important of these are:

1. *The Promotional Campaign* Delegates need plenty of warning of forthcoming events. The norm is six to eight weeks for a one-day seminar, to six months or more for an international event. This is discussed in greater detail in the next chapter.

2. *Administrative Considerations* It takes much longer to plan an event than most people realize. It is a complicated task to agree dates with perhaps a dozen or more speakers, and to tie these in with venue selection, the preparation, design and printing of brochures and the many administrative procedures involved. It is easy to underestimate the time these procedures take, with the result that the marketing campaign is mounted too late and the success of the event jeopardized. At least three months should be allowed before the marketing campaign in which to set up a small one-day seminar – and even this might be too little in some cases. A major international event takes years to prepare.

3. *Competitive Activity* It is essential to keep an eye on the activities of competitors. To quote one professional organizer: 'We spend a lot of time planning and researching ideas for conferences and many putative ones are aborted at that stage due to the activity of competitors. We are often surprised when we come up with something good only to find that a lot of other people come up with the same idea.'

When this happens it may not be necessary to abandon the idea. It may be that a different slant can be put on the subject, or the timing altered so that two similar events do not run at the same time. Terrible mistakes are often made. Two almost identical conference and exhibition events in the computer and business efficiency fields were scheduled for the same month and year, and the conference and travel businesses managed to overlap their annual events which inevitably affected attendance at both. Even if there appears to be no direct competition, it is necessary to research other events which may attract people from the chosen market segment. For example, a major conference is organized for personnel management every autumn. However attractive an event you mount for personnel managers at that time, your attendance will be affected not only because many of your target audience will be in Harrogate, but also because few can afford the time or money to attend two events in the space of a matter of weeks even if your event does not clash directly.

4. *The Timing of the Event may be Part of its Attraction*   One major organizer of international management training events invariably runs several in London in late November/early December because they know people will be as attracted by the opportunity to do Christmas shopping as by the event itself. As a footnote to this – they also show time in the programme for shopping (usually by finishing early on Thursday so delegates can take advantage of late night shopping in the West End). They know that if they did not make this provision in the programme delegates would skip sessions anyway.

5. *Cancellation due to Insufficient Support*   This consideration also affects timing, but in a different way. Many, but not all, venues carry cancellation clauses in their contracts. Thus, some may demand a deposit which is forfeited if the event is cancelled, while others raise cancellation charges on a time basis. Thus, one London venue will not raise cancellation charges if an event is cancelled more than 56 days beforehand, but the charges gradually increase during the 56-day period so that an event cancelled less than seven days beforehand attracts a 100% cancellation charge on room hire and all services including food and extra staff. The conference organizer must be fully aware of such conditions and plan to make timely decisions on whether or not to proceed.

Fortunately, if a marketing campaign has been properly mounted to schedule, this is not difficult. The response curve for registrations after a mail-out or advertisement for a public event is nearly always in the shape of a bath-tub, with a quick return of initial registration, falling to a steady flow and then rising again shortly before the event.

Thus, if the initial response is good, it is usually possible to forecast whether the break even point will be reached. However, if the response is poor – or even if, as sometimes happens, there is no response at all – then the likelihood of reaching break even is remote and the decision whether or not to proceed must be taken.

Such a decision is not always easy. If the response is poor, but there will still be enough delegates to produce a viable event in terms of the number attending, it may be worthwhile proceeding and at least receiving some income. One company only received 20 registrations for a one-day seminar for which their break even figure was 60 delegates. They decided to proceed since the income from the 20 delegates more than covered the cancellation charges and, indeed, recovered at least a third of the set-up costs. It was therefore less costly to proceed than to cancel. The style of the event was changed from a series of formal presentations to a round-the-table, less formal event with the accent on discussion and delegate participation. The participants were not aware of the change and the event was so successful that the formula was subsequently repeated. The set-up costs were reduced by running a less ambitious marketing campaign and the value of the informal discussions was stressed in the publicity material. The lower break even figure ensured the profitability of the subsequent events and the original disaster turned to modest success.

There are other reasons for avoiding cancellations. News of them soon gets round and the sponsor's reputation may be damaged in the marketplace. This may affect the response to future activities. In addition, speakers do not like being let down and may be reluctant to co-operate in future venues if they fear further cancellations may occur. Many speakers are wary of associating with unsuccessful or unproven sponsors for this reason.

If one event in a series is cancelled, it is worth offering places 'in lieu' of other events when notifying delegates. Registrations are often transferred and the business not wholly lost.

PRICING POLICIES FOR DELEGATES' FEES

The price charged for the event is important not just because it dictates the financial viability and profitability of the venture but also because price is an important factor in the eyes of the potential customer. In Chapter 4 we saw that the price charged for an event should be considered in two ways, by calculation and from the delegate's standpoint. The calculated price is used by many associations to fix the delegates' fees for events offered to their members and this explains the extraordinarily good value of some association conferences. However, as we indicate elsewhere, some associations and professional bodies subsidize their events either in cash or in kind (for example, the free use of the organization's administrative facilities) in order to keep delegates' costs down. These apart, when events are being organized on a purely commercial basis and the objective is to make the best possible return on the investment, it is more sensible to price the event from the delegate's standpoint.

The delegate will look at the cost in terms of the commercial value of the benefits offered to him or his organization (and here, some benefits are perceived rather than real. For example, a company may allow an executive to attend a certain conference not for the value of the information he will receive, but as a reward for past performance and an incentive for the future). It is therefore advisable to base the cost of the event on such notions as 'what the market will bear', the activities of competitors and price quality perceptions.

The idea that a product should be priced according to market rather than cost considerations is not new, but many companies enter a pricing decision by talking about the costs rather than about the market. In a sense this is understandable as costs are tangible inputs, quantifiable (even if sometimes misleadingly so) in any decision process. Market factors are usually harder to pin down. Getting a feel for what the market will bear can really only come through experience. We are usually able to identify broad bands within which the price will be acceptable to the majority of the chosen markets. We would normally conclude that the potential customer sets two price limits – a lower limit below which he would distrust the quality of the event, and an upper limit beyond which he would judge the event unduly expensive. These limits will vary depending on whether the customer will be paying out of his own pocket or whether price is forced right down, a factor which greatly influences the pricing policy for most association and professional body conferences.

Price also has a qualitative dimension. That is to say, we *position* the event by the price we charge. We can deliberately charge a high fee and aim our event at the top end of the market (implying comparatively high returns from small numbers of delegates) or we can aim at the popular market, charging a lower fee to increase potential numbers but at a lower net contribution per delegate.

There is therefore a framework within which the registration fee can be set and, provided the range of options is above the break even figure, the primary decision is a matter of discretion influenced by a variety of factors.

PROMOTION

The last element of the marketing mix. It is said that if you invent a better mousetrap, people will beat a path to your door. This is patently a half-truth: if no-one has heard of your invention, no-one will come to buy it. Promotion is concerned with communicating with your market: promoting public events is discussed in the next chapter.

FEEDBACK

It is usually easy to tell whether an actual event is going well. Signs of success are a high degree of delegate participation, the level of conversation during breaks and the general atmosphere. Signs of failure are sullen silence and hostile questions from the floor. However, the conference organizer needs to know why a particular event is a success or failure so that future events can be tailored to meet delegates' needs.

It is therefore worth giving delegates a reportback form on which they can record their immediate comments, and it may also be worth following up a proportion of the delegates some time after the event. In this way it is possible to identify subjects for future events and find out what improvements can be made to programmes and so on. Post-event evaluation is discussed further in Chapter 13.

EXECUTIVE CHECKLIST

- ◆ Do you treat the public event as a product which is to be sold in a competitive market?
- ◆ Do you consider all elements of the 'product' – content, programme, speakers, venue and timing?
- ◆ Do you identify the appropriate market segment for each of your events? Is each one viable and can it be reached at a reasonable cost?
- ◆ Does your event match the needs of potential customers in the chosen market segment?
- ◆ Do you vet registrations and reject 'unsuitable' participants in order to preserve the quality of your audiences?
- ◆ If delegates from overseas want to shop when they come to your events, do you make provision for this activity in the programme?
- ◆ What is your policy about cancellation due to poor support?
- ◆ Do you ensure that your events do not clash with other similar events and that the chosen segment of the market is not involved in some other activity at the time you intend to hold your event?

10

PROMOTING THE EVENT

Once we have established our 'product' and identified our market segment, we need to communicate with our customers to tell them about our event. Many people refer to this process as 'marketing' the event. More correctly, this chapter is concerned with *promoting* your event, 'marketing' being covered by this and the previous chapter taken together.

There is a range of techniques available which we should seek to deploy singly and in combination for the maximum effect within our given budget. The major media, as they are called, which are widely available and which might be considered for promoting a public event, are:

♦ national and regional newspapers;
♦ trade and professional magazines;
♦ direct mail;
♦ public relations;
♦ personal selling;
♦ the Internet.

Other media of the communications mix, which are less likely to be of interest to the conference organizer, are:

♦ national, regional and European radio and television;
♦ exhibitions;
♦ point-of-sale literature and packaging.

NATIONAL AND REGIONAL NEWSPAPERS

These appear daily or weekly (typically within just one country but a number of international links between the serious or quality dailies have developed in recent years). Advertising conferences and meetings in national papers is expensive and is therefore not used extensively. Indeed, the only example of the extensive use of the national press for advertising meetings has been a series of inserts and advertisements, primarily in the colour supplements of some Sunday newspapers, promoting a series of seminars for salesmen. The organizer of these seminars was, at least for a short time, able to use high cost promotion to reach a mass-market for his reasonably priced seminars. It is worth considering placing advertisements for the larger conference and for events which might have a wide interest. Different newspapers reach different markets and some offer regional advertisements, particularly in colour supplements. The *Financial Times* has a very high business readership while the *Mail on Sunday* has very wide cover of the so-called middle classes. Some papers often carry special reports and supplements on particular industries, technologies and businesses. It is sometimes possible to advertise to good effect in a relevant report or supplement.

TRADE AND PROFESSIONAL MAGAZINES

These cover everything from architects' materials, computers, caravans and model railways to the accountancy and medical professions. They offer an excellent entrée to specialist segments. Most accept leaflet and brochure inserts in addition to advertising.

DIRECT MAIL

This term is used to describe circulars or leaflets which are sent through the post or, in some applications, are delivered door-to-door. It is a widely misunderstood promotional tool mainly on account of the 'junk mail' so many of us receive through our letter boxes selling everything from timeshares to double glazing. As one senior executive exclaimed, 'In this company we don't use direct mail'. When asked whether they wrote to customers – and to potential customers – the answer was affirmative.

It is also a myth that most people throw direct mail letters into the wastepaper basket without even opening the envelope. The fact is that most people open the envelope and read on if the contents interest them: over 94 per cent of businessmen say that they like receiving direct mail when it is about something in which they are interested.

The fact is that direct mail is a very powerful tool provided it is used properly. It is widely used to promote conferences, and is discussed in greater detail later in the chapter.

PUBLIC RELATIONS

This covers everything from the dissemination of information to the press and television to the general development of an organization's image. News releases can be used to considerable effect to promote conferences and other events. One company had organized a seminar on a specialist computer language. The direct mailing had generated a very poor response but there was a surge of interest and bookings after the event had received editorial cover in a weekly magazine which had a wide readership in the computing industry. Editorial and news cover cost almost nothing and local – and even national – television and radio is often hungry for news of local or unusual interest. When the subject is topical or unusual in some way, a PR campaign can produce good results. Press releases and press conferences should therefore always be considered by the organizer of a public event. Access to the press, arranging press conferences and writing press releases is not easy for the layman and it may therefore be worth employing the professional services of a PR consultant to deal with these matters.

PERSONAL SELLING

Although last in the list of media which conference organizers should consider, this is by no means the least important. It is normally considered to embrace the activities of representatives travelling on regular journeys to seek out customers to collect orders. However, the use of a telephone sales approach is becoming increasingly common in the conference industry. A telephone call to follow up a direct mail shot can often clinch a sale. Even if the response is negative, valuable information can be obtained about the reason for the failure to attract the customer.

In trying to communicate with our customers, we have to decide which of the available media can be deployed. One on its own will seldom suffice. The brochure mail-out should be supported by a press release and, possibly, some advertising. Telephone selling should always be considered as a further promotional tool. The effective marketing organization is continually experimenting with the mix of communications media it employs to find out how to make a fixed expenditure more effective or, alternatively, to reduce its budget and achieve a similar level of effect.

INDIRECT COMMUNICATION

The above forms of communication are termed 'direct'. Organizations also communicate with their customers in a series of less obvious ways which we can term 'indirect'. In the last chapter, we intimated that the well established organizations have a better chance of being successful when they promote public events. This is, in part, due to the image which these organizations have in the minds of potential customers prior to receiving any new message about them. That image will have been built up from a range of past experience and hearsay and will affect the way in which customers perceive any particular communications. Thus the brochure from the well known organization is likely to be better received than that from some new, unknown company.

This indirect communication of the image is supplemented or reinforced by the way any enquiry or order is handled. The manner in which each customer contact is handled influences the customer and is very important. Indeed, being in a service industry, the promoter of public events shares a characteristic which distinguishes the marketing of services from manufacturing. In selling a service, we can never finally 'manufacture' the product we wish to sell: the customer himself plays an important part in actually forming the offering he receives. Nor can management in a service industry limit customer contact to a dedicated group of customer-oriented specialists such as a sales force. Research shows that, on average, 90 per cent of a service organization's staff have direct contact with the customer; the comparable figure for a manufacturing organization is only 10 per cent.

Thus, in a conference company office, the majority of the staff will have a direct impact on customers through contact of some kind: perhaps in answer to a telephone enquiry, or in handling a registration. For the most part, staff are recruited not for their contact skills, but for their technical or administrative abilities. Yet it is from these contacts that customers gain their impression of the organization *and its offering*: marketing or sales specialists, paradoxically, often have less direct contact with customers than the great majority of staff – including some not under direct control of the event organizer (such as venue staff, AV operators and even some speakers: all of these people are, in the eyes of the customer, representative of the organizer of the event).

The message therefore is that, in a service industry, marketing is not simply the bridge to the customer which conventional management theory implies, but is a key part of the total staff's activity. Their interaction with the customer is a crucial element in the 'product' or 'service package' which the company is offering, and is critical to success.

Price is also an extremely meaningful communications cue to customers. In unsophisticated markets where customers are unsure of the precise nature of and criteria for judging a product or service – for example, wines, restaurants, or hotel accommodation – price will frequently be used as an indication of quality. As the customer becomes more certain of himself he begins to rely more on his judgement and takes a more discriminating view of price. Where the price is known to colleagues or friends, however, the fact that it has been paid can also act as a communications message to such people about the customer himself. Selection for, or the authority to attend, say, a prestigious over-seas conference can do much to enhance a person's status and reputation at work and socially. Price can also say much about the quality of the event. A top executive event will be expected to be more expensive than one for junior managers. Indeed, if the price is well below the expected level, then the quality of the event will be doubted. The market orientated approach to pricing has been discussed in more detail in Chapters 4 and 9.

Perhaps here the benefits of word-of-mouth communications should be mentioned. These are closely allied to the reactions of people who have attended previous events. On their return they will discuss the event with their colleagues and, if they have enjoyed it or felt it was worthwhile, this message will be transmitted to them. Such opinions are seen as much more objective than advertising or the direct mail brochure. In user terms they usually are. If an organization can also get satisfied customers and users communicating for it in this way, it is indeed blessed.

THE MESSAGE

The media outlined above provide a means of putting a message across to the chosen market segment. What should the message be? What advocacy should we employ to persuade people to buy our 'product'?

It is seldom sufficient merely to inform people of an event. The exception to this 'rule' is, possibly, the association or professional body conference which a proportion of members habitually attend once they know the event is to take place. When we are trying to attract people from the 'open market' something more than information about the event is needed. This is because people have attitudes. If an attitude is well entrenched, people will have a distorted perception of any information which is at variance with it in order to make it fit the attitude in question. Hence, persuasive appeals must either create fresh attitudes or build upon those which are there already and which are used by the potential customer to evaluate the event of which he has become aware. Once the relevant attitudes have been identified and understood, it is not normally necessary to give both sides of an argument. Advocacy, effective advocacy, is what most of us wish to hear. If the audience is well disposed, it will use the advocate's information to confirm and reinforce its own prior attitudes. It is reassuring to know that one is right, a point which must not be overlooked after the purchase either. The registration literature and the content of the event itself should give the desired reassurance.

A company decided to set up a series of seminars on new industrial production technology based on automation and the micro-processor. It was well known that many people in industry needed to know about the opportunities and problems presented by the new technology. It was also known that people felt threatened by the technology, were ignorant about the subject and were afraid to admit their ignorance. The organizers realized that it would not be sufficient to market the seminars by merely stating that the events would tell people what they needed to know about the new technology. Such a message would have fallen on stony ground. It was decided to exploit the fears, and the publicity material asked 'Can you afford to ignore these imminent developments?' This message traded on the fears but turned them into a reason for attending the event, using the argument that few people had had the chance of receiving informed expert advice and that, unless such advice was taken, expensive mistakes would be made. The overall message, by reinforcing the attitudes already held, was able to persuade potential customers to attend the event.

It is impossible to give more than the most general advice on this aspect of marketing public events since each is very different. Some association conferences sell out regularly regardless of content. Many international congresses are sold as much by the venue location as by the programme content (hence the tourist information so often included in the event brochure). Well established organizations often do better than newcomers because of their reputation and the goodwill they have established in the market. In this context, a sustained multi-media campaign for a series of events helps to position the product in the market and make the parent organization's activities more widely known and accepted.

Sell benefits – not features

In the previous chapter, we saw that events with a high information content can be sold to a particular market segment by virtue of the benefits to be gained from attending. It is, of course, essential to communicate those benefits to the potential customer. Unfortunately, most people fall into the trap of selling the features of their events, and not the benefits to be gained from them. What does this mean?

When customers buy a product or service (and a seminar or conference is, of course, a service), they are not primarily interested in the physical or objective attributes of the product itself, but in the benefits these attributes bring with them. Thus, when you, the reader, purchased this book, you bought it not because it was 'n' pages of printed paper bound together, but because it contained a promise to bestow certain insights about organizing conferences. Those who buy books seek specific benefits that are not limited to the physical product, in this case the printed page. If those benefits are provided more effectively by some other product or service, then the consumer is likely to use the new product in preference to the old. Thus, certain segments of the book-buying public may well find that other information technologies, such as the Internet, serve their information needs more efficiently than books can. If this happens, book publishers will lose part of their market.

The difference between benefits and features is not just a question of semantics. It is crucial to success in selling meetings. If people buy services for what they will do for them, that is, the benefits of using the service – then we must sell those benefits rather than the objective features of the service.

Every meeting has features such as: the speakers, the programme, individual sessions, the price, the venue, perhaps a social programme and so on. Many brochure copy writers fall into the trap of merely describing these features. This is not surprising: if such detail is not given, the customer might doubt the quality of what is on offer.

However, merely describing the technical detail is not enough. The customer may not be able to work out the benefits which particular features bring and it is therefore essential to explain the benefits which accrue from every feature mentioned.

A simple formula to ensure this customer-oriented approach is always to use the phrase 'which means that' to link a feature to the benefit it brings. The following examples illustrate what is meant:

'The event is a unique blend of plenary sessions and workshops which means that participants will have the chance to explore issues of particular interest in greater depth in a smaller group.'

'There is an extensive social programme which means that delegates will have plenty of opportunity to meet other delegates and to see the tourist attractions of this famous city.'

'The programme ends at 1 pm on Friday so that delegates can be back in London by early evening.'

Note that the alternative phrases such as 'so that' instead of 'which means that' can add variety and avoid repetition.

With this approach in mind, we can ensure that the event brochure is not just a catalogue of features but a living statement of the benefits the event will bring.

It is good practice to include a summarizing statement which begins: 'After this event, participants will...' (this is followed by a positive statement of the new knowledge and/or skills the participant will take away with him).

Timing the message

A company obtained the rights to run a seminar on computer security which had been very successful in North America. There was an identified need for the programme and the organizers had high hopes for success. Administrative and other difficulties delayed the mail-out until about three weeks before the event. Interest was high, but the notice was so short that the date was already taken up in people's diaries. Few bookings were received and the event therefore had to be cancelled.

The timing of the publicity campaign can therefore be critical There can be no hard and fast rules, but an awareness of the factors which must be taken into account is needed. A campaign – mailshot, advertisements, inserts and so on – must be sufficiently early for there to be a good chance that the dates will still be free in people's diaries. This implies about an 8- to 12-week notice (provided holiday periods are avoided in the case of non-recreational events). Sufficient time must also be allowed in which the customer's organization can process the bid. People may have to obtain their superior's permission to attend or seek financial authority for the expenditure. These administrative procedures can be lengthy. Most people advocate 12 to 14 weeks' notice for run-of-the-mill public conferences and seminars. Delegates to larger international events need much more notice, mainly because the travel and administrative arrangements are more complicated. Most people advocate at least six months notice for major international conferences.

This lead-time generates administrative problems. If you want a mailshot to arrive by a certain date, printing, envelope stuffing and postage must be arranged early on. Large mailshots are usually posted second or economy class and delivery can take 7 to 10 days in some areas of the country. Overseas mailing takes much longer, especially when surface mail is used.

Current events might affect the timing of the mail-out and other advertising effort. It is sometimes possible to plan the campaign to coincide with a related event or with the publication of a particular report, government white paper, or an anniversary or similar occasion. This can help increase impact and underline the relevance of the event. One organizer was able to market a one-day seminar on a new computer language immediately after the language was released for publication. Being first in the field, he was able to cash in on the topicality and relevance of his seminar.

PUBLICITY MATERIAL

Having defined our product, the market segment, the message and the media we would use, we can think about the production and distribution of our publicity material.

The brochure

Some form of printed brochure, leaflet or booklet is normally prepared to publicize the public event. Distributed either by post or as a magazine or journal insert, the brochure is a critical element of the publicity plan. The style, content, size and cost of a brochure can vary greatly. Some are expensive and elaborate multi-coloured booklets. Others are reply-paid slips which double up as delegates' registration cards.

The type and style of brochure used depends on many factors. One for a large, international conference might be a comprehensive booklet published in more than one language. It would contain full details of the event, the formal and social programmes, the speakers, accommodation and travel arrangements and even the sort of details of the host country that are more usually found in travel brochures. In contrast, the leaflet for a one-day seminar may just be a folded A4 sheet containing brief but succinct information about the event.

Large or small, the brochure should contain most, if not all, of the following details:

- ◆ The title of the event.
- ◆ The subject.
- ◆ Who should attend – and why.
- ◆ The benefits participants will receive ('after this event, participants will know how to…' and so on).
- ◆ Where and when the event will take place (including a map showing how to find the venue).
- ◆ The outline programme and speakers.
- ◆ Cost – and what the cost covers.

- Payment details (eg, whether credit card payment is accepted and so on).
- How to register – including a registration form.
- Essential administrative details (for example, timings, travel and accommodation).
- Any special terms and conditions (cancellation charges, discount schemes, etc).
- The name, address and telephone number of the organizing body, along with the company name, registered number and address. It is also useful to give the VAT number.
- Disclaimer notice (usually in the form: 'The organizers reserve the right to make such changes to the programme and speakers as may be necessary due to conditions outside their control').

Most of the above items are self-explanatory, but the last few are often omitted. The company details are required by law on publicity material offering goods or services for gain and the disclaimer notice is to protect the organizer in the event of changes to the published event having to be made (for example, speakers being ill or otherwise unavailable, necessary programme changes and so on).

The brochure should look good and it is worth considering the use of the professional services of advertising agencies or PR consultants to this end. The brief on which these people work is very important. They must understand exactly what the brochure is for and they must appreciate what the cost and other limiting factors are; otherwise you are likely to be disappointed and they frustrated.

The style, artwork and layout of the brochure should reflect the type of event being publicized. A rather conservative style is often used for professional and senior management events, while more adventurous layouts are used with great effect elsewhere. Whatever the style, the brochure must:

- attract (demand?) attention;
- present the necessary information clearly and concisely;
- be well produced.

The size of the brochure is, of course, determined to a great extent by the quantity of information and illustrative material it contains. Nevertheless, there is still some choice of size available – A4, A5 and so on. Some people avoid A4 brochures because they tend to be crumpled in the post. This can be overcome by using a heavier weight of paper, but the overall weight of the brochure can also be critical. Some journals and magazines demand extra payment for inserts over a specified weight and it is sensible to keep postage weights within as low a stamp cost as possible. If a brochure is to be sent out by post it should be of a size and design which will withstand transit without being damaged. This usually precludes a large, thin publication. The weight allowance for minimum first and second class post (60 grammes) is generous. The majority of mail uses only about one-third of the available weight. If type-setting and printing costs permit, it is worth considering increasing the information in the brochure – or perhaps paper grade – to use the full permitted weight.

Weight allowances are less generous when brochures are to be sent overseas. For example, the weight for the minimum postage rates to European and overseas destinations is only 10 grammes. These limitations should be taken into account at the brochure design stage.

Most brochures contain a registration form. The design of this form is discussed in Chapter 11. Some people advocate using a 'Reply Paid' or 'Freepost' service to facilitate the return of the form. There are arguments against this. The cost is not great in terms of the Royal Mail Licence, but its use restricts the registration detail to one side of a card not much larger than a postcard. This limits the information which can be requested, can make the form difficult to fill and makes it impossible to attach the necessary payment (payment with registration should be actively encouraged). The truth is that if someone wants to attend an event he or she (or a secretary) will be prepared to return the form in an envelope and to pay the postage. Indeed, the Royal Mail admits that a significant proportion of reply paid cards posted by businesses are meter-franked by mailing-room operators anyway!

The registration form should be easily detachable – a perforation is recommended. The rest of the brochure should stand alone after the registration form has been detached. This means that some information, such as addresses and fees has to be repeated on both parts of the brochure.

Letters/Direct mail

Many events are publicized by *direct mail* letter – either a stand-alone letter or as a covering letter for a brochure. The latter can be good practice. The average person is exposed to hundreds of possible advertising impressions every day. Most go unnoticed. The personal character of direct mail, however, ensures that almost all of it is opened and read. As mentioned earlier, contrary to a widely held belief, a direct mail piece is rarely dropped into the wastepaper basket unopened. It is usually the quality of the contents which determines whether the material will pass the secretarial filter and reach the actual addressee. This implies the use of the more sophisticated techniques and laser printing to incorporate the addressee's *correct* name and address in the letter. Nothing is worse than the 'Dear Sir or Madam' greeting. Letters, like brochures, will have greater impact if they are well written and well typed. Everybody thinks he can write a good letter. Most people in business write dozens of them a week and this, not unnaturally, seems a good enough training. In fact, writing a simple sales letter is a task full of pitfalls. Unlike the business letter, which is addressed to an individual and deals with a specific subject, the direct mail letter has to communicate to several hundreds or even thousands of people. Letters need to be short and to the point and get into the subject right away. They must contain the relevant facts and invite a response. Long, wordy letters, with the emphasis on 'we' instead of 'you' are unlikely to hold the reader's interest and will end up in the wastepaper basket. The opening words are very important.

Distribution

Mailing lists   We have already discussed the need to identify the target segment for each event. It is theoretically possible to reach almost any trade, business and professional segment through the post. How can you assemble the mailing list for your particular target segment? It is seldom difficult to track down a mailing list which targets the segment you want to reach. Sources include professional bodies and trade associations which will either mail members on your behalf or supply pre-addressed labels. Alternatively it will probably be possible to have a loose insert placed in the relevant journal.

Commercial mailing lists   Many firms specialize in 'selling' mailing lists. These commercial lists are claimed to be up-to-date and accurate. In reality, they are not always quite as good as they are claimed to be.

You can be reasonably confident in mailing lists you rent from a reputable list broker (the word 'rent' is important: you cannot usually purchase a list outright – rather, you rent it for a particular mailing or series of mailings; you are not allowed to re-use it later). In the United Kingdom, the safest course is to approach a member of the DMA (Direct Marketing Association). The Association has about 530 members who are governed by a code of practice designed to protect you, those on the lists and the list owners. List brokers' business is to negotiate the rental of privately owned lists. Between them, the DMA members have access to a very large number of lists covering virtually the entire range of professions, industries and many individual interests. Some suppliers will undertake to build up special lists to the advertiser's specific requirements. This may involve original research, but more likely will involve merging one or more existing lists and 'deduplication' or 'merge and purge' – a control process whereby no matter how many times the same address appears within a list, it will be acceptable for a mailing only once.

The cost of these lists varies with the quality of the list, and prices are normally quoted per thousand addresses – typically £70–£90 per thousand for business lists.

You can usually have your list supplied in the form of pre-printed, self-adhesive labels although it is becoming increasingly common for lists to be available on disk or CD ROM. All DMA brokers adhere to the provisions of the Data Protection Act and if you are mailing to consumers (ie, individuals at their private addresses) the brokers will be registered with Mailing Preference Service (MPS) which allows members of the public the option of not receiving direct mail or only of receiving direct mail on products and services they wish to know more about. List brokers will also be able to operate Mailsort (see 'postage' below).

Not all mailing list vendors will let you have master lists and so you may not know to whom you have written. Most lists are a little 'blunt', that is to say their coverage tends to be blanket rather than selective, even within a particular group or segment. For example, a list to members of one of the larger professional bodies will cover all members, practising or not, over a wide geographical area. If you are only interested in reaching practising members in a limited geographical area, the selection methods may not be sufficiently sophisticated. This tends to increase the size of your mail-out with corresponding increases in postage, printing and handling charges. Nevertheless, some organizations offer very selective lists, especially when selection is on a geographical basis. The aim must always be to achieve a 'rifle shot' list which hits exactly the target segment, rather than a 'shot gun' list which peppers the whole market. There is one problem in asking for a selection from a larger list. It is sometimes difficult to predict how long the list will be until it is actually run off the computer. It is therefore better to print rather more brochures or leaflets than you think you will need rather than risk running short. The run-on cost of printing brochures is comparatively low compared with the initial set up costs and the extra thousand or so brochures will not unduly harm the budget.

Another feature of the commercially produced mailing label is that it is usually instantly recognizable for what it is – a print-out from a standard list. This reduces the degree to which the envelope looks like a personal rather than a circular letter. There are ways round this. For example, you can use a laser printer to produce your letters with the address and salutation merged with the text (this process is known as 'lasering' in the trade); these can then be despatched in window envelopes. Another possibility which is really only suitable for larger mailshots is to use what is called the 'closed-faced' process where an address is printed directly onto paper which is then turned into an envelope. This gives an authentic 'typewritten' appearance. However, such techniques are the domain of specialized mailing houses.

Mailing houses   Also known as 'lettershops', these will handle your mailshot on your behalf. They take your letters, brochures and labels, collate them, stuff them into envelopes and handle the mailing. Their charges are very reasonable and save a great deal of time and disruptive work – handling even a small mailshot in-house is, as anyone who has done it will tell you, a major task. Mailing houses can accept 'cheshire labels', ie, labels designed to be fixed to envelopes by machine, and can also operate Mailsort.

If you are not VAT registered, do ensure you pre-pay the postage, otherwise you will be liable to VAT on the postage if it is charged on to you retrospectively.

DIY research   What if you cannot find a mailing list which meets your requirements or what if you are one of the sceptics who do not believe commercial mailing lists are good enough? You are then faced with a time-consuming research project – time-consuming because it takes hours to extract and accurately record the information you need, even after you have found a source which gives the addresses you want. Most public libraries carry comprehensive reference sections and even the more restricted publications can be ferreted out if you have sufficient patience and tenacity. Company files can be another source of names and addresses. Customers' invoices, sales contacts and correspondence can all be searched for information. Another rich source of names and addresses is attendees at previous events. Satisfied customers not only buy again, they also recommend events to colleagues and friends (a process which, incidentally, can be encouraged by offering discounts for repeat business and people from the same organization). The lists extracted need frequent revision and constant expansion and it is advisable to keep the information on a computer to facilitate change. In time, the 'home-made' list will become a valuable asset, so valuable that many companies actually rent their lists to list brokers or to other organizations operating in non-competitive markets. Note, however, that you must be registered under the Data Protection Act if you intend to compile your own mailing lists. What is more, EC legislation is being introduced to regulate further the use of direct mail.

Size of mailing   The size of the mailing list is important for two reasons. Firstly, the cost of the mail-out is directly proportional to the numbers involved and, with postage rates constantly going up, the sums involved can be very large. Secondly, the number of responses is a fraction of the size of the mail-out. A response of under 1% is said to be normal for the majority of direct mailshots. Thus, if we want 150 delegates we need a mail-out of 15,000 to 20,000. However, when associations and trade organizations use their own lists to promote their own conferences, the response rates are much higher. Association mailings often attract a 10% response; some achieve response rates as high as 20%.

Postage   The Royal Mail estimates that it handles some 9 million direct mail letters every day, or 2,372 million per year – which amounts to a total expenditure of around £1,000 million. About one-third of all direct mail is business-to-business. This is an enormous quantity of mail.

Some people in key business appointments receive 8 to 10 items of direct mail every day. One training director of a large international company who receives these quantities says the average item receives scant attention unless its message is particularly clear and relevant. Mailshots for small events, directed at specialized market segments, may be numbered in hundreds rather than thousands, and it is rare for mail-outs for even the largest conference to exceed 50,000. Your material is thus competing for attention against high numerical odds. The Royal Mail publishes a booklet containing advice on direct mailing techniques (*The Royal Mail Guide to Successful Direct Mail*) and on the service it offers. The Royal Mail used to offer discounts on larger quantities of pre-sorted second class letters. These have now been replaced by Mailsort.

Mailsort enables you to obtain significant discounts on the postage cost of mailings of 4,000 letters or more at any one time: the savings range from 13% to 34% depending upon the quantity and level of service selected. Mailsort offers three delivery options:

- Mailsort 1: first class, target delivery next working day.
- Mailsort 2: second class, target delivery within three working days.
- Mailsort 3: economy class, target delivery within seven working days.

As always, you do not get something for nothing. In order to qualify for the available discounts, you have to pre-sort and bundle your letters by postcode so that the Royal Mail can despatch them to its main Delivery Offices without further sorting. They provide the Mailsort Database free to contract holders. Most – if not all – mailing houses are Mailsort contract holders so that, if your organization does not handle sufficient mail in-house to make it worth operating Mailsort, you can still have access to the discounts.

Another feature of Mailsort is that the postage pricing is not based on price steps according to weight. Instead, a 'straight line' pricing system is adopted so that, if your mailshot is just a few grammes over, say, the

60 gramme limit, you only pay pro-rata for the extra weight rather than the full cost of the next 'step' of the normal letter scales.

The table below summarizes the principal discounts available from Mailsort:

Mailsort 1
– standard discount	13%
– early posting discount (for postings before 1 pm)	15%

Mailsort 2	13%

Mailsort 3
– 4,000–250,000	25%
– over 25,000	28%
– over 1 million	32%

> *Note:* these discounts apply to postings sorted by Delivery Offices. The residue (smaller bundles) attract smaller discounts. For full details, contact the Royal Mail (see address section at end of book).
>
> If you can provide envelopes and addresses suitable for OCR (Optical Character Recognition) processing you will be able to obtain an additional 2% discount.

Other tips and ideas   It has already been mentioned that it is sensible to use the full available 60 grammes in a mailing. Other tips which the Royal Mail recommend include putting the sender's name and address on the envelope. This makes it easy for the Royal Mail to return undelivered letters and for the sender subsequently to update his mailing lists. The envelope can also be made to work to attract attention. In some cases a plain white envelope with the recipient's name and address neatly typed may be the most appropriate. On other occasions, colour and design can be used to make the letter stand out from the rest of the mail. A message can be printed on the envelope to draw attention to the importance of the content or to further publicize the event.

Another effective way of attracting attention is to time the mail-out so that it coincides with a first day cover. One conference organizer was fortunate enough to discover that a stamp issue relevant to his event was to be made at the time of his planned mail-out. He arranged a specially printed envelope which gave details of his conference and the first day cover. Although it was difficult to measure the benefits of this gimmick there is no doubt that it attracted a lot of attention.

The Royal Mail encourages the use of specialized mailing houses which are used to stuffing, addressing and handling large quantities of mail.

Indeed, when faced with a mail-out of several thousand brochures, any wise organizer would use professional help.

That said, if you are faced with doing it yourself, it is worth remembering that the Royal Mail will machine-frank bulk postings of 50 or more letters, eliminating the need to buy and lick large quantities of stamps, and that your local sorting office will collect mailings of 1,000 or more second class letters free of charge. These services are not widely known and it is well worth finding out about these and some of the other less well publicized Royal Mail services.

Overseas mailings   If you are mailing overseas, you can make considerable savings over Royal Mail postage charges by using private companies such as TNT who will collect your mailing and deliver it to individual addresses overseas. The savings can be as high as 50% over standard Royal Mail rates even for modest numbers.

Another possibility is to send the mailshot in bulk to an overseas address for posting, taking advantage of cheaper local rates.

Inserts

As mentioned earlier, most trade, professional and business publications accept inserts. This can be a comparatively inexpensive way of reaching a target market. The cost is dependent on the circulation (often the rate is quoted per 1,000 inserts, with a specified minimum number) and the weight of the material to be inserted. Some organizations will only accept inserts which have received prior clearance (this restriction is placed to protect the organization from becoming involved in promotions of an unsuitable kind). Inserts can be very effective but their impact can be reduced if the publication concerned habitually carries large numbers of them. However, in spite of what people say, most inserts receive a glance before they are discarded, and if your message is good enough it has a fair chance of attracting a response. Nevertheless, inserts do soon become separated from the parent publication and library and business circulation copies of such publications seldom retain them for very long.

Inserts Versus Advertising   Opinion is divided as to whether inserts are more effective than advertisements. The degree to which advertising pays depends on the type of event and the chosen publication. We have seen that advertising in national newspapers can be expensive and, in terms of cost per sale, very disappointing. Advertising in specialist publications is much less expensive and, because these magazines tend to be read by the customers in the target segment, can be highly cost-effective.

However, advertisements can only carry a limited amount of copy – certainly much less than a brochure. This is one argument for using an insert. In addition, it is usually possible to be selective when placing inserts – for example on a geographical basis. This facility is only rarely available to advertisers. Finally, an inserted brochure can be used within the receiving organization to support a request for permission to attend the event or, perhaps, a request for an allocation of funds.

For these reasons, inserts almost invariably work better than advertisements. That said, advertising has its uses as a means of creating awareness of your event – see 'Initial awareness' below.

A BALANCED PROMOTIONAL EFFORT

None of the promotional tools described above is likely to be successful in isolation. You need to mix and match the various methods to work in unison. How might this work in practice?

Initial awareness   Whilst a mailshot of a letter and brochure can create the initial awareness and, possibly, clinch the sale, it is best not to rely upon this.

Display advertising and good PR can each, in their own way, create an initial awareness which can mean that the subsequent brochure – be it sent by post or inserted in a relevant publication – will be received by at least a luke-warm audience. Most display advertising is concerned with creating awareness rather than in actually selling the product. Of course, display advertising leads to some sales, but display advertising – as we have already seen – rarely works on its own when selling conferences.

PR creates awareness in a different way. Editorial comment, unlike advertising, is seen to be unbiased by the reader and as such is thought to be objective. The reality is often that the copy has been taken (albeit in an edited form) from the press releases issued by the organizer or his PR agent.

The sales tools   The brochure is the principal sales tool for most events, but even when this has been preceded by advertising and PR, further efforts are often necessary to clinch the eventual sale. Follow-up telephone selling can be very effective, but it is expensive and it requires good telephone selling skills. It may be worth subcontracting this task to a company which specializes in telephone selling.

Some organizers do a double mailshot, the second being designed to jog the recipient's memory. How effective this is depends upon many factors but one pitfall is the risk of alienating the recipient especially if the mailing list you have used is not very 'clean' and contains duplicate addresses. As one manager wrote back, 'Thank you for the six brochures promoting your seminar. Although the subject matter interests me, I will not be attending since if the event itself is as badly organized as your mailshot it will be a disaster.'

Promotional schedule   The final promotional schedule will therefore be a carefully timed programme of advertising, PR, direct mail, e-mail and/or inserts and telephone selling. Of course, the overall promotional effort will depend upon the money available. Promotional activities are expensive – advertising particularly so (although the experienced – or canny – buyer can often 'snatch buy' display advertising at short notice at heavily discounted rates). Thus, in the end, the actual schedule will have to be a compromise with the brochure and postage absorbing the lion's share of the budget.

WILL YOU BE SUCCESSFUL?

A management consultant decided to market an executive training programme. Years of experience in business and a great deal of consultancy and research had confirmed that there was a need for the programme he offered. The programme itself was well thought out and supported by excellent speakers, exercises and case material. A high quality brochure was produced and mailed under cover of a personal letter to the people who needed the training. Success seemed assured. But the mail-out of 3,000 brochures failed to generate a single positive response. This failure is by no means unique. As mentioned at the start of Chapter 9, many public events do not succeed. Why not?

If our efforts fail to persuade the people we think the event will attract we should re-examine our product and our marketing strategy. Was what we offered right? Was the event too long, too expensive, too technical or not technical enough? Was the timing wrong, or the location? Did we promote the event to the right people – ie, had we identified the right segment and did we reach it? In short, we are back where we started.

Is it possible to carry out any research to test our ideas before we go to the expense of a full market campaign and hence perhaps avoid such failures? Some research and pre-testing might be possible. A company based in the Midlands decided to promote and sell programmes on public speaking, report writing and communication skills. The form of the programme was worked out and then a number of industrial and commercial companies were approached to seek their views. As a result of the comments received the sponsors shortened the programme and altered its content. The revised 'product' was subsequently successfully marketed to many of the companies whose opinions had been sought. Would it have been successful without the prior consultation which enabled the sponsors to match the product with the wants of the customers? Probably not. Some form of research like this can be inexpensive and can save a lot of wasted time and money. Sometimes it is worth carrying out a test market. An idea can be tried out by arranging a pilot event to gauge the response. We can also draw on the experience of experts in the chosen field and seek their advice on the event and the needs of the potential customers. There is much we can do to improve our product through research and seeking professional advice in order to reduce the subsequent risks.

The task of the organizer of the public event is to match what he or she can arrange with what the customer wants. A marketing manager will talk about the 'four Ps'. He tries to plan, co-ordinate and control the *product* offered, the *price* that is charged, the style of the *promotion* and the *place* where the product is made available. In doing so, his concern is to master not only the separate effects of these four Ps, but also their interactive effects. If we aspire to market conferences or meetings commercially we should adopt a similar approach.

EXECUTIVE CHECKLIST

- Is all your publicity material clear and does it contain all the necessary information? Is it produced to the highest standards?
- Do you prepare a marketing plan? Is your event promoted in sufficient time beforehand?
- Do you seek professional help over the content and design of your publicity material?
- Do you use more than one of the available media to communicate with potential customers?
- Do you use direct mail to best effect? Are your direct mail letters addressed personally?
- Do you take advantage of Royal Mail Mailsort discounts?
- Do you capitalize on your own mailing lists?
- Have you investigated using private companies for overseas mailings?

11

PAPERWORK AND ADMINISTRATION

'To do our work we all have to read a mass of papers. Nearly all of them are far too long. This wastes time, while energy has to be spent in looking for the essential points' (Sir Winston Churchill).

Paperwork is a vital element of any conference or meeting. Plans, schedules, programmes, minutes, invitations, orders, invoices, letters, reports, name badges, brochures, sketch maps, registration forms... a never-ending catalogue of printed papers without which the event could not take place. This chapter describes the more important paperwork generated by the typical conference, and how a PC can help in so many areas.

Things we say are soon forgotten. Things we write down are much more permanent. Paperwork communicates information. It does something else as well: it tells others a great deal about the originator. A neat, well produced letter not only *looks* better than a scruffy, badly produced one which is full of errors – it *is* better. We are often judged by people we may never meet who will base their opinions on the quality of paperwork. Things we commit to paper must therefore not only be clear, concise, accurate and readily understood by the reader, the paperwork itself must also look good.

HOUSE STYLE

Most large conferences have a logo, and even if the event itself does not have a logo the sponsor organization probably will. The logo and agreed house style should, if possible, be consistent throughout the event. Delegates' papers, programmes, visuals, venue signs, brochures, folders, pens and even menu cards should all reflect the house style and sport the logo. In this way a theme runs through the event, which not only adds to the professional image but also immediately identifies the event itself. This point is not lost elsewhere. Each Olympic Games seems to have its own logo incorporating the Olympic rings, while the 1951 Festival of Britain logo is still to be seen on some village nameplates throughout the country.

ROUTINE CORRESPONDENCE

'If language is not correct, then what is said is not what is meant. If what is said is not what is meant, then what ought to be done remains undone' (Confucius).

The conference organizer has to write a large number of letters. Nearly all will be detailing things which must be done. If these letters are badly written and contain incomplete or faulty information they will be misunderstood and the intended action will go wrong. However busy, the conference organizer and his staff must pay meticulous attention to detail in all routine correspondence.

Information technology

Ever since the introduction of fax machines, e-mail and mobile telephones the general tempo of business life has increased and the conference organizer has had even less time for the first aspect of an event (the planning stage) and almost the last (the event itself) and of course everything in between. Hosts, suppliers and delegates have all been struck by the 'I need it yesterday' syndrome – what a pity they didn't think about it the day before!

The quill pen went at the turn of the last century, the typewriter has been and gone, the word processor stayed for a while, but now every meeting planner has a personal computer on their desk or in their briefcase and e-mails are taking over from faxes, which replaced telexes. What next? Who knows? But what we do know is that meeting planners have been in the vanguard of using new technologies to make it easier to do what they always had to do: put simply, to plan their events.

Repetitive letters and registration   All conferences involve the despatch of repetitive or semi-repetitive letters, often in large numbers. Registration acknowledgements and briefings to speakers are typical examples of such letters. Most conference offices use software packages to handle registrations. Conference software is discussed in a later paragraph.

Some conference organizers accept e-mail registrations, others send out joining instructions on disk, the aim in each instance being to cut out unnecessary paperwork.

Delegate lists   The PC can automatically reproduce registration information in a variety of different formats – for example, delegate lists sorted alphabetically by name, by company, by hotel at which participants are staying and so on. These lists can, of course, be updated on a daily basis (even during the event itself if you have your system on site). If you use laser printers, the output copy will be near print quality.

Speakers' papers   These can be reproduced in a standard format using desktop publishing (DTP) or a word processor. To avoid the time and expense of re-keying, OCR (Optical Character Recognition) can be used to capture the text from hard copy provided by the speakers, or you can arrange to receive speakers' papers on floppy disk (or via e-mail – provided you have the necessary software and modem on your system).

Camera ready copy can then be produced for litho-printing or photocopying without a delay for proof-reading. A laser printer is essential if you opt for desktop publishing – even if you do not use DTP, a laser printer will give a far higher quality reproduction than an old fashioned daisy-wheel or dot matrix printer.

Some organizers now make speakers' papers available on disk, and others – for example, Emap – publish conference papers on the Internet. The advantages are obvious: delegates do not have to go away from the conference burdened with a heavy folder of paper, they can select and print off only those papers of interest to them; and organizers are spared the task of printing, binding and distributing sets of papers for each and every delegate.

Personal computers (PCs) are ideal for storing, manipulating and using information such as spreadsheets, invoices, sales records, address lists and all the detailed information associated with the typical conference. Indeed, one wonders how organizers of the larger events coped before they became available.

Today, there are several commercial conference management PC-based software packages on the market. These systems have been designed to assist meeting planners in all the stages of event management: planning, registration, financial, budgetary and management control, logistics reporting and communications. The premier systems ensure that organizers only ever have to enter data once – oh what bliss! – and when information is held on the system it can be collated with any other data and presented in any format for delegates, hosts and suppliers as well as for the organizers!

For instance, from the single entry of a medical or religious dietary requirement information can be sent to hotels, airlines and banqueting functions with rooming lists, flight manifests and seating plans.

The main off-the-shelf systems currently available are Visual IMPACT, ConQuest and Conference Management System. All three are sold as multi-user or single user packages, can be run from a laptop (ideal for on-site work) and are compatible with dot matrix, inkjet or laser printers. Each system is menu-driven so that the operator always has a series of instructions or prompts, to follow. Training programmes are an integral part of the after sales service. Visual IMPACT, which runs on any MS Windows platform, is probably the best of the bunch: it is very user friendly and the software has clearly been designed by both meeting planners and computer specialists with the needs of the users very much in mind. They have also led with the new hands-free registration via the Internet.

Costs vary; typically, a single user package will cost around £2,700–£4,000. Multi-user packages are more expensive, the overall cost depending upon the eventual number of workstations.

Desktop publishing (DTP) has already been mentioned. Using software packages such as Microsoft Publisher on a PC with a laser printer, you can produce print quality copy ready for photocopying or litho-printing. The finished product is very professional and is much cheaper and quicker than using the services of a printer to typeset everything.

Conference newspaper   It is good practice to publish a conference 'newspaper' during larger events. It can be used to promulgate administrative changes and important news. Desktop publishing (above) enables a professional-looking publication to be produced quickly and cheaply on site.

REGISTRATION

The process of registration involves a lot of detailed paperwork and is full of pitfalls. The word 'registration' is somewhat confusingly used to describe two separate processes:

1. Action before the event to receive and acknowledge bids or nominations for places on the event.
2. The reception procedures at the actual event.

In this chapter we are mainly concerned with the former. Registration at the event itself is discussed in Chapter 13.

An accurate record of who is coming to an event will be needed, and delegates must always be told where they have to be – and when. Every meeting therefore needs at least a basic registration procedure. Public events need a more elaborate system and registration for the largest conferences is a major task (even if you have a computerized registration system). Most of the following remarks are concerned with registration for public events where money is to be received from the delegate, but many of the principles can also be applied to the in-company event.

Three general principles should be followed in setting up the registration system:

1. *Simplicity* – because most of us are very bad at completing forms, reading detailed instructions or following complicated routines. Only the simplest procedures will therefore work.
2. *Foresight* – to anticipate and eliminate possible causes of error and confusion.
3. *Common sense* – to avoid silly and unnecessary mistakes.

It is worth remembering that the efficiency or otherwise of the registration procedure will itself carry a message to the delegate. If acknowledgements are slow, administrative instructions obscure and other information inaccurate or badly produced, the delegate will feel that the event itself will be poorly organized. Conversely, an excellent response will sharpen the delegate's anticipation and may even induce him to persuade colleagues to register.

The registration form

Most bids for places on public events are submitted on the registration form published by the organizers. The design of this form is critical to the effectiveness of registration procedures. Get it wrong and either the delegate or you and your staff – or even both parties – will face severe problems. The form must be clear and simple for the delegates to complete and easy for the registration staff to process. The registration staff may be dealing with large numbers of forms, perhaps for more than one event at a time.

The main points to consider when designing the registration form are:

1. The form must seek to obtain all the information needed by the organizers.
2. The registration form should contain sufficient space in which the delegate can write the required information. This sounds obvious but how often are we faced with forms which leave far too little space for some answers and, perversely, too much for others? Space should also be left for any control material which has to be added by the registration staff.
3. The form must look attractive. If it does not it will be thrown away, and a letter, containing inadequate information, will be returned instead, thus creating exception handling (see page 320) and causing inconvenience and loss of valuable time.
4. Forms for different events should be printed on different coloured papers to simplify identification and sorting.

Computer Forms   Even if the information on the registration form is going to be fed into a computer data bank there are strong arguments for avoiding a form which is obviously to be used to this end. The special boxes so often associated with computer forms are less easy to fill in than conventional forms. It is almost impossible to type the information into the boxes and quickly scribbled capital letters can be very difficult to decipher. Another argument against making it obvious that the information is to be fed into a computer is that some people do not like to have their names and other details used in this way. Delegates may be sufficiently put out to avoid registering altogether if the registration form is obviously designed for ease of computer input. However, it does make sense to order the questions/information on the registration form so that it can be input straight onto the computer.

If you do store – or intend to store – information about delegates on a computer you must register under the terms of the Data Protection Act.

Registration information

The accuracy and completeness of information submitted on a registration form is directly related to the design of the form. If information is requested in a logical sequence then organizers stand a very good chance of receiving accurate data.

Remember that information will nearly always be completed by hand so wherever possible allow delegates to tick boxes or circle alternatives rather than have to write down their selections.

Information needed for a registration may include:

1. Title (Mr/Mrs/Miss/Ms/Dr/Prof/Sir, etc).
    First name – names for name badges.
    Last name prefix (van, von, de la, etc).
    Last name.
    Qualifications and awards (Phd, BSc, MBE, etc).

2. Company or organization name.
    Job title.
    Full address and a mailing address if different.
    Communication details – telephone number, fax number, e-mail address, mobile number.

3. Nationality.
    Preferred conference language.
    Country of origin.
    Passport number and expiry date (when taking delegates overseas).
    Dietary requirements.
    Any special requirements – wheelchair access, facilities for dogs for the blind or deaf, etc.

4. Type of delegate (full, student, honorary member, etc).

5. Date of arrival and time (if before normal check-in time).
    Date of departure.
    Travel – details or requirements.
    Guest details (spouse, partner, colleague, children (ages for cots etc).
    Name format as for delegates.

6. Required options.

7. Plenary sessions.
    Optional sessions.
    Visits – business tours.
    Social activities – cultural visits, city tours, sporting functions, etc.
    Banqueting functions – welcome cocktails and reception, gala dinners.
    Pre- or post-conference tours.

8. Accommodation.
   Dates required if different to arrival/departure dates.
   Specific hotel if offered or grade of hotel.
   Type of room(s): single, double, twin, junior suite, etc.

9. Payment details.
   Method of payment – cheque, bank transfer, credit card.
   Fixed currencies.
   Deposit or full payment dates.
   Cancellation and refund policies.

Throughout the form of course all charges must be clearly shown with VAT rates and service charges. However delegates register (mail, fax or e-mail) it is essential that the organizer confirms all the requirements that have been noted back to the delegate, with either an invoice or a receipted statement. The onus for checking is then passed back to the delegate.

Processing registration forms

Registrations should be acknowledged quickly – preferably by return of post. The acknowledgement for the event (ie, those promoted six to eight weeks beforehand – see page 261) should include:

◆ a welcome letter;
◆ a programme for the event;
◆ details of when and where to register (to include, for larger events, how – by a number, alphabetically, by name, etc);
◆ how to get to the venue and, if necessary, to the hotel (a sketch map is always useful to the delegates);
◆ admission and social function tickets (if needed);
◆ invoices (receipted if payment accompanies registration). The invoice should state the event, the name(s) of the delegate(s), VAT payable, the balance due and details of any under- or over-payments.

As mentioned earlier, some of the above information may be sent out on disk.

For international events, which have a lead time of six months or more, it is usual to arrange two responses:

– the first, which is sent out when the registration if received, acknow-ledges the bid and contains the admission card and invoice and/or receipt;

Confirmation letter with finance

2 July 1999

Mrs Maisie Blyth   Ref: CV2104/89
Hospital Equipment & Laboratory Products
Unit 5
Bounds Green Industrial Estate
London N11 0JG

Dear Mrs Blyth

RE: The Millennium – The Millennium Dome
Friday 31 December 1999 – Wednesday 5 January 2000

Thank you for your recent registration to attend the above event.

In accordance with your booking requirements we have pleasure in confirming your full registration details below. In the event that any of the information contained herein is incorrect then please contact our Conference Department immediately. Please quote your booking reference number as detailed above in all communications.

Attendee Type:	Full Delegate Fee
Dietary Requirements:	Vegetarian
Preferred Language:	English

Guest(s)
Mr Derek Blyth   Spouse   No nuts

Flight Reservations		Class	Departure Details		Arrival Details		Seats
EZ123	30/12/1999 IN	CL	14:45	Schiphol	15:45	London Luton	1
EZ987	05/01/2000 OUT	CL	20:00	London Luton	22:00	Schiphol	1

Accommodation Reservations	Grade	Room type	Arrive/Depart	Nights	#Rooms	Occupancy
The London Hilton	5	EXEDBL	31/12/1999–05/01/2000	5	1	2
Park Lane, London, United Kingdom						

Option Bookings		Timings	Description and Location	Tickets
31/12/1999	01/01/2000	18:00–02:00	Gala Dinner – Welcome to the New Century The Banqueting Hall	2
02/01/2000		10:00–18:00	Tour of the Dome The Dome	1
03/01/2000		09:00–11:30	The New Millennium and Religion The Main Hall	2
04/01/2000		10:00–12:00	Future Developments The Main Hall	1
05/01/2000		13:00–15:00	The Automobile The Main Hall	1

Financial Summary

Total Amount Invoiced	£2,648.66
Total Amount Received	£734.40
Balance Due	£1,914.26

May we take this opportunity to thank you for your reservation and we look forward to meeting you in the very near future.

Yours sincerely

John Robinson
Event Co-ordinator

Nearer the event a detailed itinerary and conference programme with travel instructions (even tickets), hotel vouchers, function tickets, etc will be sent out to the delegate.

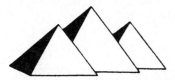

EVENT MANAGEMENT SYSTEMS
Computer Software – Setting The Pace

The Millennium
The Millennium Dome
Friday 31 December 1999 – Wednesday 5 January 2000

Event Itinerary

Name: **Mrs Maisie Blyth**
Company: **Hospital Equipment & Laboratory Products**

Arriving at the Event:

30/12/1999	13:45	Check-in for Flight EZ123
30/12/1999	14:45	Flight EZ123 departs from Schiphol
30/12/1999	15:45	Flight EZ123 arrives at London Luton

Accommodation Reservations

31/12/1999   The London Hilton – Room type 'Executive Double' booked for five nights

Option Bookings

31/12/1999	18:00–02:00	Gala Dinner – Welcome to the New Century	Banqueting Hall
02/01/2000	10:00–18:00	Tour of the Dome	The Dome
03/01/2000	09:00–11:30	The New Millennium and Religion	The Main Hall
04/01/2000	10:00–12:00	Future Developments	The Main Hall
05/01/2000	13:00–15:00	The Automobile	The Main Hall

Departing from the Event

05/01/2000	19:00	Check-in for Flight EZ987
05/01/2000	20:00	Flight EZ987 departs from London Luton
05/01/2000	22:00	Flight EZ987 arrives at Schiphol

– the second which is sent out nearer to the event (say 4–6 weeks beforehand), contains the welcome letter, details of where to register and how to get to the venue, and – possibly – the programme (although this is sometimes handed out on the day because changes in the programme can take place at the last minute and it is some-times quite bulky. Furthermore, many delegates forget to bring it and therefore ask for a replacement when they arrive).

Changes   Delegates will change their minds, submit new information and make substitutions. All these changes must be recorded and it is necessary to send out a duplicate receipt/admission card acknowl-edging the change in booking.

Processing Registrations   A foolproof system is needed. A control number should be given to each form and a record of processing, invoicing and so on should be kept. Cheques, postal orders, etc, must be properly handled and it is sensible to make the invoice number the same as the process control number for ease of identification at a later date. As already mentioned, most organizations already use computers to process registrations.

LIAISON

The need to confirm everything in writing, especially when dealing with hotels, was stressed in Chapter 2.

The venue needs:

◆ a detailed timetable/administrative schedule;
◆ a delegates' list and, for residential events, a rooming list;
◆ confirmation of menus, special dietary needs and so on;
◆ detailed billing instructions.

Some of the above merit further explanation:

Timetable/Administrative schedule

There is no 'right' or 'wrong' way of preparing this. Some of the better venues have their own proformas, but even these can omit important detail. The best advice is to prepare as simple as possible a guide on a day-by-day basis, specifying what happens room by room and covering every detail such as AV equipment, timings of breaks, menus and so on.

There is one snag: all too often, venue staff fail to assimilate much of the finer detail. Sometimes, they ignore important details or substitute standard venue practices for specific requests. Hence the need to check and check again and, for large events, for a daily conference with key members of the venue management to go over and confirm the day's plan.

Rooming list

This can be the cause of endless confusion and problems, especially if bills are to be split (eg the delegates pay for their own extras, but the main accommodation is paid for by the conference organizer).

The format on page 286 shows a layout produced by one meeting planner on his computer system:

Bookees and Residents within Accommodation Groups
<u>The Millennium</u>
<u>The Millennium Dome</u>
<u>Friday 31 December 1999 – Wednesday 5 January 2000</u>

The London Hilton
Park Lane
London
United Kingdom

Bookee	Arrive–Depart Dates	# of Nights	Assigned Residents
Executive Double			
Beasley – David	31/12/1999–05/01/2000	5	Mr David Beasley
Blyth – Maisie	31/12/1999–05/01/2000	5	Mrs Maisie Blyth
			Mr Derek Blyth
Laarsen (van) – Arthur	31/12/1999–05/01/2000	5	Mr Arthur van Laarsen
Long – Adrienne	30/12/1999–05/01/2000	6	Ms Adrienne Long
Mayes (van) – Jenny	31/12/1999–01/01/2000	1	Ms Jenny van Mayes
Pearson – Peter	31/12/1999–05/01/2000	5	Mr Peter Pearson
			Mrs Julie Smithson
Reid – Desmond	31/12/1999–05/01/2000	5	Mr Desmond Reid
			Mrs Anne Arkwright

No. of Assigned Residents for Room Type: Executive Double = 10

Bookee	Arrive–Depart Dates	# of Nights	Assigned Residents
Executive Single			
Bourne (van) – Franca	31/12/1999–09/01/2000	9	Ms Franca van Bourne
Boxall – Jerry	31/12/1999–05/01/2000	5	Mr Jerry Boxall
Venison – Barbara	31/12/1999–05/01/2000	5	Dr Barbara Venison

No. of Assigned Residents for Room Type: Executive Single = 3

Bookee	Arrive–Depart Dates	# of Nights	Assigned Residents
Executive Suite			
Carter (van) – Tristan	31/12/1999–05/01/2000	5	Dr Tristan van Carter
Cerezales – Oscar	31/12/1999–05/01/2000	5	Mr Oscar Cerezales
Hudson – Rocky	31/12/1999–05/01/2000	5	Mr Rocky Hudson
Polson – Roy	30/12/1999–04/01/2000	5	Mr Roy Polson
			Ms A N Other
Provis – Alison	31/12/1999–05/01/2000	5	Miss Alison Provis
Reid – Desmond	31/12/1999–05/01/2000	5	Mr Desmond Reid
			Mr William Armstrong

No. of Assigned Residents for Room Type: Executive Suite = 8

NAME BADGES

There are almost as many opinions about name badges as there are conference delegates and the variety of products is astonishing. People have their own preferences, but the main requirements are:

1. The name must be legible: see 'Legibility' below.
2. Information on the badge must be accurate. Names, job titles and company details must be spelt correctly and verified against the registration form.
3. It must be possible to produce replacement badges on site during the conference: this is because:
   (i)   there are inevitable late substitutions for people on the original list;
   (ii)   however careful you are, one or two spelling errors will escape notice until the delegate registers; and
   (iii) people lose their badges and ask for replacements. The badges produced on site should look the same as those produced before the event: see 'Legibility', below.
4. The badge must be durable enough to last the event. A stick-on paper badge might last out a one-day event but is certainly not suitable for longer. It is worth considering giving each delegate a second badge to save having to replace mislaid badges during the conference.
5. The badge must be simple to fix securely without damaging the delegates' clothing. This is a demanding requirement. Pins are unpopular with women and top-pocket badges may be alright for the men, but what do women do? There are many makes of badge holder, some good, some bad, some cheap and some expensive. Some are very novel. For example, one pocket type has room for the event timetable on the pocket insert – an easy ready reference for the delegate. Perhaps the best advice is to test the market and obtain several samples from suppliers before making a final choice.
6. If possible, the badge should carry a logo or other 'house' design – this adds a touch of professionalism. Name badges should be colour coded to differentiate delegates, speakers and administrative staff.
7. The problem of quickly finding a delegate's badge at registration should not be overlooked when deciding what sort of badge to adopt. The time taken to find badges is often a major cause of delay during registration, although the problem can be eliminated by filing name badges with other delegate papers – see the section on 'Conference Kit' below and Chapter 12.

Legibility

This is likely to be your biggest problem – one which can really only be solved by investing in appropriate technology.

Even today, it is not uncommon to see name badges in the form of sticky labels with typewritten – or even handwritten – names. These are really not acceptable. Even the well-sighted have to bend down to read the typewritten names – the less well sighted have to lean forward to peer at the label, thereby invading the wearer's 'body space' and causing embarrassment.

Handwritten labels look unprofessional. Other methods such as neat calligraphy, phototypesetting or desktop publishing, plastic tape and so on can be used. All these have their disadvantages, either in terms of cost, ease of production, legibility or the time needed to produce replacements. (As we saw in 3 above, the reception desk at the event should be capable of producing instant replacements or new labels in the same style as the pre-prepared labels. This implies having the methodology which produced the original labels on the registration desk.)

Fortunately, modern technology has done much to overcome the name badge problem. If you have a PC and laser printer, it is a simple matter to produce labels like the one illustrated below (reproduced actual size):

EVENT MANAGEMENT SYSTEMS

MAISIE BLYTH

Hospital Equipment & Laboratory Products UK

EVENT MANAGEMENT SYSTEMS
5 Bucklersbury · Hitchin · Herts · SG5 1BB · UK
Tel: +44 (0) 1462 420780 · e-mail: enquire@eventmanagementsystems.co.uk

Example of a delegate's name badge (see page 287)

If you use one of the event management software packages mentioned on page 277, you will be able to produce labels using the software without having to re-key the delegates' names – the perfect solution to the problem?

There are also specialist machines which produce typeset quality copy on clear adhesive tape which can be stuck onto colour coded or pre-printed card (see also 6 above). Another, the Brother PT-8008 Lettering System, can produce up to five lines of text (eg, name, job title, company and so on) on a variety of tapes up to 24mm wide. The machine, which is mains or battery powered, is fully portable (it weighs about 2kg and is the size of an A4 ring binder) and has a conventional keyboard with LCD display and a built-in thermal printer.

PLACE NAME PLATES

These are often required for training courses and smaller meetings. Rather than produce handwritten name plates (or even ask delegates to write their own!), you can use your PC to produce legible and professional looking cards. If you use 'tent card' name plates, print the delegates' names on both sides of the card so they can locate their seats without having to lean over the table to find out where they are sitting.

As with name badges, you need to be able to alter/replace name plates on site to accommodate late changes (and even mistakes!).

DELEGATES' LISTS

It is common practice at public events – and at many in-company meetings – to produce a list of delegates which is given to each person attending. In the past, the task of producing this list was a headache to the organizers. It had to be accurate and up to date. Late changes were inevitable but time had to be left to type or typeset and reproduce the final list. There was an inevitable conflict between the time needed to prepare an accurate, well-produced list and the need to delay as long as possible to incorporate late changes. An addendum for late changes often had to be produced at the last moment or even during the event. Today, thanks to computerized registration, these problems are things of the past.

It is necessary to decide what information should be shown on the list and in what order. Should delegates be listed in alphabetical order by name, or by company? Should they be shown grouped in their different departments? Is it necessary to produce plenary *and* sectional or syndicate meeting lists? The list for large, residential conferences where delegates are accommodated in more than one hotel should, if possible, show at which hotel each delegate is staying. This simplifies out-of-hours social contact and relieves the organizer of the need to answer constant queries about this subject. That said, female delegates in particular can – rightly – be sensitive to having this information available to other delegates.

It is worth remembering that the full names and addresses of the delegates attending an event can be commercial valuable information. For this reason it is rare to give full addresses on delegates' lists, both to protect delegates from unsolicited correspondence and direct mail advertising material after the event and because the sponsor may wish to generate extra income by selling the requisite lists. As mentioned earlier, you must be registered under the Data Protection Act if you store personal information on computer.

Delegates' lists seldom give full addresses (this is to protect delegates from receiving unwanted attention after the event). However, to encourage 'networking', it is sensible to have the facility to make addresses available to those who wish to exchange this information. At some conferences, delegates' business cards are collected in, photocopied and distributed during the event.

CONFERENCE KIT

A 'pack' of information is nearly always given to each delegate. A typical conference kit might be made up of:

- a document case or wallet;
- notepaper;
- pen or pencil;
- programme (if not sent out in advance);
- exhibition catalogue;
- delegates' lists;
- venue site plan;
- speakers' papers (if to be circulated beforehand);
- promotional material, tourist information and so on.

Name badges and other individual items are sometimes included but it is advisable to handle these separately. Packing, handling and distributing large numbers of kits is no small task and most organizers prefer to have a standard run of identical folders for all delegates and keep the individual items such as name badges and tickets separate, usually in an envelope addressed to the delegate himself. This simplifies handling procedures during registration at the conference – see also Chapter 13.

It is sometimes worth having two packs per delegate at the longer residential conference. One, containing social and local interest information, town maps, etc, can be placed in the delegate's hotel room. This can make a visitor feel very welcome in a strange city. If you do this, the conference folder itself then only needs to contain essential business material and can be given to delegates as they arrive at the venue.

CONFERENCE PAPERS

Delegates expect to receive copies of speakers' papers. They do not just need the papers for their own record of the conference: delegates are often expected to write a report on conferences they attend and draw on handout material when they are preparing their documents. The production of speakers' papers can cause difficulties.

Obtaining copy from individual speakers

Papers should be reasonably full summaries of the main points and supporting arguments rather than copies of actual scripts. Some speakers are very slow at drafting their papers and firm deadlines must be established and followed to avoid a last minutes rush to produce combined bound volumes to distribute to delegates. Some speakers will not release their papers until they have delivered the speech. This is particularly the case if the speech is newsworthy or controversial. In such cases delegates would need to be told that the text or summary would be circulated later.

The 'Abstract' and 'Poster' techniques are used in some larger technical conferences – see Chapter 3.

Reproduction

It is advisable to specify the layout and possibly also type styles so that contributions can be reproduced without retyping and reformatting. The preparation of numbers of papers can be a major task and some organizers even ask speakers to submit the required number of pre-printed papers. However, quality control is lost in this case and, if the appearance of the final papers is really important, the conference organizer is faced with the task of rekeying, typesetting and printing all the papers. Fortunately, modern technology has made this task much easier: OCR (Optical Character Recognition) can be used to capture the text without re-keying and, as already mentioned, desktop publishing can be used to ensure a quality end product. Also, as previously mentioned, papers can be published on the Internet or made available on disk.

Distribution

Papers can either be sent to delegates beforehand, distributed with the conference kit or be given out afterwards. Each course has its own advantages and disadvantages:

1. *Distribution beforehand*   This has the advantage of giving delegates time to study the papers before the event and to prepare questions. However, pre-conference distribution pre-empts the speakers' presentation, and is costly and unreliable. It also reduces the time available in which to print and collate the speakers' material. Many delegates – especially those from overseas – will arrive without their papers either because they forgot them or because their copies have been delayed in the post. Extra copies may have to be prepared for them, adding to costs.

Some events (especially training programmes) have pre-reading material which has to be issued beforehand. Sadly, much of this is unread – assuming it actually reaches the participant in time!

2. *Distribution at the event*   This method is simplest and cheapest provided speakers can produce their copy in sufficient time. However, delegates may only receive their papers as they arrive at the hall and there is a danger that they will be reading and shuffling papers instead of concentrating on the session in hand. As already mentioned, at some major conferences, papers – or, more usually, summary extracts or abstracts – are displayed on 'poster boards'.

Some organizers make papers available for collection/distribution during the event but in loose leaf form after each session so that delegates can build up their folder as the event unfolds. This technique is almost invariably used on training programmes. Care has to be taken to ensure the folder (usually a 4-ring binder) is big enough for all the papers. At one recent London conference the volume of paper was almost twice as great as the folder could contain – what is more, not all the material was 4-hole punched! Electronic distribution of papers (Internet or on disk) obviates the problem.

3. *Distribution after the event*   Papers can be given out after each session or they can be posted to delegates after the event. This method has a number of disadvantages. Postage costs apart, it is often unpopular with delegates since, if they do not know how comprehensive papers will be, they will not know whether or not to take notes during sessions. It is also unpopular with some delegates since they like to take the papers home to prove they attended the event. Nevertheless, distribution after the event does give a chance to include post-conference reports of proceedings and to summarize question and answer sessions and other discussions.

If you decide to distribute the papers after the event, you should do so as soon as possible. We saw earlier that delegates often use the speakers' papers when they prepare their own post-conference reports: they naturally do not like this task to be delayed due to their not having the speakers' papers to hand.

Post-conference reports

Sponsors sometimes ask for full records of their conference proceedings. Some even ask for full verbatim reports. The only satisfactory way of producing full reports is to have shorthand writers present to note everything down. Tape recordings and speakers' personal notes can be used to check and verify anything which is not clear, but these are not always completely satisfactory methods of producing verbatim reports. Tape recording quality cannot be relied upon, especially during question and answer sessions, and there is no guarantee that speakers will follow their scripts. Reports can either be in the form of full reported speech, with all asides and remarks included, or sequence summaries covering the essential points. The latter type of report is less bulky and easier to read. However, certain proceedings have to be fully reported and in these cases full verbatim records are prepared.

On other occasions, summaries of the proceedings are sufficient. Writing minutes of meetings or summaries of discussions at seminars or workshops is not easy. The author must have knowledge of the subject and be skilled at writing sequence notes. He must also be fully briefed so that he knows, for example, whether to simply record decisions or whether supporting arguments and discussions are also to be summarized.

Many organizations generate extra income by selling copies of conference papers after the event. If this is intended, copyright agreements must be negotiated with the speakers.

OTHER PAPERWORK

In addition to the major items listed above, there is a whole range of other accessories to consider: menus, tickets to sessions and functions, invitations, information packs, air ticket folders and luggage labels, to name but a few. Conference newspapers are sometimes produced, especially at major events, but these are expensive. A daily news sheet can be a useful way of promulgating routine administrative announcements and even a one-off newspaper can be used to highlight the themes of the event. (This, as we saw earlier in the chapter, is easily accomplished with the aid of desktop publishing.) A venue plan is a useful document. The layouts of many hotels and the larger conference centres such as Wembley, the Barbican (famous – or infamous – in this respect), ICC Birmingham or the ICC Berlin are confusing to the stranger and a personal plan, over-printed with details special to the event, will be appreciated, help reduce delegate movement time and relieve the information desk of many direction-seeking enquiries.

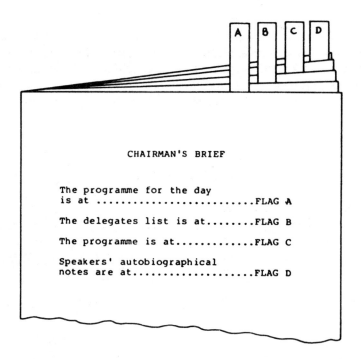

CHAIRMAN'S BRIEF

The programme for the day
is at ....FLAG A

The delegates list is at........FLAG B

The programme is at............FLAG C

Speakers' autobiographical
notes are at...................FLAG D

Example of use of flags to identify elements of a brief
– in reality there would be much more text detail than illustrated

BRIEFS

Chairmen, speakers, exhibitors (if there are any), visitors and VIPs all need to be briefed. Exhibitors at large exhibitions need comprehensive briefs covering timings, access, set-up procedures, services, security, cleaning, etc. The professional exhibition organizer usually produces an exhibitors' handbook to cover all the information and instructions exhibitors need (see Chapter 7 for further details).

Briefs for chairmen, speakers and VIPs are best prepared in the form of a short paper giving the person all the essential information (timings, where to go, who will be there, etc) with all the background information (autobiographies, statistics, useful extra information, etc) attached in the form of appendices. It is good practice to use the Civil Service 'flag-up' method to identify essential supporting information (see diagram on page 294).

Speakers' briefs

Speakers are notoriously difficult to 'discipline'. They must be carefully briefed, especially if they cannot attend a speakers' meeting before the conference. With a good brief, you are in a stronger position to insist they follow your instructions, especially if they are receiving a fee for speaking.

SCRIPTS

Few people have the ability to speak at formal occasions without using scripts or notes. A script is essential at the larger event where AV aids are cued to the speakers' words and where, perhaps, interpreters will be using scripts to help them make their simultaneous translations. Most speakers will produce their own scripts but they will need advice on the cuing symbols for AV aids. Television prompt scripts are usually prepared by the firm which provides the prompt equipment. (See Chapter 6.)

EXECUTIVE CHECKLIST

- Are you satisfied with the quality of paperwork produced for your events?
- Do you use either off-the-shelf or your own computer software for event management?
- Is your house style or corporate image properly reflected throughout?
- Are your registration forms well designed? Do you have a trial run to test the registration form before it is printed?
- Are registrations acknowledged quickly? Do acknowledgements help foster a good image of the event?
- Are the name badges you use really acceptable, and are the names on these and delegates' lists correct?

- ◆ Do you brief chairmen, speakers and VIPs properly?
- ◆ Do you give delegates a conference kit containing notepaper, pen, delegates' list, programme and any other useful material?
- ◆ Do you prepare conference papers and identify the most suitable time and method for distributing them?
- ◆ Do you make full use of technology for managing your events and for all the 'paperwork'... and can you replace paperwork with electronic copy?

12

DEALING WITH HOTELS

'We're about to settle the account for last month's training course at the Park Hotel, and I'm ringing to ask your advice. Should we add anything for service when we settle?'

The caller, a 'first time' buyer of hotel conference facilities, was consulting the agency which had handled the booking on his behalf. His problem was that he had been sailing in what were, for him, unchartered waters. Right from the outset he had been conscious that he did not know the ropes when it came to dealing with hotels and his uncertainty about gratuities was the latest and, he hoped, the last of the difficulties he had encountered.

This is a common problem. For most of us, our experience in dealing with hotels is confined to holidays (which, more often than not, have been booked through a travel agent) or to being delegates at events organized by someone else. We may be familiar with the rules (such as they are) regarding tipping and service charges on meals. But when it comes to all the ramifications of running a conference in an hotel we are less than sure of the rules of the game.

This is not surprising. The organization behind what we, the public, sees in an hotel is quite properly hidden from view. Our dealings are confined to (hopefully) well-trained managers and staff. What goes on behind the scenes only concerns us when something goes wrong. Even then, it is rare for us to have access to whoever is responsible: we continue to be faced with the 'front-of-house' staff.

But unless we know what makes the organization 'tick', and unless we know the limitations as well as the capabilities of hotels in terms of accommodating conferences, we could be courting disaster.

This chapter is designed to help you in your dealings with hotels so that, aware of their limitations (as well as their strengths) you can avoid some of the potential pitfalls and maximize the advantages of using hotels for your conferences.

HOTELS ARE NOT CONFERENCE CENTRES

The first thing to understand is that hotels exist to feed, water and accommodate their guests. They are organized to that end. Guests – especially residents – are 'processed' as individuals or in small groups of three or four. Larger groups – weddings, banquets and receptions – are processed *en bloc* and only stay on site for a short time (those who do stay on in the hotel afterwards revert to individual patterns of behaviour once the event is over).

Conferences – especially residential conferences – are by their very nature different and thus present hotels with a number of difficulties. The guests behave less as individuals; they are on site throughout the day; and they – and the event organizers – tend to be more demanding than individual guests. Often, the hotel facilities – which are not designed for conference use – are less than adequate, and, perhaps most important of all, the needs of conference delegates and organizers place simultaneous demands on different departments of the hotel – departments which tend to be autonomous in the way in which they are managed and run.

Conference centres, on the other hand, are organized and run to cater for groups. Paradoxically, they are not organized to cater for individuals and many do not accept single bookings for that reason.

But, for reasons we have already discussed in Chapter 2, the majority of conferences take place in hotels, and we need to be aware of the inherent organizational and management difficulties our events present to these establishments.

How are hotels organized?

First and foremost, we need to know how hotels are organized: this knowledge will, in itself, help us avoid many misunderstandings in our dealings with them.

Whilst not peculiar or unusual in their organizational structure, hotels follow very conservative operating patterns which distinguish them from most other commercial organizations. There are many reasons for this – some obvious, some not so obvious.

First, hotels operate round-the-clock. There are no set opening hours (although, of course, some facilities are only available at certain times). Second, managers and staff work long hours, many of which are 'anti-social'; pay is not generous; a large amount of casual labour is used on an 'on demand' basis to cover periods of peak activity and staff turnover rates are often high. The task of the personnel manager in a large hotel in terms of recruitment and training must be a constant nightmare and, although most managers and staff move within the industry (ie, from hotel to hotel), the lack of continuity is a major feature – one we must recognize (and one for which we must legislate) right from the outset.

Management and organizational structure

Most major hotels – by which we mean larger hotels, especially those owned by the major chains (Granada, Hilton and so on) – are organized along functional lines as follows:

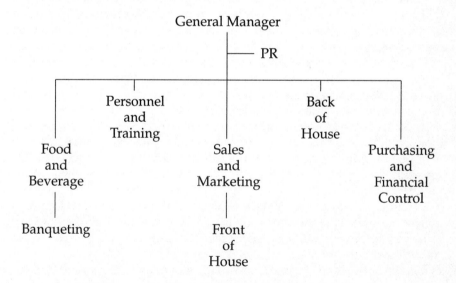

Note: Some of these departments are combined in smaller hotels.

Each department has its own manager, and departments tend to be autonomous. This is an important point. Communications between departments are not always as good as they could be which means that it is dangerous to assume that things you agree with one manager will be relayed accurately (if at all) to someone in another department.

The General Manager is, quite literally, next to God. Your chances of meeting him (or, occasionally – but ever more often, her) are, in the average hotel, practically zero. Staff (and other managers) seem to hold him in awe and he certainly wields considerable power. Of course, in some hotels the 'GM' is not only very visible, he is also very approachable and helpful. In *privately owned* hotels, the proprietor often fulfils this role. In these cases, the involvement is almost invariably very personal (even to the point of idiosyncrasy in some instances).

Sales and Marketing   This department is discussed in detail first not because it is the most important, but because it is usually your first point of contact when you make your initial approach. Well groomed and personable, their *sales executives* are just that – no more and no less. Their job is to win your business and, like any salesperson, they will do all within their powers to persuade you that *their* hotel is the place for *your* event and that whatever you need the hotel will provide.

But, beware! Like so many salespeople they do not have any responsibility for delivery. Indeed, by the time your event takes place, they may have moved onto pastures new – having left no record of the promises they so eagerly made to persuade you to sign on the dotted line.

This may sound harsh. It is certainly not always the case, but it is better to be safe rather than sorry and to make sure that you discuss the detailed plans with those who *will* be responsible for the eventual delivery *before* you sign on the dotted line.

And this is *vital:* make sure you confirm everything in *writing* – and seek written confirmation back from the hotel. Then there should be no misunderstanding (provided, in the turnover already discussed, the file for your event is not lost for the want of a handover – it has been known!).

To mitigate our comments about the hotel industry, technology has improved internal communication and now hotel staff only have to tap into the computer system to view files or add information to the event file. We strongly recommend that you attend the briefing, close to the event, when the hotel group co-ordinator will relay all relevant details to the different departmental heads. The group co-ordinators are often junior members of staff with a huge amount of responsibility, and the organizers' attendance adds weight to the briefing and ensures that the hotel and the organizers are working 'together' for the benefit of the event attendees.

Banqueting   In most hotels, the banqueting department is responsible for all functions from, as the name implies, banquets to weddings and from conferences to dinner dances. What this means in practice is that they plan, set up, run and (not to be forgotten) clear functions... and so on to the next. Hotels like to maximize the use of their banqueting rooms ('conference rooms' from our particular viewpoint) which means, in turn, that banqueting managers and staff are usually very busy and are working to tight schedules – setting up rooms with tables, chairs, cutlery, linen, glass; hiring and briefing casual staff, dealing with the kitchens and other hotel departments, also with outside sub-contractors (everything from toast-masters to bands and set constructors to audio visual suppliers) and, last but not least, with the organizers.

The planning horizons of banqueting managers tend to be short – tomorrow, the day after and next week. *Your* conference may be many months away. This disparity in planning horizons can be a problem but, provided you can win his attention, you should be able to obtain a lot of useful advice and ideas from the banqueting manager – after all, he has seen it all before... or has he?

A year or so ago, a group of hotel banqueting managers were attending a seminar entitled, 'Do you really know what conference organizers want?' In mid-morning a lively debate was in progress and the seminar leader, realizing the value of the discussion, let it run on to 11 o'clock – well after the scheduled time for coffee (10.30 am). Every conference organizer will recognize this sort of situation: sometimes it is just not possible to follow a rigorous timetable to the exact minute. But this was a revelation to the banqueting managers, one of whom exclaimed that he would never, in future, stand outside a conference room as the coffee went cold saying it served them right for over-running.

The point is that, more often than not, neither the banqueting manager nor his staff have any idea of what goes on inside the meeting room. Perhaps, if you brief them and involve them, they will be more under-standing. Make sure the hotel management and staff know about your event and its importance to you and to the delegates: they will then be much more supportive than if you exclude them or – even worse – ignore them.

As a post script to the above story about the seminar for hoteliers, the organizer made the participants sit all day on standard (armless) banqueting chairs – the sort which are acceptable for a dinner but not for sitting on all day. That, too, was a salutary lesson for the banqueting managers, all of whom admitted that their hotels invariably used these chairs for conferences (at least they used to: perhaps proper conference chairs have been provided by now... perhaps...).

Food and Beverage   As the name implies, this department is responsible for the kitchens and for wines and the hotel bars. In some hotels, food and beverage are combined with banqueting; in others – especially in

London hotels – the food and beverage manager is also the deputy general manager.

Food and beverage is a 'behind the scenes' operation. To be sure, we consume the end product (often to excess) but it is not usual for us to deal with the food and beverage manager over the choice of menus and wines for meals – this is part of the banqueting manager's remit (all the food and beverage manager is responsible for is providing what you have ordered).

That said, there may be occasions where the standard range of banqueting menus does not suit your event. When this happens you would do well to ask to discuss the matter either with the food and beverage manager or, better still (for food), with the chef.

Now, in many hotels, the chef is a feared individual, and many staff and managers would prefer to upset you than to upset the chef. There is a delightful (and true) story of how a guest at one top-class restaurant wanted to meet the chef but was told that would be difficult to arrange: 'I suppose,' said the head waiter, 'that the best way to get madame out of the kitchen would be to send something back. But if you did, she would come out preceded by a couple of knives!'

It is not surprising that chefs are sometimes temperamental. They have a difficult and demanding job; the working conditions are invariably hot, humid – and often cramped, and the pace can be frenetic. Good chefs are also almost literally worth their weight in gold. Hotel managers therefore do all they can to keep the peace and to hang onto them – hence the unwillingness to acceded to your request for non-standard menus. But if you ask to discuss the matter with the chef, you may find he relishes the challenge of doing something different and of showing off his skills. When faced with what looks like a rather uninspiring set of conference menus it may therefore pay dividends to request a meeting with the chef.

A question to ask is: 'Will the chef be here for my event?' Now that chefs are often celebrities it is worthwhile checking that he won't be working with the PR department that day.

Some further factors to consider when choosing menus are discussed later in the chapter.

Front of House   Apart from the obvious task of taking room bookings, allocating rooms and registering guests on arrival, this department is also responsible for the concierge and housekeeping. Conference organizers often want to control – or at least have some say in – the allocation of bedrooms to delegates. Most want their senior managers or VIP guests and speakers to have the 'better' rooms and suites (and most organizers ensure they have good rooms for themselves!). Rooming lists are discussed further in Chapter 11. You may also want to put flowers, conference papers and even personal messages in rooms before your delegates arrive. If you are not careful, these matters may fall between sales, the hotel conference office (usually part of sales), banqueting (who may be your main point of contact) and the front of house management and staff.

It is worth taking particular trouble ensuring these minor but important matters do *not* fall between front of house and the other parties. A brief meeting with the front of house manager can pay dividends and you can use the occasion to agree how guests should be received and procedures for checkout (including what happens about vacating rooms by 11 am on the last day of a conference which has been meeting all week – you may not be able to keep the rooms, but it should be possible to store suitcases until the end of the event). By the same token, you need to negotiate access to bedrooms on arrival. It can be very inconvenient for delegates arriving a 9 am for a residential programme and being told their rooms will not be available until midday: where do they put their suitcases, and what if they need to change their clothes or wash or shave? Oddly enough, this is often a bigger problem on a Monday morning, not because hotels are busy on Sunday evenings (as a rule they are not), but because they are not busy and so do not bring staff in over the weekend to make rooms up, gradually working through all the bedrooms instead.

Another important matter to agree direct with the front of house department is how messages will reach you and your delegates. In particular, you must make sure that sessions are not interrupted by incoming messages.

And, during the event, keep in touch with front of house staff. Make sure they know who you are, where you are (at all times) and how they can reach you.

Other departments   You are unlikely to be involved with other departments except for the Accounts Office – and with the latter after rather than before the event. Of course, the invoicing instructions and who pays for what have to be worked out and agreed before the event (see also Chapter 4), but most of the serious problems seem to occur when the final account arrives after the event. *Check the final account in detail.* This can be a nightmare, not only because of the way in which computer driven hotel bills are presented (you almost need to be a trained accountant to understand them!) but also because gross errors can, and often do, occur. One common cause of dispute is the allocation of delegates' 'extras' – things like telephone, drinks and newspapers which are charged to the main account in error (or by design because the individuals have checked out without settling their bills). Problems of this nature can be reduced by good planning and careful delegate briefing and control.

The problem of disputes over errors in the final bill can be mitigated (even if not entirely eliminated) by having the final bill made up before departing at the end of your event. You may not be popular (especially if it is late on a Friday afternoon) and you may have to wait. But at least problems can be rectified there and then – especially as the supporting chits will be available for cross-checking and verifying individual transactions. Whatever goes wrong (in your view) do not be afraid to challenge items with which you do not agree, and do not settle the final account until you are completely satisfied. Which brings us to the question, how do hotels make their money?

HOW DO HOTELS MAKE THEIR MONEY?

Having read the foregoing, you might be tempted to think 'with difficulty' or by overcharging the account. And in any case surely they are in business to make a profit, so why does it matter to you from where their profit comes provided their prices are fair and their accounts accurate?

The fact is, it matters a great deal to the conference organizer: armed with this knowledge, you are better placed to obtain real value for money and to avoid making false economies.

The first thing to understand is that some activities are far more profitable to the hotel than others. These are discussed below in the context of conferences and similar activities.

Accommodation prices

In most hotels, accommodation sales are the single most important source of revenue. The reason for this is quite simple – the marginal costs associated with letting a room (laundry, soap, toiletries coffee/tea-making kit, chambermaid and cleaning services and a comparatively little electricity) are very low compared with the revenue generated from the sale – typically between 7 per cent and 25 per cent depending on the room rate (weekday, weekend and so on). So the contribution from room sales is substantial.

The prices a hotel charges for a conference will depend upon a number of factors, and need not reflect the rates in the published tariffs.

The *rack rates* are the standard published room rates – normally quoted inclusive of Value Added Tax (VAT) and, in the provinces, breakfast (usually 'full English') but in London *exclusive* of breakfast.

There was a time when the rack rate bore no relationship to conference rates, but in recent years, particularly in London, hotels have tended to drop the *24-hour conference rate* (see below) and charge a *day-delegate rate* (also see below) plus the overnight rack rate for residential meetings. The reasons for this are complex. There are certain times of the year in London when demand for hotel rooms exceeds supply: the height of the tourist season and during special events (eg the Wimbledon fortnight). At such times, hotels do not need to offer discounted rates for conferences (and the 24-hour conference rate is, in effect, a discounted rate) since they can easily let the same rooms at full price.

However, at these times the conference/banqueting rooms tend to be under-utilized, so hotels will do their best to fill these with day events or, if they do accommodate a residential event, by charging the rack rate they will do so without loss of revenue from room sales.

24-hour conference rate   Often also called the 24-hour delegate rate, this is an all-in rate which covers overnight accommodation, breakfast (usually full English), room hire, morning coffee and biscuits, lunch, afternoon tea and biscuits and a three course dinner. The service charge and VAT are also usually included although there is an increasing tendency to exclude VAT from the advertised figure, especially in London: see also 'Value Added Tax' below. In most provincial hotels the once common practice of including flip chart and OHP (overhead projector) and screen hire in the 24-hour rate is still maintained.

When comparing rates it is therefore important to check what is and is not included. In particular, check whether you will have the use of your meeting room on a 24-hour basis. It is not always safe to assume that this is the case unless you specify this requirement in advance. Indeed, some busy London hotels may well apply a surcharge for 24-hour use of meeting rooms. This is because they can let these rooms for private functions (which can be very profitable – well worth the hassle of clearing your room when you break at the end of the day and relaying it before you return next morning).

The 24-hour rate is often less than the advertised rack rate for an overnight stay. How – and why – are hotels able to offer such 'value for money' conferences? There are several reasons:

- conferences tend to be held in what are otherwise off season times of the year – if the hotels did not have this business they would be practically empty, especially on weekdays. The 24-hour rates are thus a simple marketing ploy to attract business;
- delegates to residential conferences tend to buy more drink than ordinary guests – wine with meals, and drinks at the bar (often with

useful and earnest discussion late into the night), provide valuable additional revenue which can, in fact, even make good the discount.

Other factors include the value to the hotel of comparatively long stays – a typical residential conference may extend over three nights – training programmes often last a full working week. What is more, many training courses are repeat business. All these lead to significant savings in promotional and other marginal costs.

Day delegate rate Hotels treat this as an 8-hour rate. It is similar to the 24-hour rate except that the associated overnight accommodation and meals (dinner and breakfast) are excluded.

36-hour conference rate Some hotels now offer a 36-hour package to cater for the event which runs from 8 am on day one to late on day two – allowing maximum work time and only one night's accommodation costs.

The 24-, 36- and day delegate rates are often not offered for smaller numbers (typically for groups smaller than a dozen), charges being based on a fixed room hire cost and the actual consumption of food and beverages. The reason for this is that, with these small numbers, the room hire element of the rate is insufficient to cover the costs associated with using the room.

By the same token, for larger numbers the contribution from the room hire element is considerable and generates a significant margin of profit. For this reason, if you are taking large numbers to an hotel for an event and are being charged a packaged-delegate rate, you should be able to negotiate a discount. Some hotels offer stepped discounts for larger numbers (eg 5 per cent reduction on rate for 100–200 delegates, 7½ per cent for 201–300 and so on). See also 'Discounted rates' below.

Additional facilities You may also be charged for additional facilities (eg use of syndicate rooms, hire of audio visual equipment and flip charts) and for any other extras. Although many hotels include simple AV aids and even one syndicate room in their rates, some do not. And beware of hidden extras, for example mineral water at lunch may not be included – and may prove an expensive extra if waiters are 'heavy handed'.

As we have already seen, care must be taken to ensure that the individual extra charges incurred by delegates (telephone, newspapers, drinks and so on) are not charged to the main account if this is your policy (some organizations allow these to be charged to the main account on the grounds that delegates are away from home and should not be penalized in this way).

Value Added Tax We have seen that, as a general rule, hotels quote rates which include VAT. Of course, business users who can reclaim VAT can discount the appropriate rate from their budgets (but not from their cash flow forecasts).

Remember too, that some hotels no longer quote VAT inclusive rates (see '24-hour conference rate' above).

Discounted rates Conference organizers often feel that they should be able to negotiate over rates: they feel that they are bringing a substantial amount of business to the hotel and that this should be recognized in the form of a price reduction. Attempts to negotiate discounts in this way will meet with varying success.

At peak times, when the hotel can easily fill the rooms, they rightly feel they do not need to offer any discount. However, if you are holding your event at a slack time – perhaps in August or over a weekend – then you may well be able to negotiate substantial discounts. And you may be able to negotiate discounts if you can be flexible over dates or if you are booking at short notice. For example, if you can move your event to a different week, or vacate by a particular time, you may be able to benefit from a 'short notice' discount (simply because, if the hotel cannot win your business, it may not be able to let the rooms in question – 'a bird in the hand is worth two in the bush').

What else is negotiable? Even if the conference rates are not negotiable, you should be able to add value to your package:

- ◆ *Free upgrades* You may be able to negotiate free room upgrades from standard to executive bedrooms or suites (perhaps the latter for a small number of senior executives). If your event is occupying all the conference facilities and the hotel is not otherwise busy, the free upgrade will not cost the hotel anything, but your delegates will appreciate the better facilities.
- ◆ *Free rooms* If you have a large group – say 60 or more – you can expect to be given a 'free' room. This is in line with the free room they offer couriers of coach parties and should be scaled up for larger groups (ie 2 for 120, 3 for 180 and so on). However, you will not be offered it unless you ask!
- ◆ *Free use of leisure facilities/fitness club.*
- ◆ *Free access for set up* If your meeting rooms are not in use the day or evening before your event you should be able to negotiate free access to set up – the cost to the venue is negligible but could be valuable to you.
- ◆ *Variations to menus* to add value.

How to negotiate: IF... THEN   You will notice that many of the negotiable items listed above are of low cost to concede to the hotel but are of high value to you. Hotel sales staff – who usually have revenue targets – will therefore readily make concessions on low/nil cost items to protect their rates. Trade on this when you negotiate:

'*If* you cannot discount the rate *then* what about free upgrades?'

You will usually be able to negotiate a bundle of concessions in this way to your mutual satisfaction (classic 'some win: some win' negotiation).

Of course, if you have the buying power of several events to offer, or if your event is very large and valuable to your venue, you are in a stronger position to negotiate over rate:

'*If* I can guarantee three more similar events *then* will you offer a reduction in your rates?'

Always include the 'low cost' items in the negotiation: you should be able to end up with some or all of those *and* a reduced rate. See also 'Corporate Rates' below.

Corporate rates   Some large companies – for example ICI and British Telecom – are able to negotiate specially reduced corporate rates, usually with one hotel chain. The advantages to both parties are clear: the buyer wins a discounted price for all its hotel bookings and the hotel chain, in return, not only wins a lot of business, it also wins business which might otherwise have gone to competitors. However, smaller organizations are less likely to be able to negotiate business on these terms.

Agency discounts   It is a well-known fact that travel agents and conference placement agencies receive commission on business they introduce to hotels. Commission rates are typically 8–10% on pre-booked accommodation (and sometimes on pre-booked food and beverages as well). Some buyers believe that, if they deal direct with hotels, they will be able to 'win' a similar reduction. They are unlikely to be any more successful than if they book an airline ticket direct with the airline rather than through a travel agent. It is not in the interests of hotels to cut out agencies: agencies are a far too valuable source of business to them to risk antagonizing them in this way.

Gratuities and service charges   Most conference rates include a service charge so, to answer the question posed at the start of this chapter, there is no need to add on anything for service when you settle the final bill. This raises the question of whether these gratuities are actually passed on to staff. Hotels claim that gratuities are included in the wages they pay to their staff but, in the end, you have no way of knowing whether this actually happens.

You may therefore be tempted to offer cash gratuities during your event either to reward people who provide exceptional service or simply to 'oil the wheels' (ie to buy that 'extra' degree of attention and service). How effective is this?

In theory, any gratuities which staff receive should be handed over to a central kitty – called the tronc – to be divided amongst all staff according to an agreed formula. The tronc master, usually the banqueting manager, will probably receive the largest 'cut', and others will receive diminishing sums according to seniority, length of service and so on. Thus, a cash tip to an individual member of staff may not have quite the impact you might have expected (although the banqueting manager may be slightly better disposed towards you).

Of course, some individuals 'forget' to put all their gratuities into the tronc in which case you will almost certainly be rewarded with a little extra attention.

In the end, the whole question of gratuities is a bit of a minefield. Hotels seem ambivalent about tipping. They recognize that gratuities add to individual earnings and can act as an incentive, but they also know that the Inland Revenue regard all such payments with suspicion, and any prosecutions (even of individuals) can be bad for staff morale and for the image of the establishment.

In short, there is a degree of ambiguity associated with the question of gratuities, but at least if you know the form you can decide how to behave.

Guarantees and cancellations

When you book an event in an hotel, you will be required to forecast your numbers and, once the booking is confirmed, you may be liable to charges if you cancel the event or if your numbers fall short.

Numbers guarantees   When you place an event, it is accepted by the hotel on the basis of the number of delegates you say you will bring. It is essential, right from the outset, that you are honest with your figures: the hotel will plan the event on your numbers and if these are subsequently reduced, they stand to lose valuable income (they might have done better to refuse your event and accept another instead). It is therefore not surprising that they will charge you for any shortfall.

Cancellation   You will also be charged if you cancel the event (unless the hotel is able to relet the space).

Charges   The charges for lower than anticipated numbers or for cancellations depend upon the notice you give. Most hotels operate a sliding scale from 100% for a very late cancellation to lesser percentages depending on what costs the hotel has actually incurred and, as mentioned above, on whether or not the space is relet. Thus, a cancellation a few days before the event will not incur a full 100% charge if the food has not been bought or casual labour engaged. A cancellation charge 72 hours before the event may be 90% of the charge – still a significant sum.

It is essential that you make sure you read the contract before you confirm your booking so that you know the potential liabilities. You should always insure your event against unforeseen late cancellation (see also Chapter 4 for more information on insuring your event).

'Predictable' shortfalls   However well you forecast your numbers, there will always be some 'no shows'. This is because people fall ill and because sometimes they cannot be spared from work. And during longer conferences (as opposed to training courses) a number of delegates skip meals – and some sessions. Some professional conference organizers build late cancellations and 'no shows' into their forecasts: for a large event this figure might be as high as 5%. If their forecast turns out to be wrong, it is usually possible for the venue to cater for a few late additions. The hotel is pleased with the additional income and the organizer is spared the cost of late cancellations.

Food and drink prices

Food   The old adage, 'you get what you pay for' does not apply to hotel food quite as you might expect and it is not safe to assume either that the more you pay the better the quality you will receive, or that in hotels the more expensive foods are necessarily the most luxurious or exotic. What are the reasons for this?

The first thing to note is that hotels are not able to sell food at the same mark-up as other items so that the contribution from food is at best marginal: often it is sold at a loss. This is because preparing and serving food are labour intensive activities and, because the kitchens and restaurants have to function even if there is only one guest in the hotel, the overhead costs of catering have to be spread in such a way that the one guest is subsidized by the many on busy days.

The problem is made worse by the limit to which the price of food can be 'loaded' with these overheads. We tend to know what food costs us at home and if the mark-up is too outrageous we will not pay.

As a result, the cost of food in a typical hotel will amount to about one-third of the total cost of the menu.

Thus, if a hotel suggests a banqueting menu of, say, £20 including VAT, the food will cost about £6, labour (at about 30%–35% turnover in the banqueting department) another £6, VAT £2.97 (at rate of 17½% – current at the time of writing), leaving a balance of about £5 to cover everything else: gas, electricity, laundry, breakages and fixed overheads. No wonder there is not much profit to be gained from a typical hotel restaurant!

Drink   The contribution from sales of drink on the other hand is much greater. The mark-up may be less – 100%–150% – but the marginal costs are very low (probably less than 5%). As a result, the profit from sales of drink subsidizes the restaurant and banqueting operations.

So what?

All the above may be very interesting, but how does this knowledge help the conference organizer?

Choice of food   Always remember that you want your delegates to enjoy their food: if they don't they will spend more time whining about the food than they will on thinking about why they are there. So you want good food, and you want value for money. Here are a few tips:

-   Some things are more expensive for hotels to produce than others. For example, smoked salmon costs much less to produce than hors d'oeuvre because a small serving of smoked salmon, with a garnish, slice of lemon and brown bread, costs less than the ingredients of an hors d'oeuvre.
-   A small quantity of a luxury item (such as smoked salmon – above) will be just as acceptable as a decent portion of, say, sole because, although the former costs more per pound, the portion weight of the latter has to be greater, so that it actually costs more. In other words, the weight of the serving is a key factor, especially when the basic ingredients are expensive.
-   Do not, however, judge the value of the menu solely on the cost of the ingredients. Another consideration is how delegates judge the menu: it is often better to offer things they are unlikely to eat at home – and these need not be expensive.
-   When offered a standard menu, do not assume that one with an expensive item (for example, duck) is better value than another with a less expensive item (chicken). The hotel will price the overall menu and the latter will almost certainly have 'better' starters and sweets.
-   Don't be afraid to ask for non-standard menus, or to change items on standard menus. As mentioned previously, chefs often relish the

challenge of doing something different and, paradoxically, the difference in price will be based on the difference in cost of the ingredients: the extra preparation time is unlikely to be considered, so variations or individually designed menus can offer much better value for money.

Choosing drinks   While your decisions on foods will be concerned with 'value for money', those concerning drink will be more to do with cost limitation. The drinks you choose – and the way they are served – will have a major bearing on the eventual bill.

When you plan consumption, you can assume the following norms:

- 5 or 6 glasses of wine per bottle;
- 32 measures of gin or whisky per bottle;
- 30 measures of port of liqueur;
- 12–15 measures of sherry.

The average consumption of wines with a meal is 1½ – 2½ glasses (more if heavy handed waiters keep topping glasses up – but waste in terms of unconsumed wines left in glasses seems to rise correspondingly). The lower figure applies if only red *or* white wine is offered, the upper if both red *and* white are offered. It is best to set a limit on the number of bottles of wine to be served, perhaps with a fail-safe of allowing more bottles to be opened if consumption is higher than planned but only with the organizer's permission.

Spirits can be more difficult to control. People seem to become very greedy when spirits are on offer, especially if they are served by waiters carrying trays (having to go to a bar or serving point slows consumption down).

Insist that optics are used to measure out spirits – otherwise heavy handed waiters will give double measures, to the delight of your delegates and the ruination of your budget.

Whatever you do, you cannot afford to let the flow of drink run dry. It is therefore sensible to limit the length of time, and to consider not offering canapés (people drink more when they can eat at the same time). Alternatively, you may consider serving champagne (or a sparkling wine – many people cannot tell the difference). Champagne is still perceived to be 'exciting'. It is, of course, expensive but in fact it costs less overall because most of us can only manage a glass or two at a time.

A free bar after a dinner presents different problems. Again, people tend to take advantage of the situation and consume a great deal of alcohol. But this social period is often a vital part of the conference (this is particularly true of residential training programmes where it is common practice to offer a free bar after the course dinner). To shut the bar – perhaps quite early on because a pre-determined limit has been reached – can destroy the occasion, and to make participants pay for their own drinks after a set limit or time can seem parsimonious. There is, perhaps, no way out – but do make sure you are not being 'ripped off' by the hotel – see 'Dirty tricks' below.

DIRTY TRICKS

The wine was being served at a course dinner in a well known hotel. The menu stated that the white was a rather fine (and expensive) Puligny-Montrachet. The wine had been brought, with typical showmanship, for the course organizer to taste. A few moments later the organizer noticed that a different wine was being poured at the other end of the table: it was instantly recognizable as the house white they had been drinking the night before.

'Oh dear! A terrible mistake – I do apologize, sir!' said the embarrassed head waiter when the error was pointed out to him *there and then* by an angry organizer.

A mistake – or a dirty trick? No-one can be sure. Most people, and most hotels, are very honest (it is more than their reputation is worth not to be). But mistakes can (and do) happen, and there are some people who will cheat you. The majority of dirty tricks centre round the drink items – probably because they are easiest to fiddle.

It is therefore as well to be on your guard and to build your protection into your plan.

Setting Limits The practice of setting limits on consumption has already been discussed.A strict limit makes it much more difficult to cheat you or to be heavy handed. Where there is no limit (and hence consumption is considerable) it is much easier to 'hide' leakage (ie, theft).

Stock Controls Your first protection is to physically check the stock before and after the function. The wines for a dinner, and the spirits for your bar, will be counted out of stock before your function, and the unconsumed bottles will be counted back afterwards. You will be charged for the difference – ie, for what you consumed... or did you?

A number of dirty tricks can be played:

– *Staff may help you drink your stock* It is surprising how much Scotch a few hardened drinkers can get through in a very short space of time. This practice can be difficult to spot and it is equally difficult to control. The best you can do is say what your rules are (eg, the only drinks staff may consume are those offered by you) and to make sure everyone knows you are alert to the problem.

- *Substituting empty bottles for full bottles*   It is an easy matter to substitute empty bottles for full ones during your function. The hotel will almost certainly have empties from previous functions and the practice can be difficult to detect. One way round it is to personally mark/number every bottle that comes out of store and to check all the empties at the end of the function. Any bottle not bearing your mark is clearly a substitute.
- *Substituting cheaper stock*   This is what happened at the course dinner described on page 313. The substitute may be a cheap bottle from an off-licence which is sold to you at the hotel price, or it may only be a different vintage wine sold to you at the same price as a more expensive vintage of the same wine. Bottle marking – and careful checking beforehand – can eliminate these dirty tricks.
- *Deliberate heavy handedness*   This problem has already been discussed: that of the waiters who keep topping up glasses to boost consumption (not only of wine but also mineral water). Hotel management might encourage this practice (in order to increase income). Again, by setting a limit and checking stocks you can do much to legislate against it.
- *Fiddling the figures*   This may occur if you do not physically check the stock as suggested above. After the event it is your word against the duty barman or duty manager's if the consumption is in dispute.
- *Opening too many bottles*   This can cause problems. The hotel may open more bottles of wine than are actually consumed – especially red wine to allow it to 'breathe' beforehand. Should you pay for what you do not consume? The good hotel will not charge you, but if they do you might as well remove the opened stock or use it next day. The important point is to agree the 'rules' beforehand.

There are many other fiddles – probably enough to merit a book of their own. But our purpose here is to alert you to the dangers. If the dishonest hotelier realizes you are an astute and knowledgeable buyer he will probably back off and not even try to cheat you. After all, there are plenty of naive people they can trick without risking being caught by you!

A few final points on dirty tricks:

- If you suspect anything, draw it to the attention of the most senior hotel manager present *there and then*. If you leave it until later it becomes much more difficult to prove.

- If you do uncover dishonesty, the hotel management will probably be more than pleased to co-operate. They, too, suffer from dishonest staff and are grateful when someone uncovers something of which they are unaware.
- *Beware being taken for a ride* Unplanned expenditure can turn out to be very expensive: on one recent course, it was someone's 50th birthday and the course organizer ordered a special cake with the afternoon tea. The gesture was much appreciated by the course, but the bill – £60 + VAT – was a rip-off. The organizer should have obtained a quote beforehand – and, if necessary, agreed to a less expensive alternative.

Never be embarrassed to ask about prices or to insist upon the sort of measures we have discussed in the above paragraphs. Some people think they will make themselves unpopular with the hotel. They need not worry – the professional hotelier will respect your professional approach. Paradoxically, if you do seem too trusting or naive, you may not win his respect, nor that of his staff, with the result that you will be more rather than less vulnerable.

ACCEPTING HOSPITALITY

As a conference organizer or, from the hotel's point of view, a potential buyer, you will almost certainly be offered hospitality. This may be in the form of a *facility visit*, or a *meal* when you inspect the hotel.

Some people wonder whether they should accept such hospitality for fear of becoming obliged to the hotel in return. These fears are understandable but groundless.

The normal sales executive or banqueting manager knows that he has a better chance of winning your business if they can show you their hotel and answer your questions. They also want you to sample their fine foods and to meet other members of staff. The meal, or the facility visit, is part of this process.

Do not be fooled into thinking that the hospitality you receive during your meal or on a facility visit reflects the true standards for conferences and meetings. Everyone will be making a special effort which may not carry through to the normal day-to-day routine.

Nevertheless, hospitality and facility visits are useful opportunities to find out what particular hotels are like. And, provided you do not 'free load' (ie, accept hospitality from hotels you have no intention of using), you should accept these invitations without feeling under any subsequent obligation.

EXECUTIVE CHECKLIST

♦ When discussing detailed arrangements for your events, do you deal with sales managers or with the staff who will be responsible for running your event?

♦ Do you confirm everything in writing – and seek written confirmation back from the hotel?

♦ Do you involve the banqueting manager in your planning – seeking his help and advice *and* making sure he fully understands your event?

♦ Do you discuss your menus with hotel chefs?

♦ Do you liaise directly with the front of house managers?

♦ Do you check all accounts in detail?

♦ Do you ensure you agree the best pricing structures for your events and, where possible, negotiate discounts?

♦ What policy do you have regarding cash gratuities during the event?

♦ Do you understand your obligations in terms of cancellation charges – and do you protect yourself with insurance?

♦ Do you get best value for money when planning menus?

♦ What do you do to limit expenditure on drink?
  - do you set limits on consumption?
  - do you personally do stock checks to verify consumption?

♦ Do you ensure hotel managers and staff appreciate that you cannot be cheated over drink consumption? If you suspect something is wrong, do you raise the matter there and then?

♦ Do you accept hospitality as a useful way of finding out about the hotel? And can you honestly say you *never* 'free load'?

13

THE EVENT

The event itself is the culmination of months – sometimes years – of preparation and planning. The very largest events have a planning cycle of two, three or even four years and a simple one-day seminar can take up to 12 months to arrange. At the end of so many months of effort, waiting and anticipation, everyone – delegates, speakers and organizers alike – will be keyed up and anxious for success. The degree of success depends to a great extent on the quality of the original plan and the effectiveness of the preparatory work. However, the best laid plans can go astray and what actually happens during the event ultimately decides whether or not success is achieved. Many a fine plan has failed to work in practice and sometimes suspect plans succeed in brilliant fashion, thanks to the manner in which they are carried out.

There is no magic formula for success but much can be done to legislate against the more obvious causes of failure and to prepare for the inevitable catastrophes which will occur however good the plan. This chapter recommends principles for the management of meetings and highlights some of the more important organizational procedures.

MANAGING A MEETING

Very small meetings almost run themselves. Being small, the group will normally accept a degree of informality which would not be appropriate at larger events. It takes a great deal of detailed organization to control the activity, movement and administration of a large body of people. The event is much more likely to be successful if it runs smoothly and this, in turn, depends on the effective management of what happens both inside and outside the conference hall.

The sponsor (that is, the person who set the objectives) will generally want to see that these objectives are met. He will therefore be mainly concerned with what happens inside the conference hall. The sponsor may act as programme chairman, but even if he does not he will usually attend sessions to observe and participate in the proceedings. He should be left free to concentrate on the business of the event and should not have to worry about administrative matters. The marketing director who decides to hold a sales conference or product launch should be able to devote all his attention to what happens in front of the audience. If he is worrying about the timing of the next meal, noise from the kitchens or whether the next speaker has arrived, he will be distracted to the extent that he will not be able to relax and concentrate on the business in hand, and will not be effective in his main role.

It is therefore essential to divide the responsibility for an event:

◆ The meeting itself should be managed by a person whose prime interest is to ensure that the objectives are achieved.
◆ Responsibility for administration should be given to someone else.

These two people will work closely together, but the task of the administrative organizer is to ensure the event runs smoothly so that the necessary business can be completed without disruption.

It is usual to appoint a programme chairman to manage the conference proceedings. His role and function are described in Chapter 14. In an ideal world, the person who organized the conference would only be responsible for administration during the actual event. However, in many cases the conference organizer *has* to be involved in the actual proceedings. For example, the marketing director mentioned previously may well have been responsible for organizing the event but would also have to play a leading role in it. In this case he should appoint someone from the organizing team who is familiar with the plan to take on the administrative task. This person should not take part in the actual proceedings.

As noted in an earlier chapter, conference organizers should not be tempted to rely on hotel and venue staff to handle administration on their behalf. Venue staff can only be responsible for venue matters. Their involvement before the event will always be limited since, in the build-up period, their day-to-day task is to handle other events at their venue. Some venues claim to be able to act as conference organizers for their clients. For the reasons just given they can seldom give the necessary attention to a specific event until shortly before the actual day. Even then they are likely to be more concerned with the smooth running of the venue than with the wider problems faced by the conference administrator. It is therefore always necessary to have your own administrator to look after the specific interests of your event.

The larger companies and associations which have their own in-house conference officers or even full-time conference departments are very fortunate. The in-house staff will usually, as a matter of routine, handle all the administration both in the planning period and during the event.

The professional conference organizer provides much the same service, leaving the sponsor's staff free to carry on with their normal work before the event and to participate on the day, free from worry about administrative matters.

THE ADMINISTRATIVE TASK

What are the administrative responsibilities of the conference organizer during the event? His function is to ensure that everything which happens outside the meeting room runs smoothly and that the meeting itself has all the administrative support it needs. The main tasks are described in the following paragraphs.

Registration

The delegates' first impressions when they arrive at the venue are very important. They will become disgruntled and impatient if they have to queue to get in and their reception is badly organized – hardly the best frame of mind in which to enter the conference hall. The registration procedures must therefore be efficient, the staff courteous and pleasant, and registration desks must be *tidy*.

Each delegate has to be processed individually to give him his name badge, function tickets and to keep a record of actual attendance. A single desk with one or two staff is sufficient to cope with up to about a hundred people attending a smaller event. Several desks will be needed for larger numbers: as a rough guide, one registration point should be provided to every 50 delegates. Each desk can be geared to handle a pre-planned number of delegates. The method of splitting delegates into groups for registration – perhaps alphabetically by name or by numbers – must be clearly stated in the joining instructions. Each desk should carry an identification sign (for example a number, or the appropriate letters). These signs should be suspended above the desks so that they can be read over the heads of other waiting delegates.

The registration procedure must be quick. It is usual to have a standard run conference folder or pack for each delegate (see Chapter 11). These folders can be stacked behind the desks and handed to delegates as they register. In addition, each desk should have a small indexed box or file of individual delegate envelopes containing personal items such as name badges and function tickets. Standard run and individual items are separated in this way to avoid having to hunt through piles of bulky folders to find a particular personal pack. It is much easier to sort through a comparatively small file to find an individual envelope and to take a standard folder from a separate pile, thereby saving time during the registration process.

The envelope system also avoids the need to lay out delegates' name badges on the table. The scene of registration staff and delegates bending over an array of name badges trying to find individual badges is all too familiar – and all too inefficient and time wasting.

Computerized registration

Some major venues offer access to venue computer systems for registration; AMK's system in Berlin, called BUSY, covers all aspects of conference management including delegate registration, room, hall and exhibition stand bookings and even mailings and invoicing. Some of these systems use bar-coding and laser scanning to speed up registration.

Exception handling

Any delegate who asks for information or has a problem of any kind should be directed to a separate desk specially staffed to handle such queries. In addition, if the organizers have queries to raise with particular delegates – for example, under-payments, travel and hotel problems – the individual's envelope should be marked 'Exception' and he should be directed to a separate desk. Exceptions can then be processed without interrupting the flow of other delegates.

Similarly, *new* registrations should be taken at a separate desk. It is essential that they are processed with considerable care in order to ensure that names, addresses, invoices and other details are recorded accurately. The procedure should never be rushed.

Registration desks will need a supply of stationery, a PC and the means of producing new delegates' name badges.

Messages and information

An information point is needed. It must be staffed at all times. An information and messages board should also be set up in the reception area. The information board should display the event programme and, possibly, delegates and accommodation lists. There will always be a number of telephone messages for delegates. It may be necessary to page the delegate if a particular message is urgent. Other messages can either be placed in individual delegate pigeon holes, or a message can be prominently displayed on the messages board asking the delegate to contact the information desk. Special announcements should also be displayed on these boards.

Very urgent messages can be projected onto the screen during breaks between plenary sessions – perhaps using an OHP (overhead projector).

Organizers should not be too despondent if some messages remain uncollected. It is a fact that some people register for a conference, turn up for on-site registration but then attend few, if any, sessions. Delegates from overseas use conferences as a means of getting to, for example, London and, once there, prefer sight-seeing and shopping.

Signing

It is often difficult to find the conference rooms when you first arrive at the venue. Hotel conference suites, in particular, are often tucked away at the back of the hotel or on another floor, and standard signing within venues is often inadequate (the signing in the Barbican in the early days was a bad joke!). It is therefore usually necessary to put in special signs, bearing the conference name and logo, to direct delegates to registration, the conference hall and the break-down rooms, tea and coffee areas and so on.

Some hotels are very fussy about having conference signs up in their smart foyers: this is a matter for negotiation and compromise during a visit to the hotel.

Never forget that *people* – be they your own or the venue staff – are much more welcoming and efficient than signs at directing people (if only because they can answer questions!). Do make sure, in hotels in particular, that receptionists and doormen are fully briefed and can welcome and direct delegates as they arrive.

Reception of VIPs and speakers

VIPs expect special treatment and a separate reception procedure must be established for them. Hosts should be nominated to meet VIPs and to take them to meet senior staff from the organization. It is sometimes a good idea to entertain VIPs in a separate room (although segregation can upset other delegates if they think they are receiving sub-standard treatment).

Speakers may not expect special treatment but should nevertheless be singled out in much the same way as VIPs. The start of one conference was delayed because a speaker could not get through the crush of delegates to find anyone to tell him where to go or what to do. He was eventually located patiently waiting at the exception handling desk while a pedantic visitor in front of him had numerous detailed queries answered.

Rehearsal Room   It is good practice to set aside a rehearsal room where speakers can sit quietly and go over their scripts, brief projection staff and load slide magazines. On no account should speakers be allowed to enter the projection booth during another speaker's session. A production manager is often appointed to receive speakers and coordinate the presentations.

Press and TV

Reporters attend some of the more important events. A separate public relations officer should be appointed to handle and brief press and TV staff. The conference organizer cannot be expected to deal with this additional burden. It is usual to provide a separate press office with telephones, food and refreshments and special tables may be needed in the actual meetings rooms (see also Chapter 2).

Routine administrative tasks

Several things should be checked by the administrative staff before each session:

Layout   Lecterns, the chairman's and speakers' seats, etc should be correctly positioned. Layouts often change during a long event. For example, different layouts are needed for panel discussions and speaker presentations. It may be necessary to prepare a schedule if a large number of changes of layout are needed.

AV Equipment   Sound volumes, microphone positions, light levels and the focus and positioning of projectors (especially overhead projectors) must be checked and adjusted before each session.

Scripts Several people need up-to-date copies of the speakers' scripts. The projection staff, interpreters and chairmen may all need copies and it is essential to check regularly that they have them and that they are about to use the right script for the right session. Simultaneous translation has been thrown into confusion by out-of-date or even incorrect scripts on more than one occasion and speakers can be put off their stride if the slide cues on the projection room copy are not the same as those on their own.

Heating and Air Conditioning These must be regularly checked throughout the event. The heat output from several hundred bodies is significant. Even in winter the hall will soon become stuffy and delegates drowsy if the air conditioning is not switched on. In Chapter 2 a conference centre was mentioned where the noise of the heating fans drowned speakers' voices. The staff at that venue had developed a slick routine for turning the heating on and off over every break and even when short films were being shown.

Smoking There are many more non-smokers than smokers these days and non-smokers find cigarette and cigar smoke irritating and distracting.

It is become standard practice to ban smoking during plenary sessions in smaller meetings. Some organizers permit smoking in larger venues. Prominent 'no smoking' notices should be displayed and ample breaks allowed for delegates to indulge in their habit.

It is also usual for hotels to offer smoking and non-smoking bedrooms and to reserve sections of restaurants for non-smokers. Similar courtesies should be extended to delegates.

Housekeeping Ashtrays must be regularly emptied, iced water jugs topped up and dirty glasses replaced. Stray coffee and tea cups must be collected and a great effort is needed to keep the whole area clean. Although the quantity of litter in a conference hall is unlikely to match that left by the typical cinema audience, it is still necessary to sweep up each time the conference hall is vacated. Special cleaning contracts with outside firms have to be arranged for larger events.

Lights should be regularly checked and bulbs replaced. Blackout, when needed, must be effective. A single shaft of sunlight can ruin a screen image and, because people open windows and peer behind curtains out of curiosity, regular checks are needed before each session. Pointers (either hand or laser type) should be replaced in position near the lectern and any papers left by previous speakers should be collected.

If the event involves sensitive material contained, for example, in papers and flip charts, the organizer must ensure these are regularly collected for disposal *by the organizer* – it is imprudent to rely on venue staff to destroy such material (the chances are it will end up on a skip, eventually to blow round the street or rubbish dump for anyone to see).

If you wish flip charts to remain in place during the event, make sure the venue staff are told. One organizer of a training programme was dismayed to find all the flip charts from the previous days had been removed from the walls. They were eventually located in the hotel dustbins covered with other dirt and litter.

Noise   In Chapter 2 we saw that noise is a major enemy of the conference organizer. Outside noises can distract delegates' attention. Kitchen noise, the clatter of coffee cups being laid out and chatter by people outside the hall must be eliminated – something which is easier said than done. The organizer must establish close liaison with the venue staff and must have a predetermined line of communication for sorting out problems. Beware the private 'conference' by waiters and venue staff. Upset them when you ask them to be quiet and they may take their revenge during the next meal break!

Sounds from outside the venue can also cause problems. Regular traffic noise cannot be avoided although, in choosing the venue, its level should have been checked. It is often possible to do something about unexpected noise. A word to the site engineer can sometimes silence a noisy pneumatic drill, while the inevitable hammering and knocking noises can usually be traced and silenced.

Signs on doors carrying the message 'Quiet Please – Meeting in Progress' can be effective. They certainly stop strangers barging in. However, to maintain their impact, they should only be displayed while sessions *are* in progress.

Liaison with Venue Staff and Caterers   The need to exchange schedules with the venue was mentioned in Chapter 11. Close liaison is needed between the organizer and the venue staff and caterers during the event itself. They must be warned of changes in timing, particularly those of meals and coffee breaks. Even if it only becomes apparent at a very late stage that a session is likely to overrun, the catering staff should be told so that they can hold last-minute preparations and arrange to keep food warm.

Most venue problems arise out of poor communication between the organizer and the venue staff. The organizer should always remember that his event, which is unique and important to him, is just one of hundreds to the venue staff. If he is enthusiastic and makes sure the staff know what his event is about and why it is important, he will do much to ensure that he receives better than average treatment. All too often no one tells the venue staff anything about the event. No wonder they, in their turn, are not interested.

'Thank you' is easy to say – and yet is so often left unsaid. People respond to recognition and thanks. Some waitresses were overheard talking to each other after the well-known chairman of a large international company had taken the trouble to talk to them and thank them for their efforts. 'I like it when they show an interest', said one. 'Yes', was the reply, 'usually they are so damned snooty you might just as well be part of the furniture.'

Gratuities   This, as already mentioned in Chapter 12, is always a difficult subject. In some countries, particularly in the Middle and Far East, an attempt to give a tip may cause offence. In other countries, for example the US, gratuities may be *expected* (and must therefore be incorporated in the budget). Where a service charge is included in the bill additional gratuities need only be given to particular individuals who have been exceptionally helpful.

However, whom to tip, and how much is, in the end, a matter of personal taste. If in doubt, you can always consult the hotel or venue management to determine local custom and practice. Always try to give gratuities in person – in local currencies.

Letters of thanks, to individual staff and managers, are always appreciated.

Troubleshooting   The administrator can never relax. He must be constantly on the alert, checking arrangements, looking for potential problems and ready for speedy action when something goes wrong. If a problem or potential problem – for example, a speaker arriving late or a meal behind schedule – is likely to affect what happens inside the conference hall, the chairman must be forewarned to give him time to decide how to handle the situation. He will not thank you if you spring a major crisis on him at the last moment.

Regular liaison between the administrator and the programme chairman is essential in order to exchange information and discuss how the event is progressing. Being outside the hall, the administrator often has no way of knowing what is actually happening unless he has access to a projection booth with monitoring speakers. If it is too hot or cold in the hall, or other problems are bothering delegates or speakers, the chairman must tell the administrator so that he can take remedial action.

SECURITY

Physical security

All gatherings are potential targets for thieves, terrorists and other extremists.

People   Before the event it is essential to assess the potential threat to speakers, VIPs and/or delegates. Although the in-house event is unlikely to be threatened unless the organization is the target of particular groups, public events are a different matter, especially if foreigners are attending. Delegates from Middle East and Third World countries can be particularly vulnerable to terrorist and extremist activity and it is the responsibility of the conference organizer to do everything possible to arrange the necessary protection. Similarly, VIP visitors must be protected.

Close liaison should be established with the police over security arrangements. They will advise on all aspects of personal security including the control of access to the venue and the protection of delegates outside the conference hall.

Security can be a major consideration when choosing a conference venue. Indeed, for some events security may be an overriding factor. Many top level gatherings are held in venues which can be isolated from the outside world. Leeds Castle was mentioned in Chapter 2 as an excellent example of a venue which can be made completely secure. It is surrounded by water, is set in private grounds well away from the nearest main road, and has only one access. By the same token, the QE II Conference Centre in London has excellent security, and, within the Centre, certain parts are secure in themselves for added protection.

Certain VIPs, especially royalty and senior politicians, are given permanent protection. The police and national security staff will liaise with conference organizers over their security.

Access to the Venue   It is often necessary to control access to the venue. Delegates, venue staff and visitors may be admitted by ticket only and, when the threat is serious, may have to be searched each time they enter the building. All entrances have to be guarded and public and vehicle access to the immediate vicinity of the venue may be restricted. Security staff can be hired from specialist security firms to help with this task. Most of the specialist security firms will advise on all aspects of security and draw up necessary security plans.

Venue Searches   The venue must be thoroughly searched before the event to check for unauthorized people and packages which may contain explosives. The venue must be completely sealed from public access while this search is being carried out and, when it is complete, the full access control plan should be put into action. In addition, the venue should be searched each day to ensure that there has been no unauthorized access during the silent hours.

Equipment   Arrangements must be made to safeguard against the theft of equipment and valuables. This applies during 'open' hours and at night. Specialist firms should be engaged if the problem of security against theft is likely to be significant.

Espionage

Industrial espionage is big business conducted on an international scale. In-house events are often a target for industrial espionage since confidential matters will almost certainly be discussed either during sessions or informally at the bar. A security plan is needed to guard against such eavesdropping:

1. *Electronic Eavesdropping*   The venue must be 'swept' for electronic listening devices (sometimes called 'bugs'). A small device, the size of a cigarette packet, can be used to transmit everything that is said in the hall to an outside receiving station. Specialist security firms have detectors which can locate such devices. Once the building has been electronically 'swept' it must be guarded round the clock.

2. *Spies*   Anyone not connected with the regular organization must be regarded as a threat. Spies may infiltrate bar, catering, sub-contractor and venue staff. Delegates must be warned not to discuss confidential matters within earshot of strangers, and venue staff who have access to the conference proceedings must be vetted and cleared beforehand.

   Papers and AV material may also be targets for espionage. A safe may be needed for storing videos, visuals, papers and so on. Records should be kept as each item is booked in and out of the safe and only authorized persons should be able to take papers from safekeeping.

   It is advisable to brief delegates about the security risk. Delegates should be told not to leave confidential papers in their hotel rooms or in the conference halls and that facilities are available for the safe storage of their papers.

3. *Post event problems*   It is essential to ensure all sensitive material is removed after the event. Danger areas include:

- flip chart pads (material is often left behind – often to be discovered during a session of the next event!);
- material left in waste paper baskets;
- loose papers (the author found a complete copy of a major company's marketing plan after an event at one venue).

Valuables

Most hotels offer to look after personal valuables. If the service is not available the organizers should make suitable arrangements.

Emergencies

Bombs   These are a very real threat these days, especially at some overseas locations and also, from time to time, in the UK (no-one will ever forget the IRA bomb attack at the Tory Party Conference in Brighton in 1984). A search routine when people enter the building (see above) will help deter attempts to bring explosives into the venue. Nevertheless, should a warning be received, delegates must be able to vacate the building quickly. The evacuation routine can be explained at the beginning of the conference and, if the danger is very great, the routine should be practised.

The building should be regularly patrolled and searched. Any unattended package should be treated as suspicious until proved otherwise. One delegate's briefcase was blown up by bomb disposal experts after he left it unattended in a government building. A hard way to learn a lesson – but most effective!

Fire   We tend to be blasé about fire risks in public building but terrible fires do claim lives from time to time – usually because exit doors are illegally locked. Organizers should check that all emergency exit doors function properly and are not locked. It is also advisable to see that fire escapes and stairways are free of rubbish and other obstructions.

Power Cuts   All public halls must, by law, have emergency lighting but this is usually battery run and, even if the batteries are in good condition, they will only provide a low level of illumination for a very limited time. Organizers should at least consider what they would do in the event of a power failure. Sometimes more positive action is needed. Planned power cuts are occasionally threatened as a result of industrial action. One important conference was to be held during what was said to be a 'high risk' period for power cuts. A generator was hired and connected to the system so that, in the event of a power cut, it would have been possible to throw a switch to restore power. Nevertheless, the sponsor was still not satisfied. What, he wanted to know, would happen if the generator broke down? He insisted that paraffin pressure lamps should be obtained and that these should be kept outside the hall 'just in case'. Delegates were reassured about the power supply and told of the reserve generator. They were clearly impressed. The sight of the lamps, which they saw as they left the conference hall, caused much merriment. In fact, the sponsor was a showman and the lamps were no doubt part of the show as much as braces to back up the belt.

Equipment Spares   Equipment will fail from time to time. It is always advisable to have spare projector bulbs and even spare projectors to hand. Someone who knows how to make operator repairs should always be available. If you are using hired-in equipment you should also pay for an operator. For smaller events this will not normally be necessary but you must ask yourself what would happen if, say, a vital video recorder failed at the last moment. How long would it take to obtain help or a replacement?

You may wish to consider hiring spares of vital pieces of equipment if you cannot be certain that on site assistance will be reliable – or even available.

Lost and Found   A system is needed to deal with lost and found property.

MOVING LARGE NUMBERS OF PEOPLE

Anyone who has failed to hear the five-minute bell at the theatre or been caught in the crush of a large crowd will be aware of some of the problems involved in moving large numbers of people. One major difficulty facing the organizer is that of attracting delegates' attention and actually getting them to, say, leave the coffee area and return to their seats. It is worth considering novel and dramatic ways of attracting attention – for example, a school hand-bell and a loud voice can be very effective. It is not advisable, however, to go so far as one senior executive who wanted to gather his workforce together at short notice. He decided to ring the fire alarms since he knew people, on hearing the alarm, would all assemble in front of the building. The plan worked exceedingly well but, just as he began to speak to the assembled company, the distant but increasingly loud sirens of approaching fire engines drowned what he was saying!

Conference organizers should also allow plenty of time for people to move in and out of the conference hall. It always takes much longer than expected. If over-optimistic timings are put into the programme the event will consistently overrun.

Novel methods for communicating information to delegates inside the conference hall should also be considered. Tea and coffee breaks can be announced by using a slide and a 'signature tune' and the technique of dimming lights can settle delegates at the end of a break. There are a number of short, witty videos which can be used to the same effect. These can be commercially hired at a very reasonable cost.

EXTRAS

The organizer should use his imagination when planning venue layout and administration. If you are not holding an exhibition alongside your event (or if a full exhibition would not be appropriate), delegates will always be interested in displays of equipment, photographs and so on. It is worth considering having an official photographer and displaying proofs of his pictures in the reception area.

A post box and public telephones are useful for delegates. Beware of letting delegates use the organizer's or venue telephones. All too often you find you are faced with bills for long calls to business colleagues – or even friends – in the far-flung corners of the world.

STAFF

Large events absorb a lot of staff. Registration and information desks, guides, escorts and office staff will be needed. It is possible to hire experienced exhibition and conference staff on a temporary basis, but as many staff as possible should be provided from the sponsor organization's own resources. Secretaries and other junior staff enjoy the break and the privilege of participating and are more likely to be committed to the event and the sponsor organization than short term, temporary staff. It is always a good idea to provide staff with some form of identifying 'uniform'. This need not be elaborate. One organizer buys sets of dresses for female staff from a chain-store. These look better than quasi-uniforms, and are cheaper but still easily identifiable.

FOOD AND DRINK

Conference catering presents a special challenge to catering staff. Food and drink should be planned to fit the programme in terms of the types of food and drink, quantities, production and the logistics of serving the food quickly. And the choice of food and drink should be related to the overall budget. (See also Chapter 12, 'Dealing with Hotels'.)

The type of food

Delegates expect good food. Indeed, if the food is poor at a residential conference, little else will be remembered after the event. Catering managers can advise on what dishes are best suited for particular meals. As a general rule midday meals should be light (see Chapter 3). More sumptuous food can be provided in the evenings.

Make sure you understand and agree with the venue all the charges for food and beverages and whether or not VAT or local taxes, service and extra staff charges are included. If you are holding private receptions and dinners, find out whether you will be charged extra for room hire, bar staff and so on.

If there are delegates from different parts of the world, their tastes must be catered for, and the caterer must also be aware of any delegates who, for medical or religious reasons, have particular requirements. Menus should offer a choice for the health conscious delegates as well as those with more conventional tastes. Not many hotels provide skimmed milk and decaffeinated coffee unless requested to do so.

Any foods chosen should be suitable for bulk preparation and should be quick and easy to serve.

Serving methods

The organizer should decide whether to opt for buffet or sit-down meals and between self-service and waiter service. Buffet lunches are popular with conference organizers but the food must be suitable for buffet handling and consumption. Finger or fork dishes are fine but a cold chicken salad which requires the use of a knife and fork poses problems for the delegate who cannot sit down, especially if he also has to contend with a glass of wine. Self-service is usually quicker than waiter service at table but portions are easier to control in the latter case. As discussed in Chapter 3, a good compromise is to allow self-service for the main course and waiter service for the others. For example, the starter can be pre-positioned, then delegates can collect the main course and a plated sweet and coffee can be served at the table.

The layout of self-service buffets, coffee and teas is important. A poor layout causes congestion and wastes valuable time. If there are several service points on a long table, staff need to direct delegates to prevent everyone queuing in one line. It is good practice to have several separate serving points. Sugar, milk and biscuits should always be placed on separate tables to speed up service, especially during short breaks.

Drink

A difficult problem. Some delegates at residential events expect to do a lot of social drinking. There is nearly always time in the programme for this and it is not necessary to provide much to drink between sessions or at lunchtime unless there is a specific need to do so – for example, for VIPs or during an incentive event.

Controlling expenditure   Whenever drinks are provided out of the event budget as opposed to being paid for by individual delegates, there are potential problems in controlling expenditure.

Firstly, as mentioned in Chapter 12, when drink is 'free', delegates tend to consume more – sometimes very much more than they would normally. Secondly, it is difficult to be sure everything charged is actually consumed. It is an unfortunate fact of life that bar staff and wine waiters are sometimes less than honest and 'load' bills accordingly. A guest speaker at a recent 'end of course' dinner at a hotel in Glasgow declined to join delegates in a foray to a local pub after the formal dinner. Left alone in the private dining room, he asked the waiter what should be done about signing for the private bar and wines. 'You can leave it to us… or you can call the duty bar manager.' He insisted on the latter (to the evident dissatisfaction of the waiter!) and, after about 30 minutes, the bar manager arrived. The guest carefully supervised the reconciliation of the spirits. 'Oh, and there were 22 bottles of wine,' said the bar manager. The speaker had taken the precaution of counting the empty bottles and replied, 'Well, I wonder where the other four empties have gone?' The by now embarrassed bar manager muttered something about having miscounted and amended the total.

The moral is clear. Watch venue bar staff like a hawk. Insist on counting the empties, and sign for drinks round-by-round. Your final bill will be more accurate and, lower, than if you adopt a trusting or *laissez-faire* attitude.

SUPPORT SERVICES

The large conference will employ many sub-contractors. Coaches to transport delegates; audio-visual staff; outside caterers; photographers; security staff; receptionists; travel agents; set construction companies; flower arrangers and cleaning staff, to name but a few. All sub-contractor staff should be briefed well before the event but all will have to be met at the venue and be briefed in detail. Decisions on location of equipment, furniture, lights, projectors and other items will be needed and sub-contractors may have to be fed and administered. The conference organizer must be prepared to handle all these people and must have the authority to answer queries and to take decisions.

It is advisable to set aside a room for coach and car drivers and to provide them with food, coffee and tea. Drivers seem to have a habit of disappearing just when they are wanted and, while it is not always possible to prevent this, a well appointed rest room reduces the chances of their straying from the venue. One canny operator always puts a television in the drivers' waiting room. This is sometimes the most popular room in the venue, especially during major sporting events. Incidentally, when major sporting or other events are in progress it is a nice touch to relay news to the conference hall from time to time. An OHP slide showing the latest test score or the result of, say, the Derby, is easy to prepare and can be shown during a short break in proceedings.

It is necessary to provide simultaneous translation at some international events. The equipment requirements are mentioned in Chapter 2. Interpreters need special handling. They must have up-to-date copies of speakers' papers well beforehand and both speakers and interpreters need mutual briefing on their separate needs and requirements and delegates will need instruction on how to operate individual language selection controls. If the event is lengthy, several interpreters will be needed for each language, and rest and refreshment rooms must be provided. There are several companies which specialize in simultaneous translation – see the list of Useful Addresses at the end of this book.

OFFICE

The need for an organizer's office was mentioned in Chapter 2. If he is to cope effectively with all the responsibilities described in this chapter, the organizer will need an office, secretarial and, possibly, executive support along with at least one telephone. A 'bleep' device for the organizer and key staff is useful for the larger event so that they can always be contacted in an emergency.

KEEP IN TOUCH

The organizer will be very busy during the event. So busy that, if he is not careful, he will seldom mix with delegates to find out how they are enjoying themselves and what problems or complaints they have. It is easy to keep in close contact with venue staff, the chairmen, speakers and sub-contractors. However, it is worth remembering from time to time that the event is primarily for the *delegates*. A conscious effort has to be made to get feedback from them to gauge how things are going. Strange to say, the things that bother the organizers will often not even be noticed by the delegates. This is partly because the organizers are almost over-critical of everything and it is worth remembering that the delegate is often unaware of minor disasters. However, the reverse is also true. There may be things which are bothering delegates of which the organizers know nothing. These problems often come to light only when the organizers actually talk to the delegates.

EVALUATING THE EFFECTIVENESS OF THE EVENT

Everyone, either consciously or unconsciously, evaluates every meeting of which he or she is a part. However, the perceptions of organizers, chairmen, speakers and delegates will usually be different. Some sort of formal evaluation is essential to find out whether the objectives have been met and for use when planning future events.

That said, it is surprising how many companies make no attempt to evaluate their events. A recent survey revealed that 65 per cent of companies either failed to evaluate their events or, if they did, most ignored the results. The reason for this attitude seems rooted in fear – fear of negative feedback.

There are three principal opportunities to evaluate your event which can be used singly or in combination:

- at the end of the event;
- after the event;
- during the event.

Evaluation at the end of the event   This is the most common form of evaluation. Delegates are asked to complete a questionnaire and to hand it in before they leave. You will achieve a high rate of return with this form of evaluation provided the questionnaire is not too long and complicated.

However, because the feedback is immediate, it may be distorted by general euphoria or, conversely, it could be distorted in the opposite direction by a single irritator – a poor meal or one poor speaker – which could cloud the overall perception of the event.

Some organizers give the feedback forms out at the end of the event and ask delegates to return them by a specified date – usually about two weeks later. Although the return rate will drop if you do this, the feedback will be more considered and objective, and the distortions mentioned above will have less impact.

Evaluation after the event   This form of evaluation involves sending your evaluation questionnaire to delegates some time after the event – say 4–6 weeks later. It is usual to send forms to a 'sample' of delegates rather than to everyone. In selecting the sample size it should be remembered that the return rate is likely to be significantly less than that which will be achieved by immediate evaluation at the end of the event. Nevertheless, the feedback will be more objective since you will achieve a more accurate measure of what delegates actually remember some time later. By then, only the salient points will be recalled, and the 'clutter' of immediate feelings at the end of the event will have been forgotten. There is another reason for undertaking this sort of evaluation: it strengthens the delegate's feeling that the meeting was for him and that what he says is important.

Evaluation during the event   This usually has a somewhat different purpose to the other forms of evaluation already discussed. Its purpose is to determine what, if anything is going wrong so that immediate remedial action can be taken.

Thus, if delegates feel the objectives are not being met, or that there are venue failings (poor service, poor food, noise and so on) it may be possible to put matters right. It may be difficult (but not impossible) to persuade speakers to alter their approach if delegates feel the event is not meeting their objectives, but it is often possible to persuade a venue to make changes to rectify administrative problems.

Evaluation during the event can be informal – just go round asking questions and seeking delegates' views 'so far'. Formal evaluation during the event is less usual unless some form of deliberate testing is to be used. Where formal evaluation or voting is to be involved it may be worth putting in special audience response systems (see Chapters 6 and 14) or using a low-cost feedback system that will run on a PC, as described overleaf.

What to evaluate?

You need to be clear what your evaluation is intended to achieve: is it intended to determine how much participants have learnt, how much they enjoyed themselves, what they thought of the venue, the administration and so on? And why do you need this information? Is it to improve future similar events – or is it to determine whether further action is needed in order to meet the stated objectives? In reality, you will probably want feedback for a combination of reasons.

The sort of questions which might be asked include:

1. What did they expect and hope for from the meeting?
2. How well did the meeting fulfil their expectations and hopes?
3. What gaps in information, experience and so on did the delegates see as unfulfilled?
4. How useful did the delegates consider the meeting?
5. What did delegates think of the chosen subject matter?
6. What did delegates think of the standard of the speakers?
7. What did they think of the presentation methods?
8. How well did the delegates feel that *their* problems were dealt with?
9. What use, if any, do delegates plan to make of the material from the meeting?
10. What did delegates think of the venue, organization, food and accommodation?
11. What did delegates think of the pre-event information they were given?

There are now some feedback systems designed specifically for meeting planners. One of these, a low-cost solution called Visual INSIGHT, which runs on PCs, not only analyses the markings but helps you prepare your questionnaire from your library of questions.

We have included two questionnaires with a selection of questions and a sample Rated Response Report to help you with your search for feedback information. You will note that in all instances an even number of multichoice boxes has been used. If you use an odd number your respondents will be likely to tick the middle course!

CROWN HOTEL & RESORTS
GUEST SATISFACTION REPORT

Please mark the statement which best describes the following aspects of your stay.

1. **Cleanliness and hygiene of the public area of this hotel.**

Excellent	Good	Average	Poor
☐	☐	☐	☐

2. **Cleanliness and hygiene of your room.**

Excellent	Good	Average	Poor
☐	☐	☐	☐

3. **The speed and efficiency of your check-in.**

Excellent	Good	Average	Poor
☐	☐	☐	☐

4. **The safety and security of the hotel.**

Excellent	Good	Average	Poor
☐	☐	☐	☐

5. **The temperature control in your room.**

Excellent	Good	Average	Poor
☐	☐	☐	☐

6. **The use of the telephone to dial direct.**

Excellent	Good	Average	Poor
☐	☐	☐	☐

7. **The physical condition of the following areas of the hotel**

	Excellent	Good	Average	Poor
Lobby/Reception	☐	☐	☐	☐
Public corridors	☐	☐	☐	☐
Your room	☐	☐	☐	☐
Your bathroom	☐	☐	☐	☐
External surroundings/garden	☐	☐	☐	☐
The Business Centre	☐	☐	☐	☐

8. **Have you used a restaurant for breakfast/lunch/afternoon meal?** ☐ Yes   ☐ No
   If yes, please specify the restaurant name and describe the service you received.
   Restaurant name: _____

	Excellent	Good	Average	Poor
Quality of food	☐	☐	☐	☐
Variety of menu	☐	☐	☐	☐
Availability of healthy choices	☐	☐	☐	☐
Quality of service	☐	☐	☐	☐
Atmosphere/Ambience	☐	☐	☐	☐

9. **Which statement best describes each member of staff with whom you have had contact?**

	Excellent	Good	Average	Poor
Front desk/reception	☐	☐	☐	☐
Concierge	☐	☐	☐	☐
Telephone operators	☐	☐	☐	☐
Bar staff	☐	☐	☐	☐
Room service	☐	☐	☐	☐
Fitness Centre	☐	☐	☐	☐
Business Centre	☐	☐	☐	☐
Maintenance department	☐	☐	☐	☐

10. **Overall which statement best describes this hotel?**

Excellent	Good	Average	Poor
☐	☐	☐	☐

11. **Have you stayed in other hotels in this city?**   ☐ Yes   ☐ No

12. **Which of the following factors influenced your decision to choose this hotel for this trip?**   *(please tick one or more boxes)*
    - ☐ Personal experience of this hotel
    - ☐ Recommendation by a friend/colleague
    - ☐ Advertising/Special promotion offer
    - ☐ Someone else made the decision for me
    - ☐ Company policy or recommendation in HOME city
    - ☐ Hotel included as part of inclusive package deal
    - ☐ Other factor *(please write in)* _____

13. **If you return to this city will you use this hotel again?**   ☐ Yes   ☐ No

14. **Length of your stay**   ☐ One night   ☐ 2–4 nights   ☐ 5 or more nights

15. **Purpose of your trip**
    - ☐ Individual business traveller   ☐ Individual leisure traveller
    - ☐ Meeting/Conference delegate   ☐ Group leisure traveller
    - ☐ Other factor *(please write in)* _____

16. **Your age**   ☐ Less than 30   ☐ 30–50   ☐ 51–60   ☐ Over 60

17. **Your sex**   ☐ Male   ☐ Female

FIVE YEAR PLANNING – MARCH '99
PART TWO QUESTIONS

Please use this scale to evaluate the following questions

Strongly disagree	Disagree	Agree	Strongly agree
1	2	3	4

SECTION 1

Workshops

The format was effective in eliciting knowledge, ideas and concerns	1	2	3	4
The presentations challenged my thinking	1	2	3	4
The content provided me with information that will be helpful in my work	1	2	3	4

Making it happen – George Brown

The speaker demonstrated good speaking skills	1	2	3	4
I can apply what I learnt in my job	1	2	3	4
The content was relevant to my work	1	2	3	4
The speaker identified important issues	1	2	3	4
The speaker thoroughly answered participants' questions	1	2	3	4

Conference overall

The programme was appropriate for my job experience	1	2	3	4
My understanding of 'Leadership and continuous improvement' was enhanced	1	2	3	4
I can apply what I learnt on the job	1	2	3	4
The programme was well organized	1	2	3	4
I was made to feel welcome	1	2	3	4
I would rate the facility highly	1	2	3	4
The conference was very effective	1	2	3	4

	Yes	No
Should we conduct a similar conference in 2000?	1	2

SECTION 2

1. When you return to your business unit, will the information you receive at this conference have an impact on how you do your job? Please explain.

_____

_____

2. What was the strongest aspect of this conference?

_____

_____

3. What was the weakest aspect of this conference?

    _____

    _____

4. What, if anything, should have been included that was not?

    _____

    _____

5. Do you have any suggestions for improving next year's conference?

    _____

    _____

    _____

To which type of organization do you belong?   **Are you**

    Hospital   1   An executive?   1

    Consultancy   2   A manager?   2

    General practice 3   A supervisor? 3

                                                 Other?   4

RATED RESPONSE REPORT

Event   : 1999 Annual Meeting
Session   : George Grown
Location   : The Grand Hotel
Date   : 1st March '99

DELEGATE TYPE: ALL

Number of Responses: 80

	Mean	Strongly Agree 1	2	3	Strongly Disagree 4
1. The speaker demonstrated good speaking skills	2.99	8	18	21	33
2. I can apply what I learnt in my job	2.66	9	19	42	10
3. The content was relevant to my work	2.61	15	16	34	15
4. The speaker identified important issues	3.46	2	10	17	51
5. The speaker thoroughly answered participants' questions	3.51	1	5	26	48
OVERALL	3.04				

Follow evaluation up!

It is obvious that feedback from evaluation should be acted upon (sadly, the survey mentioned earlier discovered that in a high proportion of instances *nothing* was done as a result of evaluation feedback).

Furthermore, it is good practice to let delegates know (1) the results of the overall feedback and (2) what action is being taken as a result. This will further reinforce the effectiveness of the event. All too often, good ideas which emerge from conferences are subsequently lost because no-one follows them up. Good evaluation and after-action can prevent such lapses.

POST-MORTEM

The organizers should contact a 'post-mortem' after the event. The following questions should be asked:

- Were the objectives of the whole meeting and of each session clear and realistic? Were they achieved?
- Did we analyse delegates' expectations correctly?
- Did delegates feel that the meeting was for them? Did they participate in it?
- Were our presentation methods suitable?
- Did everyone enjoy the event?

If the answers to these questions are positive, the chances are that the meeting was a success. It is no accident that these questions are all about the meeting and not about the administration of the event, although it might seem strange to pose them at the end of a chapter which deals mainly with administrative matters. The point is that the answers are less likely to be positive if the event has been an administrative failure. The questions are also raised here because we must never forget what the administrative staff should be striving to achieve – an event which meets its objectives. All their work and all their planning are directed to this end. In the ultimate analysis, all the administration and planning are purely the vehicles for success in the conference hall.

EXECUTIVE CHECKLIST

- Do you try to administer meetings in which you participate? Should you appoint a separate administrator?

- Are people kept waiting when they register for your events? Do you:
  1. Have sufficient registration points to deal with the flow of delegates quickly?
  2. Divide hand-out material into standard and individual runs for ease of handling?
  3. Have a separate exception handling desk?
- Do you set up an information and message system?
- Do you arrange separate reception of VIPs and speakers?
- Do you provide a rehearsal room for speakers?
- Do you carry out session checks – room layouts, AV equipment, scripts, lighting, heating, cleanliness, noise, etc?
- Do you maintain close liaison with the venue staff, caterers and sub-contractors? Do you brief them and thank them?
- Do you provide suitable food and refreshments?
- Do you monitor and physically check the consumption of wines and spirits?
- Do you draw up security plans to protect people, valuables and equipment and against espionage?
- Do you have spares for vital equipment such as projectors and bulbs?
- Do you appoint a troubleshooter to deal with emergencies?
- Do you have plans for fire, bomb alerts, power cuts and equipment failures?
- Do you evaluate your meetings?
- Do you, if necessary, follow up evaluation with appropriate remedial action?
- Do you subsequently let delegates know the results of the evaluation exercise?

14

THE ART OF CHAIRING A CONFERENCE

'My Lord, ladies and gentlemen. Pray silence for our president...' with these immortal words, a toastmaster opened an association annual conference in London. The management of that event was a disaster. In the right context toastmasters can lift the proceedings from the mundane to memorable heights. But it is not fair to expect a toastmaster to take on the role of a conference link-man – or chairman – for the task goes far beyond that of merely introducing the next speaker. Chairing any meeting, be it a small round table discussion or a full-blown international conference, demands skills and knowledge which only a few people possess. A good programme chairman can make the difference between a conference going well and being a disaster. Steering an event to success is an art that requires preparation, skill, quick thinking, confidence and knowledge. In this chapter we identify and define the role of the chairman and give advice on how someone nominated for the job should prepare himself for the task and carry it out.

The chapter is not concerned with the task of chairing committee meetings. This is not only a different discipline, it also requires somewhat different skills. The art of chairing such meetings has been described in many books and articles and the subject is well covered in any good public library. What we are concerned with here is the task facing the person chosen to hold together the event which involves a number of speakers. We normally call this person the chairman or

343

programme chairman although, naturally, he might be referred to by other titles according to his position in the particular organization.

THE ROLE OF THE CHAIRMAN

The chairman has a number of roles to play. First and foremost in terms of the audience's perception of the role, the chairman is a ringmaster. His task, as a ringmaster, is to announce speakers, events and matters of interest. He also has to link the elements of the event together, helping thereby to weld a number of separate elements in to a whole. He is also a guide to help speakers and audience through the programme. In this respect he is also the time-keeper, ensuring that the programme runs smoothly and to schedule. His other roles are more subtle and less obvious to the audience but are none the less fundamental to the success of the event. These are described below.

An important task of the chairman is to help the audience interpret and understand in terms of the objectives the information being given by the speakers. This is not to say that the chairman should try to alter the meaning of what has been said by a speaker, nor should he make critical or contentious comments. Rather, the chairman should help the audience focus on the relevant issues. This is discussed in greater detail later in the chapter.

The chairman sometimes has to act as a referee, either between the audience and speakers or between speakers themselves. This role is most clearly manifest during question and answer sessions either between individual speakers and the audience or between speakers during, for example, a panel discussion. However, the chairman may also have to cope with situations where speakers' papers are at variance with each other or with the objectives of the event. These occasions require firm but tactful handling by the chairman. Failure to act as a referee at these times can prejudice the potential success of the event.

It must be remembered that, throughout the event, the chairman is a participant. It is not enough to introduce a speaker and then relax with the mind in neutral. The chairman must concentrate, listen, think about the subject in hand and actively participate in everything which takes place. This does not mean that the chairman should try to dominate the proceedings – far from it. The chairman, above all, should act as the cata-lyst, bringing both speakers and audience to life. The good chairman will do this through the occasional summary and the question which throws discussion open, and not by imposing his views and personality on either speaker or audience. Perhaps the best advice which can be given to any chairman is 'be yourself'. Do not try to be funny if you are naturally serious or to be dominant if you are naturally retiring. If you know the subject in hand and are properly briefed, you should be able to fulfil the necessary chairman's role without forcing yourself to act in an uncharacteristic manner.

The role of the chairman, then, is a complex one. Certainly, the chairman must have natural authority and intelligence. He or she should know the subject to hand and the needs of the audience. This is why the toastmaster at the conference described at the beginning of the chapter was so inadequate in the role of chairman. It was unfair to expect him to do anything more than call for silence for the next person to speak. How can a toastmaster, who has little or no technical knowledge of the subject, be expected to interpret the proceedings and act as referee and catalyst?

CHOOSING THE CHAIRMAN

The choice of the programme chairman is a crucial decision. If the wrong person is selected, the meeting can fail to achieve the desired objectives. Sometimes we have no choice. The elected chairman of an organization, who may be excellent in that role, may be wholly inadequate as a conference chairman. Similarly, the managing director of the in-company event – however good he is as managing director – may be unable to perform the role of chairman of an incentive or sales conference. One senior executive regularly chaired conferences and seminars in his organization and his summaries and thanks after speakers had delivered their papers were rambling, confusing and embarrassing to speakers and audience alike. No-one in the organization had the courage to point out his inadequacies to him. In the end it took an outsider, who could afford to ignore the internal politics, to suggest that he stood down in favour of someone more suitable. The irony was that he was only too happy to do so. He had secretly suffered agonies every time he had acted as chairman, but had carried on because he felt it was his duty and responsibility to do so.

Fortunately, the choice is often less restricted. A little research may be needed to find someone who has the necessary attributes. As a general rule, the chairman will be comparatively senior. It is usually only the more senior person who has the experience and authority to handle the task. A senior person is also more likely to have the requisite knowledge. The chairman needs a degree of specialist knowledge of the subject in question. He should also be a person who can identify and have sympathy with the aims of the event. If there is conflict between the chairman's personal beliefs or professional obligations and the aims of the conference, the chairman is not able to conduct the proceedings in a sympathetic and understanding way. When this happens it is highly unlikely that the objectives will be satisfied. One would not expect a doctor of the Roman Catholic faith to chair an event calling for the use of contraception, nor could a Conservative politician be expect to chair a conference calling for the abolition of private medicine. These may be extreme examples, but they illustrate cases where the chairman would experience personal conflict which would reduce his credibility and effectiveness.

The chairman needs to be experienced in public speaking. A person with the attributes previously described would normally have this experience, but this is not always the case. A person who is poor at speaking in public is unlikely to be able to hold the event together. There is a further reason for selecting a reasonably accomplished speaker. Many of the other speakers will be nervous immediately before they perform. Their anxieties are unlikely to be allayed by a chairman who is equally nervous and hesitant. The chairman must instil confidence in everyone: speaker, audience and even supporting staff. In short, the chairman needs to be an experienced leader. The chances of the meeting going well will always be enhanced when the chairman has these attributes.

THE TASK

How should you approach the task if you are asked to chair a conference? A lot of preparation is needed to equip yourself for the role and your responsibilities during the event are considerable.

The chairman must ensure that he fully understands the aims of the event. This must be done early on because if he does not have sympathy with these aims he should not continue. He must also appreciate the *needs* of the audience. People attend conferences for a variety of reasons. They may be seeking to learn something new; or they may be there to exchange information with other delegates; they may be there to be rewarded for good performance or they may be attending in order to reinforce the feeling of belonging to a particular group – perhaps a professional body, an association or some other organization. There are many other reasons. Each reason generates different audience needs. The delegate of an incentive event will expect entertaining sessions. The delegate who is there to learn will expect a more serious, academic event while the member of an association or political party may be in need of a morale-boost. By appreciating the needs of his audience the chairman can pander to these needs and, in so doing, guide the event towards achieving its objectives. A lack of appreciation of audience needs can have a disproportionately adverse effect. A chairman of a seminar caused a storm of protest when he refused to allow a speaker to be questioned by an audience which had been excited and motivated by a particular talk. In his anxiety to avoid overrunning at a point in the programme where in fact an overrun would not have had any serious consequences, the chairman deprived the delegates of the chance of cross-questioning a leading politican who had spoken on a particularly controversial subject. Such was the frustration of many delegates that they walked out of the rest of the event. Had the chairman allowed a limited number of questions (the speaker had been willing to take questions from the floor) and then curtailed the proceedings, everyone would have been satisfied.

A chairman must also anticipate audience reaction. Indeed, a failure to do this caused the problem just described. If an audience is likely to be hostile, puzzled or even bored, the chairman can do much to smooth the way with a skilfully worded introduction, a well-timed intervention or a request for a further explanation.

A leading Socialist politician was due to speak at a conference of social workers whom he could reasonably have expected to support his party's policies. During his preparatory research, the chairman discovered that a group of delegates due to be in the audience was vociferously opposed to some of the policies which were to be discussed. The chairman forewarned the speaker who was able to prepare himself and minimize the disruptive effect of the protests – a good example of how, by anticipating audience reaction, the chairman is able to keep the event 'on track'.

The chairman must review the strengths and weaknesses of his panel of speakers. Have they the necessary knowledge? Are they attractive speakers? How good are their presentational skills? The chairman of an event is often (but not always) asked to help choose his speakers and can thus influence these matters. Where he has no choice, he can at least anticipate problems which might occur. Further, if he has a prior knowledge of the speakers' strengths and weaknesses the chairman can discuss these matters with them beforehand. If he knows that a particular speaker, although an expert on his subject, is not a good presenter, he can encourage him to use visual aids to enhance the session.

The chairman should avoid taking a key speaking role in addition to his duties as chairman. The only exceptions are a keynote opening or closing address. This apart, the chairman already has plenty on his hands without taking on the additional burden of speaking at a main session. This cannot, of course, be a hard and fast rule and is one which is often broken. Nevertheless, the roles of speaker and chairman are best kept separate.

Briefing speakers

The chairman should be involved in the speakers' briefings. A good conference organizer will handle this on the chairman's behalf (see Chapter 15) but the chairman will wish to see the speakers' synopses well before the event to help him assess each speaker's contribution. Without this prior knowledge it is difficult to imagine how the chairman can effectively prepare himself.

A personal discussion between speakers and chairman, either individually or in a group, is always useful. One well known businessman who is often invited to chair seminars and conferences invites his speakers to dine with him at his London club. This is a very civilized way of introducing speakers to each other and helping them tie their contributions together. In meeting his speakers, the chairman is also able to form an even better impression of their strengths and weaknesses and, having met them socially, is able to bring a more personal note into his autobiographical remarks when he introduces each speaker.

Personal preparation

Having completed your research, seen the speakers' synopses and, possibly, met the speakers, you are in a position to prepare yourself for the actual event. This involves identifying the various links and themes. At several points in this chapter we have seen that the chairman should be instrumental in welding together the individual elements of the event. If the programme has been well constructed and the various sessions reflect the objectives of the event, this should not cause undue difficulty. Nevertheless, each speaker's contribution is a single unit. Indeed, the average speaker goes to great lengths to build his session into a coherent unit, with its own summary and conclusions. It is the chairman's task to build continuity between these individual elements.

By studying each speaker's contribution the chairman can identify development points which he can use throughout the event. It is usual for certain themes to appear and reappear in several different sessions and the chairman can use these as bridges between sessions, either during his summary remarks or by steering discussion periods towards these themes. The chairman should decide upon which aspects of each speaker's contribution he wishes to place emphasis in his summaries in order to maintain the desired continuity.

When the event is a symposium or some other more open session with discussion between delegates (and speakers) and is intended to reach specific conclusions, the chairman should try to anticipate the likely outcome of the discussions. This is not to suggest that an autocratic approach should be taken in order to ensure that certain conclusions are reached. The chairman's role is to meet the objectives of the event. The objectives of any discussion event are usually conducted in general terms ('to discuss' or 'to decide what should be done'), rather than by defining what the decision or conclusions of the discussion should be. However, although the chairman may wish to see certain conclusions and may try to steer discussion accordingly, the real reason for his forecasting likely conclusions is to arm himself to handle the decision and discussion process, not to influence it. To take an extreme case, if the conclusions turned out to be something the chairman had not even thought of, it is possible that he might have been intellectually unable to grasp the point at all. At least forewarned is forearmed!

THE EVENT

Having fully prepared yourself well beforehand you are almost ready to take the chair. Almost... but not quite.

Preparation at the venue

The chairman should arrive early and well before the speakers and delegates. This may involve travelling the night before to avoid the risk of being late due to transport delays and other problems. An early arrival enables the chairman to make a number of valuable last minutes preparations. First, he should liaise with the organizer and discuss the programme, delegates lists, late changes and so on. The good organizer will give the chairman a brief (see Chapter 11) and show him around the venue. The chairman must know the geography of the conference hall and the immediate area so that he can inform delegates where coffee and meals will be served and where they can obtain information, make telephone calls and so on. In addition, the chairman should meet projection room staff, interpreters, shorthand writers and any other suppliers of supporting services.

It is necessary to finalize the layout of the conference room. Where will the chairman sit? Where will speakers sit before they are introduced and from where do people speak? Are there any special controls which the chairman and speakers need to understand – light switches or dimmers, projector controls, volume controls and the like? Are there warning signals for speakers who overrun? What are they? How do they work? Who will control them? Is there a visible clock? Does it tell the right time? These are just some of the things the chairman should check so that, fully briefed himself, he is able to pass on information to other speakers and delegates.

Speakers   The chairman should meet the speakers as they arrive (this is not always possible when speakers arrive after the event has begun, in which case the organizer has to stand in). The speakers should be introduced to each other if they have not met before and the chairman should use this opportunity to check autobiographical details and, perhaps, obtain further information. He should also discuss the links he intends to use with each speaker and tell them the main themes he will be developing during the event.

Conducting the session

Introducing the Conference   The chairman will usually be the first person to speak and his opening remarks, and the manner in which they are delivered, are therefore very important. The chairman should welcome delegates and if any particular people or groups of people (for example, new members or overseas delegates) deserve special mention they can be singled out at this early stage.

It is then good practice to dispense with any administrative points although these should be kept to a minimum. If the organizers have done their job properly and given delegates a good briefing with their conference papers, there should be little to add. However, it may be necessary to explain the layout of some facilities and the operation of headsets and controls of interpretation equipment and other individual seat controls (TV, lights and so on).

The purpose of the event must be reaffirmed and its relevance stressed. This point is important. It is often possible to mention recent events or press interest in the subject to underline the importance or relevance of the event. Press or TV coverage of the event itself might be mentioned in this context and if reporters are present they should be identified to the audience. Special messages can be read out – for example, a message from a royal patron or some other important person. All these can help to create a conference atmosphere at an early stage – a sense of occasion and a feeling of belonging to a unique or important body.

Introducing the Programme and Speakers   Although delegates will have copies of the programme, the chairman will normally wish to explain certain aspects. For example, it may be necessary to stress the informality of the proceedings or to explain how the main group will be split into syndicates or sub-groups later on. Delegates should be forewarned if speakers' papers are to be given out to save them from unnecessary notetaking. The speakers should be briefly introduced at this stage, along with any VIPs. Their status and expertise can be explained and their contributions stressed. Finally, the chairman should explain how and when questions will be taken – at the end of each paper or in panel sessions – and whether questions have to be submitted in writing beforehand (a technique not recommended if spontaneity is to be maintained).

One of the chairman's more obvious roles is to introduce speakers. This is not the simple task it may seem. A delicate balance is needed between saying enough to introduce the speaker and his subject and saying so much that time is taken out of the sessions and the audience begin to lose interest. It is also important not to pre-empt what the speaker is about to say.

The following points should be covered:

1. *Introduce speaker*   A few words about his or her expertise and knowledge in the area and a brief biographical résumé is usually sufficient. Long-winded biographies are boring and unnecessary. Only highlight the more interesting and relevant points and stress his or her knowledge and achievements in the subject area.

2. *Link each paper with the previous one*   The chairman should explain the link between the coming contribution and what has gone before. It is essential to avoid pre-empting the speaker's paper when handling this part of the introduction.

The chairman must be careful not to distract the audience while the speaker is on his feet. This is sometimes difficult. The chairman often sits in full view of delegates and any movement will be seen. Obvious fidgeting and signs of boredom must be avoided. The chairman must appear to be attentive and interested throughout the session in order to encourage both speaker and audience. The chairman should make notes of points he wishes to remember or, perhaps, take up later on. He should also observe the audience to gauge how they are receiving the session. A good speaker holds the audience spellbound to such an extent that it becomes silent and still. Such occasions are, sadly, rare. Noise and movement in the audience are much more common and are signs that the speaker or his subject (or even both) have failed to capture attention. On the whole, there is little the chairman can do unless the event is a private function of the type where a call to order would be appropriate.

The chairman has to ensure that speakers keep within their allotted times. This is important. Subsequent speakers are delayed if individual sessions overrun. This is discourteous, and will often play havoc with the nerves of even the most accomplished speaker. There is often a temptation to erode discussion times or coffee and meal breaks. This, too, is undesirable. Delegates will begin to lose concentration when they notice the time and those who had hoped to make urgent telephone calls during the breaks will become agitated and annoyed. Finally, a chairman should never let the day overrun the advertised time. Delegates may miss trains or start to drift away before the end of the session if this happens. Prompt lights and similar devices are often used to warn speakers that they are near the end of their time. These are often ineffectual because speakers either fail to notice them or even deliberately ignore them. If a speaker is overrunning badly a verbal reminder that time is up will normally suffice.

When the speaker does finish, the chairman should lead applause. Applause when the speaker finishes is better than invited applause at a later stage ('... and I suggest we show our appreciation in the normal manner'). The former has a degree of spontaneity which will please the speaker. The latter, if perfunctory and not really genuine, is embarrassing. A second round of applause when the speaker leaves the platform will always follow naturally if he has been particularly impressive.

Questions

The organizer must decide whether questions will be permitted and, if they are, when they will be taken. Some people keep question sessions separate, often inviting them to a panel of all the speakers at the end of the day. This course has the merit of giving delegates time to think about what they have heard and to ask questions about points they wish to follow up. On the other hand, by the end of a long day, people may be more interested in leaving to go home than in asking questions. Thus a question session immediately after a paper has been given can be useful for clearing up immediate queries. Perhaps a combination of the two is the best way to deal with this problem, but you will always run the risk of seeing your audience melt away if the concluding discussion session is allowed to last too long or, worst of all, if it overruns.

When the chairman invites questions he should focus on those topics which are of particular relevance or interest. This can often be done by asking the first question himself. This directs the focus and sets the ball rolling, avoiding a long embarrassed silence before someone in the audience plucks up sufficient courage to speak. When a question has been asked the chairman should relay it to the speaker or panel. This ensures that everyone in the room has heard and understood the question – something which might not have been possible when the delegate spoke – and also gives the speaker or panel time to think about a reply.

The chairman also has to control questions. He must decide which person to call upon when several people wish to speak and he must ensure that the delegate does actually ask a question and not make a statement or give his own lecture. If a delegate is being long-winded or fails to ask a question the chairman should call him to order and ask him to come to his point quickly so that others may also have a chance to put their questions. Noise, interruptions and separate discussions amongst delegates should also be dealt with firmly. Although rare, it is sometimes necessary to ask people to sit down or even leave the hall – a sight sometimes seen at the annual party political conferences.

Modern voting systems are available which can greatly assist the chairman in controlling questions from the floor – especially at larger conferences. For example, the Philips DCN system – whilst principally designed to obtain accurate voting and spontaneously test audience reactions – also has a facility to control and manipulate contributions from the floor. Every delegate's voting keypad has its own microphone; the chairman's control unit tells him who wants to speak and how many are waiting. Each delegate has a PIN card to activate his or her keypad which means the chairman can call up people by name and, thanks to the individual microphone, everyone can hear the question. Finally, the system can be linked into simultaneous translation systems so that questions can be translated as they arise.

Closing the session   The chairman generally concludes the session with a short summary. If this is to follow the question session it is important to time this closing properly. It is better to cut the session a little short than to drag it out when there are obviously no more questions. In his summary the chairman may re-emphasize the more important points that have emerged from the speaker's paper and the subsequent questions session. However, the chairman should avoid adding his own points. This is discourteous to the speaker and often annoys the audience. The summary should always be short and should include a word of praise and thanks to the speaker.

Closing the conference

The exact form which the end of the event takes will depend on a number of factors. There may be a closing ceremony or an address by a key figure. The chairman, however, usually has an opportunity to make his own closing remarks. Indeed, on many occasions the chairman's final remarks are the only way in which the conference is brought to a close.

The chairman should thank the speakers for their contributions. He should also remember to thank the audience. A good audience contributes a great deal, especially during question and discussion sessions, and recognition from the chair of this contribution is always appreciated. The chairman should also thank them for giving their time and for their interest. Interpreters and backroom staff such as projectionists and information staff and, perhaps, the organizer, may well be thanked at this juncture.

The achievements should be confirmed and the highlights recalled. If a particular speaker gave an outstanding performance, this should be recalled along with any events or happenings which were of note. Even disasters can be mentioned and their memories used, possibly in a humorous way, to reinforce the spirit and enthusiasm generated by the conference. Likewise, any noteworthy achievements such as record attendance, agreements about contentious issues and so on should be mentioned.

Finally, the chairman should relate the event to the future. It is not possible to give detailed advice on how this should be done as the link to the future depends entirely upon the aims of the individual event and the degree to which they have been achieved. A surge of new confidence or the use of new information can easily be related to the future activities of either the individual delegate or the group as a whole.

Dealing with calamities

Something will always go wrong however well the event has been planned and rehearsed. The chairman is in the hot seat when a calamity occurs. Backroom staff may be reponsible for putting things right and the calamity might be totally outside the control of the chairman. But the chairman is the person who has to take the initiative to restore the situation.

Speakers Late or Absent   This is always a potential problem. If a speaker is late but is known to be coming, the chairman can act accordingly, either extending a break or reshuffling the programme. An absent speaker causes far greater problems. In a perfect world there would be a stand-in for each speaker waiting in the wings for just such an eventuality. In the real world this is seldom possible and the chairman has to decide what to do. In the worst case he may have to deliver the paper himself, using the material in the delegates' papers. Or he can explain the problem to the delegates, invite them to read the paper in their folders and then throw the subject open for a general debate. Whatever he decides to do, the chairman should at least consider the possibility of a speaker failing to attend and be ready with some alternative, even if the standby action is less valuable than the original.

Another fairly frequent problem is the speaker who becomes ill or dries up. If the speaker is too ill to continue, the situation is much the same as in the case of the absent speaker – the chairman has to decide how to proceed without him. The speaker who dries up is a different matter. There are normally two reasons for the silence: nerves or the speaker has run out of things to say. A careful prompt or encouragement from the chairman is often sufficient overcome the problem of nerves. The latter is more serious because, for whatever reason, the speaker will probably have failed to cover the ground in sufficient depth. In this case there is little alternative to opening up a discussion in the hope that the speaker will respond to the rather less formal atmosphere and that the necessary information will be drawn out of him.

Conference Not Being Successful   An even more difficult problem arises when it becomes obvious that the conference is not being successful. The signs of audience unrest and dissatisfaction will be all too apparent. The chairman's best course is to consult the organizers and, possibly, the speakers at the next break to decide what should be done. It may even be worthwhile asking some of the delegates why they think the event is not working well. Armed with this knowledge it may be possible to rearrange the programme or session contents to improve matters. Sometimes the problem is a fundamental misunderstanding by one side or the other. A one-day seminar was advertised on 'Novel Uses for Closed Circuit Television (CCTV)'. The advertisement appeared in the educational press and attracted a good number of delegates. The event itself was a near disaster. The speakers were there to talk about CCTV's potential as a propaganda weapon – a far cry from the educational interests of the delegates. Even the most brilliant chairman would have had difficulty in bridging that gap although, with good preparation, he might well have prevented the situation from happening at all.

Technical Hitches   These are, in many ways, the least of all the chairman's problems. When a film breaks or the lights fuse the reasons for the failure are understood and the audience is usually patient provided the organizers seem to be on top of the situation. The chairman of an important company conference wanted to 'make an entrance' at the beginning of the event. It was planned that, as he rose to speak, the stage curtains would open to reveal the company logo on the screen. After several rehearsals the timing was perfected. On the actual day the curtains remained obstinately closed. As soon as the chairman realized this was due to a technical failure and not a human error, he immediately ordered some of the junior executives present to tear the curtains down – no mean task as they were heavy velvet stage curtains on complex runners. The beginning was even more dramatic than planned, but the chairman gained more credit and respect than he might have done had he reacted differently.

The chairman need not be afraid of technical hitches, but he should certainly think about them beforehand so that he can at least be partially prepared for every eventuality.

PREPARATION IS THE KEY

The enduring lesson to be learnt from this chapter is that good preparation is the hallmark of the good conference chairman. The well prepared chairman will know his subject, the programme, the venue, the speakers and the aims of the event. Armed with this knowledge he will be able to handle the event with confidence and authority and guide it towards the desired objectives.

EXECUTIVE CHECKLIST

- Prepare thoroughly before the event:
  1. Determine the needs of the audience and anticipate its reaction.
  2. Review the speakers' strengths and weaknesses.
  3. Brief speakers.
  4. Identify links and themes.
- Arrive early on the day:
  1. Get to know the geography of the venue.
  2. Liaise with the organizer.
  3. Introduce speakers to each other.
  4. Check biographical details.
  5. Inform/check links and themes.
  6. Be prepared for calamities and have plans to deal with them.
- Include the following in the opening remarks:
  1. Welcome.
  2. Administration.
  3. Purpose of the event.
  4. Relevance.
  5. Introduce speakers, their status, expertise and contribution.
  6. Introduce the programme.
- During each session:
  1. Introduce the speaker.
  2. Link with previous session.
  3. Time keep.
  4. Lead applause.
  5. Invite questions (if required).
  6. Summarize.
- When closing the conference:
  1. Thank speakers, audience and support staff.
  2. Confirm achievements.
  3. Recall the highlights.
  4. Relate to the future.

15

THE CONFERENCE ORGANIZER

Having read the previous chapters, you may feel that organizing meetings is a daunting and thankless task and one to be avoided at all costs. In fact, the reverse can be true. The workload is certainly considerable, but the task itself is varied, challenging and rewarding. Unlike many, the conference organizer has the pleasure of seeing the end-product of his labours, and the satisfaction to be gained from success can be considerable.

Only a few organizations are sufficiently active in the field to warrant a conference department or even one full-time specialist. The job is usually given to the hard-pressed manager of the department closest to the theme of the conference or to someone who happens to be under-employed (and how many of an organization's best managers ever find themselves in *that* position?). The result is that the responsibility for many meetings is pushed down the line to inexperienced people who have neither the knowledge nor the resources for the task. This failure to involve top management is partly due to the ill-defined nature of the activity. Meeting, communicating and conferring are part and parcel of everyday business life. At what point do we need special expertise and responsibility to ensure that they are done properly?

Perhaps the answer lies in the need for meetings to be successful. What are the consequences of failure? The cost of assembling an important audience (and who wants to assemble an unimportant audience?) is only one factor to take into account. What does the conference balance sheet look like if you end up by puzzling or depressing a workforce you had intended to motivate, or if you put on a drab incompetent display to a group of buyers you were trying to impress with the quality of your products or the liveliness of your service? The real cost of failure can be very high. Considerable demands are therefore placed upon the conference organizer. Arranging a successful meeting cannot be regarded as a routine administrative task. True, the basis of successful conference organization is punctilious housekeeping: planning, checking and re-checking every detail of the physical arrangements. That certainly is within the competence of company personnel if they take it seriously enough. But the task is much broader than this. To do the work well, the conference organizer has to perform various roles in meeting the complex needs of his organization or the organization to which he is a consultant. He has to be:

- an administrative executive;
- a planner;
- a co-ordinator of information;
- a presentation specialist;
- a consultant to management.

Of these roles, the first four would probably be immediately accepted as the prerogative of the conference organizer. The fifth, that of a consultant to management, is less obvious. It is also often the most important role and one which, significantly, the junior and inexperienced will feel least able to play. In any event, each role requires somewhat different skills and abilities. In a small organization the conference organizer may have to attempt to perform all these functions. In a larger organization a department head might well be a consultant to management for planning the meeting, while those on his staff design, administer and conduct the actual event.

In Chapter 1 we posed five simple questions to be answered when a conference or meeting is being considered: (1) Why do we need to hold a conference? (2) What is to be achieved? (3) Who should attend? (4) When should the event be held? (5) Where should it take place? We saw that unless these questions are answered in a logical and disciplined manner the event is unlikely to be successful. Those who initially decide to hold an event may only have a half-formed idea of what they actually wish to achieve. If the conference organizer is an experienced and relatively senior executive, he can act as a consultant to work with management to:

1. Identify the objectives for the event.
2. Decide the type of meeting needed to meet these objectives.
3. Develop the meeting plans.
4. Explore appropriate resources to implement the meeting plan.
5. Evaluate the event.
6. Decide the follow-up steps needed after the meeting.

When acting as a consultant, the conference organizer must understand the nature of this aspect of the work and the way it should be performed. It is not necessarily difficult. In a sense, everyone is a consultant. We all have to give advice from time to time. Teachers, parents and friends are consultants, as are business colleagues and partners. Further, we all at times feel the need for help. The key to a working relationship between consultant and consulted is mutual trust and respect. Both parties need certain skills, knowledge and awareness which, taken together, form an effective and complementary relationship.

The conference organizer will normally be dealing with people who have considerable expertise in their own fields. While it is not necessary for the organizer to be an expert in these fields, he must certainly be able to relate to the experts and understand their requirements and difficulties. He therefore needs experience, a background in management, and abilities which go far beyond the limited skills of the junior administrative executive so often chosen for the task of organizing conferences and meetings.

The real lesson is that, whether large or small, a conference consumes considerable quantities of two of an organization's most precious resources: time and people. This fact cannot be over-stressed. Conferences and meetings should receive the same top management backing and attention that is automatically given to other corporate activities with budgets of the same order. Objectives will then be set more clearly, higher standards will be demanded and controls will be more tightly applied.

Organizations bent on DIY conference organization should ask themselves two questions:

◆ Can we really afford to divert the time and energy of those executives who have enough *authority* to do the job?
◆ If so, have these executives the *expertise* to do it well?

If the answer to either question is 'no', outside help is needed.

The questions is, what sort of help – and where do you find it?

The answer lies in the 'professional conference organizer' (PCO).

THE PROFESSIONAL CONFERENCE ORGANIZER

There are plenty of people who claim to be conference organizers or who will tell you they can organize your event(s) for you – but beware, they are not all quite what they seem:

Hotels   As we saw in an earlier chapter, hotels often state in their promotional material that they have 'trained conference organizers' on hand to ensure the success of your event. What they *mean* is that one of the assistant managers (probably from the conference office – possibly from the banqueting department) will be appointed to liaise with you just before and during your event. They should be able to 'make things happen' and sort out problems – but that is about all. In truth, the term 'conference organizer' is a misnomer in this instance. The truth is that the venue will have a very short-term view of your event: it only becomes really important when it becomes the next function in the schedule and the venue staff have to plan the next set of menus and room layouts. You, on the other hand, will have been planning the event for months – possibly for a year or more. No hotel can help you with the longer-term planning – nor with the actual content of your event.

PR companies and advertising agencies may also claim to be able to organize a conference for you. In reality, they are straying into areas which are beyond their purview. True, they can organize press conferences and yes they often become involved in product launches. But this does not mean that they can offer a full conference organizing service (although they are well placed to offer advice on some aspects of the task).

Travel agents will also loosely talk of offering a conference organization service, especially for events overseas. In fact, their stock in trade is arranging all the travel and dealing with the ground handling both in the UK and at the destination venue. Because they are used to this work, and because they can help you in your dealings with the venue, hotels, social functions and so on, their support is invaluable. But when it comes to what goes on inside the conference hall then they are out of their depth just as you would be out of your depth if you tried to handle the detailed local travel arrangements.

Production houses exist to produce 'shows' – ie events like product launches and presentations with special sets, a high degree of audio-visual and possibly live 'entertainment' in the programme. Production houses vary in size and capacity. Some offer a comprehensive service.

Others specialize in audio-visual presentation. The latter will probably have their own in-house creative and technical personnel but will hire in freelance talent, equipment and so on when needed.

Professional conference organizers (PCOs) tend to divide into two categories: the larger companies which specialize in organizing big events (for example, major international conferences) from within their own resources and the 'smaller' PCOs who often work alone with, possibly, only a secretary. The latter will sub-contract and hire in a range of support services according to the event in hand. Both have their places in the industry, but care needs to be exercised when selecting the 'one man band'. Anyone can call himself a conference organizer: there are no professional exams to pass and no controlling professional body which lays down standards or enforces a code of practice. This is not to say that every small operation has to be viewed with suspicion – some independent PCOs have excellent track records.

It is no use asking which is 'best' – it depends upon the specific requirements of the 'client', that is, the organization hiring the professional.

Choosing a professional conference organizer

Identify the tasks which cannot be handled by your own resources before approaching a professional conference organizer. Do you need just specialist advice and knowledge or do you want someone to take over the whole task? Is the professional expected temporarily to dovetail into your organization or to work virtually independently?

Even when you have decided roughly what you want it can still be difficult to decide which outside services are truly capable of providing help which will effectively augment your own organization's efforts. A few professionals will have the full range of capabilities you need – others will certainly not.

The best thing to do is to approach several and:

1. Discuss your needs *vis-à-vis* the services they claim to offer. Visit the supplier instead of always permitting him to visit you. In this way you will find out the quality of his staff and how big his organization is. Is the person you see a 'front man'? Will he, or someone else, be supporting you?

2. Find out whether he is able to provide all the skills and resources you need. In particular, does he have the managerial experience and knowledge to act as a consultant to your organization? Will he and your organization's link person be able to form the necessary working

relationship? To discover this it may be necessary to hold several lengthy discussions with the supplier. In these discussions, is he frank, helpful and able to relate to the problem?

3. Check that your organizers are supported by a computer system so that they can react to changes – to the programme, to attendees and to their requirements, and to enable them to produce letters, labels, lists, rosters, name badges and financial and management reports very speedily.

4. Find out exactly what the supplier does and what he sub-contracts. There is nothing wrong with sub-contracting – it can ensure that you will always use the very best suppliers (but decide what criteria you use for 'best' – which, for example, is most important to you: cost, quality or speed of response?).

5. Ask the organizer for the names of some clients – follow them up and ask for references. The successful organizer will be delighted to provide this information. Others may be evasive. Ask yourself why!

6. Ask if you or a senior colleague can visit a similar event the organizer is running for someone else. If you see him in action you can judge his actual competence and ability.

7. If relevant, ask to see some of his work – a complete AV presentation from an AV house and, from the organizer, programmes, brochures, delegates' papers and so on.

8. Ask for a quotation and find out exactly what is and is not included. An estimate of unquoted expenses should be given and the basis for charging travel, accommodation and other expenses should be agreed. You do not want to pay for your supplier to fly on Concorde or stay at a more expensive hotel than you!

9. Find out whether your supplier is obtaining commissions from hotels and other facilities used for your event. This is a controversial subject, but if the organizer is to act on your behalf it seems reasonable that he should do just that and not have financial interests elsewhere. Many professional conference organizers disagree, especially those who are primarily placement agencies. They use their commissions to defray or even eliminate fees to their clients. However, the client still pays in the end! Members of the Association of British Professional Conference Organisers (ABPCO) – see below – are obliged to inform clients if they are taking commission from suppliers: this is a refreshingly honest policy which others ought to follow.

Most organizations will take this sort of care when purchasing other goods and services and it is good sense to do the same when engaging a conference organizer. Such precautions will not guarantee success but they will greatly reduce the risk of a costly fiasco – or paying someone to do what, with a little care, you and your staff could have done just as well yourselves.

Professional bodies Although there is no overall professional body for the conference industry – say the equivalent of ABTA (The Association of British Travel Agents) for the travel industry, or the BMA (British Medical Association) for the medical profession, there are some associations to which you can turn for advice.

The Association of British Professional Conference Organisers (ABPCO) was set up as a forum within which PCOs could exchange information, arrange training and work to improve standards. Members of ABPCO have to demonstrate a proven track record before being accepted into the Association. There is also an International Association of Professional Conference Organizers (IAPCO) which only admits established PCOs and which has similar aims to its smaller British counterpart.

The Association of Conference Executives (ACE International) seeks to bring together 'buyers' and 'suppliers' in the conference industry. It has a code of practice, but anyone can join: the Association does not seek to impose standards – rather it encourages training and, through social functions and facility visits, it facilitates the process of introducing suppliers to buyers.

There are other associations of interest to conference organizers, two of which deserve particular mention:

- The Meetings Industry Association (MIA) is the recognized trade organization for the conference industry in the United Kingdom.
- The International Visual Communications Association (IVCA) is the professional association of visual communication users and suppliers.

The MIA's principal aims are (1) to improve the quality of service and facilities offered by its members and (2) to encourage the maintenance of the highest professional standards within the meetings industry. Other activities include training and 'Parliamentary Liaison'. The Association has introduced what it calls the 'Meetings Magna Carta' to which its members are obliged to conform. The model terms and conditions and standards for conference packages incorporated in the document are what they call 'buyer led' initiatives. Copies of the 'Magna Carta' can be obtained from the Association and if you are a regular buyer it would be worth obtaining a copy so that you are aware of the industry norms (whether they are sufficient for your needs is for you to decide – you can always negotiate your own terms if they are not in accordance with your particular requirements).

Addresses of all the above are included in the list of Useful Addresses at the end of the book.

THE 'TYPICAL' CORPORATE CONFERENCE ORGANIZER

In reality, in the great majority of companies it is the senior secretary who ends up being responsible for organizing corporate conferences. They may be the PA to the managing director, marketing manager or sales manager – or they may work for the company training department. They initially become involved because their boss wants the conference, and they soon become *very* involved. To their surprise, they find they enjoy the work – the added responsibility, freedom to make decisions and to organize a variety of resources add to their job satisfaction.

As mentioned in the Preface, these people usually learn as they go along, with little or no outside help and guidance, and they seldom have the opportunity of meeting other people who organize conferences. And yet many of them arrange very large meetings – and in surprisingly large numbers – with few or even no additional resources in terms of secretarial support. If you are one of these people, this book will probably have reassured you.

However, you should consider joining one of the bodies listed on page 363. Most company conference organizers tend to join ACE International, but you may be eligible to join ABPCO. You might also consider joining MPI (Meeting Professionals International) – this American body has an active European Chapter which organizes training courses and 'professional qualifications' for conference organizers.

To keep up to date with what is going on in the industry, with venue news, the latest equipment, overseas and domestic destination reports and case histories of events large and small, you should register to receive one or both of the excellent trade publications *Conference and Incentive Travel* and *Meetings and Incentive Travel*. Both are free in the UK to qualifying conference organizers.

Other activities worth pursuing are attending one of the few courses available to conference organizers, and visiting the annual exhibitions of the conference industry. Taking courses first, Management Centre Europe (MCE – address at the end of the book) offer programmes for conference organizers: these are held in both London and Brussels. The two exhibitions – Confex, at the time of writing held each year in February and MEIT (Meetings and Incentive Travel Show) which is held in June – are well worth attending whatever your interest. Both events are held in London.

THE TASK

The task of the conference organizer is what this book is all about. What will probably strike the reader is the sheer quantity of things to do and remember. No-one can possibly remember everything, but perhaps, having read this book, when a similar problem or situation confronts the reader a bell will ring in the memory. A solution may then be found more easily than would have been the case without prior knowledge. Prior knowledge and experience help – but they do not tell you how to begin. The following tips may be useful:

Checklists

There must be hundreds of checklists available to the would-be conference organizer. Each is designed to a purpose. Many are claimed to be comprehensive – few are. Someone else's checklist is of little use unless it is rewritten for your own specific event. In short, you will have to prepare your own plan for your own event.

A suggested approach

In effect, arranging a conference is like drawing together to a single point a large number of threads of different lengths and from different places. People and suppliers of goods and services have to be briefed, informed, bullied and persuaded. Lead times are interdependent and variable. It is the perfect task for network analysis, but few would wish to adopt this method – perhaps justifiably, for it is not the plan but the *result* which counts in the end.

However, even the most competent organizer needs an administrative schedule. This is not a complicated document but a sequenced statement of what has to be done and by whom. An extract from a typical schedule is reproduced in Figure 15.1. It shows some of the actions during part of the work-up period of a typical event. The tasks to be undertaken week by week are listed, and the responsibility for action stated.

The administrative schedule, which is held by all who have action to take, is used by each person as a working document. It is amended and updated weekly and completed tasks are ticked off as shown.

The venue will need a *venue schedule* for the event. This specifies the detailed arrangements and lays down the responsibilities. The schedule for a fairly small meeting is reproduced in Figure 15.2. One for a larger meeting would, of course, be much more detailed and complicated, but the same principles apply. Good venues produce a similar schedule which they pass back to their clients. The two documents must agree

366 How to Organize Effective Conferences and Meetings

February		Action		
w/e 7 Feb	Obtain speakers' papers	DS	✓	8/ii
	Brochure mail-out	DS/DY	✓	10/ii
	Set up internal registration files	DY	✓	"
	Pay venue deposits	Client	✓	"
	Copy to signwriter for venue signs	DY	*delay until 21/ii*	
w/e 14 Feb	Edit speakers' papers	DS/DY		
	Copy to computing dept for visuals	DS		
	Press release	DS/PR		
18 Feb	Monthly co-ordinating meeting:			
	Client's office at 10 a.m.	All		
	Obtain quotes for printing papers	DY		
	Obtain quotes for delegate folders	DS		
w/e 21 Feb	Receive and process first registrations	DY		
	Start weekly reports to Client	DY		
	Order staff uniforms	DS/DY		
	Attend AV preview	DS		
	Obtain artwork for papers' covers	DS		
21 Feb	*Copy to signwriter*	*DS*		

Figure 15.1 *Extract from administrative schedule*

and it is always comforting for the organizer to receive a detailed, correct summary of his requirements – an indication that the venue staff are 'on the ball'. Note, however, that you will need to go over everything in detail when you arrive at the venue. Again, at a good venue, the banqueting manager/duty manager/venue conference manager will go through the venue's schedule with you. This schedule is usually a standard internal form and it is essential that everything on your schedule has been properly transposed. Even then it is not always safe to assume that what is on the venue schedule has been communicated to every member of the venue staff concerned. One conference organizer gets round this problem by giving key people (coffee waiters, kitchen staff) copies of his own schedule. The venue staff love to have this sort of detail but take care you do not upset the venue management by appearing to interfere.

ABC plc: Sales Course: 12–16 February

Sunday 11 February	3 delegates (Mr Jones, Mr Smith and Ms Tarr) will arrive approx 9 pm: overnight accommodation required.	Charge rooms to main account.
Monday 12 February	From 0830: coffee available in Conference Room. Delegates check in by 0900 (remaining 15 course members + Tutor (Mr Brown))	Please: (1) Have all rooms ready for occupation on arrival (15 delegates). (2) Advise delegates of coffee arrangements when they check in. Billing: • room (24 hr/day delegate rates) to main account • individual extras to personal account except Tutor (Mr Brown) to main account.
	0900 Conference commences 1030 Coffee (Restaurant bar area) (19) 1300 Buffet lunch (20) 1530 Tea (Restaurant bar area) (20) 1730 Conference breaks approx 1930 Dinner (19) 2030 Evening work in syndicate rooms	Conference room layout: see attached diagram. 3 × syndicate rooms each with flip chart and pens. 6 seats. (**NB:** see changes to syndicate room layout on Thursday.) Mr Jackson joins group for lunch and tea. Sparkling mineral water (3 bottles) as well as squash, please. 2 vegetarian. House wines (3 × red, 3 × white) and mineral water (3 bottles) with meal to main account. 1 vegetarian. Limits only to be exceeded with Mr Brown's authority.

Figure 15.2 *Venue schedule*

Other schedules may be required for transport, accommodation, personnel and equipment. But all these schedules are only pieces of paper. The way in which the plan works out in practice depends on the conference organizer and his team. The organizer's commitment to the event, and his or her dynamism and dedication will, to a great extent, determine the success or otherwise of the whole occasion.

Fay Pannell, one of the first commercial conference organizers in Britain, once said: 'Most people reach for the moon: the conference organizer has to get there.' This means checking and re-checking arrangements to ensure that the plan is working. Privately, the conference organizer can trust no-one. It is not enough to have a written contract or a letter confirming a plan. Suppliers, venues, colleagues and clients all have to be constantly reminded, persuaded, cajoled and bullied – a process which may make the organizer unpopular but which will earn respect and, with luck, will make the plan work. The organizer cannot do everything in this process. He or she is the leader of a team of colleagues, helpers, sub-contractors and suppliers who weld a series of elements – many of which are outside their direct control – into an integrated whole. Responsibility for various tasks has to be delegated and a team spirit created. Indeed, the organizing team do much to create the 'spirit' of the actual event. If the team is always cheerful and willing, sets high standards and is patently efficient, it creates an aura of success and professionalism which will hallmark the whole event.

However big or small the event, it is – or should be – important for those who come. They may have travelled a long way and spent of lot of money. To them we should offer a sense of a unique occasion and this, above all, is generated by the spirit of the organizers. It will be manifest in the way in which delegates are welcomed, by the appearance of the venue, the presentation of the sessions, the quality of the programme, the chairman, the speakers, the paperwork and the trouble-free way in which the event appears to run.

IS IT ALL WORTHWHILE?

You will often ask yourself this question during the run-up period and during the event. The answer, in the end, should be 'yes'. The satisfaction of seeing everything work out and go well is considerable. If the delegates enjoy themselves and, at the same time, the objectives are achieved, then those who originally decided to hold the event will also be satisfied.

You, the conference organizer, will have played the major part in creating this success. Whether or not your role is publicly acknowledged does not matter. Your real reward is not public recognition, nor is it financial gain. It is the pleasure of knowing that all your work, all your care and all your concern were worthwhile.

GOOD LUCK!

EXECUTIVE CHECKLIST

- Is the person responsible for organizing your events sufficiently senior?
- Is he or she capable of fulfilling the role of consultant to management in your organization?
- Can you spare the necessary resources to organize your meetings?
- If not, have you considered using a professional conference organizer?
- Do you/would you vet outside suppliers properly?
    1. Does the supplier possess the necessary skills and knowledge?
    2. Can a close working relationship be formed between the two organizations?
    3. Does the supplier use sub-contractors?
    4. Do you ask for references and follow them up?
    5. Do you visit an event the supplier is organizing?
    6. Do you ask to see samples of the supplier's work?
    7. Do you obtain a quotation, find out what is and is not included and agree the basis for costing expenses?
    8. Do you find out whether the supplier is on a commission basis with other suppliers to the event?
- Do you attend trade exhibitions, read trade publications and belong to one of the industry's professional bodies?
- Do you prepare administrative schedules for each event?
- Are *your* conferences and meeting successful and effective? If not, why not?

APPENDIX: USEFUL ADDRESSES

This list is not intended to be a comprehensive guide. Inclusion in the list does not indicate any endorsement of the services of a particular organization; exclusion does not indicate that unlisted bodies are wanting in any respect.

The list is up to date at the time of going to press.

Author
David Seekings
Fairfield
St Catherine's
Ely
Cambridgeshire
CB6 1AP
Tel: 01353 665558

Co-author
John Farrer
7 The Ridgeway
Hitchin
Herts
SG5 2BT
Tel: 01462 434948

Professional bodies
When looking for a list of suppliers in a particular discipline, the relevant professional body will normally be able to provide a list of members. They are not in a position to recommend the services of particular members.

Association of British Professional
    Conference Organizers (ABPCO)
Hon Secretary: Mr Peter Weston
PO Box 286
Worcester
WR2 6YA
Tel and Fax: 0704 405 5207
Web site: www.abpco.co.uk

Association for Conferences & Events
    (ACE International)
General Manager: Peter Worger
Riverside House
High Street
Huntingdon, Cambs
PE18 6SG
Tel: 01480 457595
Fax: 01480 412863
e-mail: ace@martex.co.uk

Corporate Hospitality and Event
    Association (CHA)
Arena House
66–68 Pentonville Road
London
N1 9HS
Tel: 020 7278 0288
Fax: 020 7837 5326
e-mail: cha@agnet.co.uk

International Congress and Convention
    Association (ICCA)
Entrada 121
1096 EB Amsterdam
The Netherlands
Tel: 00 31 20 398 1919
Fax: 00 31 20 699 0781
e-mail: icca@icca.nl

International Association of Professional
  Congress Organizers (IAPCO)
Executive Secretary: Ghislaine de
  Coninck
40 Rue Washington
B1050 Brussels
Belgium
Tel: 00 322 6407105
Fax: 00 322 6404731
e-mail: N/A

Management Centre Europe
Rue de l'Aqueduc 114–118
B1050 Brussels
Belgium

Meetings Industry Association (MIA)
34 High Street
Broadway
Worcs
WR12 7DT
Tel: 01386 858572
Fax: 01386 858986
e-mail: mia@meetings.org

Meeting Professionals
International European Bureau
Avenue E Mounier 83
B-1200 Brussels
Belgium
Tel: 00 322 772 9247
Fax: 00 322 772 7237
e-mail: N/A

Exhibitions:
British Exhibition Contractors
  Association (BECA)
Kingsmore House
Graham Road
Wimbledon
London
SW19 3SR
Tel: 0181 543 3888
Fax: 0181 543 4036
e-mail: info@beca.org.uk

Interpreters:
International Association of Conference
  Interpreters (AIIC)
General Secretary: Mrs Barbara Wilson
12 Vicars Road
London
NW5 4NL
Tel: 020 7284 3112
Fax: 020 7284 0240
e-mail: info@aiic-uk-ireland.com

Production/Audio Visual:
International Visual Communications
  Association Limited (IVCA)
Bolsover House
5/6 Clipstone Street
London
W1P 8LD
Tel: 020 7580 0962
e-mail: info@ivca.org

**Conference venues: Principal sources
  of information (see also 'Conference
  placement agencies' below)**
British Association of Conference
  Destinations (BACD)
Director: Tony Rogers
1st Floor
Elizabeth House
22 Suffolk Street
Queensway
Birmingham
B1 1LS
Tel: 0121 616 1400
Fax: 0121 616 1364
e-mail: info@bacd.org.uk

British Tourist Authority (BTA)
Thames Tower
Black's Road
Hammersmith
London
W6 9EL
Tel: 020 8846 9000
Fax: 020 8563 0302
e-mail: 101657.335@compuserve.com

British Universities Accommodation
  Consortium (BUAC)
Box No 1389
University Park
Nottingham NG7 2RD
Tel: 0115 950 4571
Fax: 0115 942 2505
e-mail: buac@nottingham.ac.uk

Connect Venues
The Workstation
15 Paternoster Row
Sheffield S1 2BX
Tel: 0114 249 3090
Fax: 0114 249 3091
e-mail: info@connectvenues.co.uk

Useful periodicals:
Association Meetings International
Conference & Travel Publications Ltd
Ashdown Court
Lewes Road
Forest Row
East Sussex RH18 5EZ
Tel: 01342 824044
e-mail: cat@cat-publications.com

Conference & Exhibition Fact Finder
Batiste Publications Ltd
Pembroke House
Campsbourne Road
Hornsey, London N8 7PE
Tel: 020 8340 3291
e-mail: N/A

Conference & Incentive Travel
Haymarket Marketing Publications Ltd
30 Lancaster Gate
London W2 3LP
Tel: 020 7413 4222
e-mail: tim.waldron@haynet.com

Meetings & Incentive Travel
Conference & Travel Publications Ltd
Ashdown Court, Lewes Road
Forest Row
East Sussex
RH18 5EZ
Tel: 01342 824044
e-mail: cat@cat-publications.com

Directories:
Conference Blue and Green Books
Miller Freeman Ltd
Riverbank House, Angel Lane
Tonbridge
Kent
TN9 1SE
Tel: 01732 377586
Fax: 01732 367301
e-mail: cbg@unmf.com

Corporate Event Services
Showcase Publications Ltd
38C The Broadway
Crouch End
London
N8 9SU
Tel: 0181 348 2332
Fax: 0181 340 3750
e-mail: N/A

The Right Solution
Canada House
272 Field End Road
Eastcote
Middlesex
HA4 9NA
Tel: 020 8866 4400
e-mail: rightsolution@msn.com

The Venue Directory
Berry Marketing Services Ltd
Berry House
11–13 Stone Street
Cranbrook
Kent
TN17 3HF
Tel: 01580 715151
Fax: 01580 715588
e-mail: bms@venuedirectory.com

The White Book (Production Directory)
Inside Communications
1st Floor, Bank House
23 Warwick Road
Coventry
CV1 2EN
Tel: 01203 230333
Fax: 01203 252241
e-mail: N/A

Worldwide Convention Centres
  Directory
Conference and Travel Publications
Ashdown Court
Lewes Road, Forest Row
East Sussex RH18 5EZ
Tel: 01342 824044
Fax: 01342 824030
e-mail: cat@cat.publications.com

AV equipment and operators:
Sharp Electronics (UK) Ltd
Sharp House, Thorp Road
Newton Heath, Manchester M40 5BE
Tel: 0161 205 2333
Fax: 0161 205 7076
e-mail: custinfo.@sharp-uk.co.uk

**Computerized conference management
  systems:**
Visual Impact and Visual INSIGHT
Event Management Systems
5 Bucklersbury, Hitchin
Herts SG5 1BB
Tel: 01462 420780
Fax: 01462 422335
e-mail: enquire@eventmanagement
  systems.co.uk

Conference placement agencies:
Expotel Hotel Reservations
Kingsgate House
Kingsgate Place
London NW6 4HG
Tel: 020 7328 9841
Fax: 020 7328 8021
e-mail: lores@expotel.co.uk

Peter Rand Group
6 Station Square
Coventry CV1 2GT
Tel: 01203 555383
Fax: 01203 256264
e-mail: N/A

Insurance:
Conference & Exhibition Insurance
  Services
33 Harbour Exchange Square
London
E14 9GG
Tel: 020 7538 9840
e-mail: caroline.jordan@rtib.co.uk

Insurex Expo-sure Group
Pantiles House
2 Nevill Street
Tunbridge Wells
Kent
TN2 3UH
Tel: 01892 511500
Fax: 01892 510016
e-mail: insurex@expo-sure.com

Woodgates & Partners Limited
Brishing Court Barn
Brishing Lane
Maidstone
Kent
ME17 4NF
Tel: 01622 744666
Fax: 01622 741747
e-mail: woodgates@btinternet.com

Miscellaneous:
Royal Mail Help and Advice
Customer Service Centre
Tel: 0345 740740
Sales Centre
Tel: 0345 950950
or see the display advertisement in your
  local telephone directory.

GLOSSARY

Note: This glossary gives definitions for some of the more common jargon and terms you will come across when dealing with audio-visual production and when using modern technology in support of your events.

3-D   Three dimensional images.
8mm   A compact and versatile video format that has image definition suitable for role play or experimental video production. Not really good enough for corporate productions, however.

Acetate   Overhead projector 'slide' or 'transparency'.
Action   Enactment of a script on stage or before cameras. The call to commence performance in a film/video.
Active matrix   When showing animations or video on LCD panels and projectors, an active matrix (or TFT) is the type of panel used as its fast reacting electronics make it suitable for moving images. Active matrix systems cost more than passive matrices.
Ad lib   An unscripted remark. Also used as a verb: 'Ad lib your welcome to the delegates, will you?'
AF   Auto-focus, usually found on slide projectors. The benefit is mainly found with non-glass mounted slides which can pop (*qv*).
Ambient light   The existing or normal light levels in a room or other environment, normally referred to in terms of projection. High ambient light levels can wash out the appearance of a projected image.
Aniforms   Trade name. System whereby an animated cartoon character on screen can hold an ad lib conversation with speaker or audience.
ANSI lumen   A unit of measurement of projector brightness, calibrated and clarified by the American National Standards Institute.
ASCII (pronounced phonetically as 'Askey') American Standard Code for Information Interchange.
Aspect ratio   The relationship between the height and width of an image, usually described as a ratio with the width first, eg 4:3 for PAL video or 16:9 for High Definition TV.
Audio conferencing   Individuals and small groups of people at two or more locations are linked into what effectively becomes the same telephone line, using nothing more complicated than the phone on their desks.

Autocue Trade name. System which enables a speaker to dispense with script or notes. The script is typed onto a narrow roll of paper. An operator backstage feeds this through a machine at the speaker's speed of delivery, slowing as he slows, pausing when he pauses. The words on the roll are transferred by closed-circuit television to a television receiver concealed in the base of the speaker's lectern. A clear glass screen above the lectern reflects the moving lines of the speech. These are only visible from the speaker's side. The speaker may thus address his audience 'eye to eye' and seem to be speaking without notes. The monitors alone may be incorporated into stage modules such as desks, or be free-standing in convenient places.

Autoscan Projectors and LCD panels need to be atuned to the frequency of the incoming signal to be able to show an image. Autoscan systems will automatically find the correct frequency.

Auxiliary microphone (or 'mike') Any separate microphone that can be plugged into a camera to replace its built-in mike.

AV Audio-visual. The combining of pictures and sound.

Backlight A light set slightly behind and above the subject to give a rim of light around the edges, creating a depth by separating the subject from the background.

Back projection (or 'rear projection') The projecting of slides and film where the screen is between the audience and the projection source. A special screen material is used.

Bandwidth Measure of the amount of information a system can transmit without error or loss.

Betacam Sony's video acquisition and editing broadcast-quality video format, widely used in the corporate sector.

Betamax ½" video cassette format, developed by Sony.

Blank A black slide. *Colour blank:* a coloured slide used to avoid an otherwise 'dead' screen, or as a base on which to superimpose information.

Brightness Brightness in projection usually describes the amount of light emitted from a surface such as a screen. Brightness is measured in watts or watts per square meter.

Broadcast quality High quality video (compared with domestic quality output from home video equipment).

Bubblejet A Canon-developed technology that deposits tiny bubbles of ink onto paper to produce images. Capable of good quality colour images in excess of 300 dpi resolution.

Build Usually referred to as build slides or transparencies, where images are built up point by point, so that the audience concentrates on the point in hand, rather than racing ahead by reading the whole visual. Builds can be achieved (in slides) by producing a new image with the latest point highlighted (or the previous ones dimmed), or (with OHTs) by adding overlays. An alternative is a reveal (*qv*).

Business television   You can broadcast your own live or pre-recorded material from a central location to audiences of any size at any number of locations, using satellite and microwave links.

BVU   Broadcast quality U-matic video.

CAD/CAM   Computer Aided Design/Computer Aided Manufacture. The interaction between computers used for designing and those used for manufacturing a product.

Caption generator   Can be built into camera or purchased as an optional extra. Produces lettering and numbers in different colours and sizes, which can be superimposed over the image on screen. May also have stopwatch and dating functions.

Carousel   A Kodak trademark, the Carousel is a round slide storage system that is used in all professional-standard slide projectors. Also known as a rotary tray, it uses gravity feed to drop slides into the projector's gate.

CCD   See Charge Coupled Device.

CD   Compact disc, a Philips-invented digital storage medium that holds more than 550 MB on a single 5.25 inch disc.

CD-A   Compact Disc-Audio, a variation of CD specially formatted for audio storage. As bought in Virgin Megastores, etc.

CD-i   Compact Disc-Interactive, an interactive format of CD developed by Philips that allows the mass write-once storage of linked text, graphics, video and animations.

CD-R   Compact Disc-Recordable, a type of CD that can be recorded to using a desktop CD writer linked to a computer. CD-R discs can be replayed on most CD-type formats, depending on the information stored.

CD ROM   Compact Disc-Read-Only Memory. The basic mass data storage medium.

CD-Video   A new format that allows the storage of full motion video on CDs, using compression techniques. A feature film would require two discs.

Charge Coupled Device (CCD)   A high resolution micro-chip which replaces the bulky video tubes used in earlier generations of video equipment and permits today's high performance, lightweight cameras.

Chippie   Carpenter.

Closed Circuit Television (CCTV)   Television transmission by cable to limited audience, (as opposed to broadcast television).

Condenser microphone   Microphone using an electrostatic element in place of the more conventional diaphragm, requiring a power supply, and characterized by better high-frequency and transient response.

CPU The Central Processor Unit: the main chip on a PC's mother-board.

Crew Technical personnel.

Crop To edit a photograph by reproducing only a part of it.

CRT Cathode-ray tube as used in television sets. In audio-visual projection, CRTs are used in CRT-type projectors to form the red, green and blue images that comprise a full colour picture.

Cube wall A videowall (*qv*) that uses rear projection cubes in a stacked configuration. The image quality is extremely good, and text is handled well as there is practically no gap between screens.

Data projector Generally a projector that handles common computer signals up to VGA level. Better systems are usually referred to as graphics projectors.

Digital A signal made up of two states ('On' and 'Off'). Stored on computer in binary format – giving the ultimate in image or sound quality, for example, as files can be instantly accessed and manipulated.

Digital imaging This is the process of digitizing photographs, nega-tives or slides and then manipulating the image on screen using a computer.

Dissolve The process of gradually fading one image as another gradu-ally brightens to take its place, with a variable degree of image overlap, usually found in slide projection (and controlled by a dissolve unit). This transition process requires at least two slide projectors, with consecutive slides carefully split between them. Dissolves are also found as features in electronic presentations software, where an electronic dissolve is made on screen. Other transition effects found in these packages include wipe, curtain and pixelation.

DOS Disk Operating System. The interface between machine level instructions and the computer user.

dpi Dots Per Inch, the measurement of a printer's resolution – the maximum number of dots that can be printed per square inch of page.

Drift The slow process where CRT projectors go out of alignment. It's a simple matter to realign the three tubes to refocus, usually using the remote control system.

DTP Abbreviation for Desk-top Publishing computer software, providing the design, layout and printing of documents using a desktop computer and a laser printer.

Dye-sublimation A process in colour printers where colours are diffused into a base material to give superb high-resolution continuous tone images, ideal for presentation printers or OHTs.

Ektalite Kodak trade mark for lenses for EKTAPRO projectors.

EKTAPRO   The trade name of Kodak's replacement of the Carousel projector.

Electromagnetic focus   A method of focusing the image from a CRT tube in a CRT projector that allows extremely fine adjustment for edge to edge sharpness. Found on the most expensive projectors.

Electronic presentation   A presentation created on a computer and presented via an electronic device (eg LCD panel, data projector) that does not involve the production of hard copy (eg slides, transparencies). The whole process is digital.

Electrostatic focus   A method of focusing the image from a CRT tube in a CRT projector, found in the majority of such projectors.

e-mail   Electronic mail.

e-mail address   To send e-mail you need to know the receiver's address, a series of numbers, letters and dots with an '@' symbol in the middle.

ENG   Electronic News Gathering.

File size   An image's resolution and dimensions determine its file size (ie how much storage space it takes up). It is expressed in kilobytes (k) or megabytes (Mb).

Film recorder   Small CRT-based systems which focus the image from a CRT tube onto slide film for outputting computer files. The red, green and blue elements are drawn individually, at resolutions of between 2,000 and 16,000 lines.

Fixer   An organizer, but specifically one who provides musicians and singers for recording sessions.

Focal length   The distance from the optical centre of the lens to the surface of the image sensor, with the lens focused on infinity. In practice, a lens with short focal length is a telephoto; a variable focal length is a zoom. On OHPs, the focal length varies little from model to model.

Font   The size and shape of any character produced on slides or computers, etc.

Fresnel lens   Used to focus light, particularly in OHP assemblies. The particular property of a Fresnel lens is that it is virtually flat – its convex lens properties come from the radically-cut variations in its surface topography. They are also, incidentally, used in lighthouse light assemblies.

f-stops   Numbers that refer to the size of the aperture on a camera.

Gaffer   Film slang for chief electrician.

Get-In   The process of importing sets and equipment at the venue.

Get-Out   The reverse operation.

Good viewing area   Area within which audience sees a good picture on the screen.

Graphics projector A projector that handles high-resolution signals from graphics workstations or engines above the normal VGA level.

Graphics standards Graphics standards on your computer determine the number of colours and the definition you can expect to achieve. But the definition you actually get on a projector is equally dependent on its own resolution capability – you can't get more than 640 × 480 resolution out of a basic LCD panel with a high-resolution graphics workstation, for example. Consult the table below to determine your systems and requirements.

Computer graphics standard	Resolution/pixels	Horizontal scan frequency/kHz
CGA	640 × 200	15.7kHz
EGA	620 × 200/350	15.7/21.8kHz
PGA	640 × 400/480	30.5kHz
VGA	640 × 480	31.5/35.5kHz
XGA	1,024 × 768	48kHz
Apple Mac Quadra	640 × 480	35kHz
CAD system	1,280 × 1,024	64kHz
Standard PAL	625 lines	15.7kHz
HDTV	1,125/1,250 lines	32kHz

Graphics tablet A digitizing device that uses a pen or cross-hair pointer to trace over images so that they can be reproduced in drawing software on a computer. Can also be used as an alternative to a mouse, or for freehand drawing.

Grip Film slang for handyman.

GUI Graphical User Interface: a user-friendly computer interface introduced by Apple and emulated by Microsoft's Windows, which uses symbols (icons) to represent computer functions, and a point-and-click mouse for manoeuvring around applications.

Hard disk The term used for either an internal or external rigid disk used for storing and reading computer data. Its capacity is measured in megabytes (Mb).

HDTV High Definition Television. A system that shows CRT-based images in either 1,125 or 1,250 lines resolution, as compared to standard PAL signals of 625 lines.

Hi8   An enhanced 8mm video tape format with excellent sound quality. Probably the minimum requirement for corporate production. Inexpensive desktop editing systems are available.

Hologram   3-D photograph produced and viewed using lasers or other coherent light sources.

Holograph   Plate on which the interference pattern for above is stored (each part of the plate contains all the information, therefore *Holo*graph).

Inkjet   A low cost printing/proofing system that spurts microscopic drops of ink onto paper to form full-colour images.

Instant playback   Lets you view the material you have recorded at once through the camera viewfinder or television without needing a VCR.

Interactive   An adjective that describes the technology of the same name. Interactive refers to types of (usually) computer-based equipment used in training, presentations and information systems. Rather than being a linear presentation, in which the user simply watches passively, an interactive presentation invites the user to make choices which influence how the programme continues.

Interface   The piece of cable and connectors by which a computer or other device is connected to another. Avoiding incompatible or incorrect interfaces is especially important when giving portable presentations.

Internet   The name given to a vast global collection of *inter*connected computer *net*works. It is made up of many separate networks, belonging to universities, businesses, and Internet Service Providers. You access the Internet from your PC and a modem connected to a telephone line.

Internet Service Providers (ISPs)   Companies that provide subscribers with temporary telephone connections to the Internet for a modest fee. ISPs also provide other services such as e-mail, *post restante* and Web Servers.

ISDN   Integrated Services Digital Network: a special type of telephone line designed for transmitting digital information.

Keystone   The ratio between the width at the top and bottom of a projected image.

Keystone distortion   A type of distortion in a projected or TV image whereby a square pattern appears larger at the top than at the bottom. This is caused by the plane of projection not being aligned to that of the screen.

'Kill' (as in, 'Kill that spot!'   Indicates that a particular light, prop, furnishing, is no longer required.

Lamp   A light bulb. A light source inside a lantern.

Landscape   A picture format (usually 35mm × 24mm) for slides where the width is greater than the height. *Portrait* where the slide is rotated through 90° to produce a picture where height is greater than the width.

Laser   *L*ight *A*mplification by the *S*timulated *E*mission of *R*adiation. Used for visual effects of 'solid' non-spreading light-beams in grid or other patterns projected on screen and/or spread over stage and auditorium, varied and split via combinations of lenses and mirrors.

LCD   Liquid Crystal Display. LCDs have the unique property that they reorientate themselves depending on whether or not they are subject to an electrical voltage. This polarity allows layers of microscopic crystals to act like millions of tiny light shutters, all working together to form a larger, detailed image. By adding filters to the crystals, full colour images can be built up.

Lectern   The speaker's desk equipped with support for script, lights, prompting and cueing devices, timers, hand rests, etc.

Level   Sound volume. A Soundman will ask 'May I have a level?' This means that the speaker should read a few sentences at the volume and pitch he intends using so that the equipment may be adjusted accordingly.

Light valve   A system in projectors whereby an image is transferred to another technology so that its naturally low light levels are amplified. This is used in some LCD projectors, for example where the CRT image is transferred to an LCD, and arc lamps are used to transmit the LCD image.

Line doubler   An electronic processing system that improves the smoothness of a 625-line video image by interpolating extra information between the lines, in order that it can be projected at very large magnifications.

Linear video   Refers to real-time videotape-based presentations. The linear aspect refers to the fact that tape must be spooled to position, and takes time; the converse, digital video, has instant access. Linear video editing systems are therefore much slower than their digital counterparts.

Live   Not recorded. Actual presence in the flesh. Live action.

Lumen   A unit for measuring the brightness of (usually) a CRT projector. A typical video projector would have a brightness of more than 600 lumens.

Lux   Measurement of illumination at a surface. Used to indicate the sensitivity of a camera's system to light.

Magazine   The removable section of a slide projector that stores the slides and presents them to the side gate in sequence. A slide magazine usually refers to a long straight system, rather than a carousel (*qv*).

Master   Original scripts and tapes from which copies are made.

Metal halide   A type of projector lamp that gives out a particularly bright and clear white light. Their power is not directly comparable to those of, say, quartz lamps – a 50 watt metal halide bulb might be as bright as a 400 watt quartz lamp.

Microprocessor   Electronic chip that controls data-handling devices.

Modem   MODulate and DEModulate: a device which converts digital signals into analogue for transmission down telephone lines.

Morphing   A video graphics program which creates an apparently seamless transition from one image to another, eg sequence ageing from child's face to old man's.

Multi-image   A slide technique where very high quality photographic and graphic images are computer-controlled to give a semi-animated effect, often widescreen, backed by an emotive audio track. Generally used for large presentations such as product launches.

Multimedia   The storage and replay of all presentation elements, such as video, graphics, audio and still pictures, from a computer drive and its peripherals.

Newton's Rings   Visual interference pattern or 'rainbow' effect caused by refraction when two surfaces are in imperfect contact with one another; slide mounts may have one side of their glass coated to prevent this phenomenon.

NiCad   A rechargeable-battery technology based on Nickel and Cadmium.

NTSC   American standard for TV transmission. (National Television Standard Committee.)

NTSC4.43   The video output of video tape or disk players used mainly in Middle East countries.

OHP   Overhead Projector. Established and familiar presentation device that uses transmissive (*qv*) and reflective technology to project images from transparency materials as well as LCD panels.

OHT   Overhead Transparency. Also referred to as an overhead foil, these are the (usually) A4 films that can be drawn on with special pens, or passed through a copier or laser/colour printer (certain film types only).

Overlay   1. Projected image superimposed over another. 2. Artwork prepared on transparent cell so that it can be added to a base piece of artwork.

PAL   European (excluding France) TV standard. (Phase Alternating Line.)

Passive matrix In LCD panels, these are LCD pixels that react slowly to electronic changes. They are not suitable for moving images such as video, but are cheaper to produce.

Photo-CD A CD format developed by Kodak and Philips that stores high quality photographic images on CD, for printout or replay via monitors or TVs.

Pin registration A technique used in rostrum camera slide production (*qv*) that ensures each slide is in perfect register. Small pins inside the slide mount hold the slide precisely in a position.

Pixel A single dot on a computer display or in a digital image. The combination of thousands of dots on your screen creates the illusion of an image. A high quality 10 × 8 inch print would contain around five million pixels.

Podium Speaker's rostrum on which a lecturn may stand, but used incorrectly as synonym for lectern.

Popping When slides are placed in the gate of a slide projector, they are subject to intense heat from the lamp system and the expansion causes the film to bow in the middle. An autofocus projector can counter the resulting loss of focus to some degree, but the best method is to use glass mounted slides.

PostScript Adobe's page description language that allows printing devices to interpret complex graphics and print them successfully.

Prompting devices These permit speakers or actors facing film or television cameras, standing at a lectern or in movement on-stage, to dispense with scripts. Several systems are in use internationally, a description of one is given under Autocue.

Radio-mike A microphone that broadcasts via a small transmitter also on the person. The signal is picked up, amplified and broadcast through loudspeakers. Thus the need for cabling is eliminated.

Rake The slope of stage or auditorium that aids those in the latter to see those on the former.

RAM (Random Access Memory) A part of memory configured to store information in computers. Its contents are lost when the computer is switched off.

Rear projection A method of projecting images from behind onto a translucent screen. The major benefit is that the equipment is kept out of sight, while the image will remain bright even in high ambient light conditions.

Rear screen (or rear projection screen) A translucent panel. Light from the projector(s) travels through the screen and forms an image on the other surface.

Reflective OHP A flat-based OHP system that is extremely portable, as the lamp is in the lens head assembly – the beam passes through the

OHT and is reflected by a Fresnel lens/mirror combination back through the lens and onto the screens. These systems cannot be used with LCD panels.

Resolution   It is measured by the number of dots per inch (dpi) or pixels per inch (ppi). The higher the number of pixels in an image, the more detailed it is, and the higher its resolution.

Retro   A CRT projector-based rear-projected presentation system usually with a 40–46 inch screen (domestic TV types) or 60 inch screens (professional grade).

Reveal   1. Used specifically of a product launch to describe the moment when the new product is seen for the first time. Invariably this is a climax of the show. 2. In speaker support-type audio visual presentations, the reveal is a gradual device where portions of an image or message are shown bit by bit or line by line, building up to the full message. Using an overhead projector, a simple reveal device is a piece of opaque card, moved down a transparency to show one detail at a time. The main purpose of reveals is to prevent an audience reading ahead of what the presenter is discussing.

RGB   Red, green, blue – the description of the components of white light that are used in varying proportions to create any colour imaginable. In video, it refers to a component (ie split up) signal, and RGB signals are the purest.

ROM   Unlike RAM, Read-Only Memory (ROM) can only be read. Its contents are permanently stored in the chip. ROM chips are usually used for fundamental bits of software. The contents of ROM survive after power is turned off.

Rostrum   A platform. Portable sections that combine to form a stage.

Rostrum camera   A table platform with special lighting and vertical camera column. A still or video camera is mounted on the column, and can move up and down. Items to be photographed are placed on the platform. Rostrums with damped (smooth) lateral movements are available. Video footage can be gathered of inanimate objects and for slide production the creative possibilities are endless, often seen in multi-image shows.

Rotary slide tray   A round slide tray and storage system – see 'Carousel'.

Scan converter   An electronic processing system that converts the frequency of a signal so that it is suitable for a particular piece of projection equipment. For example, a converter might reduce the 64kHz rate of a CAD (computer aided design) system, enabling it to be shown on a VGA projection device at 32kHz.

Scan rate Refers to the frequence of a projector, monitor or signal. All computer signals 'scan' across the screen, building up the image. For example, a 32kHz system will scan a single line once every 1/32,000 of a second, or will scan 32,000 lines each second.

Scanner A flatbed, hand-held or drum device that uses a diode to read colour or mono images into rasterized form at resolutions of 300 dpi or more. These images can then be manipulated in software packages on a computer, or incorporated into a presentation.

SECAM French TV standard (Sequential Couleur à Memoire), also used in the Independent Repubics (formerly USSR).

Session An unbroken period of conference. A day that is divided by lunch and morning and afternoon tea/coffee breaks would consist of four sessions.

Show Synonym for conference whether or not it contains show business elements.

Sightline View a spectator has of events on stage; thus the entire audience must be contained within the sightlines (and things the audience should not see must be *outside* the sightlines).

Sparks Electrician.

Special effects generator Electronic device that processes video signals to produce a variety of effects (eg, wipes, superimposition, key effects).

Spike (1) To mark the stage floor position of props, furniture, etc. (2) Momentary electronic interference in the mains.

Storyboard Sequence of drawings suggesting proposed artwork. Film/video: drawings identifying proposed action and camera positions. Slide: the document that shows all slides in sequence.

SVGA Super VGA. See 'Graphics standards'.

S-VHS A hi-bandwidth video standard.

Teleconferencing Generic term used to describe audio conferencing, video conferencing and business television (*qv*).

Transmissive OHP A conventional box-shaped OHP is described as transmissive, as the light source is under the platen (*qv*) and passes through the image before being projected through the lens. These systems are the only type suitable for use with LCD panels.

Turnkey A completely installed and usable system with little or no user knowledge or experience required for operation.

U-matic An obsolescent but still widely used Sony ¾" video format, ideal for corporate and broadcast use.

VCR Video Cassette Recording/Recorder.

VGA The Video Graphics Array: See 'Graphics standards'.

VHS   Video Home System, developed by JVC, is the most popular cassette format, using ½" tape. VHS-C is a compact version, developed for use in camcorders and which can be played back on standard VHS format machines with an adaptor.

Video   The signal that is used by display devises, such as projectors, to generate a picture. This term also refers to the video output of video tape or disk players or computers.

Video 8   Video cassette format, developed by Sony, that uses 8mm tape in small cassettes. Capable of recording hi-fi sound and both standard and long play.

Video conferencing   Enables individuals and small groups at two or more locations to see and hear each other, face-to-face, over live video links.

Video for Windows (VfW)   Microsoft's system for allowing video clips to run on Windows computers in a multimedia environment.

Videowall   A configuration of stacked CRT monitors or projection cubes, with little space between the screens, on which a large image is shown. A single image can be split across a number of screens. Such systems are often used as backdrops to presentations, or can be effective for video-only presentations.

Viewing angle   Screens do not reflect equally in all directions. Most light is reflected in a conical volume. This cone is centred around the 'line of best viewing' or along the 'on axis', on which a viewer sees maximum brightness. A viewer located along the surface of the cone sees only 50% of the maximum brightness. The horizontal and vertical angles are the horizontal and vertical angles of the cone. Curved screens usually have smaller viewing angles than flat screens.

Virtual Reality   A system which, at present, consists of a helmet worn by an individual: tiny TV screens in front of the eyes create computer driven images in 3-D. Sensors attached to the body are relayed to the computer so that the images change accordingly. In spite of relatively crude images, Virtual Reality is exciting considerable attention.

Visual   A picture, usually on screen. *Visual aid:* picture/diagram/text that assists comprehension.

VTR   Videotape recording/recorder.

Web/Web sites   Families of Internet multimedia information pages and programs which are provided at 'web sites' and are owned by corporate or individual users.

Web Browser   Internet user software.

Web Server   Web browser (*qv*) software sends out requests to Web Servers which provide text. Each page on the Web has its own address which is usually written beginning with characters 'http://'

Windows Microsoft's PC architecture, based on a graphical user interface (GUI) like the Apple Macintosh.

Wipe An electronic effect in which one scene progressively replaces another by moving from one edge of the frame. A 'wipe to black' involves the progressive blacking out of the screen.

wysiwyg (pronounced 'wissy-wig') Stands for What You See Is What You Get, and refers to the relationship between the screen display on the computer and the final output.

XGA IBM's proprietary high definition graphics system. See 'Graphics standards'.

Zoom lens A lens with a variable range of focal lengths. Focus may sometimes be automatically maintained as the length is altered.

INDEX

Ford Motor Company   8, 188

gala dinners   97–98
green considerations   40
Green Flag International   40
green tourism, traveller's guide
    leaflet (GFI)   40
Guild of Business Travel Agents
    225

Higher Education
    Accommodation Consortium
    (HEAC)   50
hotels   6, 47–49, 297–316
    Conrad International   40
    Forté Hotels   189
    Hilton International   40
    Holiday Inn hotels   190
    Holiday Inn Worldwide   40
    Intercontinental Hotel, London
        189
    Inter-Continental Hotels   40
    Marriott   40
    Renaissance   40
    Sheraton   40
hotels, departments
    accounts   303–04
    banqueting   300–01
    food and beverage   301–02
    front of house   302–03
    general manager   300
    sales and marketing   300
hotels, food and drink prices
    310–11
    choice of food   311–12
    choice of drinks   312–13
    'dirty tricks'   313–15
    free bar   312–13
    setting limits   313
    stock control   313–15
hotels, hospitality, accepting   315
    management and
        organizational structure
        298–304, 299

IBM   188
IMS Health   94
incentive   11
    destinations   40
Incentive Travel and Meetings
    Association (ITMA)   226
Inland Revenue   188
inspection visits   54–66
    checklist site/venue survey
        report   56, 69–78
    checklist venue evaluation form
        56, 79–81
    checklists   56, 60
    failure   65
    first impressions   57
    furniture   60
    lavatories   61
    noise   61
    seating space   60
    soundproofing   61
    standards   57
    viewing area   60
insurance   67, 131–33
    cancellation   67, 132–33
    failure to vacate   132
    public and employee liability
        132
    risk   132
    travel   230
insurers, specialist   132
Insurex-Exposure   67
Intelsat (International Satellite
    organization communications
    satellites)   143
internal events (in-house, in-
    company)   12
International Equestrian
    Federation   216
International Hotels and
    Environmental Initiative
    (IHIE)   40
International Standards
    Organization (ISO)
    111